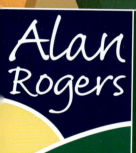

Alan Rogers

GW01326626

the best campsites

2010 EDITION

in **Italy**

PLUS **Croatia & Slovenia**

INSPECTED SINCE 1968 & SELECTED

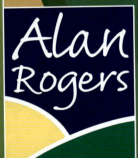

Compiled by: Alan Rogers Guides Ltd

Designed by: Paul Effenberg, Vine Design Ltd

Additional photography: T Lambelin, www.lambelin.com
Maps created by Customised Mapping (01769 540044)
contain background data provided by GisDATA Ltd
Maps are © Alan Rogers Guides and GisDATA Ltd 2010

© Alan Rogers Guides Ltd 2010

Published by: Alan Rogers Guides Ltd,
Spelmonden Old Oast, Goudhurst, Kent TN17 1HE
www.alanrogers.com Tel: 01580 214000

British Library Cataloguing-in-Publication Data:
A catalogue record for this book is available
from the British Library.

ISBN 978-1-906215-27-9

Print managed in Great Britain by DPI Print & Production Ltd
and printed by Stephens & George Print Group

Mixed Sources
Product group from well-managed
forests and other controlled sources
www.fsc.org Cert no. SGS-COC-003625
© 1996 Forest Stewardship Council
FSC

INSPECTED
SINCE 1968
& SELECTED

Contents

Alan Rogers – in search of 'the best'

Alan Rogers Guides were first published over 40 years ago. Since Alan Rogers published the first campsite guide that bore his name, the range has expanded and now covers 27 countries in five separate guides. No fewer than 20 of the campsites selected by Alan for the first guide are still featured in our 2010 editions.

This guide contains impartially written reports on over 330 campsites in Italy, including many of the very finest, each being individually inspected and selected. We are including reports on almost 80 of the very best sites in Croatia and Slovenia, destination countries which have seen a substantial surge in interest in recent years. We aim to provide you with a selection of the best, rather than information on all – in short, a more selective, qualitative approach. New, improved maps and indexes are also included, designed to help you find the choice of campsite that's right for you. We hope you enjoy some happy and safe travels – and some pleasurable 'armchair touring' in the meantime!

How do we find the best?

The criteria we use when inspecting and selecting sites are numerous, but the most important by far is the question of good quality. People want different things from their choice of campsite so we try to include a range of campsite 'styles' to cater for a wide variety of preferences: from those seeking a small peaceful campsite in the heart of the countryside, to visitors looking for an 'all singing, all dancing' site in a popular seaside resort. Those with more specific interests, such as sporting facilities, cultural events or historical attractions, are also catered for.

The size of the site, whether it's part of a chain or privately owned, makes no difference in terms of it being required to meet our exacting standards in respect of its quality and it being 'fit for purpose'. In other words, irrespective of the size of the site, or the number of facilities it offers, we consider and evaluate the welcome, the pitches, the sanitary facilities, the cleanliness, the general maintenance and even the location.

" …the campsites included in this book have been chosen entirely on merit, and no payment of any sort is made by them for their inclusion."

Alan Rogers, 1968

INSPECTED SINCE 1968 & SELECTED

Expert opinions

We rely on our dedicated team of Site Assessors, all of whom are experienced campers, caravanners or motorcaravanners, to visit and recommend campsites. Each year they travel some 100,000 miles around Europe inspecting new campsites for the guide and re-inspecting the existing ones. Our thanks are due to them for their enthusiastic efforts, their diligence and integrity.

We also appreciate the feedback we receive from many of our readers and we always make a point of following up complaints, suggestions or recommendations for possible new campsites. Of course we get a few grumbles too – but it really is a few, and those we do receive usually relate to overcrowding or to poor maintenance during the peak school holiday period. Please bear in mind that, although we are interested to hear about any complaints, we have no contractual relationship with the campsites featured in our guides and are therefore not in a position to intervene in any dispute between a reader and a campsite.

Independent and honest

Whilst the content and scope of the Alan Rogers guides have expanded considerably since the early editions, our selection of campsites still employs exactly the same philosophy and criteria as defined by Alan Rogers in 1968.

'telling it how it is'

Firstly, and most importantly, our selection is based entirely on our own rigorous and independent inspection and selection process. Campsites cannot buy their way into our guides – indeed the extensive Site Report which is written by us, not by the site owner, is provided free of charge so we are free to say what we think and to provide an honest, 'warts and all' description. This is written in plain English and without the use of confusing icons or symbols.

Looking for the best?

HIGHLY RESPECTED BY SITE OWNERS AND READERS ALIKE, THERE IS NO BETTER GUIDE WHEN IT COMES TO FORMING AN INDEPENDENT VIEW OF A CAMPSITE'S QUALITY. WHEN YOU NEED TO BE CONFIDENT IN YOUR CHOICE OF CAMPSITE, YOU NEED THE ALAN ROGERS GUIDE.

- SITES ONLY INCLUDED ON MERIT
- SITES CANNOT PAY TO BE INCLUDED
- INDEPENDENTLY INSPECTED, RIGOROUSLY ASSESSED
- IMPARTIAL REVIEWS
- OVER 40 YEARS OF EXPERTISE

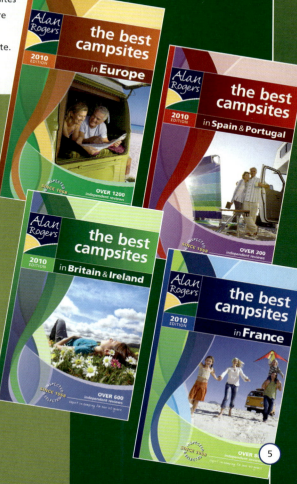

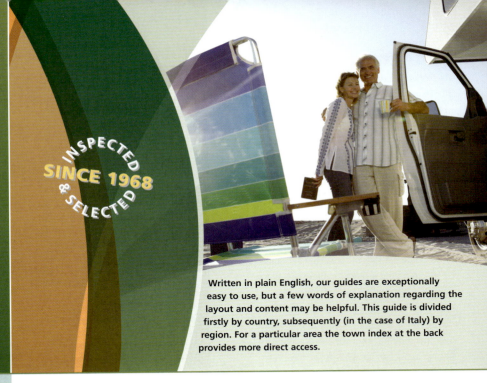

INSPECTED SINCE 1968 & SELECTED

Written in plain English, our guides are exceptionally easy to use, but a few words of explanation regarding the layout and content may be helpful. This guide is divided firstly by country, subsequently (in the case of Italy) by region. For a particular area the town index at the back provides more direct access.

The Reports – *Example of an entry*

Index town

Site name
Postal address (including region) T: **telephone number**. E: **email address**
alanrogers.com web address (including Alan Rogers reference number)

A description of the site in which we try to give an idea of its general features – its size, its situation, its strengths and its weaknesses. This section should provide a picture of the site itself with reference to the facilities that are provided and if they impact on its appearance or character. We include details on pitch numbers, electricity (with amperage), hardstandings etc. in this section, as pitch design, planning and terracing affect the site's overall appearance. Similarly we include reference to pitches used for caravan holiday homes, chalets, and the like. Importantly at the end of this column we indicate if there are any restrictions, e.g. no tents, no children, naturist sites.

Facilities

Lists more specific information on the site's facilities and amenities and, where available, the dates when these facilities are open (if not for the whole season).

Off site: here we give distances to various local amenities, for example, local shops, the nearest beach, plus our featured activities (bicycle hire, fishing, horse riding, boat launching). Where we have space we list suggestions for activities and local tourist attractions.

Open: Site opening dates.

Directions

Separated from the main text in order that they may be read and assimilated more easily by a navigator en-route. Bear in mind that road improvement schemes can result in road numbers being altered.

GPS: references are provided as we obtain them for satellite navigation systems (in degrees and minutes).

Charges 2010 (or a general guide).

Maps, campsite listings and indexes

For this 2010 guide we have changed the way in which we list our campsites and also the way in which we help you locate the sites within each region.

We now include a map immediately after our Introduction to that region. These maps show the towns near which one or more of our featured campsites are located.

Within each regional section of the guide, we list these towns and the site(s) in that vicinity in alphabetical order.

You will certainly need more detailed maps for navigation, for example the Michelin atlas. We provide GPS coordinates for each site to assist you. Our three indexes will also help you to find a site by its reference number and name, by region and site name, or by the town where the site is situated.

Facilities

Toilet blocks

We assume that toilet blocks will be equipped with a reasonable amount of British style WCs, washbasins with hot and cold water and hot showers with dividers or curtains, and will have all necessary shelves, hooks, plugs and mirrors. We also assume that there will be an identified chemical toilet disposal point, and that the campsite will provide water and waste water drainage points and bin areas. If not the case, we comment. We do mention certain features that some readers find important: washbasins in cubicles, facilities for babies, facilities for those with disabilities and motorcaravan service points. Readers with disabilities are advised to contact the site of their choice to ensure that facilities are appropriate to their needs.

Shop

Basic or fully supplied, and opening dates.

Bars, restaurants, takeaway facilities and entertainment

We try hard to supply opening and closing dates (if other than the campsite opening dates) and to identify if there are discos or other entertainment.

Children's play areas

Fenced and with safety surface (e.g. sand, bark or pea-gravel).

Swimming pools

If particularly special, we cover in detail in our main campsite description but reference is always included under our Facilities listings. We will also indicate the existence of water slides, sunbathing areas and other features. Opening dates, charges and levels of supervision are provided where we have been notified. There is a regulation whereby Bermuda shorts may not be worn in swimming pools (for health and hygiene reasons). It is worth ensuring that you do take 'proper' swimming trunks with you.

Leisure facilities

For example, playing fields, bicycle hire, organised activities and entertainment.

Dogs

If dogs are not accepted or restrictions apply, we state it here. Check the quick reference list at the back of the guide.

Off site

This briefly covers leisure facilities, tourist attractions, restaurants etc. nearby.

Charges

These are the latest provided to us by the sites. In those cases where 2010 prices have not been provided to us by the sites, we try to give a general guide.

Reservations

Necessary for high season (roughly mid-July to mid-August) in popular holiday areas (i.e. beach resorts). You can reserve many sites via our own Alan Rogers Travel Service or through other tour operators. Or be wholly independent and contact the campsite(s) of your choice direct, using the phone or e-mail numbers shown in the site reports, but please bear in mind that many sites are closed all winter.

Telephone numbers

Italy: All numbers assume that you are phoning from within Italy. To phone Italy from outside that country, prefix the number shown with the relevant International Code: 00 39. Do NOT drop the first 0 of the area code.

Croatia and Slovenia: The numbers given assume you are actually IN the country concerned. If you are phoning from the UK remember that a first '0' is usually disregarded and replaced by the appropriate country code: Croatia 00 385, Slovenia 00 386.

Opening dates

Are those advised to us during the early autumn of the previous year – sites can, and sometimes do, alter these dates before the start of the following season, often for good reasons. If you intend to visit shortly after a published opening date, or shortly before the closing date, it is wise to check that it will actually be open at the time required. Similarly some sites operate a restricted service during the low season, only opening some of their facilities (e.g. swimming pools) during the main season; where we know about this, and have the relevant dates, we indicate it – again if you are at all doubtful it is wise to check.

Sometimes, campsite amenities may be dependent on there being enough customers on site to justify their opening and, for this reason, actual opening dates may vary from those indicated.

Some campsite owners are very relaxed when it comes to opening and closing dates. They may not be fully ready by their stated opening dates – grass and hedges may not all be cut or perhaps only limited sanitary facilities open. At the end of the season they also tend to close down some facilities and generally wind down prior to the closing date. Bear this in mind if you are travelling early or late in the season – it is worth phoning ahead.

The Camping Cheque low season touring system goes some way to addressing this in that many participating campsites will have all key facilities open and running by the opening date and these will remain fully operational until the closing date.

F248   Our Accommodation Section

Over recent years, more and more campsites have added high quality mobile home and chalet accommodation. In response to feedback from many of our readers, and to reflect this evolution in campsites, we have now decided to include a separate section on mobile homes and chalets.

If a site offers this accommodation, it is indicated above the site report with a page reference where full details are given. We have chosen a number of sites offering some of the best accommodation available and have included full details of one or two accommodation types at these sites. Please note however that many other campsites listed in this guide may also have a selection of accommodation for rent.

Whether you're an 'old hand' in terms of camping and caravanning or are contemplating your first trip, a regular reader of our Guides or a new 'convert', we wish you well in your travels and hope we have been able to help in some way. We are, of course, also out and about ourselves, visiting sites, talking to owners and readers, and generally checking on standards and new developments.

We wish all our readers thoroughly enjoyable Camping and Caravanning in 2010 – favoured by good weather of course!

THE ALAN ROGERS TEAM

Trentino-Alto Adige
page 64
Friuli-Venézia Giúlia
page 79
Lake Garda
page 42
SLOVENIA
page 210
CROATIA
page 220
Veneto
page 86
Lombardy
page 37
Piedmont &
Valle d'Aosta
page 16
Emila-Romagna
page 111
Marche
page 155
Ligúria
page 29
Tuscany
page 120
Umbria
page 147
Abruzzo & Molise
page 171
Lazio
page 162
Campania
page 178
Puglia & Basilicata
page 182
Sardinia
page 201
Calabria
page 187
Sicily
page 192

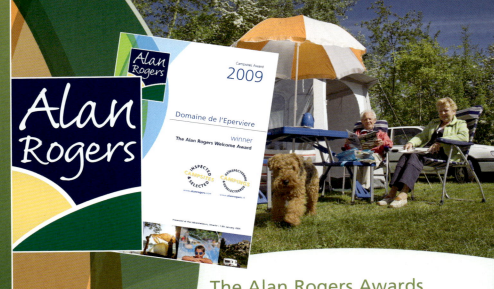

The Alan Rogers Awards

The Alan Rogers Campsite Awards were launched in 2004 and have proved a great success.

Our awards have a broad scope and before committing to our winners, we carefully consider more than 2,000 campsites featured in our guides, taking into account comments from our site assessors, our head office team and, of course, our readers.

Our award winners come from the four corners of Europe, from southern Portugal to Slovenia, and this year we are making awards to campsites in 13 different countries.

Needless to say, it's an extremely difficult task to choose our eventual winners, but we believe that we have identified a number of campsites with truly outstanding characteristics.

In each case, we have selected an outright winner, along with two highly commended runners-up.

Listed below are full details of each of our award categories and our winners for 2009.

Our warmest congratulations to all our award winners and our commiserations to all those not having won an award on this occasion.

THE ALAN ROGERS TEAM

Alan Rogers Progress Award 2009

This award reflects the hard work and commitment undertaken by particular site owners to improve and upgrade their site.

WINNER

FR40180 Le Vieux Port, France

RUNNERS-UP

FR29050	L'Orangerie de Lanniron, France
AU0265	Park Grubhof, Austria

Alan Rogers Welcome Award 2009

This award takes account of sites offering a particularly friendly welcome and maintaining a friendly ambience throughout reader's holidays.

WINNER

FR71070 Domaine de l'Eperviere, France

RUNNERS-UP

NL6970	't Weergors, Netherlands
UK0805	Woodovis, England

Alan Rogers Active Holiday Award 2009

This award reflects sites in outstanding locations which are ideally suited for active holidays, notably walking or cycling, but which could extend to include such activities as winter sports or water sports

WINNER

SV4200	Bled, Slovenia

RUNNERS-UP

FR29010	Ty Nadan, France
CZ4720	Frymburk, Czech Republic

Alan Rogers Motorhome Award 2009

Motorhome sales are increasing and this award acknowledges sites which, in our opinion, have made outstanding efforts to welcome motorhome clients.

WINNER

DE3003	Wulfener Hals, Germany

RUNNERS-UP

NL5675	Vliegenbos, Netherlands
DE3833	LuxOase, Germany

Alan Rogers 4 Seasons Award 2009

This award is made to outstanding sites with extended opening dates and which welcome clients to a uniformly high standard throughout the year.

WINNER

ES87420	La Marina, Spain

RUNNERS-UP

FR74230	Le Giffre, France
ES89650	Picos de Europa, Spain

Alan Rogers Seaside Award 2009

This award is made for sites which we feel are outstandingly suitable for a really excellent seaside holiday.

WINNER

IT68200	Baia Domizia, Italy

RUNNERS-UP

CR6765	Kovacine, Croatia
NL6870	De Lakens, Netherlands

Alan Rogers Country Award 2009

This award contrasts with our former award and acknowledges sites which are attractively located in delightful, rural locations.

WINNER

NL6285	Wildhoeve, Netherlands

RUNNERS-UP

FR85260	La Guyoniere, France
UK2030	Wareham Forest, England

Alan Rogers Rented Accommodation Award 2009

Given the increasing importance of rented accommodation on many campsites, we feel that it is important to acknowledge sites which have made a particular effort in creating a high quality 'rented accommodation' park.

WINNER

FR34110	Yelloh! Village Le Club Farret, France

RUNNERS-UP

SV4210	Sobec, Slovenia
DK2010	Hvidbjerg Strand, Denmark

Alan Rogers Unique Site Award 2009

This award acknowledges sites with unique, outstanding features – something which simply cannot be found elsewhere and which is an important attraction of the site.

WINNER

IT60370	International Jesolo, Italy

RUNNERS-UP

AU0525	Fisching 50+, Austria
PO8030	Rio Alto, Portugal

Alan Rogers Family Site Award 2009

Many sites claim to be child friendly but this award acknowledges the sites we feel to be the very best in this respect.

WINNER

IT60200	Union Lido, Italy

RUNNERS-UP

FR83020	Esterel Caravaning, France
HU5370	Napfeny, Hungary

Alan Rogers Readers' Award 2009

We believe our Readers' Award to be the most important. We simply invite our readers (by means of an on-line poll at www.alanrogers.com) to nominate the site they enjoyed most.

The outright winner for 2009 is:

WINNER

ES83900	Vilanova Park, Spain

Crossing the Channel

One of the great advantages of booking your ferry-inclusive holiday with the Alan Rogers Travel Service is the tremendous value we offer. Our money-saving Ferry Deals have become legendary. As agents for all major cross-Channel operators we can book all your travel arrangements with the minimum of fuss and at the best possible rates.

Just call us for an instant quote

01580 214000

or visit
www.**alanrogers.com/travel**

Let us price your holiday for you
instantly!

The quickest and easiest way is to call us for advice and an instant quote. We can take details of your vehicle and party and, using our direct computer link to all the operators' reservations systems, can give you an instant price. We can even check availability for you and book a crossing while you're on the phone!

Please note we can only book ferry crossings in conjunction with a campsite holiday reservation.

When you book with us, you will be allocated an experienced Personal Travel Consultant to provide you with personal advice and manage every stage of your booking. Our Personal Travel Consultants have first-hand experience of many of our campsites and access to a wealth of information. They can check availability, provide a competitive price and tailor your holiday arrangements to your specific needs.

- Discuss your holiday plans with a friendly person with first-hand experience

- Let us reassure you that your holiday arrangements really are taken care of

- Tell us about your special requests and allow us to pass these on

- Benefit from advice which will save you money – the latest ferry deals and more

- Remember, our offices are in Kent not overseas and we do NOT operate a queuing system!

The aims of the Travel Service are simple

- To provide convenience - a one-stop shop to make life easier.

- To provide peace of mind - when you need it most.

- To provide a friendly, knowledgeable, efficient service – when this can be hard to find.

- To provide a low cost means of organising your holiday – when prices can be so complicated.

HOW IT WORKS

Choose your campsite(s) – we can book around 500 across Europe. Look for the yellow coloured campsite entries in this book. You'll find more info and images at www.alanrogers.com/travel

Please note: the list of campsites we can book for you varies from time to time.

Then just call us for an instant quote

01580 214000

or visit

www.alanrogers.com/travel

LOOK FOR A CAMPSITE ENTRY LIKE THIS TO INDICATE WHICH CAMPSITES WE CAN BOOK FOR YOU.

THE LIST IS GROWING SO PLEASE CALL FOR UP TO THE MINUTE INFORMATION.

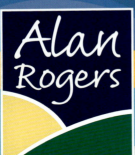

Whether you want to explore historical cities, stroll around medieval hill towns, relax on sandy beaches or simply indulge in opera, good food and wine, Italy has it all. Roman ruins, Renaissance art and beautiful churches abound. For the more active, the Italian Alps are a haven for winter sports enthusiasts and also offer good hiking trails.

Tourist Office

Italian State Tourist Board,
1, Princes Street,
London W1B 2AY

Tel: 020 7408 1254
or 09065 508925 (brochures)

Fax: 020 7399 3567
E-mail: italy@italiantouristboard.co.uk
Internet: www.enit.it

Italy only became a unified state in 1861, hence the regional nature of the country today. With 20 distinct regions each one has retained its own individualism which is evident in the cuisine and local dialects.

In the north, the vibrant city of Milan is great for shopping and home to the famous opera house, La Scala, as well as Leonardo's Last Supper fresco. It is also a good jumping-off point for the Alps; the Italian Lake District, incorporating Lake Garda, Lake Como and Lake Maggiore; the canals of Venice and the lovely town of Verona. Central Italy probably represents the most commonly perceived image of the country and Tuscany, with its classic rolling countryside and the historical towns of Florence, Siena, San Gimignano and Pisa, is one of the most visited areas. Further south is the historical capital of Rome and the city of Naples. Close to some of Italy's ancient sites such as Pompeii, Naples is within easy distance of Sorrento and the Amalfi coast.

Population
57.8 million

Capital
Rome (Roma)

Climate
The south enjoys extremely hot summers and mild, dry winters, whilst the mountainous regions of the north are cooler with heavy snowfalls in winter.

Language
Italian. There are several dialect forms and some German is spoken near the Austrian border.

Telephone
The country code is 0039.

Currency
The Euro (€).

Banks
Mon-Fri 08.30-13.00 and 15.00-16.00.

Shops
Mon-Sat 08.30/09.00-13.00 and 15.30/16.00-19.30/20.00, with some variations in larger cities.

Public Holidays
New Year; Easter Mon; Liberation Day 25 Apr; Labour Day; Assumption 15 Aug; All Saints 1 Nov; Immaculate Conception 8 Dec; Christmas 25, 26 Dec; plus numerous special local feast days.

Fringed by the French and Swiss Alps in the far north of the country home to several ski resorts, with vineyard clad-hills in the south, Piedmon* and Valle d'Aosta is renowned for its fine wines and local cuisine.

Alan Rogers

THE REGION IS MADE UP OF THE FOLLOWING PROVINCES: ALESSANDRIA, AOSTA, ASTI, BIELLA, CUNEO, IVREA, NOVARA, VERBANIA AND VERCELLI

In the heart of Piedmont is Turin, home to the most famous holy relic of all time, the Turin Shroud, and the Fiat car company. It also boasts a superb Egyptian Museum, Renaissance cathedral, elegant piazzas plus designer shops and good restaurants. In the east set in a vast plain of paddy fields along the River Po – which stretches right across northern Italy – is Vercelli, the rice capital of Europe. Further south are the wine-producing towns of Alba, renowned for its white truffles and red wines; and Asti, the capital of Italy's sparkling wine industry, where the famous 'spumante' is produced. There are numerous wine museums, vineyards and cantinas in the area, from where you can purchase wine, including those at Barolo, Annuziata and Costigliole d'Asti.

Studded with picturesque castles, the Valle d'Aosta offers great walking and skiing country with its dramatic mountains, beautiful valleys and lush meadows, most notably in the Gran Paradiso National Park. This huge park is also home to over 3,000 ibex, a relative of the deer family, 6,000 chamois plus golden eagles and rare butterflies.

Places of interest

Aosta: attractive mountain town with Roman architecture and ruins.

Avigliana: small town perched beside two lakes surrounded by mountains, medieval houses.

Biella: renowned for its wool industry.

Domodossola: mountain town of Roman origin, arcaded medieval centre, starting point of a scenic train ride across to Switzerland.

Lake Orta: set among the foothills of the Alps, in the middle of the lake rises the Island of San Guilo, with a basilica.

Saluzzo: medieval town, Gothic church, castle.

Susa: medieval town, 11th century castle and church.

Cuisine of the region

Bagna cauda: local variation on fondue, vegetables dipped into a sauce of oil, anchovies, garlic, cream and butter.

Fontina: a semi-hard cheese made in the Valle d'Aosta.

Manzo al Barolo: lean beef marinated in red wine and garlic and stewed gently.

Soupe á la cogneintze: soup with rice.

Spumone piemontese: a mousse of mascarpone cheese with rum.

Tora di Nocciole: nut tart including hazelnuts, eggs and butter.

Zabaglione: dessert made with a mixture of egg yolk, sugar and Marsala.

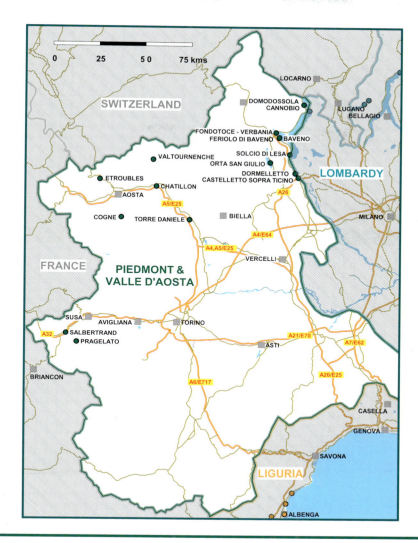

Baveno

Camping Parisi

Via Piave 50, I-28831 Baveno (Piedmont) T: 032 392 3156. E: info@campingparisi.it
alanrogers.com/IT62480

Camping Parisi is a quiet, family run site on the beautiful western shore of Lake Maggiore within the town of Baveno. The small and compact site has just 61 touring pitches which are shaded by mature trees. The site's real strength is the stunning views over the lake. It is possible to paddle and swim from the lake shore which is also good for sunbathing (but care must be taken with children – lifeguard 1/7-31/8). There are no leisure facilities, but there is direct access to a shared community complex with a restaurant and bar with satellite TV, plus some sports provision and entertainment.

Facilities

Central sanitary facilities are clean with free hot showers and British style WCs but, as yet, no facilities for disabled campers. Washing machine and dryer. No shop (town is 100 m). Freezer service. Adjacent community complex with bar, TV and restaurant and leisure facilities (from 1/5). Play area. Reception will make bookings for local activities. Kayaks for hire. Off site: Shops nearby. Boat launching 1 km. Riding 3 km. Sailing and bicycle hire both 4 km. Golf 10 km.

Open: 25 March - 10 October.

Directions

Baveno is 90 km. northwest of Milan on the western shore of Lake Maggiore, and is on the SS33 between Arona and Verbania. From A26 take Baveno exit and turn right on main road to site. From Simplon or Gothard the first site sign is in Feriolo. Site is signed to the east in the town centre.
GPS: 45.91245, 8.50555

Charges guide

Per unit incl. 2 persons	
and electricity	€ 21,50 - € 32,00
extra person	€ 5,50 - € 7,50
child (2-12 yrs)	€ 4,00 - € 5,00

Baveno

Camping Tranquilla

Via Cave-Oltrefiume 2, I-28831 Baveno (Piedmont) T: **032 392 3452**. E: **info@tranquilla.com**
alanrogers.com/IT62470

Tranquilla is a family run site on the western slopes above Baveno, close to Lake Maggiore. The site is in two terraced sections, both with electricity connections (6A). The 56 touring pitches are of average size with trees offering plenty of shade. There is a pleasant swimming pool (renovated in 2008) with an attractive new paddling pool. An unusually large restaurant with two terraces is open all season and offers a varied menu at reasonable prices and live entertainment in season. Reception is housed in an attractive old railway carriage from where the Luca family will welcome you. Excellent English is spoken. Tourist information is available and reception will book any of the local activities and facilities including watersports. The site is an ideal base from which to explore this very attractive area. The lakeside town of Baveno is about 1.5 km. away, down a fairly steep hill. About half way down are bus stops and a there is a weekly market on Mondays. Boat trips to three islands are available from the quay.

Facilities

The southern site has a recent ladies' sanitary block which includes facilities for disabled campers, whilst the male block is older. The northern side has several older, modernised blocks. All are kept very clean. British and Turkish style WCs. Laundry. Motorcaravan services. Bar. Restaurant, pizzeria and takeaway. Swimming pool (10/5-30/9). Aquarium. Play area. Excursions. Off site: Fishing 800 m. Bus service 800 m. Sailing 1.5 km. Golf, bicycle hire and riding 3 km. Shops nearby.

Open: 15 March - 15 October.

Directions

Baveno is 90 km. northwest of Milan on the western shore of Lake Maggiore, and is on the SS33 road between Arona and Verbania. Site is well signed to the west in the northern part of the town.
GPS: 45.91172, 8.49071

Charges guide

Per person	€ 5,00 - € 6,50
child (4-12 yrs)	€ 3,50 - € 5,20
pitch	€ 6,80 - € 10,00
electricity	€ 2,40
dog	free - € 2,50

Special discounts for Alan Rogers readers. No credit cards, but travellers cheques and British currency accepted.

Cannobio

Camping Valle Romantica

Via Valle Cannobina, I-28822 Cannobio (Piedmont) T: **032 371 249**
E: **valleromantica@riviera-valleromantica.com** alanrogers.com/IT62400

This site really lives up to its name! Situated in a wooded mountain valley, it was established about 50 years ago by the present owner's father, who planted some 20,000 plants, trees and shrubs. These are all now well established and maintained to make a delightful garden setting. The 164 numbered pitches for touring units are on flat grass among the trees, which provide good shade. Most have electricity (4-6A) although long cables are necessary in some parts. The site's swimming pool is in a sunny position and there are places in the river where, except after heavy rain, children can play. Used by tour operators (24 pitches).

Facilities

Three sanitary blocks provide good facilities with free controllable showers. Washing machines. Gas supplies. Motorcaravan services. Small, well stocked supermarket. Pleasant bar/restaurant with waiter service and takeaway. Pizzeria. Swimming pool (15/5-15/9). Fishing (licence required). Sailing and windsurfing schools. Fridge box hire. Off site: Bicycle hire 1 km. Boat launching and sailing 1.5 km. Golf and riding 15 km.

Open: 1 April - 13 September.

Directions

Cannobio is 4 km. from the Swiss border on the SS34 Locarno - Verbania road. Follow site signs from SS34 turning west (away from lake) at the southern outskirts of Cannobio and travel 1.5 km. to site.
GPS: 46.05758, 8.67737

Charges guide

Per unit incl. 2 persons and electricity	€ 24,00 - € 34,00
extra person	€ 3,50 - € 8,50

No credit cards.

Check real time availability and at-the-gate prices...
www.**alanrogers**.com

Cannobio
Camping Riviera

Via Casali Darbedo 2, I-28822 Cannobio (Piedmont) T: **032 371 360**. E: **riviera@riviera-valleromantica.com**
alanrogers.com/IT62450

With scenic views across the water and the surrounding mountains, this site is directly beside Lake Maggiore. Under the same active ownership as Valle Romantica, the site has a well cared for appearance and it is certainly one of the best lakeside sites in the area. Over 250 numbered pitches are on flat grass, either side of hard surfaced access roads and divided by trees and shrubs. There are 220 with 5A electricity (long cables may be needed). The site could make a suitable base for exploring the area, although progress on the busy winding road may be slow!

Facilities
The five sanitary blocks, one new and two with facilities for disabled visitors, are of good quality. Washing machines. Fridge boxes for hire. Gas. Motorcaravan services. Shop. Bar/restaurant with covered terrace, providing waiter service and takeaway. A second restaurant has an internet point. Fishing (licence required). Boat slipway. Off site: The town is only a short distance. Bicycle hire 500 m. Sailing and windsurfing schools nearby. Golf 11 km. Riding 15 km.

Open: 1 April - 18 October.

Directions
Cannobio is 4 km. from the Swiss border on the SS34 Locarno - Verbania road. It is north of the town, at the lakeside (on the east). Entrance is a few metres north of the bridge over the river. GPS: 46.06897, 8.74558

Charges guide
Per unit incl. 2 persons and electricity	€ 25,00 - € 34,00
extra person	€ 3,50 - € 8,50

No credit cards.

Castelletto Sopra Ticino
Camping Italia Lido

Via Cicognola 104, I-28053 Castelletto Sopra Ticino (Piedmont) T: **033 192 3032**. E: **info@campingitalialido.it**
alanrogers.com/IT62430

Arrival here is along the banks of the lake and there is a busy entrance. Reception, the restaurant and all other services are close to the entrance and there is an extremely pleasant beach, unusually with sand, in a quiet area that adjoins the main lake. It is a peaceful spot, apart from the occasional aircraft making for Malpensa airport. The touring pitches are all near reception with a large number of permanent pitches to the rear of the site. Pitches are of varying sizes and informally placed under trees. Most have views of the water with a few really special ones alongside the lake.

Facilities
One new (2006) sanitary block is modern and clean with British style toilets. Showers are very modern and pleasant. Facilities for children. Washing machines and dryer. Bar and good restaurant. Beach on site. Play area. Boat launching. Fishing. Off site: Watersports. Boat hire. Town 800 m. Train museum 2 km.

Open: 1 March - 31 October.

Directions
Site is on southern tip of Lake Maggiore. Use A8 from Milan taking exit for Castelletto Sopra Ticino. Follow minor road to town and site is signed from here. It is at the end of no through road where parking before entering is difficult. GPS: 45.7245, 8.61051

Charges guide
Per person	€ 4,00 - € 5,30
pitch	€ 7,20 - € 12,00
electricity	€ 2,50

No credit cards.

Chatillon
Camping Dalai Lama

Valle del Cervino, I-11024 Chatillon (Aosta) T: **016 654 8688**. E: **info@dalailamavillage.it**
alanrogers.com/IT62210

This all year site at an altitude of 1,492 metres is the dream of Renato Sartori, the owner. The theme, as the name suggests, is that of Tibet and is followed throughout the campsite. For example, the bar area is beautifully decorated in Tibetan style with a highly decorative bar front and a beautiful winter white and gold stove. Reception is operated from here in a most civilised manner. The grass pitches are on level surfaces and vary in size (80-100 sq.m) with 10A electricity. Some for motorcaravans on the upper levels are fully serviced. There are also many permanent bungalows.

Facilities
Two modern toilet blocks are kept very clean. WCs are mixed Turkish and British style and showers are large. Facilities for disabled visitors. Children's facilities and baby baths. Laundry facilities. Bar area. Excellent restaurant and takeaway (closed Nov). Indoor pool complex, spa and paddling area, sauna and gym (charged). Play area. Games room. Weekly evening entertainment. Torches useful. Off site: Town facilities 3 km. Alpine sports. Skiing. Fishing, riding and bicycle hire 6 km. Golf 15 km.

Open: All year.

Directions
Site is east of Aosta. From A5/E25 take St Vincent exit and road towards Breuil-Cervinia. At Antey St Andre take road towards La Magdeleine and then road to Promiod where the site is signed.
GPS: 45.78721, 7.60363

Charges guide
Per person	€ 8,00 - € 11,00
child (4-12 yrs)	€ 6,00 - € 8,00
pitch	€ 5,00 - € 16,00
electricity	€ 2,00

Cogne
Camping Lo Stambecco
Valnontey, I-11012 Cogne (Aosta) T: 016 574 152. E: campingstambecco@tiscali.it

alanrogers.com/IT62150

Lo Stambecco is tucked away deep in the Gran Paradiso National Park. After a very attractive mountain drive you will reach this small site with wonderful views of the mountains and glaciers. The grass pitches are informally arranged on slopes and terraces (chocks are useful) and all have great views. Electricity (3A) is available. Watch for the attractive frogs as you park up! Clean crisp air, difficult to beat views, the relaxing sound of cow bells and Alpine activities are the strengths of this site. We wanted to stay longer in this superb location. It is a site for longer stays, as the drive here makes it more than a transit site.

Facilities
The two toilet blocks are mature but clean. WCs are a mixture of Turkish and British style. Baby baths to borrow. Washing machines. Motorcaravan service point. Café/snack bar. Play area. Barbecues not permitted. Dogs are not accepted. Torches useful. Off site: Hotel 200 m. (same ownership) with restaurant and fitness facilities (charged). Riding 300 m. Bicycle hire 500 m. Alpine sports. Gran Paradiso National Park. ATM 8 km. Public transport at site.

Open: 30 May - 30 September.

Directions
Site is south of Aosta. From A5/E25 take Cogne exit south. A long scenic drive will take you to Cogne. From here take road to Valtoney where site is clearly signed. GPS: 45.58333, 7.33333

Charges guide
Per person	€ 5,00 - € 6,00
child	€ 4,00
pitch incl. electricity	€ 5,00 - € 7,00

Dormelletto
Camping Village Lago Maggiore
Via Leonardo da Vinci, 7, I-28040 Dormelletto (Piedmont) T: 032 249 7193. E: info@lagomag.com

alanrogers.com/IT62435

This site can be found on the southwestern shores of Lake Maggiore, close to the pretty town of Arona. There are 290 pitches here, of which around 90 are available for tourers. Pitches are all equipped with electrical connections and have reasonable shade. A number of brick built chalets and mobile homes are available for rent. The site has direct access to the lake and a sandy beach. On-site amenities include a well stocked shop and a bar/restaurant, which includes a pizzeria where pizzas are cooked on a traditional log stove. A wealth of sports activities is on offer on site, many based around the two swimming pools and sports field. The lake is ideal for watersports – windsurfers and boats can be hired locally. During July and August there is a lively programme of activities and entertainment.

Facilities
Five toilet blocks (a small charge is made for hot water and showers). Private family bathrooms for rent. Motorcaravan services. Bar, restaurant/pizzeria. Shop. Games room. Play area. Swimming pools. Children's pool. Sports field. Entertainment and activity programme (high season). Direct access to lake. Mobile homes and chalets for rent. Off site: Arona 3 km. Walking and cycle routes.

Open: 1 April - 30 September.

Directions
Leave the A26 motorway at the Sesto Calende exit and join the northbound SS33 as far as Dormelletto. The campsite is clearly signed from the village. GPS: 45.73333, 8.57722

Charges guide
Per unit incl. 2 persons	€ 22,00 - € 39,00
extra person	€ 5,00 - € 9,00
child (2-6 yrs)	€ 2,50 - € 5,00

Etroubles
Camping Tunnel
Via Chevriere 4, I-11014 Etroubles (Aosta) T: 016 578 292. E: info@campingtunnel.it

alanrogers.com/IT62160

This is a very small site located near the Gran San Bernado tunnel, hence its name. The views from the site are really very pleasant with green hills and towering peaks all around. There is distinct Italian feel about it and the young owners are very pleasant and both speak English. The site sits on two sides of a quiet road and steady improvements are being made. There are 150 pitches, with 50 of mixed size for touring units, on both sides of the site. All have electricity (3/6A), some have shade and most are on terraces or gentle slopes. The upper side has most of the facilities including a pretty building with bar/restaurant and terrace atop. The prices here are very good and we see this mostly as a short stay site.

Facilities
Two toilet blocks are under the main building and central to the upper part of the site. WCs are mostly Turkish, with some British style. Showers are modern in one block, basic in the other. Basic facilities for disabled visitors. Washing machine. Motorcaravan service point. Shop. Bar and restaurant (weekends only in winter). Torches useful. Off site: Fishing 2 km. Golf 7 km. Village of Etroubles.

Open: Closed for two weeks in May and November (phone to confirm dates).

Directions
Site is north of Aosta. From A5-E25 take Aosta turn and travel north on T2 E27 towards Col de Gran San Bernardo. At Etroubles the site is signed. GPS: 45.81667, 7.21666

Charges guide
Per person	€ 5,00 - € 5,50
child (3-12 yrs)	€ 3,50 - € 4,00
pitch incl. electricity	€ 5,50 - € 8,00

Feriolo di Baveno
Camping Orchidea

Via 42 Martiri, 2, I-28835 Feriolo di Baveno (Piedmont) T: 032 328 257. E: info@campingorchidea.it

alanrogers.com/IT62465

Camping Orchidea can be found on the western bank of Lake Maggiore, 35 km. south of the Swiss border and 5 km. from Stresa. This site has direct access to the lake and a sandy beach. Orchidea has recently been refurbished and has a good range of modern amenities, including a shop, bar and restaurant. Watersports are understandably popular here and pedaloes and kayaks can be rented on site. Pitches are grassy and generally well shaded, all with electrical connections (3/6A). Some pitches are available facing the lake (a supplement is charged in peak season). There are caravans and mobile homes available for rent. Stresa, nearby, is an important town with 5,000 inhabitants and has a harbour with regular boat trips to the Borromean islands, and also a cable car to the summit of Monte Mottarone, passing the stunning Giardino Botanico Alpinia, world renowned mountain gardens.

Facilities

Three toilet blocks have been modernised and all have hot and cold water throughout. Shop. Restaurant. Bar. Takeaway. Direct lake access. Pedalo and kayak hire. Fishing. Playground. Children's club. Mobile homes and caravans for rent. Bicycle hire. Off site: Walking and cycle trails. Stresa 5 km. Tennis. Riding.

Open: 15 March - 5 October.

Directions

Take Baveno/Stresa exit from A26 (autostrada dei Trafori) and head north on Via Sempione. In Feriolo follow signs to campsite. GPS: 45.9334, 8.4812

Charges guide

Per unit incl. 2 persons and electricity	€ 17,00 - € 39,50
extra person	€ 4,70 - € 7,70
child (under 12 yrs)	free - € 5,70
dog	€ 2,50 - € 5,00

Feriolo di Baveno
Camping Miralago

Via 42 Martiri, 24, I-28831 Feriolo di Baveno (Piedmont) T: 032 328 226. E: miralago@miralago-holiday.com

alanrogers.com/IT62464

Miralago is a sister site of IT62463 (Camping Holiday) and is also located on the western banks of Lake Maggiore, close to the little resort of Feriolo. Unusually, many of the pitches here have direct access to the lake or to the River Stronetta at the point where it runs into the lake. There are 74 pitches here, all of which are equipped with electricity (6A) connections. Premium pitches are available with direct lake access. On-site amenities include a bar and a play area for children. A cycle track leads from the site to Feriolo, 500 m. away. Stresa, nearby, is an important resort town with over 5,000 inhabitants and has a harbour with regular boat trips to the Borromean islands, and also a cable car to the summit of Monte Mottarone, passing the stunning Giardino Botanico Alpinia, world renowned mountain gardens. Stresa is also home to some fabulous villas, notably the Villa Ducale, dating back to 1770 and the more recent, but equally imposing Villa dell'Orto.

Facilities

Shop, bar and restaurant (all season). Play area. Tourist information. Direct access to lake and sandy beach. Off site: Feriolo 500 m. Baveno 3 km. Stresa 7 km. Golf and bicycle hire 2 km. Riding 500m. Walking and cycle routes. Watersports. Fishing.

Open: 1 April - 3 October.

Directions

Leave the A26 motorway at the Casale exit and join the eastbound S33 as far as Feriolo. Site is clearly signed from the village. GPS: 45.93388, 8.48471

Charges guide

Per unit incl. 2 persons and electricity	€ 23,50 - € 29,50
extra person	€ 5,00 - € 7,50
child (2-12 yrs)	€ 4,50 - € 6,00
dog	€ 4,50 - € 5,50

Feriolo di Baveno
Camping Holiday

Via 42 Martiri, 28, I-28835 Feriolo di Baveno (Piedmont) T: 032 328 164. E: info@miralago-holiday.com

alanrogers.com/IT62463

Camping Holiday is located on Lake Maggiore's western shores, close to the resort of Baveno and larger town of Stresa. This is a small site with direct access to a sandy beach. There are just 51 pitches, all of which are equipped with electricity (6A) and satellite TV connections. Premium pitches are available with direct lake access. There are also a number of smaller pitches, suitable for small tents. Five new mobile homes are available. Although the site is small, there is a bar/restaurant and well stocked shop. A cycle track leads from the site to the village of Feriolo, 600 m. away, and beyond to Baveno. Lake Maggiore is rightly renowned for its lush gardens and magnificent mountain scenery. The Borromean islands are a popular excursion and easily accessible from Stresa. This is also a wonderful area for mountain biking and hiking – the Monte Rosa massif is easily accessible. The lake is also understandably popular for sailing and windsurfing and hire services are available in Stresa and Baveno.

Facilities
Bar, restaurant/pizzeria and shop (all season). Direct access to lake and sandy beach. Play area. Tourist information. Off site: Feriolo 600 m. Baveno 3 km. Stresa 7 km. Golf 2 km, horse riding and bicycle hire 500m. Walking and cycle routes. Watersports. Fishing.

Open: 23 April - 26 September.

Directions
Leave the A26 motorway at the Casale exit and join the eastbound S33 as far as Feriolo. Site is clearly signed from the village. GPS: 45.93602, 8.48635

Charges guide

Per unit incl. 2 persons and electricity	€ 19,50 - € 28,50
extra person	€ 5,00 - € 7,00
child (2-12 yrs)	€ 4,50 - € 6,00
dog	€ 3,00 - € 5,50

Feriolo di Baveno
Camping Conca d'Oro

250

Via 42 Martiri 26, I-28835 Feriolo di Baveno (Piedmont) T: 032 328 116. E: info@concadoro.it

alanrogers.com/IT62485

Conca d'Oro is a delightful site with spectacular views across Lake Maggiore to the distant mountains. The first impression is one of spaciousness and colour. There are just a dozen mobile homes for rent, the rest of the 210 grass plots being good sized touring pitches. All have 6A electrical connections; they are marked by young trees and azalea bushes. The land slopes gently down to a sandy beach. An attractive restaurant serves a varied range of dishes and there is a good bar and pizzeria and a well-stocked shop. The young owners Maurizio and Alessandra are sure to give you a warm welcome. The site is close to the lakeside town of Baveno from where boat trips are available to the three small islands on this part of Lake Maggiore. Fishing and boat launching are possible from the beach at the site; sailing and other watersports can be enjoyed from various points on the lake. There are nature reserves nearby and drives out into the surrounding mountains provide opportunities for walkers, cyclists and climbers.

Facilities
Three toilet blocks provide all necessary facilities kept in immaculate condition, including controllable showers and open style washbasins; some toilets with washbasins. En-suite unit for disabled visitors. Laundry room. Motorcaravan service point. Bar, restaurant, pizzeria and shop (all season). Swimming, fishing and boat launching from beach. Bicycle hire. Dogs must be booked and are not allowed 3/7-21/8. Off site: Riding 700 m. Golf 1 km. Sailing 7 km. Shops, bars and restaurants nearby.

Open: 26 March - 27 September.

Directions
Baveno is 90 km. northwest of Milan on the western shore of Lake Maggiore. Site is on the SS33 road between Baveno and Fondotoce di Verbania, 1 km. south of the junction with the SS34 and is well signed. GPS: 45.93611, 8.48583

Charges guide

Per unit incl. 2 persons and electricity	€ 21,00 - € 40,90
extra person	€ 5,00 - € 7,50
child (2-13 yrs)	€ 3,50 - € 6,50
dog (excl. 3/7-21/8)	€ 3,50 - € 4,50

Fondotoce di Verbania

Camping La Quiete

Via Turati 72, I-28040 Fondotoce di Verbania (Piedmont) T: **0323 496 013**. E: **info@campinglaquiete.it**
alanrogers.com/IT62495

La Quiete is a small site, attractively located on the shore of Lake Mergozzo, a small lake to the west of the much larger Lake Maggiore. There are 180 pitches here, mostly well shaded and with electrical connections (6A), many of which have fine views across the lake. A number of mobile homes are available for rent. On-site amenities include a shop and bar/restaurant, as well as a sports field and volleyball court. This is excellent mountain biking and walking country and the site owners will be pleased to recommend possible routes. Verbania, nearby, is an elegant resort town on Lake Maggiore, created by the merging of the towns of Pallanza and Intra. Here, the magnificent Giardini Botanici Villa Taranto are well worth a visit. They were created between 1931 and 1940 by Scotsman Neil McEacharn who undertook substantial changes to the landscape and added over 8 km. of water pipes.

Facilities

Bar/restaurant. Shop. Sports field. Games room. Play area. Direct access to Lake Mergozzo. Off site: Lake Maggiore. Verbania. Walking and cycle routes. Watersports. Fishing.

Open: 7 March - 20 October.

Directions

Leave the A26 motorway at the Casale exit and join the eastbound S34 as far as Fondotoce. Head north here on SP54 and the campsite is clearly signed. GPS: 45.9535, 8.47745

Charges guide

Per unit incl. 2 persons and electricity	€ 22,00

Check real time availability and at-the-gate prices...
www.alanrogers.com

Orta San Giulio

Camping Orta

Via Domodossola 28, I-28016 Orta San Giulio (Piedmont) T: 032 290 267. E: info@campingorta.it

alanrogers.com/IT62420

Lake Orta is a charming, less visited small lake just west of Lake Maggiore in an area with understated charm. The site is on a considerable slope, and most of the 70 touring pitches (all with 4A electricity) are on the top grass terrace with spectacular views across the lake to the mountains beyond. There are some superb lakeside pitches across the main road (linked by a pedestrian underpass) although there is some traffic noise here. Amenities include a large games and entertainment room and a traditional Italian bar and restaurant serving good value family meals. Some English is spoken by the Guarnori family, who take pride in maintaining their uncomplicated site to a high standard. Book ahead to enjoy the lakeside pitches. If you are anxious about towing a large caravan to the top terraces, the owner will help out with his tractor!

Facilities

Three modern sanitary blocks are clean and well maintained providing mainly British style toilets, coin operated showers and an excellent unit for disabled visitors. Laundry facilities. Motorcaravan services. Excellent shop. Bar and restaurant with basic menu serving good value Italian family meals. Playground. Large games/TV room. WiFi in reception/bar area. Fishing. Bicycle hire. Boat launching. Off site: Riding, golf and sailing all within 10 km.

Open: All year.

Directions

Lake Orta is 85 km. northwest of Milan and just west of Lake Maggiore. Site is on the SR229 between Borgomanero and Omega, 600 m. north of the turn to Orta San Giulio. There is a parking area for arrivals on the lake side of the road, but reception and main entrance are on the opposite side.
GPS: 45.80188, 8.42047

Charges guide

Per person	€ 5,00 - € 6,50
pitch	€ 8,00 - € 15,00
electricity	€ 2,00

Pragelato

Gofree Villaggio Touristico Camping

Via Nazionale, I-10060 Pragelato (Piedmont) T: 012 278 045. E: info@villaggiogofree.com

alanrogers.com/IT65050

Gofree, an unusual name for a campsite, is owned by a dynamo in the form of Patrizia Laurent. She will be pleased to welcome you to this site which is open all year and is primarily a modern looking bungalow village. However, the supporting facilities are of a high quality for campers to enjoy. It is one of the very few quality camping sites hereabouts. The 40 pitches (80 sq.m) all have 10A electricity and may be at one end of the site in winter on what would be the tennis courts in summer season. Tents are placed in a field opposite. A two storey modern building houses reception, a good restaurant and a bar which are at your disposal all year. Everything here is modern and neat, and looked very new when we visited. You will also get a chance to practise your Italian with the many Italian families who occupy the bungalows. We recommend this as a stopover or to be used in the winter for skiing.

Facilities

One modern, well appointed, very clean sanitary block. British style WCs. Facilities for disabled visitors. Washing machines. Two special bungalows for campers with disabilities. Sophisticated bar and excellent restaurant/pizzeria and takeaway. Pleasant play area. Regular bus service at gate. WiFi. Off site: Town 1 km. Fishing 100 m. Bicycle hire 1 km. Riding 2 km. Golf 3 km. All mountain sports including skiing.

Open: All year.

Directions

Site is west of Torino and southeast of the Fréjus tunnel exit. From A32 take S24 towards Sestriere. Pass Sestriere and head east for Torino on the R23. Site is 8 km. along this road near the village of Pragelato and well signed. GPS: 45.01667, 6.93333

Charges 2010

Per person (over 8 yrs)	€ 8,00
pitch incl. electricity	€ 10,00

Salbertrand
Camping Gran Bosco
SS24 del Monginevro km 75, I-10050 Salbertrand (Piedmont) T: 012 285 4653. E: info@campinggranbosco.it
alanrogers.com/IT65000

This is a modern and efficiently run site very near the Fréjus tunnel. The site was chosen to host guests for the Winter Olympics of 2006, thus the amenities are very good in an area of notoriously poor campsites. A family site, now being run by the keen younger generation. It has many attractive features including a smart bar/restaurant with terrace within the clean, new building just inside the entrance and everything is open all year. The 60 touring pitches are at both ends of the site, all have 6A electricity and are on flat ground with shade.

Facilities
Two modern, well appointed toilet blocks are well placed on the site. Clean WCs are British style, showers are excellent. Superb facilities for disabled visitors. Washing machines. Motorcaravan service point. Shop. Large bar and restaurant with terraces. Play area and good games room. Children's club. Entertainment in high season. Barbecue area. Torches useful. Off site: Riding, golf and bicycle hire 10 km. Fishing 5 km. Skiing in season. Public transport 100 m. ATM 5 km.

Open: All year.

Directions
Site is east of the Italian exit of the Fréjus tunnel. From A32 Torino - Fréjus autoroute take Oulx East exit. Turn east towards Turin on the SS24 and site is at km. 75 which is 2 km. from the Oulx exit.
GPS: 45.06187, 6.866667

Charges guide
Per unit incl. 2 persons and electricity	€ 24,00
extra person (over 3 yrs)	€ 7,00

Solcio di Lesa
Camping Solcio
Via al Campeggio, I-28040 Solcio di Lesa (Piedmont) T: 032 274 97. E: info@campingsolcio.com
alanrogers.com/IT62440

Camping Solcio is a family-run site on the lakeside and has lovely views over the lakes and the green hills which surround some of the site. The neat pitches are 60-90 sq.m. with 6A electricity. Mostly shaded by trees, the 105 touring pitches are on flat sand and grass. A very pleasant restaurant and a bar back onto a large building alongside the site, and there are some views of the lake from the terraces. You will have a view of the railway halfway up the hills alongside the site, so there is rail noise at times. The lakeside is good for safe swimming and, as the site is next to a large boat repair building plus its moorings, there is no through traffic in terms of fast boats. All manner of watersports are available here and the beach is of coarse sand. An ambitious entertainment programme is arranged for children in high season, and there is adventure sport for the over 10s. This is a pleasant site with modest facilities and it may suit those who do not seek the luxuries of the larger sites. English and Dutch are spoken and the site is very popular with Dutch campers.

Facilities
One main central toilet block is smart and clean. Toilets here are British style. An older block nearer reception has mixed Turkish and British style toilets. Facilities for disabled visitors. Baby room. Washing machine. Restaurant and bar with terrace. Basic shop. Full entertainment programme in season. Play areas. Bicycle hire. Internet. Torches useful. Off site: Town facilities 1 km. Riding 5 km. Golf 10 km. Public transport 300 m. ATM 2 km.

Open: 7 March - 20 October.

Directions
Site is on the west side of Lake Maggiore. From the A4 (Milan - Torino) take A8 to Castelletto Sticino. Then north on SS33 towards Stresa and look for site sign at km. 57 marker at Lesa. Take the narrow access road to the site. GPS: 45.81586, 8.54962

Charges guide
Per person	€ 5,00 - € 7,50
child (3-13 yrs)	€ 3,70 - € 6,00
pitch	€ 8,40 - € 21,50
electricity	€ 2,50 - € 2,60

Check real time availability and at-the-gate prices...
www.alanrogers.com

Verbania Fondotoce

Camping Continental Lido

Via 42 Martiri 156, I-28924 Fondotoce di Verbania (Piedmont) T: 032 349 6300
E: info@campingcontinental.com alanrogers.com/IT62490

Continental Lido is a large, bustling site situated on the shore of the charming little Lake Mergozzo, about a kilometre from the better known Lake Maggiore. The 479 average sized touring pitches are back-to-back in regular rows on grass. All have electricity (6A) and there is shade from a variety of trees in some parts. There is a feeling of spaciousness here and the 185 mobile homes are not obtrusive. There is an impressive new pool complex and a small sandy beach slopes gently into the lake where swimming and watersports can also be enjoyed (no powered craft allowed). Pine-clad mountains and a pretty village opposite the beach provide a pleasing, scenic background. An unusual feature here is the nine-hole golf course. There is a busy programme of activities from May to September. Under the same ownership as Isolino Camping Village, this site is managed by Gian Paolo, who speaks good English.

Facilities

Five high standard toilet blocks have free hot water. Facilities for disabled visitors. Washing machines and dryers. Mini-fridges. Well stocked shop and bar/restaurant with terrace and takeaway. Swimming pool complex (26/4-14/9) with slides, rapids and waves, plus free sun loungers and parasols. Snack bars by pool and lake. TV. Tennis. Golf course (9 holes). Playground. Fishing. Windsurfing, pedaloes, canoes, kayaks. Games room. Bicycle hire. Entertainment and activities (mid-June to mid-Sept). Bus on request to Verbania. Off site: Riding 1 km. Sailing 5 km. 18-hole golf 12 km.

Open: 3 April - 21 September.

Directions

Verbania is 100 km. northwest of Milan, on the western shore of Lake Maggiore. Site is off the SS34 road between Fondotoce and Gravellona, 200 m. west of junction with SS33. GPS: 45.94960, 8.48058

Charges guide

Per unit incl. 2 persons and electricity	€ 17,70 - € 25,60
extra person	€ 4,30 - € 7,30
child (6-11 yrs)	€ 3,30 - € 5,85
No credit cards.	

Verbania Fondotoce

Camping Village Isolino

Via per Feriolo 25, I-28924 Verbania Fondotoce (Piedmont) T: 032 349 6080. E: info@isolino.com
alanrogers.com/IT62460

Lake Maggiore is one of the most attractive Italian lakes and Isolino is one of the largest sites in the region. Most of the 460 tourist pitches have shade from a variety of trees. Some are of a good size, many in long, angled rows leading to the beach. All have electrical connections (6A) and some have lake views. The bar and restaurant terraces and the very large, lagoon style swimming pool with its island sun deck area have stunning views across the lake to the fir-clad mountains beyond. The social life of the campsite is centred around the large bar which has a stage sometimes used for musical entertainment. A newly constructed amphitheatre provides a home for the programme of activities and entertainment which runs between the end of April and mid-September. The extensive poolside terrace is outside the bar, takeaway and casual eating area. In the restaurant on the floor above, some tables share the magnificent views across the lake. The site is well situated for visiting the many attractions of the region which include the famous gardens on the islands in the lake and at the Villa Taranto, Verbania. The Swiss mountains and resort of Locarno are quite near. The site is owned by the friendly Manoni family who also own Camping Continental Lido at nearby Lake Mergozzo. There is a new pool with water games and a 'canyon river'.

Facilities

Six well built toilet blocks have hot water for showers and washbasins but cold for dishwashing and laundry. Baby room. Laundry facilities. Motorcaravan services. Supermarket, bar and takeaway (all season). Swimming pool (30/4-19/9). Amphitheatre. Fishing. Watersports. Bicycle hire and guided mountain bike tours. Long beach. Internet access and WiFi. Good English is spoken. Off site: Golf 2 km. Sailing 5 km. Riding 12 km.

Open: 26 March - 20 September.

Directions

Verbania is 100 km. northwest of Milan on the western shore of Lake Maggiore. From A26 motorway, leave at exit for Stresa/Baveno, turn left towards Fondotoce. Site is well signed off the SS33 north of Baveno and 300 m. south of the junction with SS34 at Fondotoce. GPS: 45.93835, 8.50008

Charges 2010

Per unit incl. 3 persons and electricity	€ 19,35 - € 48,50
extra person	€ 4,75 - € 8,00
child (3-11 yrs)	free - € 6,60
dog	€ 3,45 - € 8,00

Check real time availability and at-the-gate prices...
www.alanrogers.com

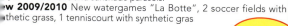

Torre Daniele
Camping Mombarone
Settimo Vittone Reg., I-10010 Torre Daniele (Piedmont) T: **012 575 7907**
alanrogers.com/IT62200

This is a small, rustic all year site alongside the SS26 road and close to the motorway from the Mont Blanc tunnel, providing a useful stop if entering or leaving Italy via this route. It has 120 pitches, with space for about 50 touring units on the grass area between the permanent units. The Peretto family take pride in looking after their guests and English is spoken. The site has a small bar and a simple, inexpensive restaurant is 50 metres away. The site is thoughtfully laid out in a valley with attractive plants, shrubs and trees for shade and is surrounded by high mountains and wooded hills, with vines bedecking the eastern slopes.

Facilities
The sanitary facilities are adequate and kept clean, with both British and Turkish style WCs and free hot showers. Washing machine. Bar. Children's pool. Fishing. Off site: Riding 5 km. Shops and restaurants nearby. Golf 30 km.

Open: All year.

Directions
From the A5 motorway take exit for Quincinetto onto the SS26 turning right; the site is almost immediately on the left. On the SS26 Aosta - Turin road, the site is between the 45 and 46 km. markers between Pont St Martin and Settimo Vittone. GPS: 45.5655, 7.8157

Charges guide
Per person	€ 4,50 - € 6,00
pitch incl. electricity	€ 8,50
No credit cards.	

Valtournenche
Camping Glair
Localitá Glair, 6, I-11028 Valtournenche (Aosta) T: **016 692 077**. E: **info@campingglair.it**
alanrogers.com/IT62170

This is a small site located in the heart of the Alps with one main function other than skiing. That is to position you for a visit to the world famous, pyramid peaked Matterhorn which towers above as you ascend the winding road towards the site. The pitches are informal, and generally you park around open paddocks. Only 2A electricity is provided and all other facilities are on a basic level. There is no supporting infrastructure here, but the town is a short walk away and there is a sports bar/café just outside the gate. The views are stunning and there is a pretty little lake to explore just a few metres from the site.

Facilities
The main toilet block is central and modern but the WCs are almost all Turkish style with one British style for each gender. Showers are modern, but by tokens. No facilities for disabled visitors. Washing machines. The chemical disposal point is a sharp climb from the motorcaravan parking area. Torches absolutely essential. Off site: The Matterhorn! Riding 300 m. Bicycle hire 200 m. Walking, climbing and skiing. Lake swimming. Public transport 1 km. ATM 2 km.

Open: All year.

Directions
Site is south of Breuil-Cervinia and the Matterhorn. From the A5/E25 St Vincent exit, take road north towards Breuil-Cervinia and, 2 km. south of the village of Valtournenche, turn right where site is signed. GPS: 45.87759, 7.62419

Charges guide
Per person	€ 4,00 - € 5,50
pitch	€ 4,00 - € 7,50
electricity	€ 2,50

Ligúria is a long, thin coastal strip nestling at the foot of olive and vine clad mountains. The Italian Riviera boasts an abundance of sandy beaches and charming seaside villages, while inland the mountain resorts offer plenty of walking and a respite from the crowds.

THE REGION HAS FOUR PROVINCES: GENOVA, IMPERIA, LA SPEZIA AND SAVONA

Ligúria divides neatly into two distinct stretches of coastline; to the west is the Riviera di Ponente and to the east is the Riviera Levante. Between the two lies Genoa, Italy's biggest port. It has a fascinating old town with medieval alleyways, and numerous palaces and churches to explore. It was also once the home of Christopher Columbus. The surrounding hills offer a quiet retreat from the city: the picturesque Valle Scrivia has several hiking routes and is easily accessible from the small town of Casella. Stretching across to the French border the Riveria di Ponente has a number of places of interest: the pretty wine producing town of Dolceacqua; the pleasant resort of San Remo; the charming seafront village of Cervo; and the medieval hilltown of Toirano. There are more coastal resorts along the Riviera Levante including Portofino, the most exclusive harbour and resort town in Italy. With sandy beaches and small coves, this attractive area also offers good walking. Further along is the coastline of the Cinque Terre (Five Lands). The name refers to five tiny villages which appear to cling dramatically to the edge of sheer cliffs: Monterosso al Mare, Vernazza, Corniglia, Manrola and Riomaggiore.

Places of interest

Albenga: small market town.

Camogli: attractive resort.

Cinque Terre: wine-growing region, picturesque villages, sandy coves and beaches.

Dolceacqua: medieval stone bridge and ruined castle.

La Spezia: museum with medieval and Renaissance art, ferry trips to Bastia in Corsica.

Lévanto: beachside resort.

Portovénere: village with three islets offshore.

Toirano: caves at the Grotte della Basura and Grotta di Santa Lucia.

Villa Hanbury: impressive botanical gardens.

Cuisine of the region

The best known speciality is *pesto*: made with chopped basil, garlic, pine nuts and grated cheese with olive oil, it was invented by the Genoese to help their long term sailors fight scurvy. Fish and seafood is readily available, often eaten with pasta. Chickpeas grow in abundance, and make *farinata*, a kind of chickpea pancake. Genoa is famous for its *pandolce*, a sweet cake laced with dried fruit, nuts and candied peel.

Burrida di seppie: cuttlefish stew.

Cacciucco: rich stew of mixed fish and seafood cooked with wine, garlic and herbs.

Carpione: fish marinated in vinegar and herbs.

Cima alla Genovese: cold stuffed veal.

Torta pasqualina: spinach and cheese pie.

Trenette al Pesto: noodles with pesto.

Ameglia
Camping River

Localitá Armezzone, I-19031 Ameglia (Ligúria) T: 018 765 920. E: **info@campingriver.com**
alanrogers.com/IT64190

Ameglia, near La Spezia, is just south of the A12 autrostada and this site is just 5 km. from the Sarzana exit. Close to Le Cinque Terre and on the banks of the Magna river, this popular site provides 100 touring pitches and about the same number for static caravans. With its own small marina and excellent swimming pools, the site provides a busy location for a short stop or a longer stay to explore Ligúria. The narrow access road will stop larger motorhomes from gaining access, but when we visited there were a large number of twin axle caravans on site. The river provides boat launching facilities and good fishing opportunities further up river. The site has direct access to the water and a small marina with docking facilities for visitors. A busy entertainment programme is provided from mid June.

Facilities

Two sanitary blocks provide toilets (some Turkish style), washbasins and unisex showers. Facilities for disabled campers. Motorcaravan service point. Restaurant and bar. Shop. Pizzeria. Swimming pool and sun deck. Boat launching. Fishing. Mobile homes and bungalows to rent. Off site: Tennis and riding 200 m. Archery. Sailing. Scuba diving. La Spezia. Le Cinque Terre.

Open: 1 April - 30 September.

Directions

Take Sarzana exit on A12 (Genoa - Livorno) and follow signs initially towards Lerici. After 3 km. follow signs to Bocca di Magra and Ameglia where the site is well signed off to the left. The final access road is narrow and has a tight bend so larger units might experience some difficulty. GPS: 44.07556, 9.96972

Charges guide

Per person	€ 4,50 - € 9,20
child (2-10 yrs)	€ 2,30 - € 7,00
pitch	€ 18,00 - € 45,80
No credit cards.	

Bogliasco

Camping Genova Est

Via Marconi Localitá Cassa, I-16031 Bogliasco (Ligúria) T: **010 347 2053**. E: **info@camping-genova-est.it**
alanrogers.com/IT64100

This wooded site is set on very steep slopes close to the Genova motorways and is east of the city. It has very limited facilities, but runs a free bus service to connect with local transport for visiting Genova. If you are extremely fit a set of steep stairs (125 m. elevation) will take you there in 15 minutes. The approach from the main road twists and climbs steeply with a tight final turn at the site entrance. There are 54 pitches for tents and mobile units with electricity available (3/6A) to the vehicle pitches. A small play area is set on a narrow terrace and children should be supervised. The restaurant/bar with terrace commands fine views over the sea and a pleasant menu, which changes daily, is offered at a good price. The Buteros who own the site both speak good English and are very enthusiastic and anxious to ensure you enjoy your stay. This is a site to be used for exploring Genova and Riviera di Levante, rather than for extended stays and is not recommended for disabled campers. It is the only site in the area.

Facilities

Two sanitary blocks provides free hot showers and en-suite cabins (WC, washbasin and shower). Washing machine. Basic motorcaravan services. Shop providing essentials. Bar/restaurant and takeaway (all open Easter - 30/9). Towing vehicle available. Gas supplies. Site is not suitable for disabled people. Free bus shuttle to local town. Scooters for hire. Off site: Beach 500 m. Fishing and boat launching 1.5 km. Bicycle hire 2 km. Golf 22 km.

Open: 15 March - 20 October.

Directions

From autostrada A10 take Nervi exit and turn towards La Spezia on the SS1. In Bogliasco look for a sharp left turn with a large sign for site. Follow narrow winding road for 2 km. to site. GPS: 44.38453, 9.07308

Charges 2010

Per unit incl. 2 persons and electricity	€ 23,10 - € 25,90
extra person	€ 3,80 - € 6,40

Less 5% for holders of a current Alan Rogers Guide.

Campochiesa di Albenga

Camping Bella Vista

Reg. Campore 23, I-17031 Campochiesa di Albenga (Ligúria) T: **018 254 0213**
E: **campingbellavista@hotmail.com alanrogers.com/IT64060**

Owned and run by the multilingual, Dutch, Kox family, this site has a crisp, neat appearance. On flat ground, the 60 pitches are in neat rows, separated in places by hedges and young trees. They are loosely ringed by bungalows rented by Italian campers. Two sizes of pitch are offered: 50 and 80 sq.m. with a sink and tap for every four pitches. Electricity (6A) is available and 17 pitches are serviced. Large units will need to exercise care when manoeuvring. This is a peaceful site where one can relax and get away from it all with the beaches 1.5 km. away.

Facilities

The single modern block is smart with British style toilets. Shower water is solar heated, washbasins have cold water only. Single facility for disabled campers although the unit doubles as a baby room with a washing machine and ironing equipment (key at reception). Shop (1/5-15/10). Bar. Takeaway (1/5-15/10). Swimming pool and separate paddling pool. Limited entertainment in season. Off site: Riding 500 m. Public transport 800 m. Beach 1.5 km. Fishing and boat launching 2 km. Bicycle hire 6 km. Golf 14 km. ATM 2 km.

Open: 15 March - 15 November.

Directions

Exit at Borghetto San Spirito onto the SS1 (via Aurelia) towards Ceriale. In Ceriale pass a pedestrians' traffic light, straight on at roundabout (by Total petrol station), right at the next roundabout into 'Via Romana' towards Castelbianco and Peagna for 1.7 km. when you turn right at the traffic lights for 900 m. to the site. GPS: 44.08333, 8.21033

Charges guide

Per person	€ 4,00 - € 8,00
child (1-6 yrs)	€ 3,50 - € 6,00
pitch	€ 5,50 - € 13,50
electricity (6A)	€ 2,50

Check real time availability and at-the-gate prices...
www.**alanrogers**.com

Ceriale
Camping Baciccia
Via Torino 19, I-17023 Ceriale (Ligúria) T: 018 299 0743. E: info@campingbaciccia.it
alanrogers.com/IT64030

This friendly, family run site is a popular holiday destination. Baciccia was the nickname of the present owner's grandfather who grew fruit trees and tomatoes on the site. Tall eucalyptus trees shade the 120 tightly packed pitches which encircle the central facilities block. The pitches are on flat ground and all have electricity. There is always a family member by the gate to greet you, and Vincenzina and Giovanni, along with their adult children Laura and Mauro, work tirelessly to ensure that you enjoy your stay. The restaurant is informal and, as no frozen food is served, the menu is necessarily simple but is traditional Italian food cooked to perfection. The restaurant overlooks a large swimming pool and there are organised water polo and pool games, as well as a half size tennis court and boules. The private beach is a short walk (or free shuttle service) and the town has the usual seaside attractions. This site may suit campers looking for a family atmosphere. If you have forgotten anything by way of camping equipment just ask and the family will lend it to you. There is a free shuttle service to Ceriale's beaches.

Facilities
Two clean and modern sanitary blocks near reception have British and Turkish style WCs and hot water throughout. Laundry. Motorcaravan services. Restaurant/bar. Shop. Pizzeria and takeaway. Two swimming pools (1/4-31/10) and private beach. Tennis. Bowls. Play area. Bicycle hire. Woodburning stove and barbecue. WiFi. Fishing. Diving. Entertainment for children and adults in high season. Excursions. Off site: Department store 150 m. Aquapark 500 m. Riding and golf 5 km. Parachuting school 10 km. Ancient town (2,000 years old) of Albenga 3 km.

Open: 20 March - 3 November, 4 December - 10 January.

Directions
From the A10 between Imperia and Savona, take Albenga exit. Follow signs for Ceriale/Savona and Aquapark Caravelle (which is 500 m. from site) and then site signs. Site is just south of Savona. GPS: 44.08165, 8.21763

Charges guide
Per unit incl. up to 3 persons	€ 25,00 - € 47,00
extra person	€ 5,00 - € 9,00
half pitch incl. 2 persons, no car	€ 16,00 - € 32,00

Discounts for stays in excess of 7 days.
Discount for readers 10% in low season.

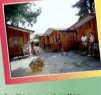

Deiva Marina
Camping Arenella
Localitá Arenella, I-19013 Deiva Marina (Ligúria) T: 018 782 5259. E: info@campingarenella.it
alanrogers.com/IT64140

Situated at the back of the town of Deiva Marina, Camping Arenella is accessed from the A12 autostrada via a twisting 5 km. of road. The site is on a hillside amongst pines and there are some good views. There are around 70 pitches for permanent units with a further 50 pitches for tourers with electricity connections available (3A). Cars must be parked in a separate area. The rustic restaurant is accessed by a long flight of steep steps and offers a varied menu along with a chioce of pizzas and spaghetti to take away.

Facilities
Two centrally situated, and quite dated sanitary blocks have predominantly Turkish style WCs. Free hot water in showers and washbasins. Laundry. Restaurant with keen prices plus small snack bar and shop (May-Sept). Satellite TV. Communal freezer. Free bus service to the beach. Off site: Beach, fishing, boat launching and watersports 1.8 km. Riding 500 m. Villages of Le Cinque Terre.

Open: All year excl. November.

Directions
Leave A12 autostrada at Deiva Marina exit and follow signs to Deiva Marina. Site is well signed and can be found before the village to the right. GPS: 44.22881, 9.53470

Charges guide
Per person	€ 7,00 - € 9,00
child (2-5 yrs)	€ 3,40 - € 4,00
pitch incl. car	€ 8,00 - € 10,00
electricity	€ 2,00

Deiva Marina
Villaggio Camping Valdeiva

Localitá Ronco, I-19013 Deiva Marina (Ligúria) T: 018 782 4174. E: camping@valdeiva.it
alanrogers.com/IT64120

A mature site 3 km. from the sea between the famous Cinque Terre and Portofino, Valdeiva is open all year. It is situated in a valley amongst dense pines so views are restricted. On flat ground and separated, most of the 140 pitches are used for permanent Italian units. There are 40 pitches for tents and touring units but in high season tourers can expect to be put onto a sloping overflow area by the road with no shade. The main touring pitches are in a square at the bottom of the site, some with shade, all with electricity (3A). Cars may be required to park in a separate area depending on the pitch and season. A small busy bar/restaurant offers food at realistic prices. There was late night noise from residents when we stayed in high season. The site does have a small swimming pool, which is very welcome if you do not wish to take the free bus to the beach. The beach is pleasant and the surrounding village has several bars and restaurants. There are very pleasant walks and treks in the unspoilt woods of Liguria nearby or the most interesting tourist option is a visit to Cinque Terre, five villages, some of which can only be reached by rail, boat or by cliff footpath. Their history is one of fishing but now they also specialise in wines. Unusually some of the vineyards can only be reached by boat.

Facilities

The toilet block nearest the touring pitches has cramped facilities. A new block is in the centre of the site. WCs are mainly Turkish, with some of British style. Shop (15/6-10/9). Washing machines and dryers. Bar/restaurant and takeaway with pizzas cooked in a traditional oven (15/6-10/9). Small swimming pool. Play area. Excursions. Free bus to the beach. Torches required. Bicycle hire. Internet access. WiFi. Off site: Beach, fishing and boat launching 3 km.

Open: All year excl. 10 Jan-10 Feb and 5 Nov-5 Dec.

Directions

Leave A12 at Deiva Marina exit and follow signs to Deiva Marina. Site signs are clear at the first junction and site is on left 3 km. down this road.
GPS: 44.22470, 9.55168

Charges guide

Per unit incl. 2 persons and electricity	€ 19,00 - € 35,00
extra person (over 6 yrs)	€ 6,00

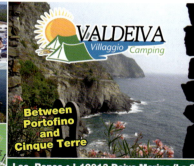

Deiva Marina
Camping La Sfinge

Localitá Gea, I-19013 Deiva Marina (Ligúria) T: 018 782 5464. E: info@campinglasfinge.com
alanrogers.com/IT64160

La Sfinge is peacefully located in the famous area of Cinque Terre and stylish Portofino, in a landscape of pine and acacia trees, with excellent panoramic views. The site is particularly suitable for tents as the pitches are located on pleasant terraces. There are many permanent residents on the site but they are separated from the touring pitches. A set evening meal is prepared at a good price or barbecues in high season. There is a free private shuttle service to the beach and to the railway station to explore the region. The owners have attempted to provide a range of communications facilities for visitors whilst maintaining a tranquil setting. The sea is just 3 km. away.

Facilities

Modern sanitary facilities including a locked WC for disabled visitors. Washing machines, spin dryers and ironing area. Small but comprehensive shop. Snack bar producing evening menu. Internet access. Animation for children at weekends in July/Aug. Free bus service to the beach (June-Sept). Tents for hire. Off site: Riding 1 km. Deiva Marina 2 km. Beach, fishing and watersports 3 km.

Open: All year.

Directions

From A12/E80 Genova - Livorno motorway take Deiva Marina exit and follow road to Deiva Marina (4 km). Site is on the right as you approach the village.
GPS: 44.22625, 9.5502

Charges guide

Per person	€ 6,00 - € 8,00
pitch	€ 9,00 - € 15,00
car	€ 3,00 - € 3,50

Framura

Camping Framura

Localitá La Spiaggetta, I-19014 Framura (Ligúria) T: **018 781 5030**. E: **hotelriviera@hotelrivieradeivamarina.it**

alanrogers.com/IT64180

Framura is an unusual, small cliff-side site of 160 pitches including just 12 pitches for touring units. These pitches are wedged in between seasonal units and are on the site of the old railway line, as is the whole steeply terraced site. The pitches themselves are fabulous as they are directly above the crystal clear waters here. Access to the site is through an old railway tunnel and there is absolutely no shade. The supporting amenities are basic but have a certain charm, some being cut into the rock face. The site is unsuitable for children and the infirm, and has no facilities for disabled campers.

Facilities

Five very mixed blocks offer basic toilets, mostly Turkish but some British style. Innovation has been used here and one very small shower block is carved into the rock face. Cold water at sinks. Washing machine. Very basic snack bar and takeaway (1/6-15/9). Bar (1/4-30/10). Small shop (15/6-15/9). Canoeing and windsurfing are possible. Fishing. Dogs are not accepted. Off site: Boat launching 1 km. Bicycle hire 3 km.

Open: 1 April - 30 October.

Directions

From A12 take nearest exit to Deiva Marina east of Portofino. Proceed to town centre. Take care to find campsite signs as the road to the north is impassable for larger units! Cross the narrow bridge and take the narrow approach road with the Italian parking. You end up facing a narrow railway tunnel. Check for cyclists in the dark interior and drive through to the site! GPS: 44.21670, 9.56440

Charges guide

Per person	€ 6,00 - € 10,50
pitch incl. electricity	€ 7,00 - € 12,50
car	€ 2,00 - € 4,00

Pietra Ligure

Camping Dei Fiori

Viale Riviera 11, I-17027 Pietra Ligure (Ligúria) T: **019 625 636**. E: **info@campingdeifiori.it**

alanrogers.com/IT64040

This is an unsophisticated site with basic facilities situated about 500 metres from the beach. The main road runs past the entrance and the restaurant terrace is overlooked by an elevated section of this road. There are 232 pitches here, mainly seasonal for Italian campers who dominate most of the site. The 60 flat touring pitches are on the lower terrace of the site, with little shade and have a two bar fence on the lower perimeter with a four metre drop into a gulley (possibly dangerous for young children). The pitches (with 3A electricity) are difficult for manoeuvring with larger units.

Facilities

Two blocks are old with a mixture of British and Turkish toilets. A new Portacabin offers better showers and toilets, but the majority are Turkish. Token-operated showers (20c) but hot water is solar heated and may be in short supply. The facilities are under pressure at peak times. Sinks have cold water only. We would not recommend this site for disabled campers. Bar/snack bar. Takeaway (June-Sept). Shop. Swimming pool (May-Sept) and fabric paddling pool. Bicycle hire. Off site: Beach 550 m. Riding 8 km.

Open: All year.

Directions

From the A10 take Pietra Ligure exit. Site is clearly signed 1 km. from the junction. Do not stray into town with large units – many restrictions and low bridges. GPS: 44.14183, 8.27833

Charges guide

Per unit incl. 3 persons	€ 20,00 - € 36,00
extra person	€ 5,00 - € 7,00
child (4-10 yrs)	€ 3,00 - € 5,00
electricity	€ 2,00

Rapallo

Camping Miraflores

Via Savagna 10, I-16035 Rapallo (Ligúria) T: **018 526 3000**. E: **camping.miraflores@libero.it**

alanrogers.com/IT64110

This site has been recommended by our Italian agent and we plan to undertake a full inspection in 2010. Camping Miraflores is located on the Ligurian coast, close to the famous resort of Portofino and the Cinque Terre. Pitches are mostly terraced with separate areas for tents (small pitches) and caravans or motorcaravans. There are mobile homes for rent. The site has recently added a small swimming pool. Rapallo is an attractive resort in its own right with an interesting old town centre. The A12 motorway is very close to the site and there may be some road noise.

Facilities

Bar. Shop. Pizzeria and takeaway meals. Games room. Playground. Swimming pool. Mobile homes for rent. Off site: Nearest beach 1.5 km. Tennis, riding, fishing, golf. Rapallo centre 1.5 km.

Open: All year.

See advertisement on page 36

Directions

Site is located very close to Rapallo exit from the A12 motorway. From this point, follow signs to Rapallo and site is well signed. GPS: 44.35772, 9.20964

Charges guide

Per person	€ 3,00 - € 6,50
pitch	€ 9,00 - € 11,50
electricity	€ 2,00

San Remo

Camping Villaggio dei Fiori

Via Tiro a Volo 3, I-18038 San Remo (Ligúria) T: 018 466 0635. E: info@villaggiodeifiori.it
alanrogers.com/IT64010

Open all year round, this open and spacious site has high standards and is ideal for exploring the Italian Riviera or for just relaxing by the filtered sea water pools. Unusually all the pitch areas at the site are totally paved and there are some extremely large pitches for large units (ask reception to open another gate for entry). All pitches have electricity (3/6A), 50 also have water and drainage, and there is an outside sink and cold water for every four. There is ample shade from mature trees and shrubs, which are constantly watered and cared for in summer. The 'Gold' pitches and some wonderful tent pitches have pleasant views over the sea. There is a path to a secluded and pleasant beach with sparkling waters, overlooked by a large patio area. The rocky surrounds are excellent for snorkelling and fishing, with ladder access to the water. The friendly management speak excellent English and will supply detailed touring plans. Activities and entertainment are organised in high season for adults and children. Excursions are offered (extra cost) along the Italian Riviera dei Fiori and the French Côte d'Azur, including night excursions to Nice and Monte Carlo. Buses run from outside the site to Monte Carlo, Nice, Cannes, Eze and other places of interest. This is a very good site for visiting all the attractions in the local area.

Facilities

Three clean and modern toilet blocks have British and Turkish style WCs and hot water throughout. Baby rooms. Facilities for disabled campers. Laundry facilities. Motorcaravan services. Bar sells essential supplies. Large restaurant. Pizzeria and takeaway (all year). Sea water swimming pools (small extra charge in high season) and whirlpool spa (June-Sept). Tennis. Play area. Fishing. Satellite TV. Internet access. Bicycle hire. Dogs are not accepted. Off site: Shop 150 m. Riding and golf 2 km.

Open: All year.

Directions

From SS1 (Ventimiglia / Imperia), site is on right just before San Remo. There is a sharp right turn if approaching from the west. From autostrada A10 take San Remo Ouest exit. Site is well signed.
GPS: 43.80117, 7.74867

Charges guide

Per unit incl. 4 persons	€ 27,00 - € 56,00
electricity (3A-6A)	€ 2,00 - € 4,00

Some charges due on arrival.
Discounts for stays in excess of 7 days.
Discount for readers 10% in low season.
Camping Cheques accepted.

Sestri Levante
Camping Mare Monti
Via Aurelia, km 469, 16039 Sestri Levante (Ligúria) T: 018 544 348. E: info@campingmaremonti.com
alanrogers.com/IT64130

Mare Monti is a neat and tidy site with 132 pitches. It is set high in the hills with spectacular views overlooking the small town of Sestri Levanti. The owner and his staff are relaxed and very friendly. The site has 35 touring pitches, all set on terraces overlooking the wonderful countryside. The remaining pitches are taken by seasonal units. A small shop and a bar with its terrace overlook a neat swimming pool. Access to the site and movement within are difficult; the site is therefore only suitable for smaller units and tents. However the rural location, together with good facilities offers a quiet and relaxing retreat away from city life. There are restaurants and shops in Sestri Levanti 2 km. away and the site provides a minibus link in July and August.

Facilities
Two refurbished toilet blocks are modern, bright and spotlessly clean. British style WCs. Hot showers. Washing machine and dryer. Small shop. Bar with takeaway. Swimming pool with separate pool for children. WiFi. Minibus to town (July/Aug). English is spoken.
Off site: Village with ATM 2 km. Fishing 2 km. Bicycle hire 4 km. Riding 5 km. Golf 8 km. Bars, restaurants and shops in Sestri Levanti 2 km.

Open: 1 March - 31 October.

Directions
From autostrada A12 take exit for Sestri Levante and follow road SP1 in an easterly direction to km. 469. Site entrance is on the left set back from road and difficult to see. The road is steep in places and winding. It is not suitable for large units.
GPS: 44.26365, 9.441901

Charges guide
Per unit incl. 2 persons and electricity	€ 20,00 - € 30,00
extra person	€ 3,00 - € 5,00

Villanova d'Albenga
Camping C'era una Volta
Localitá Fasceti, I-17038 Villanova d'Albenga (Ligúria) T: 018 258 0461. E: info@villaggioceraunavolta.it
alanrogers.com/IT64050

An attractive campsite, C'era una Volta is about 6 km. back from the sea, situated on a hillside with panoramic views. Pitches are on terraces in different sections of the site. Varying in size, most have shade from the young trees which harbour crickets with their distinctive noise. Some of the upper pitches have good views. Cars are required to park in separate areas at busy times. There are electricity connections, with water and drainage close by. Charges are high in season but the site has an enjoyable atmosphere and is a good choice for families. The charming creeper covered restaurant has a large sheltered terrace. Amenities include four excellent swimming pools in different parts of the site, open in the main season. One is large (30 m) with a paddling pool in the upper area, another, also with a large paddling pool is by the restaurant and is overlooked by the entertainment area.

Facilities
The main toilet block is modern and above average with hot water throughout. Four additional smaller blocks are spread around the site. Maintenance can be variable. Shop. Bar and pizzeria (15/5-10/9). Restaurant and takeaway (1/4-30/9). Disco (July/Aug). Swimming pools (15/5-20/9). Small gym. Fitness track. Health centre with sauna, massage and Turkish bath. Tennis. Large adventure playground. Boules. Internet. Satellite TV. Off site: Riding 500 m. Golf 2 km. Lake fishing 4 km. Beach, boat launching and sailing 6 km.

Open: 1 April - 30 September.

Directions
Leave A10 at Albenga, turn left and left again at roundabout for the SS453 for Villanova. At T-junction turn left (Garlenda), turn right in 200 m. and follow signs up a long winding narrow road beyond the Stadium. GPS: 44.04433, 8.1137

Charges guide
Per unit incl. up to 3 persons	€ 25,00 - € 49,00
tent pitch	€ 20,00 - € 38,00
extra person	€ 3,50 - € 12,00
No credit cards.	

Camping Miraflores – *see report on page 34.*

The campsite is situated in a beautiful green area, 2000 mt to the sea and 200 mt from the main road the A12. The campsite is a excellent departure to visit the "Cinque Terre". The campsite has a swimmingpool, internet point and discount prices to use the municipal pools. Renovated toiletbuildings.
Rental mobilehomes for 2 till 6 persons.
Open whole year.
Reduced prices in the low season

Via Savagna 10 • I-16035 RAPALLO (GENOVA)
Tel. and Fax 0039/0185263000 • Http: www.campingmiraflores.it • E-mail: camping.miraflores@libero.it

Check real time availability and at-the-gate prices...
www.alanrogers.com

The region of Lombardy stretches from the Alps, on the border with Switzerland, down past the romantic lakes of Como and Maggiore to the broad, flat plain of the River Po.

THE REGION IS MADE UP OF THE PROVINCES: BERGAMO, BRESCIA, COMO, CREMONA, LECCO, LODI, MANTOVA, MILANO, PAVIA, SONDRIO AND VARESE. WE FEATURE LAKE GARDA SEPARATELY.

Lombardy is one of the most developed tourist destinations in Italy, its major draw being the beautiful scenic lakes. Surrounded by abundant vegetation, Lake Como is set in an idyllic landscape of mountains; tall peaks that seem to rise directly from the water's edge. With a number of places to visit along the shores, including the prosperous towns of Como and Lecco, the area is also great for walking and in most places the lake is clean enough for swimming. Lake Maggiore has a Mediterranean atmosphere, with citrus trees and palms lining the shores, and offers a more sedate pace. There are good walks in the surrounding hills. Lying in the centre of the lake near Stresa are the Borromean Islands, of which Isola Bella is the most popular. It is home to the 17th-century Palazzo Borromeo and its splendid garden of landscaped terraces, fountains, peacocks and statues. A lesser known lake, Lake Iseo, is the fifth largest in northern Italy. Situated in wine producing country, surrounded by mountains and waterfalls, it is popular for its watersports and boasts the largest lake-island in Italy, Monte Isola. All three lakes are well served by ferries which zigzag from shore to shore, and are within easy reach of the vibrant city of Milan.

Places of interest

Bellagio: beautiful town by Lake Como, hilly old centre with steep cobbled streets.

Bergamo: hill-top town, medieval and Renaissance buildings.

Brescia: Roman ruins, 12th-century church.

Certosa di Pavia: magnificent Renaissance Charterhouse.

Cremona: where the violin was developed, home of famous violin maker Stradivarius.

Lodi: charming medieval town of pastel-coloured houses with pretty courtyards.

Milan: fashion capital, great for shopping, art museums, home of famous opera house La Scala and Leonardo Da Vinci's *Last Supper* fresco.

Cuisine of the region

Food varies considerably from town to town. Risotto is popular, the short grain rice is grown in the paddy fields of the Ticino Valley, as is green pasta and polenta. Lombardy is one of the largest cheese making regions in the country – Gorgonzola and Mascarpone are produced here.

Biscotti: biscuits flavoured with nuts, vanilla and lemon.

Cotolette alla Milanese: veal escalope.

La Casoêula: pork stew.

Ossobuco: shin of veal.

Panettone: light yeast cake with candied fruit.

Pizzoccheri: buckwheat noodles.

Risotto alla Milanese: rice cooked in meat stock with white wine, onion, saffron and grated parmesan.

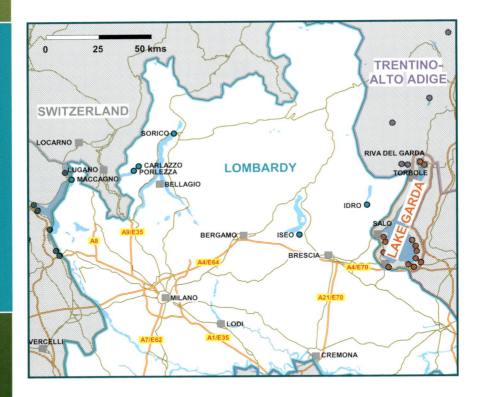

Carlazzo

Camping Ranocchio

Via Al Lago N7, Localitá Piano Porlezza, I-22010 Carlazzo (Lombardy) T: **034 470 385**
E: campeggioranocchio.campe@tin.it alanrogers.com/IT62515

This is a delightful site next to a small lake in a wetland nature reserve, surrounded by tree-clad slopes with views of distant mountain peaks. Three generations of the very friendly Cremella family are involved in the running of the site and the welcome from all of them is warm and genuine. The 180 touring pitches (all with 3A electricity) are on gravel hardstanding or grass. The restaurant, with a bar and terrace, offers a range of Italian dishes and pizzas to eat in or take away. There is a fairly small swimming pool and a paddling pool. Please see note on access below.

Facilities

Two sanitary blocks provide excellent modern facilities with warm water to some basins; showers are token operated. Good facilities for disabled visitors. Baby rooms. Motorcaravan services. Washing machines. Bar and shop (15/4-30/9). Restaurant/takeaway (15/4-15/9). Pool is charged for (€ 1) but always supervised (15/6-15/9). Gas supplies. Fishing, swimming from small shingle beach (fence and gate, but young children would need watching). Off site: Bicycle hire 600 m. Supermarket 800 km. Riding 2 km. Sailing and golf 4 km.

Open: 1 April - 30 September.

Directions

Porlezza is 14 km. east of Lugano on the SS340 to Menággio. Piano di Porlezza is a further 3 km. east, or 8 km. west from Menággio. Site is signed to the south in village. N.B. The SS340 is very narrow and winding, especially on the Porlezza - Lugano section. The Como - Menággio road is best tackled between 12.00 and 14.00 if possible! GPS: 46.04078, 9.16828

Charges guide

Per person	€ 5,00 - € 5,50
child (0-6 yrs)	€ 3,00
pitch incl. electricity	€ 9,00 - € 10,00

No credit cards.
Camping Cheques accepted.

Idro

Azur Camping Idro Rio Vantone

Via Vantone 45, I-25074 Idro (Lombardy) T: **036 583 125**. E: **idro@azur-camping.de**

alanrogers.com/IT62580

Lake Idro, one of the smaller of the northern Italian lakes, is tucked away in the mountains to the west of Lake Garda. Rio Vantone is on the southeast shore of the lake with marvellous views across the water to the villages on the opposite bank and surrounding mountains. The ground slopes gently down to the water's edge with many of the 174 touring pitches in level rows divided by hedges, with others between tall trees. All have electricity and there are 46 with water and drainage. The ones nearest the lake attract a higher charge. The lake is ideal for windsurfing, and the countryside for walking and climbing.

Facilities

The main, heated sanitary block occupies the ground floor of a large building and is of excellent quality including cabins (WC, washbasin and shower). A smaller block is also open in high season. Facilities for disabled people. Washing machines and dryer. Motorcaravan services. Gas supplies. Cooking rings. Shop. Bar. Excellent restaurant (1/6-10/9). Swimming pools. Windsurf school. Boat and mountain bike hire. Play area. Torches useful in some areas. Off site: Shops, bars and restaurants 1.5 km.

Open: 1 April - 31 October.

Directions

Idro is 45 km. northeast of Brescia. From the A4 autostrada take Brescia Est exit. Go north on SS45bis towards Saló then follow brown signs for Valle Sabia and Lago d'Idro on SS237 via Vobarno, Barghe (bypassed) and Lavenone to Lemprato. Take care not to miss right turn into narrow road after town sign for Idro. Site is north of town. GPS: 45.75418, 10.49821

Charges guide

Per person	€ 5,50 - € 9,10
child (2-12 yrs)	€ 4,00 - € 6,80
pitch	€ 7,00 - € 28,80
electricity	€ 2,80
dog	€ 2,80

Iseo

Camping del Sole

Via per Rovato 26, I-25049 Iseo (Lombardy) T: **030 980 288**. E: **info@campingdelsole.it**

alanrogers.com/IT62610

Camping del Sole lies on the southern edge of Lake Iseo, just outside the pretty lakeside town of Iseo. The site has 306 pitches, many taken up with chalets and mobile homes. The 180 touring pitches all have 3A electricity and some have fine views of the surrounding mountains and lake. Pitches are generally flat and of a reasonable size, but cars must park in the carpark. The site has a wide range of excellent leisure amenities, including a large swimming pool. There is a bar and restaurant with a pizzeria near the pool and entertainment area and a second bar by the lake. The site is near the delightful waterfront area of the town where you can enjoy classic Italian architecture, stroll around the shops or enjoy a meal in one of the many restaurants. There is a boat launching facility at the lakeside. There is a lively entertainment programme and excursions around the lake are organised, notably to Lake Iseo's three islands where you can sit at a street café or enjoy a walk while enjoying the magnificent scenery. Excursions are also organised to the wine cellars of Franciacorta.

Facilities

Sanitary facilities are modern and well maintained, including special facilities for disabled visitors. Washing machines and dryers. Bar, restaurant, pizzeria, snack bar and supermarket (all open all season). Motorcaravan service point. Bicycle and canoe hire. Swimming pool with children's pool. Bicycle and pedal boat hire. Tennis. Entertainment in high season. Off site: Golf 5 km. Riding 6 km.

Open: 16 April - 26 September.

Directions

Lake Iseo is 50 km. west of Lake Garda. Leave from A4 Milan - Venice autostrada take Rovato exit. at roundabout go north on SPX1 following signs for Lago d'Iseo for 12 km. Site is well signed to left at large roundabout. From Brescia on SS510, turn north before Iseo towards Rovato and turn right to site. GPS: 45.65708, 10.03740

Charges guide

Per unit incl. 2 persons and electricity	€ 18,30 - € 35,20
extra person	€ 5,50 - € 9,50
child (5-12 yrs)	free - € 7,90
dog	€ 2,00 - € 3,50

Reductions in low season.
Camping Cheques accepted.

Iseo

Camping Punta d'Oro

Via Antonioli 51-53, I-25049 Iseo (Lombardy) T: **030 980 084**. E: **info@camping-puntadoro.com**

alanrogers.com/IT62590

Camping Punta d'Oro, at the town of Iseo in the southeast corner of the lake, is a small, delightful campsite. It has been run by the Brescianini-Zatti family for the last 30 years and you will receive a very warm welcome on arrival. The very pretty site slopes gently down to the lake. It has 62 grass pitches (with two static caravans for hire) all with electrical connections, mainly 6A. Trees and shrubs provide some shade and there are lovely views across the lake to the mountains. Lakeside pitches are a little more expensive. There is some occasional noise from the nearby railway.

Facilities

The two small sanitary blocks have been refurbished to a high standard with a mix of British and Turkish style WCs and hot water in washbasins and showers. Suite for disabled visitors. All facilities are kept very clean. Washing machine. Motorcaravan services. Shop. Small bar serving a limited range of snacks. Games room. TV in bar. Access to lake for swimming, fishing with two narrow slipways for boat launching. Bicycle hire arranged. Internet access and WiFi. Off site: Town within walking distance. Riding 3 km. Golf 5 km.

Open: 1 April - 26 October.

Directions

Lake Iseo is 50 km. west of Lake Garda. Leave A4 Milan - Venice autostrada at Rovato, turn left to roundabout and go north on SPXI following signs for Lago di Iseo. Punta d'Oro is on northeast side of Iseo. Avoid town centre and turn northeast on SP71 for 1.5 km. before turning back north across the railway and turn right at site sign. GPS: 45.66392, 10.05583

Charges guide

Per person	€ 4,70 - € 7,50
child (1-9 yrs)	€ 3,70 - € 5,90
pitch incl. electricity	€ 9,40 - € 19,50
dog	free - € 3,70

Maccagno

Azur Parkcamping Maccagno

Via Corsini 13, I-21010 Maccagno (Lombardy) T: **033 256 0203**. E: **maccagno@azur-camping.de**

alanrogers.com/IT62390

Azur Parkcamping Maccagno is a very basic site which has great access to the lake shores through a wire fence. With hills on each side, the views day and night over the lake are spectacular. There is little in the way of entertainment or infrastructure so the site will suit those who just wish to relax on a traditional, older style campsite. The 120 rather cramped pitches vary in size (60-100 sq.m) are relatively flat and some have shade. They are numbered but the siting is a little chaotic. A small bar and snack bar are alongside the reception.

Facilities

One toilet block with old but clean facilities. Bar. Snacks. Very basic play area. Off site: Golf 20 km. Buses 500 m. Excursions.

Open: 15 March - 15 November.

Directions

Site is on the eastern side of Lake Maggiore, a little to the north of the town of Luino. Follow the SS394 towards Maccagno and Locarno. Site is well signed. GPS: 46.03333, 8.71666

Charges guide

Per person	€ 5,50 - € 8,00
child (2-12 yrs)	€ 4,00 - € 6,50
pitch	€ 7,00 - € 16,50
electricity	€ 2,50

Check real time availability and at-the-gate prices...

www.alanrogers.com

Porlezza

Camping Darna

Via Osteno 50, I-22018 Porlezza (Lombardy) T: **034 461 597**

alanrogers.com/IT62505

At the eastern end of Lake Lugano, Camping Darna is in a broad valley with a great view down the lake and mountains on all sides. It is a well run site which becomes lively in high season with plenty of entertainment for young and old; in low season it is much more relaxed. The 304 touring pitches are on flat ground, all with 3A electricity. There are 46 seasonal pitches (not along the lakeside). A pizzeria serves a full range of Italian dishes and has a bar and terrace. There is a fairly small swimming pool. Please see note on access below.

Facilities

Five sanitary blocks, some with controllable showers, are kept very clean. Facilities for disabled visitors. Washing machines and dryers. Motorcaravan service point. Shop, bar/restaurant with takeaway (all season). Swimming pool (daily charge € 5) is open to public; no paddling pool and no shallow end (1/6-30/9). Fishing, swimming and boating. Off site: Riding 1 km. Bicycle hire, shops, bars and restaurants 1.5 km. Sailing 3 km. Golf 10 km.

Open: 1 April - 31 October.

Directions

Porlezza is 14 km. east of Lugano on the SS340 to Menággio. Turn south at traffic lights in Porlezza on Via Osteno and site is 1.5 km. on the right. Note: The SS340 is very narrow and winding, especially on the Porlezza - Lugano section (not for large units). The Como - Menággio road is best tackled between 12.00 and 14.00 if possible! GPS: 46.02514, 9.12603

Charges guide

Per person	€ 6,50 - € 7,50
child (3-12 yrs)	€ 4,00 - € 6,00
pitch	€ 11,00 - € 13,50

No credit cards.

Sórico

Camping La Riva

Via Poncione 3, I-22010 Sórico (Lombardy) T: **034 494 571**. E: **info@campinglariva.com**

alanrogers.com/IT62510

La Riva lies at the northern end of Lake Como and is surrounded by mountains, close to the nature reserve of 'Pian di Spagna' and within walking distance of Sórico, a pretty town with bars, restaurants and shops. Pitches are level and of a reasonable size and many have attractive views across the river to the mountains. Most have electrical connections (6A). Reception houses a small bar, with snack bar and takeaway, and a small shop selling basics. The outdoor pool has a sunbathing terrace. Camping La Riva has a happy, friendly atmosphere.

Facilities

The centrally located sanitary building contains modern showers (tokens needed), a mix of Turkish and British style toilets and washbasins (warm water) and is kept very clean. Facilities for disabled people. Washing machine. Swimming pool (May-Sept, charged). Bicycle hire. Fishing. Water skiing. Canoe and dinghy hire. Off site: Guided walks. Cycling and walking track from site to Sorico. Riding. Golf. Local market.

Open: 1 March - 3 November.

Directions

Sórico is 100 km. north of Milan at the northern tip of Lake Como. The easiest approach is via the free SS36 dual carriageway from Lecco; just after end of motorway section turn east to Sórico. From Como the SS340 is narrow and winding and is best tackled between 12 noon and 14.00! Site is on the eastern edge of town. GPS: 46.17067, 9.39268

Charges 2010

Per unit incl. 2 persons and electricity	€ 23,00 - € 35,00
extra person	€ 6,00 - € 10,00
dog	€ 4,00

Discounts in low season.

The largest and cleanes
of the Italian lakes, Lak
Garda is also the most
popular. The low-lying
countryside of the
southern stretches give
way to the dramatic, craggy
mountains of the north, while the
western shore is fringed with oliv
groves, vines and citrus trees.

**IN THIS POPULAR TOURIST REGION WE HAVE
INCLUDED THE LAKESIDE AREAS OF THE REGIONS OF
VENETO, LOMBARDY AND TRENTINO-ALTO ADIGE**

The lake's largest town, Desenzano del Garda, lies on the southern shore. Bars and restaurants line the lakefront and a walk to the town's castle affords spectacular views. Nearby, Sirmione is popular with those seeking cures in its sulphurous springs. It has the remains of a Roman spa plus a 13th-century fairy-tale castle, which is almost entirely surrounded by water. Along the sheltered stretch of the western shore, otherwise known as the Riviera Bresciana, are lush groves and fruit trees; Salò is a good place to stock up on the local produce. Gardone is best known for its exotic botanical garden and Il Vittoriale, the home of the notorious writer Gabriel D'Annunzio, which is filled with curiosities. Up in the mountains behind Gardone is the little alpine village of San Michele, and there are good walks to the springs and waterfalls in the surrounding hills. At the northwest tip of the lake, Riva del Garda is one of the best known resorts and a favourite with windsurfers, as is Torbole, where sailing and mountain biking are popular too. On the eastern shore, Malcesine boasts a 13th-century turreted castle and a funicular which climbs to the summit of Monte Baldo giving panoramic views. Near the lively resort of Garda are white shingle beaches.

Places of interest

Bardolino: home of the light, red Bardolino wine. Festival of the Grape is held between Sept-Oct.

Gargano: olive factory, 13th-century churc good place for sailing.

Peschiera: attractive enclosed harbour and fortress.

Puegnago del Garda: home of Comincioli vineyard that has been producing wine sin the 16th century.

Torri del Benaco: considered to be the prettiest lakeside town, with old centre, cobbled streets and a castle.

Cuisine of the region

Fish is popular; there are 40 different spec in the lake including carp, trout, eels and pike. Regional dishes include trout filled with oranges and lemons, risotto with tench, and *sisam*, a traditional way of preparing lake minnows. The fruits grown on the western shore are used to make ol oil, citrus syrups and Bardolino, Soave and Valpolicella wines.

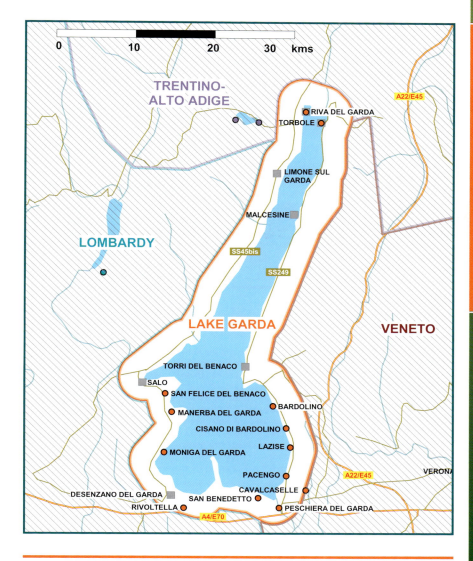

Cavalcaselle

Camping Gasparina

Via Gasparina 13, I-37010 Cavalcaselle (Lake Garda) T: **045 755 0775**. E: **info@gasparina.com**
alanrogers.com/IT62660

Gasparina is of average size for this area and of reasonable quality, but a little away from the towns around the lake. It is in a peaceful location and has the feeling of being in the countryside. As the site slopes gently towards the lake, levellers are needed in some parts. There are 363 grass touring pitches in back-to-back rows separated by gravel roads. Many trees and flowers adorn the site, with shade in most parts. The pleasant swimming pools are separated from the restaurant terraces by a neat, well clipped hedge. Just beyond the site fence is a beach and pleasant promenade. Boats can be launched here. Near reception are the supermarket and a bar/restaurant with three terraces and good prices.

Facilities

Two refurbished and one new toilet block have the usual facilities with warm water in two blocks. Facilities for disabled visitors. Washing machines and dryer. Shop. Bar/restaurant with terrace. Swimming pool. Playground. Tennis courts. Watersports. Entertainment in high season. Dogs and other pets are not accepted. Off site: Bicycle hire 2 km. Riding 3 km.

Open: 1 April - 1 September.

Directions

Leave the A4 Milan - Venice motorway at exit for Peschiera, go north on east side of lake on the SS249 towards Lazise for entrance road on your left. GPS: 45.45539, 10.7017

Charges guide

Per unit incl. 4 persons	€ 21,00 - € 39,00
extra person	€ 4,00 - € 6,00
boat trailer	€ 10,00 - € 18,00

43

Bardolino
Camping Serenella

Localitá Mezzariva 19, I-37011 Bardolino (Lake Garda) T: 045 721 1333. E: serenella@camping-serenella.it
alanrogers.com/IT63590

Situated alongside Lake Garda, Serenella has 300 average size pitches, some with good lake views. Movement around the site may prove difficult for large units (look for the wider roads). The pitches are shaded and have 6A electricity. A long promenade with brilliant views of the mountains and lake runs the length of the campsite. It is dotted with grassy relaxation areas and beach bars where snacks are served and the atmosphere is charming. The pleasant pool complex is near an older style 'taverna' where delicious, sensibly priced food is served. There is some road noise at some of the amenities and the pool.

Facilities

Five clean, well equipped sanitary blocks, include three that are more modern. British style toilets. Free hot water. Facilities for disabled visitors. Laundry facilities. Freezer. Bar/restaurant, takeaway and shop. Watersports. Entertainment programme in high season. Play area. Bicycle hire. Boat launching. Minigolf. Tennis. Satellite TV. Internet and WiFi. Dogs are not accepted. Motorcyles are not allowed. Off site: Beach, fishing and watersports. Golf 3 km. Riding 3.5 km. Town 3 km. Gardaland.

Open: 20 March - 17 October.

Directions

From E70 Milan - Venice autostrada take Pescheria exit and follow signs to Bardolino. Site is on lakeside between Bardolino and Garda, about 4 km. south of Garda. GPS: 45.55939, 10.71657

Charges guide

Per unit incl. 2 persons	
and electricity	€ 17,50 - € 36,50
extra person	€ 4,00 - € 9,50
child (4-10 yrs)	free - € 4,00

Bardolino
La Rocca Camp

Localitá San Pietro, I-37011 Bardolino (Lake Garda) T: 045 721 1111. E: info@campinglarocca.com
alanrogers.com/IT63600

This site was one of the first to operate on the Lake and the family has a background of wine and olive oil production. La Rocca is in two areas, each side of the busy A249, the upper part being used mostly for bungalows, although some touring pitches are here and these have great lake views. The remaining touring pitches are on the lower part of the site, along with the main facilities. There is access between the two parts via a tunnel. The 450 pitches are mostly on terraces with shade, 6A electricity and access from narrow tarmac roads. The site is very popular with Dutch campers and all the guests seemed happy when we visited. It is a family site and, with the pools and direct access to the lake, provides a choice of watersports. The huge Gardaland theme park is close by (free bus from gate). Many of the facilities have been renewed here and the owners are keen to please their guests. This site is not ideal for campers with mobility problems as there are large distances to cover to get to some facilities and the only access to the pool is by over 30 steps, but otherwise it is a pleasant place to spend time relaxing.

Facilities

Four toilet blocks. WCs are mixed British and Turkish style and showers are controllable. Facilities for disabled visitors but many steps to pool. Children's facilities and baby baths. Washing machines. New motorcaravan services. Shop and bakery. Restaurant, bar and takeaway with large terrace. Swimming and paddling pools (lifeguard) Sun terrace with views. Pool bar. Play area. Entertainment programme in season. Miniclub. Internet point. Bicycle hire. Games room. Watersports. Torches useful. Off site: Public transport at gate. Boat launching 20 m. Riding 8 km. ATM 1.5 km.

Open: 26 March - 3 October.

Directions

Site is on the east side of Lake Garda, on the lake ring road 249. From the A4 take Pescheria exit and the 249 north for Garda (there are many signs for Gardaland). Site is well signed approaching village of Bardolino. GPS: 45.5645, 10.7129

Charges guide

Per person	€ 4,90 - € 8,90
child (0-10 yrs)	free - € 7,50
pitch	€ 8,90 - € 19,20
dog	€ 2,60 - € 5,20

DIRECTLY ON THE LAKE
• APARTMENTS
• DELUXE MAXICARAVANS
• SPORT AND ACTIVITIES FOR CHILDREN AND ADULTS
• INTERNET POINT
• KAYAK TOUR

I-37011 Bardolino (VR) - Tel. +39 045 7211111 - Fax +39 045 7211300
www.campinglarocca.com - info@campinglarocca.com

Check real time availability and at-the-gate prices...

 www.alanrogers.com

Cisano di Bardolino

Campings Cisano & San Vito

Via Peschiera 48, I-37011 Cisano di Bardolino (Lake Garda) T: 045 622 9098. E: cisano@camping-cisano.it

alanrogers.com/IT63570

This is a combination of two sites and some of the 700 pitches have superb locations along the 1 km. of shaded lakeside contained in Cisano. Some are on sloping ground and most are shaded but the San Vito pitches have no lake views. Both sites have a family orientation and considerable effort has been taken in the landscaping to provide maximum comfort even for the largest units. San Vito is the smaller and more peaceful location with no lakeside pitches and shares many of the facilities of Cisano which is a short walk across the road. Each site has its own reception. A reader reports that a two-metre high fence separating the pitches from the beach and lake has been constructed at Cisano, with several gates, but only two that open at the moment, at the extreme ends of the beach.

Facilities

Plentiful, good quality sanitary facilities are provided in both sites (nine blocks at Cisano and two at San Vito). Facilities for disabled visitors. Fridge hire. Shop. Bar. Restaurant. Swimming pool. Play area. Fishing and sailing. Free windsurfing and canoeing. Boat launching. Internet access. Dogs are not accepted (but cats are). Motorcycles not allowed on site (parking provided). Off site: Indoor pool, bicycle hire and tennis 2 km. Riding 15 km. Golf 20 km.

Open: 20 March - 5 October.

Directions

Leave A4 autoroute at Pescheria exit and head north towards Garda on lakeside road. Pass Lazise and site is signed (small sign) on left halfway to Bardolina. Site is 12 km. beyond the Gardaland theme park. GPS: 45.52290, 10.72760

Charges guide

Per unit incl. 2 persons and electricity	€ 17,00 - € 40,00
extra person	€ 4,00 - € 10,50
child (2-5)	free - € 4,00
motorboat	€ 8,00 - € 15,00

Camping Cheques accepted.

Camping in LAZISE and PACENGO

I-37017 LAZISE (VERONA)
Tel. 0039 045 7580127
Fax 0039 045 6470150
duparc@camping.it
www.campingduparc.com

I-37017 LAZISE (VERONA)
Tel. 0039 045 7580007
Fax 0039 045 7580611
info@campingspiaggiadoro.com
www.campingspiaggiadoro.com

Loc. Bottona • I-37017 LAZISE (VERONA)
Tel. 0039 045 6470577
Fax 0039 045 6470243
laquercia@laquercia.it
www.laquercia.it

Loc. Vanon • I-37017 LAZISE (VERONA)
Tel. 0039 045 6471181
Fax 0039 045 7581356
info@campingparkdellerose.it
www.campingparkdellerose.it

Via Fossalta 42 • I-37017 LAZISE (VERONA)
Tel. 0039 045 7590456
Fax 0039 045 7590939
info@pianidiclodia.it
www.pianidiclodia.it

I-37017 LAZISE (VERONA)
Tel. 0039 045 7590228
Fax 0039 045 6499084
info@campingbelvedere.com
www.campingbelvedere.com

I-37010 PACENGO DI LAZISE (VERONA)
Tel. 0039 045 7590030 - 045 7590611
Tel. e Fax in inverno 0039 045 7580334
Fax 0039 045 7590611
info@campinglido.it
www.campinglido.it

I-37010 PACENGO DI LAZISE (VERONA)
Via del Porto 13
Tel. e Fax 0039 045 7590012
info@eurocampingpacengo.it
www.eurocampingpacengo.it

Lake Garda

Lazise

Pacengo

www.campinglazise.net

Lazise

Camping Piani di Clodia

Via Fossalta 42, I-37017 Lazise (Lake Garda) T: 045 759 0456. E: info@pianidiclodia.it

alanrogers.com/IT62530

Piani di Clodia is one of the best large sites on Lake Garda and it has a positive impression of space and cleanliness. It is located on a slope between Lazise and Peschiera in the southeast corner of the lake, with lovely views across the water to Sirmione's peninsula and the mountains beyond. The site slopes down to the water's edge and has over 950 pitches, all with electricity (6A), 250 with electricity, water and drainage, terraced where necessary and back to back from hard access roads. There is some shade from mature and young trees. The pool complex is truly wonderful with a range of pools, a pleasant sunbathing area and a bar. The whole area is fenced and supervised. At the centre of the site is a quality rooftop restaurant, a self service restaurant plus pizzeria and table service for drinks. From most of this area you will be able to enjoy the free entertainment on the large stage. The enthusiastic entertainment team provide an ambitious variety of entertainment. There is a fence between the site and the lake with access points to a private beach and opportunities for a variety of watersports. You are greeted at the gate by English speaking attendants who are keen to please, as are reception staff. The site is very close to several theme parks. Member of the Leading Campings Group.

Facilities

Seven modern, immaculate sanitary blocks, well spaced around the site. British and Turkish style WCs. All have facilities for disabled visitors and one has a baby room. Washing machines, dryers and laundry service. Motorcaravan services. Shopping complex with supermarket and general shops. Two bars. Self-service restaurant with takeaway. Pizzeria. Ice cream parlour. Swimming pools. Tennis. Gymnastics. Fishing. Bicycle hire. Large playground. Outdoor theatre with entertainment programme. Off site: Riding 6 km. Golf 12 km. Theme parks nearby.

Open: 20 March - 10 October.

See advertisement on page 46-47

Directions

Lazise is on the southeast side of Lake Garda about 30 km. west of Verona. From the north on Trento - Verona A22 autostrada take Affi exit then follow signs for Lazise and site. From south on A4 Brescia - Venice motorway take Peschiera exit and site is 6 km. towards Lazise and Garda on SS249.
GPS: 45.48272, 10.72932

Charges 2010

Per person	€ 4,80 - € 11,20
child (1-9 yrs)	€ 3,00 - € 7,30
pitch incl. electricity	€ 9,80 - € 29,20

Lazise

Camping du Parc

I-37017 Lazise sul Garda (Lake Garda) T: 045 758 0127. E: duparc@camping.it

alanrogers.com/IT62535

Camping du Parc is a very pleasant, family owned site which resembles a Tardis, in that it extends and extends as you progress further through the site. Olive groves are interspersed with the pitch areas which gives an open and green feel. The site is set on a slope which goes down to the lakeside beach of soft sand. The 150 pitches are terraced, which takes out much of the slope, and all have 6A electricity and water. Units above 10 m. long will be challenged by some of the corners here. Pitches are separated by trimmed hedges and some have shade, others views of the lake. The restaurant is on the lower level with a terrace to catch the sunsets or alternatively the pizzeria also has a patio with sea views. Relax by the beach bar or in the pool whilst the children enjoy the slides and paddling pool. This is a very good site for those who prefer peace and quiet to the noisier atmosphere of the larger sites hereabouts. Buses stop by the gate to take you to Gardaland and other tourist attractions. As a site which caters for families, there is no disco or excessive noise and when we visited there were many happy customers. Entertainment takes place in the lower sports areas and is aimed mainly at children. All facilities are open all season. The beach, accessed through a security gate, is safe for swimming and there is a lifeguard.

Facilities

Four modern sanitary blocks are well placed and have free hot water throughout. Three blocks have facilities for disabled campers, one for children and babies. Washing machines and dryers. Motorcaravan services. Well stocked small supermarket. Restaurant with lake views. Pizzeria with terrace and views. Takeaway. Beach bar. Pool bar. Swimming pool. Large paddling pool with slides. Children's entertainment programme. Play area. Tennis. Multisport court. Fishing. Internet and WiFi. Off site: Golf 10 km. Bicycle hire 500 m. Riding 1 km. Gardaland.

Open: 10 March - 30 September.

Directions

Leave A4 Venice - Milan autostrada by taking the Brennero exit to Lake Garda and then on to Lazise. At the lakeside in town turn left and follow signs for site.
GPS: 45.49833, 10.7375

Charges guide

Per person	€ 5,60 - € 8,70
child (1-5 yrs)	€ 1,50 - € 5,10
pitch	€ 11,30 - € 19,50
dog	€ 1,50 - € 5,10

See advertisement on page 46-47

Lazise

Camping Park Delle Rose

Strada San Gaetano 20, I-37017 Lazise (Lake Garda) T: **045 647 1181**. E: **info@campingparkdellerose.it**
alanrogers.com/IT63580

An orderly, well designed site with a feeling of spaciousness, Delle Rose is on the east side of Lake Garda, three kilometers from the attractive waterside village of Peschiera. The 455 pitches are of average size, most with grass and shade and laid out in 30 short, terraced avenues. The ratio of recreational area to pitches is unusually high, particularly for sites at Lake Garda. Unusually, reception is located one third of the way into the site. On approach one sees the attractive restaurant, gardens and comprehensive sporting facilities including the pool complex with its stylish terraced bar and animation area close by. There is a large car park at the modern reception centre where many languages including English and Dutch are spoken. The well stocked grocery market, general store selling fresh vegetables, and the medical centre are centrally located. At the lake a small, curved sandy beach is contained by a low wall. The water's edge is pebbled and shallow, but a long jetty extends into the water with a ladder giving easy access to deeper water. Boat launching is at the narrow end of the beach where there is a small beach bar. Ample boat and trailer parking is available behind the supermarket. Ideally designed for families, with sporting and recreational areas totally separate, leaving the pitch area as a peaceful zone.

Facilities

Five clean, modern sanitary blocks provide hot water throughout. British style toilets, some in cabins with washbasins. Private bathrooms for hire. Good baby rooms. Facilities for disabled visitors. Washing machines. Motorcaravan service point. Fridge hire. Bar/restaurant, takeaway and pool bar serving snacks. Shops. New swimming pool with flumes (mid April-Sept). Bicycle hire. Tennis. Archery. Minigolf. Play area and miniclub for children. Fishing (with permit). Beach at site. Watersports, Kayak. Windsurfing. Daily medical services. Entertainment programme in high season. Excursions. Dogs and motorbikes are not accepted. Torches useful.
Off site: Peschiera 2 km. with ATM and usual town amenities. Golf 6 km. Riding 8 km. Gardaland close by.

Open: 22 April - 30 September.

Directions

From A4 Milan - Venice autostrada take exit for Perschiera, west of Verona. Travel north towards Lazise. The campsite is on the south-eastern lakeside about 2.5 km. north of Peschiera and well signed. GPS: 45.48300, 10.73183

Charges guide

Per person	€ 4,60 - € 9,00
child (4-9 yrs)	€ 1,70 - € 5,00
pitch	€ 8,80 - € 20,00

See advertisement on page 46-47

Lazise

Camping Spiaggia d'Oro

Via Sentieri, 2, I-37017 Lazise (Lake Garda) T: **045 7580 007**. E: **info@campingspiaggiadoro.com**
alanrogers.com/IT62545

Spiaggia d'Oro is a well equipped family site near Lazise on Lake Garda's eastern bank. This is a large site with grassy pitches and a selection of chalets and mobile homes for rent. The site has its own sandy beach with a beach volleyball court. A fitness centre is a recent addition and has been developed with a good range of high specification equipment. The swimming pool complex is impressive with three pools, one for children with a slide and water games. This is a lively site in high season with a varied programme of activities and a club for children. Other on-site amenities include a snack bar with a terrace overlooking the lake and a well stocked supermarket. Lazise and Peschiera are both within easy reach and are amongst the most attractive towns around the lake. A little further afield, Verona is, of course, well worth a visit and Italy's premier theme park, Gardaland, is also close by.

Facilities

Supermarket. Bar. Snack bar. Swimming pools with waterslide. Separate children's pool. Fitness centre. Tennis. Playground. Children's club and entertainment programme. Direct access to beach. Mobile homes and chalets for rent.
Off site: Shops, cafés and restaurants in Lazise and Peschiera. Verona 35 km.

Open: 14 March -15 October.

See advertisement on page 46-47

Directions

Leave the A4 (Milan - Venice) autostrada at exit for Castelnuovo del Garda. Head north on the SR450. Leave this road at Ca Isidoro and join the westbound SP5 to Lazise. Site is clearly signed from here. GPS: 45.49716, 10.73806

Charges guide

Per unit incl. 2 persons and electricity	€ 20,00 - € 39,40
extra person	€ 5,00 - € 9,20
child (1-6 yrs)	€ 1,50 - € 5,30
dog	€ 2,00 - € 7,00
No credit cards.	

Lazise
Camping La Quercia

I-37017 Lazise sul Garda (Lake Garda) T: 045 647 0577. E: laquercia@laquercia.it

alanrogers.com/IT6255

Having celebrated its 50th anniversary in 2008, La Quercia is a spacious, popular site on a slight slope leading down to Lake Garda and is decorated by palm trees and elegantly trimmed hedges. Accommodating up to 950 touring units, pitches are mostly in regular double rows between access roads, all with electricity (6A). Most are shaded by mature trees, although those furthest from the lake are more open to the sun. Much of the activity centres around the impressive pool complex with its fantastic slides and the terrace bar, restaurant and pizzeria which overlook the entertainment stage. The daytime activities and evening entertainment are very professional with the young team working hard to involve everyone (some courses require enrolment on a Sunday). La Quercia has a fine sandy beach on the lake, with diving jetties and a roped off section for launching boats or windsurfing (high season). Another restaurant serving traditional Italian food is located closer to the beach. The site is a short distance from the delightful lakeside towns of Lazise and Peschiera, which have a wide choice of restaurants, and is a short drive from Verona, one of Italy's finest cultural centres.

Facilities

Six toilet blocks are perfectly sufficient and are of a very high standard. Laundry. Supermarket. General shop. Bar, restaurant, self-service restaurant and pizzeria. Swimming pools (small charge). Tennis. Riding. Aerobics, judo and yoga. Scuba club. Playground with water play. Organised events (sports competitions, games, etc.) and free courses (e.g. swimming, surfboarding). Canoeing. Roller-blading. Archery. Minigolf. Evening entertainment or dancing. Baby sitting service. Internet. ATM. Free weekly excursion. Off site: Bicycle hire 300 m. Golf 10 km. Gardaland, Movieland and Caneva Aqua Park nearby.

Open: 10 days before Easter - 30 September.

Directions

Lazise is on the southeast side of Lake Garda about 30 km. west of Verona. From north on Trento - Verona A22 autostrada take Affi exit then follow signs for Lazise and site. From south on A4 Brescia - Venice motorway, take Peschiera exit and site is 7 km. towards Lazise and Garda on SS249.
GPS: 45.49318, 10.73337

Charges guide

Per person	€ 5,30 - € 10,90
child (5-7 yrs)	free - € 7,20
pitch	€ 10,30 - € 29,10
dog	€ 3,50 - € 6,90

Low season discount for pensioners.

Lazise
Camping Belvedere

Via Belvedere, 9, I-37017 Lazise (Lake Garda) T: 045 759 0228. E: info@campingbelvedere.com

alanrogers.com/IT62555

Belvedere is a pleasant, family site located between Pacengo and Lazise at the south-eastern corner of Lake Garda. There is a good selection of amenities here including a restaurant with an attractive terrace overlooking the lake. Other facilities include a swimming pool, supermarket and renovated toilet blocks. Pitches are of varying sizes and are grassy, with reasonable shade. This is a popular corner of the lake and Belvedere is just 200 m. from the Caneva water park and also very close to Gardaland, Italy's largest theme park. A lively entertainment and activities programme is run during July and August, and includes a children's club. The site has direct access to the lake and its own private sandy beach as well as a pontoon for launching boats. There is a number of mobile homes and chalets available for rent. Popular excursions include Verona and Milan, and Venice is also easily accessible for a longer day trip.

Facilities

Bar. Restaurant. Snack bar. Supermarket. Swimming pool. Children's pool. Volleyball. Tennis. Play area. Direct access to lake and sandy beach. Mobile homes and chalets for rent. Entertainment and activity programme. Off site: Nearest town is Lazise with bars, shops and restaurants. Caneva water park 200 m. Gardaland theme park 3 km. Verona 35 km.

Open: 15 March - 5 October.

See advertisement on page 46-47

Directions

Leave the A4 (Milan - Venice) autostrada at the exit for Castelnuovo del Garda. Head north on the SR450 and leave this road at Ca Isidoro to join the westbound SP5 to Lazise. Site is clearly signed to the south of the town. GPS: 45.47951, 10.72278

Charges guide

Per unit incl. 2 persons and electricity	€ 18,00 - € 31,50
extra person	€ 4,00 - € 8,00
child (0-8 yrs)	€ 2,00 - € 4,70
dog	€ 1,50 - € 5,70

The Camping No. 1 of Lake Garda!

Your front line seat on Lake Garda!

VP. 2009

CAMPING LA QUERCIA, YOUR HOLIDAY FILM

Shady emplacements – Heated toilet bloks for both grown-up's and children – 24 hours Warm water – Restaurant – Pizzeria – Cocktail Bar – Funny Bar on the beach – Swimmingpools with slides – Whirlpool – Full-comfort maxicaravans and bungalows for 4-5 persons with sight on the lake – The widest sand beach on the lake – Theatre – Supermarket – Butcher's shop – Pastry- and bakers shop – Typical products of the lake – Fresh fruit and vegetables every days – Tobacconist's shop – International newspaper kiosk – Rent a car service – Fax service – Professional animators – Animation for children and teenagers – Tennis – Canoe – Archery – Surfing – Judo – Football – Fitness gym – Spinning – Horse-riding.

6500 SQUARE METRES OF CLEAN AND SAFE PRIVATE BEACH, JUST A FEW METRES AWAY FROM ALL THE AMENITIES.

900 SHADY SPOTS IN BEAUTIFULLY-TENDED GROUNDS.

18 AREAS WITH FACILITIES FOR SPORTS AND LEISURE ACTIVITIES.

Information and booking:

+ 39.045.6470577

laquercia@laquercia.it
www.laquercia.it

CAMPING ★★★★
LaQuercia
... more than a camping!

LAZISE SUL GARDA • VERONA • ITALY

Manerba del Garda
Camping Romantica
Via G. Verdi 17, I-25080 Manerba del Garda (Lake Garda) T: 036 565 4150. E: info@campingromantica.com
alanrogers.com/IT62820

Camping Romantica is a tranquil site with some lakeside pitches and terraced areas that have beautiful views across the lake to the mountains. The glittering lights across the lake at night are quite romantic and it is a pleasure to sit out and enjoy balmy summer evenings here. The pitches are of 80-100 sq.m, mostly on grass and with gravel access roads, many having shade. The long lake-front access is ideal for swimming and watersports with boat launching possible. A stylish, bistro style restaurant is situated at the front of the site serving good food in a very attractive, modern setting.

Facilities

Eleven toilet blocks all clean and pleasant with mixed British and Turkish style WCs and very good, spacious showers. Facilities for disabled visitors. Washing machines. Quality restaurant and bar with large terrace. Large supermarket and bazaar. Play areas. Boat parking and launching. Watersports. Torches useful. Off site: Bicycle hire 2 km. Riding 4 km. Public transport 100 m. in high season. ATM 2 km. Internet 2 km.

Open: Easter - 30 September.

Directions

Site is on western side of Lake Garda near the town of Manerba. From the E70 east of Brescia, take Desenzano exit and turn north for Saló on P572. Then take road to Manerba di Garda and site is well signed. GPS: 45.56639, 10.54972

Charges guide

Per person	€ 5,00 - € 10,00
pitch	€ 12,00 - € 16,00
electricity	€ 2,00

Manerba del Garda
Camping La Rocca
Via Cavalle 22, I-25080 Manerba del Garda (Lake Garda) T: 036 555 1738. E: info@laroccacamp.it
alanrogers.com/IT62830

Set high on a peninsula, on the quieter western shore of Lake Garda, La Rocca is a very friendly, family-orientated campsite. With 180 attractive touring pitches enjoying shade from the tree canopy which also protects the campers from the summer heat, this is a 'real' campsite (20 pitches are on open terraces with lake views). It has the choice of two pebble lakeside beaches, which can be accessed from the site, and a very nice pool complex. The site has all modern amenities without losing its distinctive Italian ambience. Nothing is too much trouble for the management. The owner Livio is charming and very engaging with his pleasant, halting English.

Facilities

Two sanitary blocks with smart new units for disabled campers and baby changing areas which are kept in pristine condition at all times. Washing machines. Bar with terrace also offers basic meals. Small shop. Swimming pools. Tennis. Play area. Bicycle loan. Fishing (permit). Boat launching. Music in the evenings. Miniclub (high season). Torches required on beach steps and tunnel. Off site: Bars and restaurants a short walk away. Theme parks. Riding 3 km. Golf 5 km.

Open: 20 March - 28 September.

Directions

From A4 autostrada take Desenzano exit and follow SS572 towards Saló for about 11 km. and look for campsite signs. Turn right off main road, then right again along Via Belvedere and it is the second site on Via Cavalle. GPS: 45.56025, 10.56378

Charges guide

Per person	€ 4,00 - € 7,80
child (3-11 yrs)	€ 3,00 - € 5,80
pitch incl. electricity	€ 9,00 - € 19,00
No credit cards.	

Manerba del Garda
Camping Zocco
Via del Zocco 43, I-25080 Manerba del Garda (Lake Garda) T: 036 555 1605. E: info@campingzocco.it
alanrogers.com/IT62850

Lake Garda is a popular holiday area with a number of sites well placed to explore the many attractions nearby. Zocco is an excellent site in a quiet, scenic location sloping gently down towards the lake where there is a jetty and a long shingle beach. The Sandrini family who run this site give British visitors a warm welcome and English is spoken. There are 193 pitches for tourists, all with 4/6A electricity either on slightly sloping ground off gravel roads, on terraces or around the perimeters of two open meadows.

Facilities

Three clean, tiled sanitary blocks. Two are very modern with spacious showers and toilets with seats that automatically clean. Facilities for disabled people. Washing machines. Motorcaravan services. Good restaurant/pizzeria with terrace and bar. Shop (both 1/5-15/9). Bar overlooking beach (reduced hours in low season). Pool complex with jacuzzi. Play area. Entertainment for children in July/Aug. Bicycle hire arranged. Off site: Riding and golf 4 km.

Open: 4 April - 20 September.

Directions

Manerba is on western shore of Lake Garda at the southern end. From A4 Milan - Venice autostrada take Desenzano exit and head north on SS572 towards Saló for about 10 km. Zocco is well signed to right through Manerba. GPS: 45.53967, 10.55595

Charges guide

Per unit incl. 2 persons and electricity	€ 15,00 - € 31,60
extra person	€ 3,60 - € 7,80

Check real time availability and at-the-gate prices...
www.alanrogers.com

Manerba del Garda

Camping Belvedere

Via Cavalle 5, I-25080 Manerba del Garda (Lake Garda) T: 036 555 1175. E: info@camping-belvedere.it

alanrogers.com/IT62840

Situated along a promontory reaching into Lake Garda, this friendly, traditional campsite has been landscaped with terracing to give many of the 85 touring pitches a good vantage point to enjoy the wonderful views. They are mainly on hardstanding and all have 6A electricity. From the top of the terrace a long ramp (or 56 steps) takes you to the lakeside area with access to the long pebbly beach for a relaxing swim and for boat launching. The delightful restaurant and bar with pretty flowers is under shady trees at the water's edge. The site has grass areas and attractive trees give many pitches a cool canopy. There are no facilities for disabled campers and really young children would require supervision as the terracing is unguarded in places.

Facilities

Five traditional sanitary blocks are well maintained and kept clean. Washing machine. Motorcaravan service point. Shop selling basics. Restaurant, bar and takeaway are all open most of the season. Play area. Tennis. Music and TV in bar. Fishing. Torches useful. Mobile homes to rent. Off site: Golf and bicycle hire 2 km. Riding 4 km. Watersports nearby. Bars and restaurant a short walk away. Theme parks.

Open: 4 April - 4 October.

Directions

Manerba is on western shore of Lake Garda at the southern end. From A4 Milan - Venice autostrada take Desenzano exit and head north on SS572 towards Saló for about 11 km. and look for site signs. Turn right off main road, then right again along Via Belvedere. GPS: 45.56207, 10.56315

Charges guide

Per unit incl. 2 persons and electricity	€ 15,50 - € 28,50
extra person	€ 3,75 - € 6,75
child (3-11 yrs)	€ 3,00 - € 5,40
dog	€ 2,00 - € 4,00

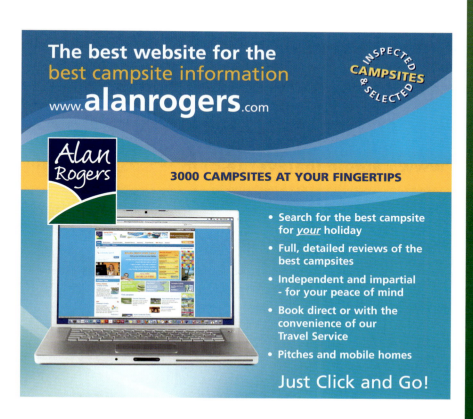
Check real time availability and at-the-gate prices...
www.**alanrogers**.com

Manerba del Garda

Camping Baia Verde

Via del Edera 19, I-25080 Manerba del Garda (Lake Garda) T: 036 565 1753. E: info@campingbaiaverde.com

alanrogers.com/IT62860

Baia Verde is a new campsite located in the southwestern corner of Lake Garda. When we visited construction was nearing completion and both the potential and the drawbacks were evident. The 69 touring pitches are in regular rows on flat, open ground where rough grass has been planted and young trees mark the corners of pitches; until these have grown there will be no shade. On the other hand, everything is being built to a very high standard and the restaurant block and the building housing all other facilities are in traditional style. All pitches are fully serviced and there are 12 'super' pitches with private facilities. Heated swimming and paddling pools are attractively designed and nearby is a play area and sports pitch. The bar and restaurant will be open all season, as will the pool complex. The lake is just two minutes' walk away; this is the quieter, less commercialised side of Lake Garda, but popular attractions such as the Gardaland theme park and Caneva water park are an easy drive away.

Facilities

Full range of high quality sanitary facilities in an impressive three storey building in the style of an Italian villa. Baby and children's rooms. Facilities for disabled visitors. Washing machines and dryers. Above will be a large TV lounge and on the roof is a sunbathing area with jacuzzi. An entertainment and activity programme in high season is planned. Bicycle hire. Off site: Manerba del Garda 1 km. Beach with fishing, swimming and boat launching 400 m. Golf and riding 2 km. Cycle and walking trails.

Open: 4 April - 25 October.

Directions

Manerba is on western shore of Lake Garda at the southern end. From A4 Milan - Venice autostrada take Desenzano exit and head north on SS572 towards Saló for about 12 km; then turn right following signs to site. GPS: 45.56155, 10.55352

Charges guide

Per unit incl. 2 persons	
and electricity	€ 22,00 - € 44,50
extra person	€ 4,50 - € 10,00
child (3-11 yrs)	€ 3,00 - € 8,00
dog	€ 3,00 - € 7,00

info@campingbaiaverde.com

NEW CAMPING

Baia Verde®
Camping

ADAC Camping Caravaning Führer 2009 Empfohlen

Camping Baia Verde • Via dell'Edera,19
I-25080 Manerba del Garda (BS)
Tel. +39 0365 651753 • Fax +39 0365 651809

www.campingbaiaverde.com

Check real time availability and at-the-gate prices...
www.alanrogers.com

Manerba del Garda

Camping San Biagio

Via Cavalle 19, I-25080 Manerba del Garda (Lake Garda) T: **036 555 1549**. E: **info@campingsanbiagio.net**
alanrogers.com/IT62870

Many changes have taken place on this previously rustic site at the tip of an attractive green peninsula surrounded by Lake Garda. Trees, shrubs and flowers have been planted, some roads have been block-paved and the general ambience is now more sophisticated. The site is steeply terraced in some parts to maximise views over the water. Some of the 165 pitches have shade whilst others are in more open positions on the water's edge. All have 16A electricity. The refurbished bar/restaurant is located on the water's edge in a charming old building with views to a little island where there is a second bar.

Facilities

The large central toilet block has been refitted to a high standard and provides excellent facilities which are kept very clean. Supermarket. Large restaurant and bar. Island bar. Play area (near water so parental supervision required for younger children). Boat launching, moorings for boats. All pitches now have access to satellite TV and the internet. Off site: Bicycle hire 500 m. Riding 5 km. Tennis and golf 5 km. Sailing 10 km. Bars and restaurants within walking distance.

Open: 1 April - 30 September.

Directions

Manerba is on western shore of Lake Garda at the southern end. From A4 Milan - Venice autostrada take Desenzano exit heading north on SS572 towards Saló for about 10 km. Look for campsite signs. Turn right off main road, right again along Via Belvedere. Site is at the end of Via Cavalle. GPS: 45.56352, 10.56638

Charges 2010

Per unit incl. 2 persons	
and electricity	€ 31,00 - € 54,00
extra person	€ 4,50 - € 11,00

No credit cards.

Manerba del Garda

Sivino's Resort

Via Gramsci 78, I-25080 Manerba del Garda (Lake Garda) T: **036 555 2767**. E: **info@sivinos.it**
alanrogers.com/IT62900

A new venture, Sivino's Resort shows great promise and the lakeside position is excellent. As yet there is just one small, brand new amenities block, a neat, modern reception and a traditional style building converted into five apartments. The 63 grass touring pitches all have electricity (6A). There is an extensive lake frontage with views of the lake from most areas and some well established trees for shade. The owners have plans for a restaurant, swimming pool and a small jetty in the future. However, it remains largely undeveloped making this a good spot for a quiet holiday.

Facilities

A small, clean, modern sanitary block is located in one corner of the site. The facilities are good although the shower cubicles are quite small with no screen or hooks so take a plastic bag to keep clothes and towel dry. Facilities for disabled visitors (although approach is uneven). Washing machine. Beach, fishing and boat launching on site. Off site: Restaurants, bar and supermarket within 1 km. Bicycle hire 2 km. Golf 4 km. Riding 6 km.

Open: 1 April - 30 September.

Directions

From A4 Milan - Venice autostrada take Desenzano exit and head north on SS572 towards Saló for 10 km. Watch for campsite signs. Turn right through Manerba, right again in Via San Sivino and continue for 2 km. along a winding road past other campsites. GPS: 45.5314, 10.5574

Charges guide

Per unit incl. 2 persons	
and electricity	€ 23,00 - € 45,00
extra person	€ 4,00 - € 9,00

Moniga del Garda

Camping Fontanelle

Via del Magone 13, I-25080 Moniga del Garda (Lake Garda) T: **036 550 2079**. E: **info@campingfontanelle.it**
alanrogers.com/IT62770

Camping Fontanelle, a sister site to Fornella (no. IT62750), is situated near the historic village of Moniga and enjoying excellent views across the lake. The site sits on the southwest slopes of Lake Garda and has 117 touring pitches on flat and terraced ground. Another 64 pitches are given over to tour operators but there is little impingement. All are marked and have electrical connections and there are some very pleasant lakeside pitches (extra cost). Some for tents and tourers are very secluded, being distant from the campsite facilities, although small blocks with toilets are close by.

Facilities

The two main toilet blocks are modern and clean, with hot water throughout. Facilities for disabled campers in these blocks. Washing machines and dryers. Motorcaravan services. Large shop with prices to compete with local supermarkets. Restaurant/bar. Takeaway. Shop. Swimming pools (from 15/5-15/9, supervised). Tennis. Electronic games. Live entertainment in high season. Boat launching. Off site: Bicycle hire 1 km. Golf 5 km. Riding 20 km.

Open: 29 April - 26 September.

Directions

Moniga is on western shore of Lake Garda at the southern end. From A4 Milan - Venice autostrada take Desenzano exit and head north on SS572 towards Saló for about 10 km. Watch for campsite signs. Turn right then right again in 3 km. GPS: 45.5253, 10.5434

Charges guide

Per unit incl. 2 persons	
and electricity	€ 22,00 - € 43,00
extra person	free - € 9,50

Pacengo
Camping Lido

Via Peschiera 2, I-37017 Pacengo (Lake Garda) T: 045 759 0611. E: info@campinglido.it

alanrogers.com/IT62540

Camping Lido is one of the largest and amongst the best of the 120 campsites around Lake Garda and is situated at the southeast corner of the lake. There is quite a slope from the entrance down to the lake so many of the 683 grass touring pitches are on terraces which give lovely views across the lake. They are of varying sizes, separated by hedges, all have electrical connections and 57 are fully serviced. This is a most attractive site with tall, neatly trimmed trees standing like sentinels on either side of the broad avenue which runs from the entrance right down to the lake. A wide variety of trees provide shade on some pitches and flowers add colour to the overall appearance. Near the top of the site is a large, well designed pool with a paddling pool and slides into splash pools. A pool bar provides refreshment and there is a fitness centre for those who wish to stay in shape. The site has its own beach with a landing stage that marks off a large area for swimming on one side and on the other an area where boats can be moored. One could happily spend all the holiday here without leaving the site but with so many attractions nearby this would be a pity.

Facilities

Seven modern toilet blocks (three heated) include provision for disabled visitors and three family rooms. Washing machines and dryer. Fridge rental. Restaurant, bars, pizzeria, takeaway and well stocked supermarket. Swimming pool, paddling pool and slides. Superb fitness centre. Playground. Tennis. Bicycle hire. Watersports. Fishing. Activity programme (high season). Shingle beach with landing stage and mooring for boats. Dogs are not accepted in high season (5/7-15/8). Off site: Bus service 200 m. Gardaland theme park.

Open: 20 March - 11 October.

Directions

Leave A4 Milan - Venice motorway at exit for Peschiera. Head north on east side of lake on the SS249. Site entrance on left after Gardaland theme park. GPS: 45.46996, 10.72042

Charges guide

Per person	€ 4,50 - € 7,00
child (3-5 yrs)	€ 3,00 - € 4,10
pitch incl. services	€ 8,60 - € 17,00

See advertisement on page 46-47

Pacengo di Lazise
Eurocamping Pacengo

Via Porto 13, I-37010 Pacengo di Lazise (Lake Garda) T: 045 759 0012. E: info@eurocampingpacengo.it

alanrogers.com/IT63010

Eurocamping is a large site at the southeast corner of Lake Garda, with direct lake access and with a pleasant beach. It is good site for launching boats as there is a little harbour/marina area adjoining the site. Expanded recently, it now includes an area of mobile homes. Most pitches, although quite small, are attractive with very good shade and all have electrical connections (4A). The new swimming pool is large and popular and incorporates a jacuzzi and a separate children's pool has a number of water features. Although not the most manicured of sites, Eurocamping is a friendly, typically Italian site. It is equipped to a good standard, although there are some older bungalows also on the site. This would be a good choice for those keen on learning the Italian language and immersing themselves in local culture. It is a very short walk to the village with its interesting bars and restaurants and the theme parks nearby.

Facilities

The sanitary blocks, although quite old, have been refurbished and are kept clean. Well stocked supermarket. Bar, restaurant and pizzeria (closed Tuesday in low season). Swimming pools (15/5-22/9). Second bar at the poolside. Large play area. Tennis. Fishing. Boat launching. Organised entertainment (July/Aug). Off site: Theme parks within 1.5 km. Riding 2 km. Bicycle hire 5 km. Golf 7 km. Sailing 8 km.

Open: 20 March - 22 September.

See advertisement on page 46-47

Directions

Pacengo is on SS249 between Peschiera and Lazise, 30 km. west of Verona. From north on A22 (Trento - Verona) autostrada take Affi exit then follow signs for Lazise and site. From south on A4 (Brescia - Venice) take Peschiera exit and follow signs for Lazise and Garda. At traffic lights in Pacengo, turn towards lake and follow road for 500 m. GPS: 45.46772, 10.71654

Charges guide

Per person	€ 3,50 - € 5,65
child (2-8 yrs)	€ 2,20 - € 3,70
pitch	€ 7,80 - € 13,00
dog	€ 1,00 - € 2,10

Check real time availability and at-the-gate prices...

www.**alanrogers**.com

Peschiera del Garda

Camping del Garda

Via Marzan 6, I-37019 Peschiera del Garda (Lake Garda) T: **045 755 0540**
E: **prenotazioni@camping-delgarda,com alanrogers.com/IT62560**

Camping del Garda is directly on the lake with access through gates which provide security at night. This is one of the largest campsites around Lake Garda and is more of a self contained holiday village with many pitches used by tour operators, although they are generally separate from the touring pitches. The mature trees provide shade for the 659 grass pitches of which 337 are for tourers. Arranged in numbered rows, all have 4A electrical connections and hedges have been cleverly trimmed for maximum attractiveness. Hard roads give access. This is a well kept site with colour added by attractive flower beds. There is a very active entertainment programme throughout the season for all ages and two good swimming pools with lifeguards.

Facilities

Eleven good quality toilet blocks have the usual facilities with free hot water in sinks, washbasins and showers. Facilities for disabled visitors in two blocks. Washing machines and dryers. Bars, restaurant and takeaway. Supermarket. Swimming pools. Tennis courts and tennis school. Minigolf. Watersports including windsurf school. Fishing. Playground. Full programme of organised activities in high season. Bowls. Dogs and motorcycles are not accepted. Off site: Gardaland, Zoo Safari, Verona, etc. Fishing 500 m. Golf and riding 2 km.

Open: 1 April - 30 September.

Directions

Leave the A4 (Milan - Venice) at Peschiera exit and travel through the town in the direction of Garda. After the second town bridge on Via Parcocatullo look for Via Marzan off the complex four road intersection. Site signs are small and difficult to see (site is on Via Marzan). GPS: 45.44797, 10.70125

Charges guide

Per person	€ 4,00 - € 10,00
child (under 5 yrs)	free - € 5,50
pitch incl. electricity (4A)	€ 10,00 - € 22,00

Peschiera del Garda

Camping Butterfly

Lungolago Garibaldi 11, I-37019 Peschiera del Garda (Lake Garda) T: **045 640 11466**
E: **info@campingbutterfly.it alanrogers.com/IT62620**

Camping Butterfly is in the town of Peschiera and has been owned by the same family for 40 years. The younger generation owner Giorgio is keen to make your holiday a success. Camping Butterfly has recently become associated with IT62630 Bella Italia and this will undoubtedly bring benefits to campers. There are 270 flat pitches on grass and sand, with 6A electricity and with some shade from mature trees. Many mobile homes are mixed randomly around the camping area, which has a distinctly compressed feel. A pleasant swimming pool with a paddling pool (and lifeguard) is available for cooling off and fun (hats are required).

Facilities

Three toilet blocks are light and bright. WCs are mainly British style with some Turkish. Facilities for disabled visitors. Washing machines. Shop. Bar and restaurant plus takeaway. Swimming and paddling pools with lifeguard. Play area. Multisport court. Entertainment programme. Miniclub. Off site: Beach 100 m. Sailing 100 m. Golf 1 km. Public transport at gate. Free transport to Gardaland from gate. Internet 700 m. All town facilities 200 m.

Open: 10 March - 28 October.

Directions

Site is on south side of Lake Garda in the town of Peschiera. From A4 take Peschiera exit and immediately pick up signs for site as you cross the attractive waterways on the 249. Take care as the signs are not that obvious. GPS: 45.44524, 10.69444

Charges guide

Per person	€ 4,00 - € 10,00
child (under 5 yrs)	free - € 5,00
pitch	€ 9,00 - € 20,00

Check real time availability and at-the-gate prices...
www.alanrogers.com

Peschiera del Garda
Camping Bella Italia
Via Bella Italia 2, I-37019 Peschiera del Garda (Lake Garda) T: 045 640 0688. E: info@camping-bellaitalia.it
alanrogers.com/IT62630

Peschiera is a picturesque village on the southern shore of Lake Garda and Camping Bella Italia is an attractive, large, well organised and very busy site in the grounds of a former farm, just west from the centre of the village. Although over half of the 1,200 pitches are occupied by the site's own mobile homes and chalets and by tour operators, there are some 400 touring pitches, most towards the lakeside and reasonably level on grass under trees. All have electricity (6A) and are separated by shrubs. There are some fine views across the lake to the mountains beyond. The pitches are grouped in regular rows on either side of hard access roads (which are named after European cities) and the wide central road which leads to the shops and pleasant restaurants. The site slopes gently down to the lake with access to the water for swimming and boating and to the lakeside public path. A feature of the site is the group of pools of varying shapes and sizes with an entertainment area and varied sports provision nearby.

Facilities
Six modern toilet blocks have British style toilets, washbasins and showers. Baby rooms and facilities for disabled visitors. Washing machines. Motorcaravan services. Shops. Bars. Waiter service restaurant and terrace and two other restaurants (one in the old farm building). Swimming pools. Tennis. Archery. Playgrounds (small). Games room. Watersports. Bicycle hire. Organised activities. Internet access. Dogs are not accepted. Off site: Fishing 1 km. Golf and riding 5 km. Gardaland, Italy's most popular theme park is about 2 km. east of Peschiera.

Open: 28 March - 11 October.

Directions
Peschiera is 32 km. west of Verona. From A4 take exit for Peschiera del Garda and follow SS11 towards Brescia. Site is at the large junction at the western entrance to the village. GPS: 45.44165, 10.67920

Charges guide
Per person	€ 6,00 - € 12,50
child (3-5 yrs)	free - € 5,00
pitch	€ 13,00 - € 23,00

Four charging seasons.
No credit/debit cards.
Camping Cheques accepted.

Riva del Garda
Camping Monte Brione
Via Brione 32, I-38066 Riva del Garda (Lake Garda) T: 046 452 0885. E: info@campingbrione.com
alanrogers.com/IT62350

Monte Brione is a municipal site situated on the edge of the small town of Riva at the head of Lake Garda. It is about 500 m. from the town centre and lakeside. There are 105 level pitches all with electricity (6A) and trees provide some shade. Some also have water and a waste water point. Terraces on the hillside take 21 tents. There are 15 mobile homes to rent, two equipped for disabled visitors. The site has a neat, well tended air and although near residential developments, there are spectacular views of the mountains from all pitches. Riva is recognised as one of Europe's windsurfing Meccas due to a combination of strong winds with flat water.

Facilities
Two refurbished sanitary blocks, one at either end of the site, have mixed Turkish and British style WCs, washbasins in cabins, and facilities for disabled people. New baby/children's room. 8 private en-suite shower rooms for hire. Motorcaravan services. Shop for basics. Bar/restaurant with covered terrace serving snacks and simple meals. Good sized swimming pool (15/6-15/9). Minigolf. TV/video. Bicycle hire. Two play areas. Off site: Fishing, boat launching, sailing 800 m. Tennis nearby. Riding 5 km. Restaurants, bars and shops in resort and many more in town centre 2 km.

Open: 18 March - 15 October.

Directions
Site is on the northeast tip of Lake Garda. From the A22 Brenner - Modena motorway, leave at Roverto Sud exit for Lake Garda north, and take SS240 for Nago, Torbole and Riva del Garda. Just before Riva, go through two short tunnels, then immediately turn right at site signs. GPS: 45.88133, 10.86148

Charges 2010
Per unit incl. 2 persons and electricity	€ 22,50 - € 28,50
extra person	€ 6,50 - € 8,50
child (4-12 yrs)	€ 4,50 - € 5,50
dog	€ 4,00

Check real time availability and at-the-gate prices...
www.alanrogers.com

Bella Italia

CAMPING BUNGALOW ★★★★

Camping Village Bella Italia, surrounded by huge trees, is directly situated on a romantic beach of Garda Lake, only a few steps from the picturesque centre of the small town Peschiera del Garda. Here you can relax in a peaceful and green landscape or enjoy our professional entertainment program. At your disposal: free windsurf courses, swimming lessons, aerobic courses, tennis lessons, cinema for kids, entertainment and plays, parties and funny evenings for everybody. **And much more... NEW FAMILY HOTEL.**

Via Bella Italia, 2 • I-37019 Peschiera del Garda (Verona)
Tel. 0039.0456400688 • Fax 0039.0456401410
E-mail: bellaitalia@camping-bellaitalia.it

www.camping-bellaitalia.it

Rivoltella
Camping San Francesco

Strada Vicinale, I-25015 Rivoltella (Lake Garda) T: 030 911 0245. E: moreinfo@campingsanfrancesco.com

alanrogers.com/IT62520

San Francesco is a large, very well organised site situated to the west of the Simione peninsula on the south east shores of Lake Garda. The pitches are generally on flat gravel and sand and enjoy shade from mature trees. There are three choices of pitch of different sizes with either 3A or 6A electricity; 76 are fully serviced. They are marked by stones but there is no division between them. A wooded beach area of about 400 m. on the lake is used for watersports and there is a jetty for boating. There are delightful lake views from the restarant and terrace. There is also a new shopping centre with a games area, bazaar and takeaway. The sports centre, pools and entertainment area are all located across a busy road away from the pitches and safely accessed by a tunnel. As with most sites in Italy, reception closes for siesta, but there is a waiting area with electricity. This is a good quality site which is great for families.

Facilities

Sanitary facilities are in two large, modern, centrally located buildings. Very clean and well equipped. Excellent facilities for disabled campers. Shop. Restaurant. Bar. Pizzeria. Takeaway and snacks. In a separate area across the road: swimming pools (1/5-19/9) and jacuzzi, sports centre and tennis. Playground. Entertainment programme, organised activities and excursions. Bicycle hire arranged. Torches required in some areas. Internet access. Off site: Riding 5 km. Golf 10 km.

Open: 1 April - 30 September.

Directions

From autostrada A4, between Brescia and Verona, exit towards Simione and follow signs to Simione and site. GPS: 45.46565, 10.59443

Charges guide

Per unit incl. 2 persons and electricity	€ 25,00 - € 44,00
extra person	€ 6,50 - € 11,00
child (0-10 yrs)	free - € 8,00

Camping Cheques accepted.

camping ★★★★ **sanFrancesco**

The camping site is located at the beginning of Sirmione peninsula. Restaurant, pizzeria, supermarket, clothes shop, winebar and take-away. The campsite is situated on a shaded surface of 104.000 sm. right by the lake, with a 300 m long beach. In the sport area you can enjoy the swimming pool with a childrens' pool and water games. In addition there is the possibility to practise more than 10 sports. To reach us follow exit Sirmione on the highway Milan-Venice. The campsite is an ideal starting point to reach Gardaland and Caneva World. New mobile homes equipped with heating and air-conditioning.

GPS: North 45° 27' 56,2" - East 10° 32' 59,3"

Strada Vic. S. Francesco - I-25015 Desenzano del Garda (BS) - Tel. 0039 030 9110245
Fax 0039 030 9119464 - moreinfo@campingsanfrancesco.com - www.campingsanfrancesco.com

San Benedetto
San Benedetto Villaggio Turistico

Strada Bergamini 14, I-37019 San Benedetto (Lake Garda) T: 045 755 0544. E: info@campingsanbenedetto.it

alanrogers.com/IT62640

Overlooking Lake Garda and in a position central to local historic attractions and theme parks, Camping San Benedetto is on a slope and has 150 reasonably sized, shaded grass pitches some with lakeside views. The restaurant and bar has a large covered terrace area and there is a comprehensive and reasonably priced menu. Additionally a beach bar serving simple meals is in a pleasant traditional building at one end of the site. A long pathway with reed beds and alternating beach and grass areas for relaxation makes an attractive promenade towards the marina and boat launching area. Two pleasant swimming pools provide a welcome cooling alternative to lake swimming.

Facilities

Four good toilet blocks provide mainly British toilets but have no facilities for disabled campers. Washing machines and dryers. Motorcaravan service point. Shop. Restaurant and beach snack bar. Two swimming pools. Aerobics. Play areas. Small boat launching. Canoe, motorcycle and bicycle hire. Sub-aqua club. Miniclub and entertainment programme all season. Off site: Fishing. Sailing 1.5 km. Golf 2 km. Riding 5 km. Launderette nearby.

Open: 15 March - 1 October.

Directions

Leave autostrada A4 at Pescheria de Garda exit and take lakeside road to Desenzano. At San Benedetto site is well signed on the right. GPS: 45.4482, 10.6697

Charges guide

Per person	€ 4,50 - € 8,50
senior (over 60 yrs)	€ 3,50 - € 7,50
child (2-10 yrs)	free - € 6,00
pitch incl. electricity	€ 6,00 - € 15,00

Check real time availability and at-the-gate prices...

www.**alanrogers**.com

San Felice del Benaco

Camping Europa Silvella

252

Via Silvella 10, I-25010 San Felice del Benaco (Lake Garda) T: 036 565 1095. E: info@europasilvella.it
alanrogers.com/IT62600

This large, modern, lakeside site was formed from the merger of two different sites with the result that the 340 pitches (about 108 for tourers) are spread among a number of different sections of varying types. The marked pitches alongside the lake are in smaller groups and closer together; the main bar, restaurant and shop are located here. The main area is at the top of a steepish hill on slightly sloping or terraced grass and has slightly larger pitches. There is reasonable shade in many parts and all pitches have electricity. A large new swimming pool complex also provides a daytime bar and restaurant serving lunches. There is considerable tour operator presence (160 pitches). There are also 50 bungalows, mobile homes and log cabins to rent. The site has frontage to the lake in two places with a beach, jetty and moorings. The private beach is very pleasant, with all manner of watersports available.

Facilities

Toilet blocks include washbasins in cabins, facilities for disabled visitors and a superb children's room with small showers. Laundry. Shop. Restaurant/pizzeria. Swimming pools (hats required) with bar. Tennis. Five-a-side soccer. Playground. Bowling alley. Entertainment (every night in July/Aug). Disco for children. Tournaments. Fishing and boat launching. First aid room. Off site: Golf 5 km. Riding 12 km.

Open: 25 April - 20 September.

Directions

San Felice is on the western shore of Lake Garda at the southern end. From A4 Milan - Venice autostrada take Desenzano exit and head north on the SS572 towards Saló for 14 km, turn right towards San Felice and follow brown tourist signs with site name (about 3 km). GPS: 45.57452, 10.53492

Charges guide

Per person	€ 4,50 - € 9,50
child (1-4 yrs)	€ 3,50 - € 8,00
pitch incl. electricity	€ 11,00 - € 21,50
pitch with services	€ 12,50 - € 23,50
dog	€ 4,00 - € 8,50

Check real time availability and at-the-gate prices...
www.alanrogers.com

San Felice del Benaco
Camping Ideal Molino

Via Gardiola 1, I-25010 San Felice del Benaco (Lake Garda) T: **036 562 023**. E: **info@campingmolino.it**

alanrogers.com/IT62650

Molino is a small, garden-like site with charm and character beside Lake Garda. It is in two main areas divided by the site buildings, and the 78 pitches vary in character, some well shaded on level ground by the lake, some for tents on terraces, and many in rows with pergolas and flowering shrubs. All have electricity, water and drainage. The excellent restaurant has superb lake views and serves traditional Italian food. A friendly family atmosphere is maintained at the site by Ingeborg, the daughter of the original owners, who speaks perfect English.

Facilities

All three small sanitary blocks have been rebuilt to a very high standard. British style WCs (some en-suite with washbasins) and adjustable hot showers and hot water to all washbasins. Facilities for disabled visitors. Laundry (attended). Motorcaravan services. Shop. Restaurant/bar. Bicycle hire. Fishing. Free organised entertainment in season. Boat launching. Boat excursions. Internet. Dogs are not accepted. Boat and caravan storage. Off site: Sailing and water skiing nearby. Golf and riding both 3 km.

Open: 15 March - 30 September.

Directions

San Felice is on western shore of Lake Garda at the southern end. From A4 Milan - Venice autostrada take Desenzano exit and head north on SS572 towards Saló for 13 km; turn right towards San Felice. Pass sign for Guardiola then follow brown signs with site name, turn right and right again.
GPS: 45.5785, 10.5542

Charges guide

Per person	€ 4,00 - € 9,00
pitch incl. electricity	€ 11,20 - € 19,00

San Felice del Benaco
Villaggio Turistico La Gardiola

Via Gardiola 36, I-25010 San Felice del Benaco (Lake Garda) T: **036 555 9240**. E: **info@baiaholiday.com**

alanrogers.com/IT62700

This small site has just 25 pitches, mainly for mobile homes, with just five available for touring. It is located at the end of a no-through road with direct lake access. The touring pitches are nearest the lake with electricity, water and drainage. The modern bar, café and reception area is small and simple, in keeping with the private feel to the campsite. The café terrace overlooks the lake. The shared amenities are of a high standard and built underground which minimises the intrusion on the beautiful views. Most of the mobile homes (to rent) now have air conditioning and four new ones have been added.

Facilities

The toilet block is just below ground level with a lift system for disabled visitors. The facilities are quite small but are adequate. Hot water is free throughout. Laundry. Small kiosk with terrace for coffee and snacks. Small playground. Fishing. Off site: Restaurants, shops, pizzerias nearby. Golf and riding 1 km.

Open: 25 March - 18 October.

Directions

San Felice is on western shore of Lake Garda at the southern end. From A4 Milan - Venice autostrada take Desenzano exit and head north on SS572 towards Salo for 13 km; turn right towards San Felice. Site is well signed (La Gardiola) before the town. Access is via a long, narrow lane. GPS: 45.57861, 10.55388

Charges guide

Per unit incl. 2 persons, water and electricity	€ 18,00 - € 40,00
extra person	€ 2,00 - € 9,50

San Felice del Benaco
Fornella Camping

Via Fornella 1, I-25010 San Felice del Benaco (Lake Garda) T: **036 562 294**. E: **fornella@fornella.it**

alanrogers.com/IT62750

Fornella Camping is one of the few campsites on Lake Garda still surrounded by farmed olive trees and with a true country atmosphere. Parts of the site have lake views, others a backdrop of mountains and attractive countryside. The 180 touring pitches are on flat grass, terraced where necessary and most have good shade, all with electricity (6/10A); 42 have water and waste as well. The owners speak excellent English. This site has a superb new pool complex, a well appointed bar and restaurant, and top class facilities for boat owners, having recently purchased the adjoining marina.

Facilities

Three very clean, modern toilet blocks have mainly British type WCs and hot water in washbasins (some in cabins), showers and sinks. Facilities for disabled people. laundry facilities. Motorcaravan services. Bar/restaurant. Pizzeria and takeaway. Shop. Supervised swimming pools and paddling pool (15/5-15/9). Tennis. Two playgrounds and animation for children in season. Bicycle hire (high season). Beach. Fishing. Small marina and boat launching. Off site: Bicycle hire 4 km. Sailing 5 km. Golf 8 km. Riding 10 km.

Open: 24 April - 26 September.

Directions

San Felice is on western shore of Lake Garda at the southern end. From A4 Milan - Venice autostrada take Desenzano exit and head north on SS572 towards Salo for 13 km; turn right towards San Felice and follow signs. GPS: 45.58497, 10.56582

Charges guide

Per unit incl. 2 persons and electricity	€ 24,00 - € 39,40
extra person	€ 6,00 - € 9,80

Check real time availability and at-the-gate prices...

www.alanrogers.com

San Felice del Benaco

Camping Villaggio Weekend

Via Vallone della Selva 2, I-25010 San Felice del Benaco (Lake Garda) T: **036 543 712**. E: **info@weekend.it**
alanrogers.com/IT62800

Created among the olive groves and terraced vineyards of the Chateau Villa Louisa, which overlooks it, this modern well equipped site enjoys some superb views over the small bay which forms this part of Lake Garda. On reaching the site you will pass through a most impressive pair of gates. There are 230 pitches, all with electricity, of which about 30% are taken by tour operators and statics. The touring pitches are in several different areas, and many enjoy superb views. Some pitches for larger units are set in the upper terraces on steep slopes, manoeuvring can be challenging and low olive branches may cause problems for long or high units. Although the site is 400 m. from the lake via a steep footpath, for many campers the views resulting from its situation on higher ground will be ample compensation for its not being an actual lakeside site. Being set in quiet countryside, it provides a tranquil environment, although even here it can become very busy in the high season. The site has a supervised pool (25 x 12 m) and a paddling pool which make up for its not actually having frontage onto the lake, and some visitors, particularly families with children, will doubtless prefer this. The large, attractive restaurant has a well laid out terrace and lawn with attractive marble statues from where there are more wonderful views.

Facilities

Three sanitary blocks, one below the restaurant/shop, are modern and well maintained. Mainly British style WCs, a few washbasins in cabins and facilities for disabled people in one. Baby room. Laundry. Bar/restaurant (waiter service). Takeaway. Shop. Supervised swimming pool and paddling pool. Entertainment programme all season. TV. Barbecues. All facilities are open throughout the season. Two play areas. English spoken. Internet points. Off site: Fishing 2 km. Golf 6 km. Riding 8 km. Windsurfing, water skiing and tennis nearby.

Open: 19 April - 21 September.

Directions

Approach from Saló (easier when towing) and follow site signs. From Milan - Venice autostrada take Desenzano exit towards Saló and Localitá Cisano - San Felice. Watch for narrow right fork after Cunettone roundabout. Pass petrol station on left, then turn right towards San Felice for 1 km. Site is next left. GPS: 45.59318, 10.53088

Charges guide

Per person	€ 5,75 - € 9,50
pitch incl. electricity	€ 15,00 - € 31,00
Camping Cheques accepted.	

Torbole

Camping Al Porto

I-38069 Torbole (Lake Garda) T: **046 450 5891**. E: **info@campingalporto.it**
alanrogers.com/IT62370

This is a small unassuming site built on what was the owner's family farm 50 years ago. It is peaceful, set back from the main road, yet only a short stroll from the waterfront and from bars, restaurants and shops. The grass pitches are level with mature trees providing shade. Hedges separate the two camping areas, one with 70 touring pitches with electricity (5A). The other area is primarily for tents (no electricity) and has a secure hut for windsurfing equipment. Near the modern reception (with wonderful historic photos on the wall) are a small bar and terrace area where basic snacks are served.

Facilities

The clean, modern toilet block has British and Turkish style WCs and hot water throughout. Facilities for disabled campers. Washing machines. Motorcaravan services. Bar with snacks. Play area. Off site: Fishing and bicycle hire 100 m. Riding 3 km. Golf 10 km. Mountain biking, hiking, climbing, canoeing, canyoning nearby. Shops a short walk.

Open: 1 April - 2 November.

Directions

From the A22 leave at Roverto Sud exit for Lake Garda north. Take the SS240 for Nago and Riva del Garda. At roundabout in Torbole, turn right (Riva). Site is signed in 200 m. before bridge. GPS: 45.87210, 10.87292

Charges guide

Per unit incl. 2 persons	€ 24,50 - € 27,50
Discounts in low season. No credit cards.	

Trentino-Alto Adige is a region of mixed Aus and Italian influences, much of it has only bee part of Italy since 1919. T landscape is dominated by the majestic Dolomites, snow-cla in winter and carpeted with Alpi plants in summer.

THERE ARE TWO PROVINCES IN THE REGION: BOLZANO AND TRENTO

Before 1919 Alto Adige was known as the South Tyrol and formed part of Austria. However, at the end of the First World War, Austria ceded it to the Italians. As a result there are marked cultural differences between the provinces as reflected in the cuisine, architecture and language (both German and Italian are spoken).

The landscape of Trentino-Alto Adige is dramatic and amongst the most beautiful in the country. With only a couple of snow-free months a year, the region is a winter sports haven, and there is also a good network of well established trails, which vary in length from a day's walk to a two-week trek or longer. Covering the whole Ortles range and topped by one of Europe's largest glaciers is the Stelvio National Park. One of Italy's major parks, it is popular with skiers, walkers and cyclists; the annual Giro d'Italia passes through here, Italy's answer to the Tour de France. It also boasts an abundant wildlife, with red deer, elk, chamois, golden eagles and ibex. There are several other parks in the region including the Panevéggio National park, a predominantly forested area with numerous nature trials and a lake.

Places of interest

Bolzano:15th-century church, archaeology museum with a 5,300 year old preserved mummy.

Canazei: mountainside town, good place for exploring the Dolomites.

Cembra: wine-producing town.

Merano: attractive spa town.

Ortisei: major centre for wood carving.

Roverto: 15th-century castle converted into a war museum.

Trento: attractive town with 13th-15th-century church, Romanesque cathedral, impressive city square.

Cuisine of the region

The food is a mix of Germanic and Italian influences. Traditional dishes include gam and rabbit with polenta, sauerkraut, and sausages with horseradish sauce (*salsa ai cren*). Desserts are often based on apples pears or plums readily available from the local orchards. The region also produces a variety of wines including the famous Pinot Grigios and Chardonnays.

Apfel strudel: apple pastry.

Canederli: bread dumplings flavoured wi smoked ham.

Soffiato alla Trentino: meringue trifle.

Strangolapreti: bread and spinach gnocc

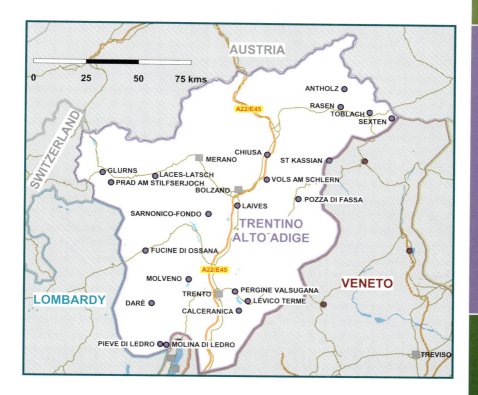

Antholz

Camping Antholz

I-39030 Antholz (Trentino - Alto Adige) T: 047 449 2204. E: info@camping-antholz.com
alanrogers.com/IT62010

Appearances can be deceptive and this is the case with Camping Antholz, an all year campsite in the heart of the Dolomites. At first sight the 130 pitches, numbered but only roughly marked out, make this a very ordinary looking campsite. All have 4A electricity and 50 have 16A electricity, water and waste water. Just inside the entrance is a pleasant looking building with reception and a smart restaurant. It is when one investigates the sanitary accommodation that one realises that this is no ordinary site, as the facilities are of an extremely high standard. High up in the Anterselva valley, there are splendid views of near and distant peaks.

Facilities

The toilet block is equipped to a very high standard with underfloor heating, in addition to the normal facilities. Hair salon. Cosmetics room with infra-red sauna. Baby room. Washing machine and dryer. Motorcaravan services. Bar, restaurant and takeaway (all year). Shop for basics. Playground. TV room. Bicycle hire. Limited entertainment programme for children in high season. Off site: Skiing and biathlon 1 km. Fishing 3 km. Riding and golf 13 km. Many waymarked tracks for walking and cycling.

Open: All year.

Directions

Antholz/Anterselva is 90 km. northeast of Bolzano. From Bressanone/Brixen exit on A22 (Brenner - Modena), go east on SS49 for 50 km, then turn north (signed Antholz) for about 12 km. Pass upper Antholz village and site is on right. GPS: 46.86442, 12.10937

Charges guide

Per unit incl. 2 persons and electricity (4A)	€ 19,20 - € 25,00
incl. full services	€ 20,70 - € 27,00
extra person	€ 5,50 - € 7,00
child (4-16 yrs)	€ 3,00 - € 5,80

Calceranica

Camping Punta Lago

Via Lungo Lago 42, I-38050 Calceranica al Lago (Trentino - Alto Adige) T: 046 172 3229

E: info@campingpuntalago.com alanrogers.com/IT62260

There is something quite delightful about the smaller Italian lakes. Lago di Caldonazzo is in a beautiful setting about two kilometres from the historic village of Calceranica which has summer time markets. This well designed campsite has 140 level, shaded pitches on grass. All of which are of a good size and have electricity (3/6A); 50 are serviced with water and drainage. Access roads are paved and the sanitary facilities are of the highest quality. A small road separates the site from the grass banks of the lake where all kinds of non-motorised watersports can be enjoyed. There are excellent restaurants within 50 m. of the gate. The site itself has a large terraced snack bar with wonderful views of the lake and the most amazing ice cream (gelato), yogurt and fruit concoctions. The campsite first opened 45 years ago and brothers Gino and Mauro continue the friendly family tradition of ensuring you enjoy your holiday.

Facilities

One central sanitary block has superb facilities with hot water throughout. Well designed bathroom and washbasin area. Excellent facilities for disabled campers and babies. Private units for rent, some with massage baths. Washing machines and dryer. Freezer. Shop. Bar/snack bar. Fishing (with permit). Modern comprehensive play area. Internet access. Cinema. TV. Off site: Town 1 km. and ATM. Watersports. Bicycle hire 1 km. Riding 3 km. Golf 20 km.

Open: 1 May - 15 September.

Directions

From A22 Bolzano - Trento autostrada take the SS47 towards Padova and then turn for Lago di Caldonazzo. Approaching town from the west beside the railway, continue along Via Donegani, turn left into Via al Lago and right at the lakeside into Via Lungolago. Site is on the right 200 m. before a sharp right turn. GPS: 46.00230, 11.25450

Charges guide

Per person	€ 6,50 - € 9,00
child	€ 5,50 - € 8,00
pitch incl. electricity	€ 10,00 - € 16,00
dog	free - € 4,00

Calceranica

Camping Al Pescatore

Via dei Pescatori 1, I-38050 Calceranica al Lago (Trentino - Alto Adige) T: 046 172 3062

E: trentino@campingpescatore.it alanrogers.com/IT62270

The enchanting small Lake of Calceranica lies just to the east of Trento in the foothills of the Dolomites amidst splendid scenery. Camping Al Pescatore is a very pretty small family campsite with a long tradition of camping and where daughter Giulia speaks excellent English. The site has a pool complex, attractive landscaping and a small poolside café with terrace. There are 200 touring pitches, all with electricity connections, on grass under tall trees. A separate area immediately opposite the entrance has one third of these pitches, however all the toilets here are of Turkish style. The lake is very popular and busy at weekends and during the summer season.

Facilities

The two toilet blocks on the main site provide the usual facilities and there is a single unisex block in the overflow section. Facilities for disabled visitors. Baby rooms. Washing machines. Shop, bar and restaurant (June/Aug). Swimming pool with spa, paddling pool and slides. Playground. Organised activities for children and music and dancing for adults in July/Aug.

Open: 20 May - 17 September.

Directions

Leave A22 (Brenner - Modena) motorway at Trento Nord, follow SS47 in the direction of Padova to San Cristoforo and follow signs to Calceranica and site. GPS: 46.01000, 11.24100

Charges guide

Per person	€ 8,50
child (3-12 yrs)	€ 7,50 - € 7,50
pitch	free - € 11,50
dog	€ 3,00

Chiusa

Camping Gamp

Via Gries 10, I-39043 Chiusa (Trentino - Alto Adige) T: 047 284 7425. E: info@camping-gamp.com

alanrogers.com/IT62080

This is a little gem of a site in every respect but one. It is situated in the picturesque Isarco valley in the mountainous, Südtirol region of northern Italy. Across the valley from the site is a tree clad hill rising to a cliff, topped by a picturesque convent. There are 80 pitches with full services including TV and internet connections. It is ideally located for a stopover on the A22 Brenner - Modena motorway, and therein lies its one drawback: the motorway passes above the site on a viaduct and there is inevitably a steady rumble of noise; more noticeable is the rattle of trains passing below the site. This aside, it is an ideal base from which to explore the mountains and valleys of this attractive region. There are numerous waymarked tracks to delight walkers and mountain bikers. Back on site the amenities are modern and equipped to a high standard. Above the pitches is an associated Gasthof with a pleasant bar and terrace plus a restaurant with an interesting menu. Here also is a small, but unfenced pool and adjacent children's play area. Camping Gamp is open all year and is well located for winter sports holidays.

Facilities

Modern toilet block with excellent facilities, including controllable showers, baby room, and special children's washbasins. Hot water to dishwashing and laundry sinks. Motorcaravan overnight area with service point. Restaurant with takeaway, shop (April-Oct). Bar (closed Jan/Feb). Music and dancing. Off site: Bicycle hire 300 m. Fishing 1 km. Riding 5 km. Golf and skiing 12 km.

Open: All year.

Directions

Klausen/Chiusa is 40 km. northeast of Bolzano. Camping Gamp is only 800 m. away from the A22 motorway (Brenner - Verona). Take exit for Klausen/Grödental, turn left and then right in 700 m. Site is well signed. GPS: 46.64083, 11.57222

Charges guide

Per person	€ 5,50 - € 7,00
child (3-14 yrs)	€ 2,70 - € 4,90
pitch	€ 10,50 - € 14,00

Family-run camping site at the entrance of the Gardena Valley

Family Schöpfer
Griesbruck 10
I-39043 Chiusa/Klausen
Tel. +39 0472 847425
Fax +39 0472 845067
info@camping-gamp.com
www.camping-gamp.com

Darè

Camping Val Rendena

Via Civico 117, I-38080 Darè (Trentino - Alto Adige) T: 046 580 1669. E: info@campingvalrendena.com

alanrogers.com/IT62135

Set in the National Park of Adamello Brenta, the only natural refuge of the European brown bear, Camping Val Rendena, is an enthusiastically run family site. There are 52 level grass touring pitches with some tree shade, all with 6A electricity. The site's location makes it an ideal base from which to explore this beautiful region, rich in flora and fauna where in summer snow still rests on peaks over 3,500 m. high. Beside the site runs the Sarca River, bordered for much of its journey by a cycle way. Surrounding the site, wooded hills with marked paths, reach up to 1,800 m.

Facilities

Two sanitary units, a small one in the reception block, a larger one at centre of site. Free hot water, controllable showers, some washbasins in cabins. Facilities for disabled people. Baby room. Laundry. Motorcaravan service area. Shop selling essential items, Solar heated swimming pool with adjoining children's pool. Large playing field. Play area and play room. Bicycle hire. Communal barbecue. Three apartments to rent. Off site: Pizza restaurant adjoins site. Thermal baths, Golf, Tennis.

Open: 10 May - 30 September.

Directions

Site is 35 km northwest of Trento. From the A22 (E45) Brenner - Verona autostrada take exit for Trento-Centro. Travel westerly on the SS45b to Sarche, then SS237 to Ponte Arche and Tione di Trento. Head north on the SS239 towards Madonna di Campiglio for about 10 km. to Darè. Immediately after entering Darè take descending slip road to right then follow camping signs to site beside river. GPS: 46.07077, 10.7197

Charges 2010

Per unit incl. 2 persons and electricity	€ 24,60 - € 28,60

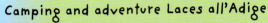

VAL VENOSTA • SOUTH TYROL

39021 LACES (BZ) • Via Nazionale, 4 • Tel. 0473623217
Fax 0473622333 • info@camping-latsch.com • info@hotelvermoi.com
www.camping-latsch.com

Camping and adventure Laces all'Adige

A taste for life, adventure and relaxation on an idyllic holiday island in the fabulous Alpine landscape of the Alto Adige region. Camping and adventure on the banks of the river with restaurant, new hotel and apartments, bungalows and all modern comforts. Open-air and covered swimming pools with waterslide, sauna, bowling and skittles. So immerse yourself in the holiday entertainment! *Special offers in winter.*

Fucine di Ossana

Camping Cevedale

Via di Sotto Pila 4, I-38026 Fucine di Ossana (Trentino - Alto Adige) T: **046 375 1630**
E: **info@campingcevedale.it** alanrogers.com/IT62110

Nestled under a castle and close to a tiny village, Camping Cevedale has a European atmosphere with very little English spoken, except by Maura, who runs the site. The 197 pitches are grouped in two areas on either side of a fast flowing river (fenced) and there is a fantastic roar from the water after rain. There are 97 touring pitches, all with electricity (only 2A). They are shaded, on grass and slope somewhat; the remainder are occupied by well kept seasonal caravans. Some campers come here every holiday and most have built little wooden chalets next to their caravans.

Facilities

Two sanitary blocks with mainly Turkish style toilets are well maintained, modern and spotlessly clean. They include hot water for showers and basins, heating in winter, washing machine and dryer. Small shop. Pleasant bar which serves snacks. Play area with tables and barbecues. Internet access. Adventure sport courses arranged. Bicycle hire. Dogs are not accepted. Off site: Shops, restaurants and bars in the two nearby villages 1 km. Riding 3 km. Skiing 10 km. Trekking, cycling, climbing, ropes courses, abseiling, canyoning, rafting, fishing nearby.

Open: All year.

Directions

Fucine is 50 km. northwest of Trento. From the A22 (Brenner - Modena) take exit for S Michele, north of Trento, then SS43 north for 43 km. to Cles. Turn east on SS42 for 26 km. to Fucine. Continue through village and turn south on SP202 (Ossana). Follow signs for campsite (ignore sat-nav!). The entrance is by the bridge just below castle. GPS: 46.31666, 10.73331

Charges guide

Per unit incl. 2 persons and electricity	€ 25,00 - € 32,00
extra person	€ 8,00 - € 9,00
child (0-8 yrs)	€ 6,00 - € 7,00
Camping Cheques accepted.	

Glurns

Campingpark Gloria Vallis

Wiesenweg 5, I-39020 Glurns (Trentino - Alto Adige) T: **047 383 5160**. E: **info@gloriavallis.it**
alanrogers.com/IT62130

Gloria Vallis is a style setter. The 80 terraced pitches (plus 12 for tents) are well grassed, level and all have electricity (10A), water and drainage. All have views and newly planted trees will provide some shade in the future. There is an elegant curved restaurant and bar with a spectacular panorama across the valley with its thousands of apple trees and snow capped mountains beyond. Another more casual eating area is across a grass field alongside a small lake which is stocked with fish. A very modern building houses the excellent sanitary facilities.

Facilities

The sanitary block with underfloor heating is equipped to the highest possible standard including showers with basin, WC and hairdryer. Excellent en-suite facilities for disabled visitors. Five private rooms for hire (€ 15 per day) with shower, toilet, basin, bidet, hairdryer, safe and music system. Excellent laundry area. Motorcaravan service point. Bar, restaurants and well stocked shop (all season). Lake for fishing. Picnic and play area. Internet access. Off site: Bicycle hire and riding 2 km. Nearby tennis, bowling alley (50% discount), sauna and health studio (10% discount) and local indoor pool (free entry for campers).

Open: 2 April - 5 November.

Directions

Glurns/Glorenza is 50 km. west of Merano via the SS38 then the SS40. Follow signs for the Reschenpass. In Sluderno/Sluderns turn west onto the SS41. Site is in about 1 km. (signed). Can be approached from north on SS40 from Austria, which appears to be a good road. GPS: 46.67317, 10.57013

Charges guide

Per person	€ 7,00 - € 9,00
child (3-12 yrs)	€ 5,00 - € 6,00
pitch	€ 14,00 - € 16,00
small tent	€ 7,50 - € 8,50

Check real time availability and at-the-gate prices...

www.**alanrogers**.com

Laces-Latsch

Camping Latsch an der Etsch

253

Reichstraße 4, Via Nazionale 4, I-39021 Laces-Latsch (Trentino - Alto Adige) T: 047 362 3217
E: info@camping-latsch.com alanrogers.com/IT62120

Gasthof Camping Latsch is 640 m. above sea level between a main road and the river, with splendid views across to the surrounding mountains. About 20 of the 100 touring pitches are on a terrace by reception with the remainder on a lower terrace by the river. They are in regular rows separated by hedges with thin grass on gravel. All have electricity and 47 also have water, drainage and TV points. Trees provide shade to some parts. A large underground car park protects vehicles from winter snow and summer sun and, if used, gives a reduction in pitch charges. An interesting feature is a water wheel which provides 3 kW. of power and this is supplemented by solar heating. Although right by a main road, the Gasthof and terracing screen out most of the noise. Mountain walkers will be in their element and chairlifts give access to higher slopes. Interesting drives can be made over nearby passes with Merano, Bolzano, the Dolomites and the duty-free town of Livigno within range. A reader's report on this site prompted a visit and we found, as suggested, a pleasant campsite, whose friendly staff speak excellent English.

Facilities

The traditional but well-maintained sanitary block is on two floors and is heated in cool weather. Excellent private bathrooms (20 with basin, shower, toilet) for hire. No facilities for disabled visitors. Washing machine and dryer. Motorcaravan service point. Shop, bar and restaurant. Small heated indoor pool, sauna, solarium and fitness room. Larger, outdoor pool. Playground. Off site: Fishing (licence) 50 m. Bicycle hire 1 km. Riding 7 Skiing 6 km.

Open: 6 December - 10 November.

Directions

Latsch/Laces is 28 km. west of Merano on the SS38 Bolzano - Silandro road. Site entrance by the Hotel Vermoi (keep on main road, don't turn off to village). GPS: 46.61664, 10.86663

Charges 2010

Per unit incl. 2 persons and electricity	€ 30,60 - € 32,80
extra person	€ 5,60 - € 7,60

Laives

Camping-Park Steiner

253

J. F. Kennedy Straße 32, I-39055 Laives-Leifers (Bolzano) (Trentino - Alto Adige) T: 047 195 0105
E: info@campingsteiner.com alanrogers.com/IT62100

Camping Steiner is very central for touring with the whole of the Dolomite region within easy reach. It has its share of overnight trade but, with much on-site activity, one could spend an enjoyable holiday here, especially now the SS12 alongside has a motorway alternative. The 180 individual touring pitches, mostly with good shade and hardstanding, are in rows with easy access and all have 6A electricity. There are also 30 chalets to rent. There is a family-style pizzeria/restaurant, and indoor and outdoor pools. This friendly, family-run site has a long tradition of providing a happy camping experience in the more traditional style – the owner remembers Alan Rogers himself who stayed here on many occasions. We met a British couple during our visit who had only intended to stay for one night but stayed for one week as it is so easy to get to different parts of the Dolomites and ideal for walking.

Facilities

The two sanitary blocks are equipped to a high standard, one having been completely refurbished. They can be heated in cool weather. Shop. Bar/pizzeria/restaurant with takeaway, (April-Oct). Outdoor pool, with paddling pool, and a smaller covered heated pool (all season, except July/Aug). Playground. Bicycle hire. Dogs are not accepted in July/Aug. Off site: Fishing 2.5 km. Riding 12 km. Golf and skiing 28 km.

Open: 20 March - 7 November.

Directions

Site is by the SS12 on northern edge of Leifers, 8 km. south of Bolzano. If approaching from north, at the Bolzano-Süd exit from A22 Brenner-Modena motorway follow Trento signs for 7 km. From south on motorway take Ora exit, then north on SS12 towards Bolzano for 14 km. GPS: 46.42955, 11.34380

Charges guide

Per unit incl. 2 persons, electricity	€ 24,00 - € 30,00
extra person	€ 3,00 - € 8,00

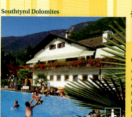

69

Lévico Terme
Camping Due Laghi

Localitá Costa 3, I-38056 Lévico Terme (Trentino - Alto Adige) T: **046 170 6290**. E: **info@campingclub.it**

alanrogers.com/IT62250

This attractive, well designed site is close to the main road but it is quiet, with mountain views and only five minutes walk from the Levico lake where it has a small private beach where one can launch boats. Hedging and a variety of trees and flowers create a welcoming garden setting. There are over 400 level touring pitches on grass, all with electricity (3/6A). Many also have water and waste water points. The site has a good pool and excellent facilities for adults and children. The attractive restaurant has good value meals and caters well for families.

Facilities

The central toilet block is very large and of good quality with British and Turkish type WCs, some washbasins in cubicles, a baby room and a unit for disabled visitors. The hot water supply can be variable. Private facilities to rent. Laundry. Motorcaravan services. Shop. Restaurant, pizzeria and café/bar with takeaway. Heated swimming pool (over 300 sq.m) and paddling pool. Animation and music in high season. Playground. Tennis. Bicycle hire. Off site: Fishing (for children) 600 m. Boat launching and sailing 1 km. Riding 2 km. Golf 12 km.

Open: 1 May - 4 September.

Directions

Lévico Terme is 20 km. southeast of Trento and site is west of the town, just off the SS47 Trento - Bassano - Padova road. Take the exit for Caldonazzo/Lévico Terme. Site is at start of ramp back onto the SS47 going west towards Trento. Look for campsite signs just as you leave the main road. GPS: 46.01217, 11.28940

Charges 2010

Per unit with 2 persons and electricity	€ 16,00 - € 34,00

Club card for entertainment, activities, etc. obligatory in July/Aug. Discounts for longer stays in low season. Camping Cheques accepted.

Lévico Terme
Camping Lévico

254

Localitá Pleina 5, I-38056 Lévico Terme (Trentino - Alto Adige) T: **046 170 6491**. E: **mail@campinglevico.com**

alanrogers.com/IT62290

Sister site to Camping Jolly, Camping Lévico is in a natural setting on the small, very pretty Italian lake also called Lévico which is surrounded by towering mountains. The sites are owned by two brothers – Andrea, who manages Lévico, and Gino, based at Jolly. Both campsites are charming. Lévico has some pitches along the lake edge and a quiet atmosphere. There is a shaded terrace for enjoying pizza and drinks in the evening. Pitches are of a good size, most grassed and well shaded with 6A electricity. Staff are welcoming and fluent in many languages including English. There is a small supermarket on site and the local village is nearby. The beautiful grass shores of the lake are ideal for sunbathing and the clear water is ideal for enjoying (non-motorised) water activities. This is a site where the natural beauty of an Italian lake can be enjoyed without being overwhelmed by commercial tourism. All the amenities at Camping Jolly can be enjoyed by crossing a pretty walkway along a stream where we saw many trout.

Facilities

Four modern sanitary blocks provide hot water for showers, washbasins and washing. Mostly British style toilets. Single locked unit for disabled visitors. Washing machines and dryer. Ironing. Freezer. Motorcaravan service point. Bar/restaurant, takeaway and good shop. Play area. Miniclub and entertainment (high season). Fishing. Satellite TV and cartoon cinema. Internet access. Kayak hire. Tennis. Torches useful. Off site: Town 2 km. with ATM. Bicycle hire 1.5 km. Boat launching 500 m. Riding 3 km. Golf 7 km.

Open: 1 April - 11 October.

Directions

From A22 Verona - Bolzano road take turn for Trento on S47 to Lévico Terme where campsite is very well signed. GPS: 46.00799, 11.28454

Charges guide

Per person	€ 5,00 - € 9,50
child (3-11 yrs)	€ 4,00 - € 6,00
pitch incl. electricity (6A)	€ 7,50 - € 18,00

Lévico Terme

Camping Jolly

Localitá Pleina 5, I-38056 Lévico Terme (Trentino - Alto Adige) T: **046 170 6934**. E: **info@lagolevico.com**
alanrogers.com/IT22280

Camping Jolly, sister site to Camping Levico, has a bright and bubbling atmosphere. It is set amidst the mountains and is very close to Lake Levico with its grassy banks which are ideal for sunbathing, swimming and non-motorised water activities. Pitches are generous, all with 6A electricity and most are shaded and grassy, although on some new, very large pitches the trees have yet to develop fully to provide shade. There is a three-pool swimming complex with a large sun deck which is very popular with families. Near reception are a small bar and terrace where snacks are served.

Facilities

Four modern sanitary blocks provide hot showers and hot water for washbasins. Mostly British style toilets. Locked unit for disabled visitors. Laundry facilities. Motorcaravan service point. Bar/restaurant, takeaway and good shop. Play area. Miniclub and entertainment. Fishing. Satellite TV and cartoon cinema. Internet access. Kayak hire. Tennis. Torches useful. Off site: Town 2 km. with ATM. Bicycle hire 1.5 km. and bicycle track. Boat launching 500 m. Golf 7 km.

Open: 20 April - 20 September.

Directions

From A22 Verona - Bolzano road turn towards Trento on S47 to Levico Terme where campsite is very well signed. GPS: 46.00627, 11.289167

Charges guide

Per person	€ 5,00 - € 9,50
child (3-11 yrs)	€ 4,00 - € 6,00
pitch incl. electricity	€ 6,50 - € 12,00
dog	free - € 5,00

Molina di Ledro

Camping Al Sole

Via Maffei 127, I-38060 Molina di Ledro (Trentino - Alto Adige) T: **046 450 8496**. E: **info@campingalsole.it**
alanrogers.com/IT62320

Lake Ledro is only 9 km. from Lake Garda, its sparkling waters and breathtaking scenery offering a low key alternative for those who enjoy a natural setting. The drive from Lake Garda is a real pleasure and prepares you for the treat ahead. This site has been owned by the same friendly family for over 40 years and their experience shows in the layout of the site with its mature trees and the array of facilities provided. Situated on the lake with its own sandy beach, pool and play area, the facilities include an outstanding 'wellness' centre.

Facilities

Superb toilet block. Five private bathrooms with shower, toilet, basin and safe. Excellent facilities for disabled people. Baby room. Laundry facilities. Freezer. Motorcaravan services. Small supermarket. Restaurant and pizzeria with terrace. Bar serving snacks and takeaway. Sun decks and snack bar at the lake. Wellness centre. Swimming pool. Play area. Bicycle hire. Boating, windsurfing, fishing and canoeing. Live music and dancing twice weekly in July/Aug. Children's club. TV room. Torches needed in some areas. Off site: Walk around lake. Riding 2 km. Golf 20 km.

Open: Easter - 8 October.

Directions

From autostrada A22 exit for Lake Garda North to Riva del Garda. In Riva follow sign for Ledro valley. Site is well signed as you approach Lago di Ledra. GPS: 45.87805, 10.76773

Charges guide

Per person	€ 6,00 - € 9,00
child (2-11 yrs)	€ 4,50 - € 6,00
pitch incl. electricity	€ 8,00 - € 16,50
dog	€ 5,00

Molveno

Camping Spiaggia Lago di Molveno

Via Lungolago 27, I-38018 Molveno (Trentino - Alto Adige) T: **046 158 6978**. E: **camping@molveno.it**
alanrogers.com/IT62140

Camping Spiaggia occupies an outstandingly scenic location at the foot of the Brenta mountains with views across the delightful lake Molveno. It is an attractive site, adorned with flowers, plants and trees and has 132 level touring pitches, all with electricity (6A). There is a similar number of seasonal caravans. The site is run on behalf of the local authority to promote the area and offers discounts on numerous tourist activities, including the adjacent sports complex with tennis courts and heated swimming pool (high season) and the funicular to Pradel in the Brenta Parco Naturali.

Facilities

An extremely high quality, modern, heated toilet block has free hot water throughout and some cabins with toilet, basin and shower. Two older blocks provide extra facilities at either end of the site. Facilities for disabled visitors. Well stocked shop (1/6-30/9) and an attractive bar/restaurant with takeaway (1/5-30/9 and holiday periods). Playground. Fishing. Off site: Football field, bowls, minigolf and pedaloes and boats for hire. Bicycle hire, sailing 1 km. Riding, skiing 5 km. Golf 40 km.

Open: All year.

Directions

Molveno is 20 km. northwest of Trento. From the A22 (Brenner - Modena) leave at exit for San Michele north of Trento and head northwest on SS43 (signed Val di Non) and then turn south on SP421 following signs to Molveno. At foot of descent into village, turn sharp right to site on left. Can also be approached from south on SP421. GPS: 46.13333, 10.95663

Charges guide

Per unit incl. 2 persons and electricity	€ 20,00 - € 44,00

Check real time availability and at-the-gate prices...
www.**alanrogers**.com

Pergine Valsugana

Camping San Cristoforo

Via dei Pescatori, I-38057 Pergine Valsugana (Trentino - Alto Adige) T: 046 151 2707. E: info@campingclub.it

alanrogers.com/IT62300

This part of Italy is becoming better known by those wishing to spend time by a lake in splendid countryside, but away from the more crowded, better known resorts. Lake Caldonazzo is one of the smaller lakes, but is excellent for watersports. Camping San Cristoforo is a relatively new site on the edge of the small town of the same name and is separated from the lake by a minor road, but with easy access. There are 160 pitches on flat grass with tarmac access roads and separated by shady trees. The pitches are of a good size and all have electricity (6A). This quiet mountain site has a well cared for air.

Facilities

The large, modern sanitary block provides some washbasins in cabins and pushbutton showers (with plenty of changing room). Dishwashing and laundry sinks. Facilities for disabled visitors. Washing machine and dryer. Motorcaravan service point. No shop (but village nearby). Attractive bar/restaurant serving reasonably priced food and takeaway. Swimming pool (20 x 20 m.) with sunbathing area and children's pool. Bicycle hire. Minigolf. Programme of activities (high season). Off site: Fishing and boating 50 m. Village 200 m. Supermarket 400 m. Riding 5 km. Golf 4 km.

Open: 1 June - 14 September.

Directions

Pergine Valsugana is 10 km. east of Trento. Site is just off SS47 Trento - Bassano - Padova road, 2 km. south of the town, near San Cristoforo. Site is signed from main road or via village. GPS: 46.03855, 11.23698

Charges 2010

Per unit incl. 2 persons and electricity	€ 15,00 - € 36,00
extra person	€ 5,00 - € 11,00
child (2-11 yrs)	free - € 7,00
dog	€ 2,00 - € 3,00

Low season discounted prices.

Pieve di Ledro

Camping Al Lago

Via Alzer 7/9, I-38060 Pieve di Ledro (Trentino - Alto Adige) T: 046 459 1250. E: mb.penner@libero.it

alanrogers.com/IT62330

Camping Al Lago is a small, unassuming site on the banks of the serene Lake Ledro, with towering hills of rock and forest on two sides. The 105 pitches (with electricity) are fairly tightly placed and the site has very limited facilities. It is very peaceful here and the friendly owner Mario will give help and guidance on what to do in the area including leading bicycle and walking tours. The site is very popular with Dutch holidaymakers. Only snacks are served in the bar behind reception but there is a choice of restaurants just 200 m. from the gate.

Facilities

A single toilet block provides a limited number of showers and toilets that are mixed British and Turkish style. Facilities are extremely busy at peak periods. Provision for disabled campers. Washing machines and spin dryers. Bar with terrace. Snacks. Bicycle hire. Kayaking. Lakeside areas. Organised walking and cycling tours. Torches useful. Off site: Riding 2 km. Sailing 200 m. Town and supermarket 500 m.

Open: 1 April - 11 October.

Directions

Site is on the north side of Lake Ledro. From the A22 near Rovereto take S240 to Riva del Garda, then S240 to Pieve di Lago. Site is well signed approaching the village. GPS: 45.8851, 10.7313

Charges guide

Per person	€ 5,50 - € 8,50
child (2-12 yrs)	€ 3,50 - € 5,50
pitch incl. electricity	€ 6,00 - € 11,00
dog	€ 3,50 - € 4,50

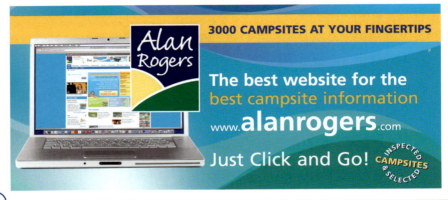
Check real time availability and at-the-gate prices...

www.alanrogers.com

Pozza di Fassa

Camping Vidor – Family & Wellness Resort

Strada de Ruf de Ruacia 19, I-38036 Pozza di Fassa (Trentino - Alto Adige) T: **046 276 0022**
E: **info@campingvidor.it alanrogers.com/IT62090**

This family-run site is in a natural setting two kilometres from the town of Pozza. Vidor had some major upgrading in 2008 with a new building housing reception, a camping shop, restaurant, pizzeria, café with terrace and lounge, indoor heated swimming pool (with whirlpool etc), beauty and 'wellness' centres, and a fitness room. There is a miniclub, indoor playrooms for children and teenagers, cinema and conference room, TV room, internet corner and cash machine. This augments the existing excellent sanitary facilities. The average sized pitches (with 1-6A electricity, water and drain) and up to 16A for full service pitches (with hardstanding), are in an attractive setting. There are slopes so chocks are advisable. A hundred metres from the site a large restaurant serves local cuisine. The local area is excellent for hiking in summer and skiing in winter.

Facilities

Two excellent hotel standard sanitary blocks provide hot water throughout and good showers with private bathrooms for hire. British style toilets. Facilities for disabled visitors. Washing machines, drying room and dryer. Bar/restaurant, takeaway and shop, wellness, heated indoor pool (all season). WiFi over whole site. Entertainment programme. Off site: Town 2 km. with usual facilities. Fishing 500 m. Ski lift 1 km. Golf 8 km. Many excursions to places of interest.

Open: All year except November.

Directions

From A22 Trento - Bolzano road take S48 to Pozza di Fassa. Take the road south to Meida and Valle San Nicola. Cross the bridge and site is well signed in 2 km. GPS: 46.41987, 11.70754

Charges guide

Per person	€ 6,50 - € 8,50
child (2-15 yrs)	€ 5,00 - € 8,00
pitch	€ 7,50 - € 15,00

Camping Cheques accepted.

Prad am Stilfserjoch

Camping Residence Sägemühle

Dornweg 12, I-39026 Prad am Stilfserjoch (Trentino - Alto Adige) T: **047 361 6078**
E: **info@campingsaegemuehle.com alanrogers.com/IT62070**

This small site in the countryside is alongside a little village and has attractive views of the surrounding mountains where skiing is popular in the winter. The grass pitches are neat and level, some have shade and most have water, electricity, drainage and pretty views. For a tiny campsite there is a lot on offer here. The indoor pool area is welcoming to cool oneself in the summer and relax in warm water after skiing in winter. The facilities are cleverly placed under the pool and include a tiny gymnasium, sauna and a TV/games room.

Facilities

The main modern toilet block is under the pool complex. All WCs are British style and the showers are of high quality. A new sanitary building has 24 private cabins for hire. Facilities for disabled visitors. Children's facilities and baby baths, plus a new second play area. Washing machines. Restaurant and bar. Indoor swimming pool. Spa and sauna. Entertainment programme in season. Miniclub. Play area. Internet. Torches useful. Off site: Town facilities. Natural spring for paddling close by. Bicycle hire 300 m. Riding 800 m. Golf 30 km.

Open: All year excl. 8 November - 19 December.

Directions

Site is west of Bolzano. From A38/S40 west of Bolzano, take exit for Pso dello Stelvio/Stilfserjoch (also marked S38) and village of Prad am Stilfserjoch. Site is well signed from here. GPS: 46.61694, 10.59111

Charges guide

Per unit incl. 2 persons and electricity	€ 29,50 - € 36,30
extra person	€ 5,00 - € 10,00
dog	€ 3,50 - € 4,00

No credit cards.

Check real time availability and at-the-gate prices...
www.alanrogers.com

Rasen

Camping Corones

I-39030 Rasen (Trentino - Alto Adige) T: 047 449 6490. E: info@corones.com

alanrogers.com/IT61990

Situated in a pine forest clearing at the foot of the attractive Antholz valley in the heart of German-speaking Südtirol, Corones is ideally situated both for winter sports enthusiasts and for walkers, cyclists, mountain bikers and those who prefer to explore the valleys and mountain roads of the Dolomites by car. There are 135 level pitches, all with electricity (16A) and many also with water and drainage and satellite TV. The Residence offers luxury apartments and there are authentic Canadian log cabins for hire. The bar/restaurant and small shop are open all season. From the site you can see slopes which in winter become highly rated skiing pistes. A short drive up the broad Antholz/Anterselva valley takes you to an internationally important biathlon centre. A not-so-young British couple who were on site when we visited had just driven up the valley and over the pass into Austria and then back via another pass. Back on site, a small pool and paddling pool could be very welcome. There is a regular programme of free excursions and occasional evening events. Children's entertainment is provided in July and August.

Facilities

The central toilet block is traditional but well maintained and clean. Additional facilities below the Residence are of the highest quality including individual shower rooms with washbasins, washbasins with all WCs, a delightful children's unit and an excellent facility for disabled visitors. Fully equipped showers for hire. Luxurious wellness centre with saunas, solarium, jacuzzis, massage, therapy pools and heat benches. Heated outdoor swimming pool (4/5-20/10). Play area. Internet. Off site: Tennis 800 m. Bicycle hire 1 km. Riding and fishing 3 km. Golf (9 holes) 10 km.

Open: 6 December - 30 March, 4 May - 31 October.

Directions

Rasen/Rasun is 85 km. northeast of Bolzano. From Bressanone/Brixen exit on A22 Brenner - Modena motorway, go east on SS49 for 50 km. then turn north (signed Razen/Antholz). Turn immediately west at roundabout in Niederrasen/Rasun di Sotto to site on left in 100 m. GPS: 46.7758, 12.0367

Charges guide

Per unit incl. 2 persons	€ 18,50 - € 26,70
extra person	€ 4,50 - € 7,30
child (3-15 yrs)	€ 3,00 - € 5,90

Saint Kassian

Camping Sass Dlacia

Localitá Sciarè 11, I-39055 Saint Kassian (Trentino - Alto Adige) T: **047 184 9527** E: **info@campingsassdlacia.it**
alanrogers.com/IT62085

Sass Dlacia is located amid the beautiful mountain scenery of the northern Dolomites, west of Cortina. Pitches here are grassy and of a reasonable size with superb mountain views on all sides. All have electrical connections (6/10A). There are a number of apartments available for rent. The site is open all year and is popular for both summer and winter holidays, offering a ski hire service to guests in the winter. On site amenities include a well stocked shop and a smart bar/restaurant specializing in local cuisine and incorporating a pizzeria, with pizzas cooked on a traditional log stove. A wealth of activities is on offer in the area, including mountain biking, hiking and rock climbing. The site's friendly owners will be pleased to recommend routes and activity ideas. Cortina d'Ampezzo is a stylish resort and former winter Olympic destination. The town is around 30 km. distant and is now well known for its designer shops and elegant hotels.

Facilities

Bar and restaurant/pizzeria. Shop. Play area. Tourist information. Apartments for rent. Off site: Nearby resort of San Cassiano. Walking and cycle routes. Rock climbing. Fishing. Cortina d'Ampezzo resort 27 km.

Open: All year.

Directions

Leave the A22 motorway at Bressanone exit and head east on SS49 to Casteldarne and then south on the SS244 and SP37 to San Cassiano, via San Martino, Badia and La Villa. Site is clearly signed after passing through the village. GPS: 46.55425, 11.96991

Charges guide

Per unit incl. 2 persons	
and electricity	€ 17,50 - € 36,00
extra person	€ 5,00 - € 7,00
child (3-10 yrs)	€ 4,00 - € 5,70
dog	€ 4,20

Sarnonico-Fondo

Camping Park Baita Dolomiti

Via Cesare Battisti 18, I-38010 Sarnonico-Fondo (Trentino - Alto Adige) T: **046 383 0109**. E: **campark@tin.it**
alanrogers.com/IT61980

Baita Dolomiti is a family campsite located in a splendid mountain region. It was very quiet when we visited in early June, but apparently becomes quite lively in high season, with plenty of organised entertainment for young and old. There is a rustic bar and restaurant providing typical local meals. The 130 grass touring pitches all have electricity (3A) and, although they are not large, there is a great sense of space. The Val di Non is a wonderful area for walking and cycling and the more adventurous can explore the canyons on foot or by boat.

Facilities

Two toilet blocks are well equipped and maintained, with a mixture of British and Turkish style WCs, controllable showers, baby room and hot water to all basins and sinks. Facilities for disabled visitors (not conveniently located). Motorcaravan service point. Bar/restaurant (all season). Swimming and paddling pools (July/Aug). Play area. Off site: Tourist train from site to various local villages. Golf 1 km. Bicycle hire 1 km. Fishing 3 km. Riding 4 km. Canoeing. Canyoning. Walking and cycling.

Open: 1 June - 30 September.

Directions

From the A22 (Brenner - Modena) take exit for San Michele/Mezzocorona. Turn right on SS43 towards Val di Non and follow signs for Cles, turning northeast after 20 km. on SS43D (Fondo). Continue 14 km. to Sarnonico where site is signed. We are told the route from Merano via the Gampen Pass is possible but Bolzano via the Mendel Pass is NOT recommended, especially if towing. GPS: 46.41889, 11.14056

Charges guide

Per person	€ 6,50 - € 8,80
pitch incl. electricity	€ 7,50 - € 14,50

75

Sexten

Caravan Park Sexten

Saint Josef Strasse 54, I-39030 Sexten (Trentino - Alto Adige) T: **047 471 0444**. E: **info@parksexten.com**
alanrogers.com/IT62030

Caravan Park Sexten is 1,520 metres above sea level and has 268 pitches. Some are very large and all have electricity (16A), TV connections and water and drainage in summer and winter (underground heating stops pipes freezing). Some pitches are in the open to catch the sun, others are tucked in forest clearings by the river. They are mostly gravelled to provide an ideal all-year surface. It is the facilities that make this a truly remarkable site; no expense or effort has been spared to create a luxurious environment that matches that of any top class hotel. Member of 'Leading Campings Group'.

Facilities

The three main toilet blocks are remarkable in design, fixtures and fittings. Heated floors. Controllable showers. Hairdryers. Luxurious private facilities to rent. Children and baby rooms. En-suite facilities for disabled visitors. Laundry and drying room. Motorcaravan services. Shop. Bars and restaurants with entertainment 2-3 nights a week. Indoor pool. Heated outdoor pool (1/6-30/9). High quality health spa. New outdoor play area for children. Good range of activities for all. Tennis. Bicycle hire. Climbing wall. Fishing. Adventure activity packages. Internet access and WiFi (whole site). Off site: Skiing in winter (free bus to 2 ski lifts within 5 km. Walking, cycling and climbing. Fishing. Riding and golf nearby.

Open: All year.

Directions

Sexten/Sesto is 110 km. northeast of Bolzano. From Bressanone/Brixen exit on A22 Brenner - Modena motorway follow the SS49 east for about 60 km. Turn south on SS52 at Innichen/San Candido and follow signs to Sexten. Site is 5 km. past village (signed). GPS: 46.66727, 12.40221

Charges guide

Per person	€ 7,00 - € 12,50
child	€ 1,00 - € 10,50
pitch (80-280 sq.m)	€ 5,00 - € 22,00
electricity per kWh (16A)	€ 0,70
dog	€ 2,00 - € 6,00

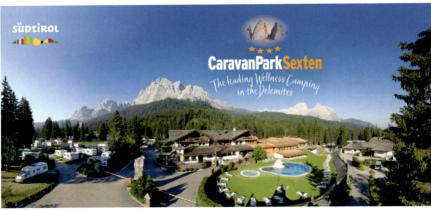

Toblach

Camping Olympia

Camping 1, I-39034 Toblach (Trentino - Alto Adige) T: 047 497 2147. E: info@camping-olympia.com
alanrogers.com/IT62000

In the Dolomite mountains, Camping Olympia maintains its high standards and is constantly being upgraded. The 314 pitches have been relaid in a regular pattern and tall pine trees and newly planted shrubs and hedges make this a very pleasant and attractive site. There are tree-clad hills on either side and craggy mountains beyond. The 238 touring pitches all have electricity (6A) and a TV point. There are 21 fully-serviced pitches with water, waste water, gas, telephone and satellite TV points. Some accommodation is available for rent, and there are 62 seasonal caravans which are mainly grouped at one end of the site. A little fish pond with a fountain and surrounded by flowers makes an attractive central feature, whilst on the far side of the site, a gate leads out into the woods where there is a little play area and a few animals. The site is an ideal base from which to explore this part of German-speaking Südtirol on foot, by bicycle (track just outside camp) or by car – and Austria is just up the road!

Facilities

The new toilet block is of a high standard. Rooms with WC, washbasin and shower to rent. Baby room. Facilities for disabled visitors. Two small blocks provide further WCs and showers. Motorcaravan service point. Shop. Attractive bar, restaurant and pizzeria (all year). Second bar with grill and terrace by pool (10/6-30/9; 20/12-Easter). Heated swimming pool (20/5-15/9). Sauna, solarium, steam bath and whirlpools. Fishing. Bicycle hire. Play area. WiFi. Programme of activities and excursions. Entertainment in high season. Off site: Tennis and minigolf nearby. Riding and golf 3 km.

Open: All year.

Directions

Toblach/Dobbiaco is 100 km. northeast of Bolzano. Site is west of the town. From the A22 Innsbruck - Bolzano autostrada, take exit for Bressanone/Brixen and travel east on SS49 for 60 km. Site signed to left just after a short tunnel. From Cortina take SS48 and SS51 northwards then turn west on SS49 for 1.5 km. GPS: 46.73330, 12.23332

Charges guide

Per person	€ 8,00 - € 10,00
child (3-12 yrs)	€ 4,50 - € 8,00
pitch	€ 8,00 - € 12,50
dog	free - € 4,50

Supplement for serviced pitch (14/7-19/8).

Widely regarded as the 'Bible' by site owners and readers alike, there is no better guide when it comes to forming an independent view of a campsite's quality. When you need to be confident in your choice of campsite, you need the Alan Rogers Guide.

- ☑ **Sites only included on merit**
- ☑ **Sites cannot pay to be included**
- ☑ **Independently inspected, rigorously assessed**
- ☑ **Impartial reviews**
- ☑ **Over 40 years of expertise**

INSPECTED CAMPSITES & SELECTED

Völs am Schlern

Camping Seiser Alm

Saint Konstantin 16, I-39050 Völs am Schlern (Trentino - Alto Adige) T: 047 170 6459
E: info@camping-seiseralm.com alanrogers.com/IT62040

What an amazing experience awaits you at Seiser Alm! Elisabeth and Erhard Mahlknecht have created a superb site in the magnificent Südtirol region of the Dolomite mountains. Catering for families and delightfully peaceful, towering peaks provide a magnificent backdrop when you dine in the charming, traditional style restaurant on the upper terrace. Here you will also find the bar, shop and reception. The 150 touring pitches are of a very high standard with 16A electricity supply, 120 with gas, water, drainage and satellite connections. Guests were delighted with the site when we visited, many coming to walk or cycle, some just to enjoy the surroundings. There are countless things to see and do here. Enjoy the grand 18-hole golf course alongside the site or join the plethora of excursions and organised activities. Local buses and cable cars provide an excellent service for summer visitors and skiers alike (discounts are available). In keeping with the natural setting, the majority of the luxury pitches are set into the hillside. Elisabeth's designs incorporating Grimm fairy tales are tastefully developed in the superb children's bathrooms that are in a magic forest setting complete with blue sky, giant mushroom and elves! A brilliant family adventure park with an enclosure of tame rabbits is at the lower part of the site where goats also roam. If you wish for quiet, quality camping in a crystal clean environment, then visit this immaculate site.

Facilities

One luxury underground block is in the centre of the site. 16 private units are available. Excellent facilities for disabled visitors. Fairy tale facilities for children. Infra red sensors, underfloor heating and gently curved floors to prevent slippery surfaces. Constant fresh air ventilation. Washing machines and large drying room. Sauna. Supermarket. Quality restaurant and bar with terrace. Entertainment programme. Miniclub. Children's adventure park and play room. Special rooms for ski equipment. Torches useful. Off site: Riding alongside site. 18-hole golf course (discounts) 1 km. Fishing 1 km. Bicycle hire 2 km. Lake swimming 2 km. ATM 3 km. Walks. Skiing in winter. Buses to cable cars and ski lifts.

Open: All year excl. 5 November - 20 December.

Directions

Site is east of Bolzano. From A22-E45 take Bolzano Nord exit. Take road for Prato Isarco/Blumau, then road for Fie/Vols. Take care as the split in the road is sudden and if you miss the left fork as you enter a tunnel (Altopiano dello Sciliar/Schlerngebiet) you will pay a heavy price in extra kilometres. Enjoy the climb to Vols am Schlern and site is well signed.
GPS: 46.53344, 11.53335

Charges guide

Per person	€ 6,00 - € 8,50
child (2-15 yrs)	€ 3,40 - € 6,80
pitch	€ 3,00 - € 11,00
electricity per kWh	€ 0,60
dog	€ 2,00 - € 4,00

Camping Cheques accepted.

Friuli-Venézia Giúlia is a beautiful border region nudging Slovenia on the east, Austria and the Carnic Alps to the north with the Adriatic to the south – forming a bridge between the Mediterranean world and central Europe.

THE REGION HAS FOUR PROVINCES: GORIZIA, PORDENONE, TRIESTE AND UDINE

Near the Slovenian border lies the atmospheric city of Trieste, with its long bustling harbour. The prime tourist site is the hill of San Giusto; at the summit is the castle and a walk along the ramparts offers sweeping views over the Gulf of Trieste. Across the bay, Múggia is only a short ferry ride from Trieste, whilst outside the city is an area of limestone uplands, known as the Carso. With an abundance of caves, including the Grotta Gigante, the world's largest accessible cave and second largest natural chamber in the world, the Carso can be easily reached by the tranvia (cable tramway). Sitting on a group of low islands in the middle of the Adriatic lagoon, Grado is attached to the mainland by a long, narrow causeway. A popular seaside resort, it has a long sandy beach and harbour plus a historic centre. A short distance from here is Aquileia, now a small town but once an important city of the Roman Empire and further inland Udine boasts galleries, fine churches, and well-preserved historic buildings. Towards the Austrian border in the north, is Carnia. With its lush valleys and flower-filled meadows, which give way to Alpine peaks, it is an area popular with walkers.

Places of interest

Aquileia: Basilica, with mosaic pavement dating from the 4th century.

Cividale del Friuli: market town, medieval walls, archaeology museum.

Forni di Sopra: thickly wooded area, popular for mountain-biking, horse-riding and hiking.

Gorizia: major shopping town, numerous parks and gardens, castle.

Pordenon: preserved historic centre.

Tarvisio: small mountain resort.

Cuisine of the region

Fish broths, made from squid, octopus, mackerel, sardines and clams, are common. Gnocchi is a Trieste speciality; gnocchi the size of eggs are stuffed with pitted prune, rolled in breadcrumbs, browned in butter and sprinkled with cinnamon and sugar. Local wines include Tocai, Ribolla Gialla, Merlot and Cabernet Sauvignon.

Brodo di Pesce: fish soup, sometimes flavoured with saffron.

Cialzons: ravioli from Carnia, usually stuffed with spinach and ricotta.

Jota: a soup of sauerkraut and barley.

Spaghetti alle Vongole: spaghetti with fresh clams in a chilli-pepper sauce.

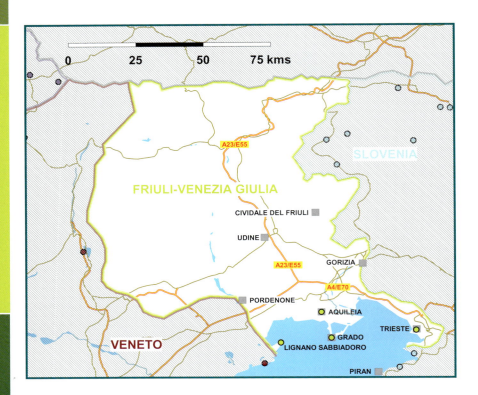

Aquileia
Camping Aquileia

Via Gemina,10, I-33051 Aquileia (Friuli - Venézia Giúlia) T: **043 191 042**. E: **info@campingaquileia.it**
alanrogers.com/IT60020

$\boxed{\text{F}}$ 254

Situated in former parkland under mature trees, Camping Aquileia, with 121 level and grass touring pitches, is a quiet site 10 km. away from the bustling coastal beaches. The pitches all with 4/6A electricity are separated from the entrance, swimming pool and play areas by tall hedges, and the more peaceful part of the site with the newer sanitary block is at the rear of the site. The now small town of Aquileia, founded in 181 BC, became one of the most important Roman military and trading posts and is now a UNESCO world heritage site. In the basilica, only a short walk from the campsite, along the former harbour, lays one of the world's most magnificent mosaics. The campsite is popular with families and for those who seek a quiet base from which to visit the beaches or tour in this interesting region. From reception, tours can be organised with the town's tourist office to the region's archaeological sites, and not surprisingly a weekly mosaic course is also on offer.

Facilities

Two sanitary blocks with free hot water, controllable showers and washbasins in cabins. Facilities for disabled visitors. Folding baby changing bench. Laundry facilities. Motorcaravan service point. Restaurant, bar and automat for drinks and ice cream. Large playing field with playground. Swimming and paddling pools. Bicycle hire. Mobile homes and chalets for rent. Off site: Supermarket opposite entrance. Riding 12 km. The historic towns of Trieste, Gorizia and the beach resort of Grado.

Open: 25 April - 15 September.

Directions

Site is 30 km. west northwest of Trieste. From the A4 (Venice - Trieste) take exit for Palmanova and travel south for 20 km. towards Grado. Just after entering Aquileia turn left at traffic lights, signed Trieste and Goriza and site is 400 m. on the right.
GPS: 45.77585, 13.37084

Charges guide

Per person	€ 5,00 - € 7,00
child (3-12 yrs)	€ 3,00 - € 4,70
pitch incl. electricity	€ 8,00 - € 21,00
dog	€ 3,00 - € 4,50

Grado

Camping Residence Punta Spin

Via Monfalcone, I-34073 Grado (Friuli - Venézia Giúlia) T: **043 180 732**. E: **info@puntaspin.it**
alanrogers.com/IT60055

Punta Spin is a large site, set between the road and a soft sand beach. When we visited in 2007, there were 500 pitches including 100 for tourers, but development should increase these numbers to 750 and 250. The flat pitches vary in size (65-100 sq.m), all with electricity (4/10A), and some are on the beach front (book early for these). A bicycle is an asset here as the sanitary blocks are up to 800 m. distant. The comprehensive amenities are clustered near the entrance and include a wellness centre where you will be pampered, and three pools, one of which is a sophisticated paddling complex.

Facilities	Directions
Three modern sanitary blocks have free hot water throughout. Mostly British style toilets. Good facilities for disabled campers. Washing machines and dryers. Motorcaravan services. Large supermarket and other shops. Bars and restaurant. Pizzeria. Takeaway. Three swimming pools. Fishing. Minigolf. Disco. Entertainment team in high season. Watersports. Wellness centre. Beach bar. Playground. Tennis. Off site: Golf 2 km. Bicycle hire 4 km. All manner of sea sports. Grado town 4 km. **Open:** 1 April - 30 September.	Site is 3.5 km. east of Grado on the beach road to Monfalcone. Take the 35L road to Grado Pineto and continue to site on same road. GPS: 45.69467, 13.45255

Charges guide

Per person	€ 5,00 - € 12,00
child (3-12 yrs)	€ 2,50 - € 8,00
pitch	€ 7,00 - € 17,00
dog	€ 3,00 - € 5,00

Grado

Camping Village Belvedere Pineta

I-33051 Grado (Friuli - Venézia Giúlia) T: **043 191 007**. E: **info@belvederepineta.it**
alanrogers.com/IT60070

Belvedere Pineta is situated on the edge of an almost entirely land-locked lagoon, 5 km. from Grado on the northern Adriatic Sea. A minor road runs between the site and the lagoon and a bridge over this connects the site with the beach of fine sand. It is a large site with 900 touring pitches arranged in regular rows with most under shade provided by the many tall pine trees which cover the site. Most are of reasonable size and all have electricity. An area of accommodation to let is to one side of the camping area. In high season a large programme of sport and entertainment for children and adults is organised.

Facilities	Directions
Most of the six toilet blocks have been refurbished to a good standard with all the usual facilities including some for children and free hot water in all basins, showers and sinks. Facilities for disabled visitors. Motorcaravan service point. Range of shops. Restaurant, pizzeria and takeaway. Swimming pools. Sports facilities. Play areas. Organised entertainment in high season. Bicycle hire. Off site: Riding 10 km. Golf 11 km. **Open:** 1 May - 30 September.	Leave A4 Venice - Trieste motorway at exit for Palmanova and go south on SS352 towards Grado. Site is signed after Aquileia on the left. GPS: 45.72867, 13.40109

Charges guide

Per person	€ 4,30 - € 8,70
senior (over 60 yrs)	€ 3,70 - € 7,50
child (2-10 yrs)	€ -2,00 - € 6,50
pitch incl. electricity	€ 10,10 - € 20,50

No credit cards.
Camping Cheques accepted.

Check real time availability and at-the-gate prices...
www.alanrogers.com

Grado

Camping Tenuta Primero

Via Monfalcone, 14, I-34073 Grado (Friuli - Venézia Giúlia) T: **043 189 6900** E: **info@tenuta-primero.com**
alanrogers.com/IT60065

Tenuta Primero was established in 1962 and has been a popular family site ever since. The third generation of the Marzola family continue to run the site and have made many improvements over the years. This is a large site with its own private beach and 800 pitches of varying sizes, including some new, large 'executive' pitches, with beach front locations, 10A electricity and a private water supply. Nine toilet blocks are dispersed around the site, some equipped with facilities for disabled visitors. There are no fewer than three restaurants here (including a pizzeria and a fish restaurant) and two bars, as well as a separate disco. Alongside the campsite is a large private marina with moorings for over 200 boats and a maintenance area. Tenuta Primero also includes an 18-hole championship golf course and a 9-hole executive course. Special rates are available for campers. Grado is a fascinating resort 5 km. away. The old town pre-dates Venice and has a similar appeal.

Facilities

Supermarket. Bars and restaurants. Pizzeria. Swimming and paddling pools. Disco. Beauty salon. Aerobics and aquagym. Windsurfing and sailing lessons. Play area. Sports pitches. Bicycle hire. Entertainment and activity programme. Children's activities. Direct access to beach. Mobile homes and chalets for rent. Dogs are not accepted. Off site: Campsite harbour. Two golf courses. Cycle track to Grado. Shops, restaurants and bars in Grado. Riding 2 km.

Open: 1 April - 3 October.

Directions

Take the Palmanova exit from the A4 autostrada and drive to Grado on the SS352 passing through Aquileia and Cervignano. Continue towards Monfalcone on the SP19 and the site is on the right after 5 km. GPS: 45.7051, 13.4640

Charges guide

Per person	€ 5,00 - € 11,00
child (3-11 yrs)	free - € 7,00
child (12-15 yrs)	€ 4,00 - € 9,00
pitch incl. electricity	€ 9,00 - € 24,00

10 % discount for CCI-members
01.04.–03.10.2010

At Grado, the most well-equipped campsite on the Adriatic. **Tenuta Primero** invites you to a enjoy your holiday in a superb natural location with entertainment, comfort and Italian cuisine.

- 800 shaded pitch sites
- 40 bungalows
- 10 suites with views over the bay and marina
- 3 take-away and gourmet restaurants
- 6 Cafès/Discos/Pubs

- 2 swimming pools
- 580 mooring sites
- 27 hole golf course
- 1000 metre beach
- Sports facilities
- Directly on the beach
- 20 mobile homes

TENUTA PRIMERO
Holiday and Sport Club

Grado/Italia – Tel. +39 0431 896900
tenuta-primero.com

Check real time availability and at-the-gate prices...

www.**alanrogers**.com

Grado
Villaggio Turistico Camping Europa

Via Monfalcone 12, I-34073 Grado (Friuli - Venézia Giúlia) T: **043 180 877**. E: **info@villaggioeuropa.com**
alanrogers.com/IT60050

This large, flat, good quality site is beside the sea and has 500 pitches, with 400 for touring units. They are all neat, clean and marked, most with shade and 6/10A electricity, 300 are fully serviced. The terrain is undulating and sandy in the areas nearer the sea, where cars have to be left in parking places. An impressive, large new Aquatic Park covers 1,500 sq.m. with two slides (100 m. and 60 m. long) and many other features. With many shallow areas it is very popular with children and there are lifeguards. A new pool bar is an attractive feature. There is direct access to the beach. The water recedes up to 200 m. from the beach, but leaves a natural paddling pool which is enjoyed by children when it is hot. A narrow wooden jetty gives access to deeper water. This is a neat, well managed site which is probably the best in the area.

Facilities

Five excellent, refurbished toilet blocks are well designed and very clean. Free hot water in all facilities, mostly British style WCs and excellent facilities for disabled people. Baby showers and baths. Washing machines. Motorcaravan services. Large supermarket, small general shop (all season). Large bar and restaurant with takeaway (all season). Swimming pools (15/5-15/9). Tennis. Fishing. Bicycle hire. Playground. Full entertainment programme in season. Internet access. Off site: Golf 500 m. Riding 10 km.

Open: 24 April - 26 September.

Directions

Site is 4 km. east of Grado on road to Monfalcone. Take the 35L road to Grado from west, continue through town to Grado Pineta on the beach road. Site is 2 km. GPS: 45.69649, 13.45595

Charges 2010

Per unit incl. 2 persons and electricity	€ 19,00 - € 42,00
water, waste water and electricity (10A) plus	€ 3,00
extra person	€ 3,50 - € 10,50

Less 10% for longer stays out of season.

VILLAGGIO TURISTICO CAMPING EUROPA
I-34073 GRADO (GO)
Tel. 0039 043180877
**   0039 043182284**
Fax 0039 043182284
www.villaggioeuropa.com
info@villaggioeuropa.com

Lignano Sabbiadoro
Camping Pino Mare

Lungomare Riccardo Riva 15, I-33054 Lignano Sabbiadoro-Riveria (Friuli - Venézia Giúlia) T: **043 142 4424**
E: **pinomare@sil-lignano.net alanrogers.com/IT60085**

This well equipped site with 1,000 pitches has direct access to a 70 m. wide, 1 km. long private sandy beach that leads down to the gently shelving waters of the Adriatic. On the beach, from where the Croatian coast is visible some 35 km. away, each of the level, mostly shaded pitches has its own numbered sun umbrella. This is a good family site with safe sea swimming (with lifeguards) and an attractive large pool complex, as well as an entertainment programme in summer. At three beach entry points there are rooftop snack bars with toilets at ground level and walkways leading down to the waters edge.

Facilities

There are 14 sanitary blocks of varying standards with free hot water. Facilities for disabled people in 8 units. Washing machines and dryers. Motorcaravan service point. Large supermarket, shop. Two restaurants, bar and takeaway. Beach snack bars. Internet point plus WiFi over site. Swimming pool complex with hot whirlpool and slides. Gym. Tennis. Direct access to the beach. Play areas. Entertainment programme and activities for children in summer. Mobile homes for rent. Off site: Shops, restaurants and bars in Lignano. Golf 1.5 km. Riding 12 km.

Open: 19 April - 21 September.

Directions

Site is 50 km. west of Trieste on the southwestern tip of the Lignano peninsula. Leave A4 at exit for and head south through Latisana to Lignano on the 354. Then follow signs for Sabbiadoro, Lignano Riviera. Site is well signed in the town. GPS: 45.64942, 13.09888

Charges guide

Per person	€ 5,40 - € 9,30
child (3-8 yrs)	€ 4,00 - € 6,20
pitch	€ 12,70 - € 22,00
dog	€ 3,00 - € 3,70

Friuli-Venézia Giúlia

Lignano Sabbiadoro

Camping Sabbiadoro

Via Sabbadoro 8, I-33054 Lignano Sabbiadoro (Friuli - Venézia Giúlia) T: **043 171 455**. E: **campsab@lignano.it**

alanrogers.com/IT60080

Sabbiadoro is a large, good quality site in two parts with separate entrances and efficient receptions. It has 1,215 pitches and is ideal for families who like all their amenities to be close by. This does mean that the site is busy and noisy with people having fun. Quite tightly packed, the pitches vary in size, are shaded by attractive trees and have electricity, TV and internet connections. You may wish to cover your car and unit to prevent sap covering it over time. The facilities are all in excellent condition and well thought out, especially the pool complex, and everything here is very modern, safe and clean.

Facilities

Well equipped sanitary facilities with free showers includes superb facilities for disabled visitors. Washing machines and dryers. Motorcaravan service point. Huge supermarket (all season). Bazaar. Good restaurant, snack bar and takeaway (15/5-28/9). Heated outdoor pool complex with separate fun pool area, slides and fountains (all season). Heated indoor children's pool. Disco. TV room. Internet. Play areas. Tennis. Fitness centre. Boat launching. Range of entertainment in the main season. Off site: Shops, restaurants and bars. Riding, sailing and golf.

Open: 6 February - 2 November.

Directions

Leave A4 at Latisana exit, west of Trieste. From Latisana follow road to Lignano, then Sabbiadoro. Site is well signed as you approach the town. GPS: 45.68198, 13.12577

Charges guide

Per unit incl. 2 persons	
and electricity	€ 19,40 - € 36,50
extra person	€ 5,20 - € 9,50
child (3-12 yrs)	€ 3,20 - € 5,20
dog	free - € 2,00

Trieste

Camping Mare Pineta

Sistiana 60 D, Duino - Aurisina, I-34019 Trieste (Friuli - Venézia Giúlia) T: **040 299 264**
E: **info@marepineta.com   alanrogers.com/IT60000**

This site is 18 km. west of Trieste and is at the top of an 80 m. cliff giving superb views over the Sistiana Bay, Miramare Castle and the Gulf of Trieste. The site has a comfortable feel and improves each year. Many of the 500 pitches are occupied by mobile homes, chalets, tour operator tents and seasonal units but there are 350 available for touring units. They vary in size and location but the most prized are on the cliff top. Others are in light woodland, and all have 3-6A electricity with water nearby. Everyone is friendly and good English is spoken. Enjoy a drink and the views at the cliff-top bar.

Facilities

Five toilet blocks have been thoughtfully refurbished (two with solar panels for hot water) and offer some washbasins in cabins. WCs are of both British and Turkish style. Facilities for disabled people. Laundry. Motorcaravan service point. Shop (all season). Bars. Pizzeria with terrace. Entertainment and disco. New swimming pool complex (1/6-15/9). Playground. Tennis. Bicycle hire. Fishing. Organised entertainment in season. WiFi. Fitness area. Information point. Off site: Riding 1.3 km. Golf 15 km. Beach 1 km. Attractive port of Sistiana.

Open: 1 April - 18 October.

Directions

From the west on the A4 take Sistiana exit and turn right on S14 towards Sistiana and then Duino. Site is 1 km. on the left past Sistiana. From the east approach on the S14. Site is well signed. GPS: 45.7725, 13.62444

Charges guide

Per unit incl. 2 persons, water	
and electricity	€ 17,00 - € 42,00
extra person	€ 4,00 - € 9,50
child (3-9 yrs)	€ 2,00 - € 6,50
dog	€ 3,50 - € 8,00

SAVE UP TO 60%

Alan Rogers Insurance Service

...we've got it covered

Low Cost Insurance
NEW from Alan Rogers

high quality, low cost insurance you can trust

We've been entrusted with readers' campsite-based holidays since 1968, and they have asked us for good value, good quality insurance.

We have teamed up with Shield Total Insurance – one of the leading names in outdoor leisure insurances – to bring you peace of mind and huge savings. Call or visit our website for a no obligation quote – there's no reason not to – and trust us to cover your valued possessions for you.

- Caravans - **Discounts up to 60%**
- Motorhomes - **Discounts up to 60%**
- Static Caravans - **Save up to 40%**
- Park homes - **Save up to 40%**
- Cars – **Discounts up to 60%** (COMING SOON)
- Pets - **1st month FREE Online**

INSTANT QUOTE
Call 0844 824 6314

www.alanrogers.com/insurance

Home to the unique ci*
of Venice, the historic
towns of Verona, Padu
and Vicenza, plus sever
fortified settlements, Ver
has an abundance of sights
keep you entertained. Situated in
northeast of Italy, it stretches fror
the flat river plains to the Dolomi

THE REGION HAS SEVEN PROVINCES: BELLUNO, PADOVA, ROVIGO, TREVISO, VENEZIA, VERONA AND VICENZA

Built on a series of low mud banks amid the tidal waters of the Adriatic, the main thoroughfare through Venice is the Grand Canal. At nearly four kilometres long, 30 to 70 metres wide, it divides the city in half and palaces, churches and historic monuments line the waterway. The Piazza San Marco is the main focal point of the city, with the Oriental splendour of the Basilica di San Marco, the Palazzo Ducale and the Bridge of Sighs. With another famous bridge and bustling markets, the district of Rialto is one of the liveliest spots, while the lagoon islands offer an escape from the crowds. Murano comprises a cluster of small islands, connected by bridges, and has been the centre of the glass-blowing industry since 1291; Burano is the most colourful with brightly painted houses and a long lace-making tradition, while Torcello boasts a 7th-century cathedral, the oldest building on the lagoon. Outside Venice, the old university town of Padua is rich in art and architecture and Verona, with its buildings of pink-tinged limestone, is renowned for its Roman ruins including the amphitheatre, which is the third largest in the world. It is also home to Casa di Giulietta, Juliet's house, a restored 13th-century inn with a small marble balcony, immortalised in Shakespeare's Romeo and Juliet.

Places of interest

Bassano del Grappa: well known for its majolica products and Grappa distilleries.

Conegliano: a wine-producing region, renowned wine-growers' school, grape festival in September, wine routes.

Euganean Hills: hot sulphur springs and mud baths.

Montagnana: fortified settlement with medieval town walls.

Padua: Basilica di Sant'Antonio, one of the most important pilgrimage destination in Italy.

Treviso: attractive town with medieval, balconied houses overlooking willow-frin canals.

Vicenza: Roman-Renaissance architecture, home of Europe's oldest surviving indoor theatre, 17th-century stone bridges.

Cuisine of the region

Risottos are popular, especially with seafood, plus pork dishes, polenta and heavy soups of beans, rice and vegetable The region is also home to Italy's famous dessert *tiramisu*, a rich blend of coffee-soaked sponge cake and mascarpone cheese. Locally produced wines include Soave, Merlot, Cabernet, Pinot Grigio an Chardonnay. Grappa is made from grape husks, juniper berries or plums.

Brodo di Pesce: fish soup.

Bussolia: ring shaped cinnamon flavoure biscuits.

Radicchio alla Griglia: red salad leaves lig grilled.

Risi e Bisi: soft and liquid risotto with fre peas and bacon.

Risotto alle Seppie: contains cuttlefish in

Map of the Veneto region showing cities and roads:

- MERANO
- BOLZANO
- CORTINA D'AMPEZZO
- TRENTINO-ALTO ADIGE
- FRIULI-VENEZIA GIULIA
- UDINE
- FARRA D'ALPAGO
- A27
- PORDENONE
- TRENTO
- ROCCA DI ARSIÈ
- VENETO
- RIVA DEL GARDA
- A4/E55,E70
- BIBIONE
- TREVISO
- CAORLE
- ERACLEA MARE
- LOMBARDY
- A31
- LIDO DI JESOLO
- CA'SAVIO
- CAVALLINO-TREPORTI
- MESTRE
- PUNTA SABBIONI
- TORRI DEL BENACO
- A22/E45
- VICENZA
- ORIAGO
- VENEZIA
- SALO
- A4/E70
- PADOVA
- FUSINA
- BRESCIA
- VERONA
- DESENZANO DEL GARDA
- LAKE GARDA
- BAONE
- SOTTOMARINA
- ISOLAVERDE
- A13
- CREMONA
- PIACENZA
- FERRARA
- EMILIA-ROMAGNA

0   25   50   75 kms

Baone

Camping Alba-Agricampeggio

Via Madonetta delle Ave 14, I-35030 Baone (Veneto) T: 390 429 4480. E: info@agriturismoalba.it
alanrogers.com/IT60570

Sheer bliss! This is a fair description of our stay at this tiny fledgling campsite tucked away close to Lake Azzurro. Very much a family site, it is part of a seven hectare farm on which are grown pears, apricots, plums for prunes and grapes. This neat site is recent (2004) and has 20 pleasant, flat pitches each with a 16A electrical supply. The entire site is surrounded by fruit trees and hedging and there are young trees on the pitches to provide shade as they grow. It is very green here and absolutely peaceful. A small peanut-shaped pool for children is alongside the pitches.

Facilities

The single modern sanitary block has hot water throughout (with a small charge for showers). British style toilets and an excellent facility for disabled campers. Motorcaravan services. Free fridge and freezer. Farm produce, bread and milk from the hotel. Traditional cooking at the hotel restaurant. Takeaway at weekends. Swimming pool for children (May-Sept). Bicycle hire. Basic playground. Hotel with four rooms. Off site: Riding 5 km. Golf 10 km. Este museum 4 km. The poet Francesca Petcacca had a house near here (open to the public).

Open: All year.

Directions

Leave A13 (Padova - Bologna) at exit for Monselice and head for Este. Continue for 4 km, then look for small campsite signs which will guide you to the site. GPS: 45.22453, 11.70349

Charges guide

Per person	€ 6,00
child (2-4 yrs)	€ 3,00
pitch	€ 8,00 - € 12,00

Veneto

Bibione
Camping Capalonga
Via della Laguna 16, I-30020 Bibione-Pineda (Veneto) T: 043 143 8351. E: capalonga@bibionemare.com
alanrogers.com/IT60100

A quality site right beside the sea, Capalonga is a large site with 1,350 pitches of variable sizes (70-90 sq.m). Nearly all are marked out, all have electrical connections, some have water and drainage, and there is good shade almost everywhere. The site is pleasantly laid out – roads run in arcs which avoids the square box effect. Some pitches where trees define the pitch area may be tricky for large units. The very wide, sandy beach, which is cleaned by the site, shelves extremely gently so is very safe for children and it never becomes too crowded. A concrete path leads out towards the sea to avoid too much sand-walking and the water is much cleaner here than at most places along this coast. A large lagoon runs along the other side of the site where boating (motor or sail) can be practised and a landing stage and moorings are provided. There is also a swimming pool on site. Capalonga is an excellent site, with comprehensive facilities.

Facilities

Seven toilet blocks are frequently cleaned. Two blocks have facilities for disabled people and very fine children's rooms. British and some Turkish style toilets, some washbasins in private cabins. Launderette. Motorcaravan services. Large supermarket. General shop. Self-service restaurant and separate bar. Swimming pool (19/5-15/9). Boating. Fishing. Playground. Free entertainment. Dogs are not accepted.

Open: 28 April - 30 September.

Directions

Bibione is about 80 km. east of Venice, well signed from afar on approach roads. 1 km. before Bibione turn right towards Bibione Pineda and follow site signs. GPS: 45.63050, 12.99358

Charges guide

Per person	€ 6,00 - € 11,00
child (1-10 yrs)	free - € 8,50
pitch	€ 11,50 - € 25,00

Bibione
Camping Residence Il Tridente
Via Baseleghe 12, I-30020 Bibione-Pineda (Veneto) T: 043 143 9600. E: tridente@bibionemare.com
alanrogers.com/IT60150

This is an unusual site in that only half the area is used for camping. Formerly a holiday centre for deprived children, it occupies a large area of woodland stretching from the main road to the sea. It is divided into two parts by the Residence, an apartment block of first class rooms which are for rent. The 226 tourist pitches (483 in total) are located amongst tall pines in the area between the entrance and the Residence. Pitch size varies according to the positions of the trees (70-100 sq.m) and all have electricity connections (6/10A). Between the Residence and the sea is a pleasant open area used for sports facilities and the two excellent pools.

Facilities

Three sanitary blocks, two in the main camping area and one near the sea, are of excellent quality. Facilities for disabled people. Washing machines and dryers. Motorcaravan services. Excellent restaurant and bar. Huge new supermarket. Swimming pools. Playground. Tennis. Gym. Fishing. Internet access. Entertainment programme in high season. Dogs are not accepted. Off site: Bicycle hire 1 km. Riding 2 km. Boat launching 2 km. Golf 10 km.

Open: 12 April - 17 September.

Directions

From A4 Venice - Trieste autostrada, take Latisana exit and follow signs to Bibione and then Bibione Pineda and site signs. GPS: 45.63330, 13.06666

Charges guide

Per person	€ 6,00 - € 11,00
child (1-4 yrs)	free - € 4,50
child (5-10 yrs)	free - € 6,50
pitch incl. electricity	€ 11,00 - € 20,50

Bibione
Camping Lido
Via dei Ginepri 115, I-30020 Bibione-Pineda (Veneto) T: 043 143 8480. E: lido@bibionemare.com
alanrogers.com/IT60130

Camping Village Lido is a quiet green site with direct access to the seafront in the centre of the town of Bibione Pineda. Of 730 pitches, 442 are for touring units. Mostly shaded, there are three sizes, all with electricity. There is convenient access to the long white sandy beach with its slowly shelving water, ideal for swimming. There are 261 high quality mobile homes available for campers who choose to fly to the site (car hire is available in a package deal). This is a simple site with good sporting and children's facilities, and an uncomplicated bar and restaurant.

Facilities

Six sanitary blocks are conveniently located and of a high standard. Car wash and motorcaravan service point. Bar, restaurant, supermarket and bazaar. Archery. Canoeing. Children's play park. Table tennis. Football. Tennis. Windsurfing schools. Boat mooring. Internet access. Dogs are not accepted. Off site: Bibione Pineda. Marina.

Open: 13 May - 17 September.

Directions

Leave E55 at Latisana exit and take 354 for Bibione. Site is well signed from afar on approach roads. 1 km. before Bibione turn right towards Bibione Pineda and follow site signs. GPS: 45.63222, 13.00132

Charges guide

Per person	€ 4,50 - € 9,20
pitch	€ 8,00 - € 18,00

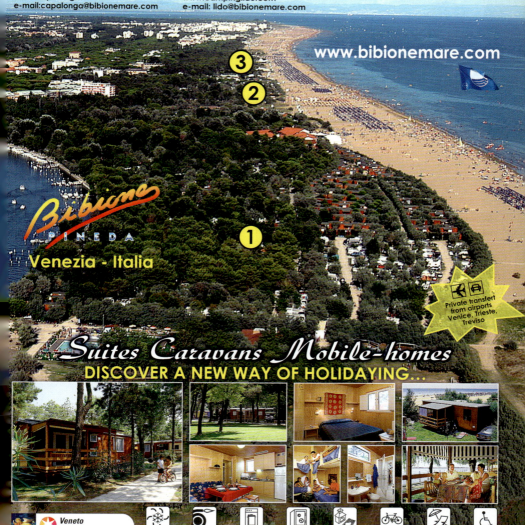

Bibione

Villaggio Turistico Internazionale

Via Colonie 2, I-30020 Bibione (Veneto) T: 043 144 2611. E: info@vti.it

alanrogers.com/IT60140

This is a large, professionally run tourist village which offers all a holidaymaker could want. The Granzotto family have owned the site since the sixties and the results of their continuous improvements are impressive. There are 350 clean pitches, many fully serviced, shaded by mature trees and mostly on flat ground. The site's large sandy beach is excellent (umbrellas and loungers available for a small charge), as are all the facilities within the campsite where English speaking, uniformed assistants will help when you arrive. The tourist village is split by a main road with the main restaurant, cinema and children's club on the very smart chalet side.

Facilities

Renovated apartments. Four modern toilet blocks house excellent facilities with mainly British style toilets. Excellent provision for children and disabled campers. Air conditioning in all accomodation. Washing machines and dryers. Motorcaravan service point. Supermarket. Bazaar. Good restaurant with bright yellow plastic chairs. Snack bar. New pool complex. Fitness centre. Disco. TV. Cinema and theatre. Internet. Play areas. Tennis. Electronic games. Off site: Bicycle hire 1 km. Riding 3 km. Golf 6 km. Fishing.

Open: 9 April - 27 September.

Directions

Leave A4 east of Venice at Latisana exit on Latisana road. Then take road 354 towards Ligmano, after 12 km. turn right to Beuazzana and then left to Bibione. Site is well signed on entering town. GPS: 45.6351, 13.0374

Charges guide

Per person	€ 5,00 - € 10,50
senior	€ 3,50 - € 10,50
child (1-5 yrs)	free - € 8,00
pitch incl. electricity	€ 9,00 - € 21,00
incl. electricity and water	€ 12,00 - € 27,00

Ca'Savio

Camping Ca'Savio

Via Ca'Savio 77, I-30013 Ca'Savio (Veneto) T: 041 966 017. E: info@casavio.it

alanrogers.com/IT60440

Ca'Savio is a large, family owned site of almost 50 years standing. It has a traditional Italian style and is set on a wide sandy beach which is safe for swimming (Blue Flag). The beach is separated from the pitches by a pleasant open area and a row of bungalows. There are many activities here, some requiring additional payment. There are 800 touring pitches (all with 5A electricity), 256 mobile homes/bungalows and around 400 tour operator pitches. Rows of pitches lead off a very busy central avenue and they are shaded, mostly flat and varying in size (70-90 sq.m). Many are a long way from water and sanitary facilities. Customers find their own pitches – leave someone there while you fetch your unit!

Facilities

Three large, new toilet blocks include many shower, toilet and washbasin units. As all the toilets are in cabins with showers and basins, at busy periods there may be a long wait. Supermarket, bazaar and other shops. Restaurants, pizzeria, café and pub. Two very large pool complexes (free). Miniclub. Bicycle and canoe hire. Minigolf. Archery. Gym. Good adventure style playground. Car hire. Internet and WiFi (at the restaurant). Dogs are not accepted. Only the site's barbecues are permitted. Off site: Boat launching 3 km. Golf and riding 5 km.

Open: 1 May - 30 September.

Directions

From A4 autostrada take Tessera exit and follow signs to Jesolo then Cavallino. Pass through Cavallino, Ca'Ballarin and Ca'Pasquali. After 3 km. in centre of Ca'Savio turn left towards beach and site. GPS: 45.44543, 12.46127

Charges guide

Per person	€ 4,80 - € 8,80
pitch and electricity	€ 9,50 - € 19,50

Min. stay 3 nights (7 from 7/7-18/8). Camping Cheques accepted.

Check real time availability and at-the-gate prices...

 www.alanrogers.com

www.capasquali.it

www.capasquali.it

CA'PASQUALI VILLAGE ★★★★ CAMPING

Via Poerio 33 - I 30010 Cavallino (VENEZIA)
Tel +39 041/966110 - Fax +39 041/5300797 e-mail: info@capasquali.it

www.velablu.it

www.velablu.it

VELA BLU Camping Village
Litorale del Cavallino
Venezia

Via Radaelli 10 - I 30010 Cavallino (VENEZIA)
Tel +39 041/968068 - Fax +39 041/5371003 e-mail: info@velablu.it

Parco Turistico di Cavallino Treporti | Veneto Between Earth and Sky | REGIONE DEL VENETO | LR. 33/02

www.vti.it

Villaggio Turistico Internazionale ★★★★

Via delle Colonie 2 - I 30020 BIBIONE (VE)
Tel +39 0431/442611 - Fax +39 0431/442699 e-mail: info@vti.it

Caorle

Camping San Francesco

Porto Santa Margherita, I-30020 Caorle (Veneto) T: 042 129 82. E: info@villaggiosfrancesco.com

alanrogers.com/IT60110

Villagio San Francesco is a large, family site with direct access to a broad sandy beach. This site has been recommended by our Italian agent and we plan to undertake a full inspection in 2010. It is a well equipped site with five swimming pools dispersed around the site and including an aqua-park. The site boasts extensive shopping and catering amenities including three restaurants. There are 687 pitches, all offering electrical connections (to 10A). The camping area is well shaded and pitches are generally of a good size. A lively entertainment and activity programme is organised here including a children's club and beach activities.

Facilities

Bars, restaurants, pizzeria and ice cream parlour. Shopping centre. Swimming pools, paddling pool and hydromassage centre. Diving school. Aqua park with waterslides. Tennis. Playground. Games room. Entertainment and activity programme, children's club. Excursions. Mobile homes and chalets for rent. Off site: Sailing and diving. Venice.

Open: 22 April - 23 September.

Directions

From A4 motorway (Venice - Trieste) take exit to Ste Stino di Livenza and follow signs to Caorle joining the P59. Site is signed from Caorle on the continuation of this road to Porto Santa Margherita.
GPS: 45.56709, 12.7943

Charges guide

Per person	€ 3,10 - € 9,80
child (3-6 yrs)	€ -2,00 - € 7,70
pitch incl. electricity	€ 7,20 - € 24,70

Camping Cheques accepted.

Check real time availability and at-the-gate prices...

www.**alanrogers**.com

Caorle

Centro Vacanze Pra' Delle Torri

P.O. Box 176, I-30021 Caorle (Veneto) T: **042 129 9063**. E: **info@pradelletorri.it**
alanrogers.com/IT60030

Pra' Delle Torri is another Italian Adriatic site which has just about everything! Pitches for camping, hotel, accommodation to rent, one of the largest and best equipped pool complexes in the country and a golf course where lessons for beginners are also available. Many of the 1,300 grass pitches (with electricity) have shade and they are arranged in zones. When you book in at reception you are taken by electric golf buggy to select your pitch. There are two good restaurants, bars and a range of shops arranged around an attractive square. Recent additions include a crèche and a supervised play area for young children. The pool complex is the crowning glory with indoor (Olympic size) and outdoor pools with slides and many other features. Other super amenities include a large grass area for ball games, a good playground, a children's car track, and a whole range of sports, fitness and entertainment programmes, along with a medical centre, skincare and other therapies. The site has its own sandy beach and Porto Santa, Margherita and Caorle are nearby. One could quite happily spend a whole holiday here without leaving the site but the attractions of Venice, Verona, etc. might well tempt one to explore the area.

Facilities

Sixteen excellent, high quality toilet blocks with the usual facilities including very attractive 'Junior Stations'. Units for disabled visitors. Motorcaravan service point. Large supermarket and wide range of shops, restaurants, bars and takeaways. Indoor and outdoor pools. Tennis. Minigolf. Fishing. Watersports. Archery. Diving. Fitness programmes and keep fit track. Crèche and supervised play area. Bowls. Mountain bike track. Wide range of organised sports and entertainment. Dogs are not accepted. Off site: Riding 3 km.

Open: 27 March - 2 October.

Directions

From A4 Venice - Trieste motorway leave at exit for Sto Stino di Livenze and follow signs to Caorle then Sta Margherita and signs to site.
GPS: 45.57312, 12.81248

Charges 2010

Per unit incl. 2 persons and electricity	€ 16,00 - € 62,40
extra person	€ 4,10 - € 9,70
child (2-5 yrs)	free - € 7,00
child (6-12 yrs)	€ 1,00 - € 8,20
Min. stay 2 nights.	

Check real time availability and at-the-gate prices...

www.alanrogers.com

Caorle
Camping Marelago
Viale Dei Cigni 18, I-30020 Caorle (Veneto) T: **042 129 9025**. E: **info@marelago.it**
alanrogers.com/IT60040

This site is just three years old and is in pristine condition. Set between the road and the beach, there is much unused space. Of two main types, one having its own kitchen and sanitary block, the other more standard, there are 177 pitches of which 115 are for tourers. All have 16A electricity. The site has limited facilities but sits within a huge holiday complex which has everything a holidaymaker would wish for. This site will grow in the next few years. All facilities are impeccably clean and the site is well organised. The pool is pleasant with a separated, safe, shallow paddling area.

Facilities
One spotless central modern sanitary block has free hot water throughout. All British style toilets and new facilities for disabled campers. Superb separate children's unit. Baby room. Washing machines and dryers. Small shop. Snack bar. Beach bars. Takeaway. Swimming pool. Fishing (permit required). Entertainment team in high season giving limited service. Basic playground. Dogs are not accepted. Off site: Golf 500 m. Bicycle hire 500 m.

Open: 15 May - 15 September.

Directions
From A4 autoroute (Venice - Trieste) take Stino di Livenza exit and follow signs for Caorle, then Lido Altanea West. Site is signed in 7 km. Beware as the site area is being hugely developed so things will change. GPS: 45.57869, 12.82704

Charges guide
Per person	€ 4,00 - € 8,00
child (6-12 yrs)	€ 2,00 - € 6,00
pitch	€ 5,00 - € 23,00

Cavallino-Treporti
Residence Village
Via F. Baracca 47, I-30013 Cavallino-Treporti (Veneto) T: **041 968 027**. E: **info@residencevillage.com**
alanrogers.com/IT60250

Camping Residence is a stylish site with a sandy beach directly on the Adriatic. It is well kept and has many floral displays. A medium size site (for this region), the 265 touring pitches are marked out with small fences or pines which give excellent shade. The pitches are in regular rows on level sand and vary in size. All have 6A electricity connections. There are strict rules regarding noise (no radios or dogs, quiet periods and no unaccompanied under 18s). A pleasant restaurant offering fine food is located in an impressive building. The beach runs the whole length of the site and shelves gradually into the sea making it safe for children.

Facilities
Three large toilet blocks are very clean with full facilities including British style WCs. Supermarket, separate shops for fruit and other goods. Well appointed restaurant with separate bar. Takeaway. Swimming pools with sunbathing areas. Playground. Tennis. Minigolf. Fitness programme. Games room. Entertainment programme. Miniclub. Bicycle hire. Dogs are not accepted. Off site: Boat moorings for hire at nearby marina. Fishing or bicycle hire 1 km.

Open: 5 May - 22 September.

Directions
From A4 Venice - Trieste autostrada take exit for airport or Quarto d'Altino. Follow signs for Jesolo, then Punta Sabbioni. Take first left after Cavallino bridge and site is 800 m. on the right. GPS: 45.48002, 12.57395

Charges guide
Per unit incl. 2 persons and electricity	€ 18,20 - € 38,40
extra person	free - € 9,20

Cavallino-Treporti
Camping Vela Blu
Via Radaelli 10, I-30013 Cavallino-Treporti (Veneto) T: **041 968 068**. E: **info@velablu.it**
alanrogers.com/IT60280

Thoughtfully landscaped within a natural wooded coastal environment, the tall pines here give shade while attractive flowers enhance the setting and paved roads give easy access to the pitches. The 280 pitches vary in size (55-100 sq.m) and shape, but all have electricity (10A) and 80 have drainage. A sister site to nos. IT60360 and IT60140, Vela Blu is a relatively new, small, family style site and a pleasant alternative to the other massive sites on Cavallino. The clean, fine sand beach runs the length of one side of the site with large stone breakwaters for fun and fishing.

Facilities
Two excellent modern toilet blocks include baby rooms and good facilities for disabled visitors. An attendant maintains the high standards. Laundry facilities. Motorcaravan service point. Medical room. Shop. Bar. Gelateria. Restaurant and takeaway. Games room. Satellite TV room. Pedalos. Windsurfing. Fishing. Bicycle hire. Entertainment. Off site Bars, restaurants and shops. Ferry to Venice.

Open: 19 April - 25 September.

See advertisement on page 91

Directions
Leave A4 Venice - Trieste motorway at exit for 'Aeroporto' and follow signs for Jésolo and Punta Sabbioni. Site is signed after village of Cavallino. GPS: 45.45681, 12.5072

Charges guide
Per person	€ 4,00 - € 8,00
child (1-10 yrs)	free - € 8,00
seniors (over 60 yrs)	€ 3,10 - € 7,00
pitch incl. all services	€ 8,50 - € 17,00
Camping Cheques accepted.	

Cavallino-Treporti
Camping Villa al Mare
Via del Faro 12, I-30013 Cavallino-Treporti (Veneto) T: **041 968 066**. E: **info@villaalmare.com**
alanrogers.com/IT60290

A charming, family site, Village Villa al Mare enjoys an unusual location, close to Cavallino's lighthouse and harbour, on the western bank of the River Sile. There is a beach of fine golden sand washed from the Dolomites. There are 134 shaded pitches varying somewhat in size and with 6A electricity, satellite TV connections, water and drainage. There is direct access to the gently shelving beach and a range of activities are organised there including daily aerobics. The pleasant restaurant has a covered area and a large patio, both with great sea views. A small pool with fountains and loungers is just inside the site.

Facilities
Two traditional style toilet blocks are kept very clean and have hot water throughout. Facilities for disabled visitors. Washing machines. Bar, restaurant and pizzeria. Shop. Swimming pool. Fishing. Playground. Jacuzzi. Children's club. WiFi. Entertainment and activity programme. Excursion programme. Direct access to the beach. Mobile homes and apartments for rent. WiFi. Dogs are not accepted. Off site: Cavallino 2 km. Punta Sabbioni ferry terminal for Venice 10 km. Aqualandia water park. Riding. Golf. Bus stop (to Venice and Jesolo) 250 m.

Open: Easter - 17 September.

Directions
From A4 autostrada (approaching from Milan) take Mestre exit and follow signs initially for Venice airport and then Jesolo. From Jesolo, follow signs to Cavallino. On crossing the large bridge in Cavallino take first left turn (Via F Baracca). Continue for 600 m. then turn left into Via del Faro. Site is at the end of this road (300 m). GPS: 45.47933, 12.58103

Charges guide
Per person	€ 2,50 - € 7,90
pitch	€ 7,50 - € 19,40

Cavallino-Treporti
Camping dei Fiori
Via Pisani 52, I-30013 Cavallino-Treporti (Veneto) T: **041 966 448**. E: **fiori@vacanze-natura.it**
alanrogers.com/IT60300

Dei Fiori stands out amongst the other small sites in the area. It is aflame with colourful flowers and shrubs in summer and presents a neat and tidy appearance whilst providing a quiet atmosphere. The 350 touring pitches, with electricity (6/10A), are either in woodland where space varies according to the trees, or under artificial shade where regular shaped pitches are of reasonable size (65-90 sq. m). Well built bungalows for rent enhance the site and are in no way intrusive, giving a village-like effect. About a quarter of the pitches are taken by static units, many for rent.

Facilities
Three sanitary blocks are of exceptional quality with British style WCs, well equipped baby rooms, good facilities for disabled people. Laundry facilities. Family rooms (key from reception). Motorcaravan services. Shops. Restaurant. Snack bar. Satellite TV. Swimming pools and whirlpool. Fitness centre, hydro-massage bath (charged in mid and high seasons) and programmes (1/5-30/9). Tennis. Minigolf. Play area. Organised activities, entertainment and excursions. Bicycle hire. Internet and WiFi. Dogs are not accepted. Off site: Riding 4 km. Fishing 7 km. Golf 15 km.

Open: 22 April - 30 September.

Directions
Leave A4 Venice - Trieste autostrada either by taking exit for airport or Quarto d'Altino and follow signs for Jesolo and then Punta Sabbioni and site signs just after Ca'Ballarin. GPS: 45.45263, 12.47127

Charges 2010
Per person	€ 3,90 - € 9,80
pitch acc. to location and services	€ 9,00 - € 24,00
tent pitch in pinewood incl. electricity	€ 7,40 - € 19,00

Min. stay 3 days in high season (3/7-21/8).

Cavallino-Treporti
Camping Silva
Via F. Baracca 53, I-30013 Cavallino-Treporti (Veneto) T: **041 968 087**. E: **info@campingsilva.it**
alanrogers.com/IT60310

Silva is a simple site, owned by the same family for many years. It is situated close to the popular beach resort of Cavallino, between the road and the beach (some road noise for the pitches near the entrance). It offers direct access to a sandy beach which is its main strength as there is little more beyond the basics of camping here. There are 278 pitches with 6A electricity (long leads needed in places) which are set on grass and sand with a canopy of mature trees providing shade. Some of the trees are positioned quite close together and, combined with vertical metal posts, the site could be difficult for large units.

Facilities
Three identically shaped blocks provide a variety of clean and respectable facilities. A mix of British and Turkish style toilets and hot water throughout. Separate facilities for disabled visitors. Motorcaravan services. Washing machine. Bar, snack bar-pizzeria. Shop. Play area. Direct access to beach. Accommodation to rent. Off site: Golf. Riding. Aqualand water park.

Open: 7 May - 16 September.

Directions
Travelling east on the A4 (Milan - Trieste) take exit for Quarto d'Altino. Follow directions for Portegrandi and Jesolo. In Jesolo follow the signs for Cavallino. Site is signed from there. GPS: 45.48150, 12.56467

Charges guide
Per unit incl. 2 persons and electricity	€ 15,00 - € 32,00
extra person	€ 2,00 - € 7,00

Cavallino-Treporti
Camping Union Lido Vacanze
Via Fausta 258, I-30013 Cavallino-Treporti (Veneto) T: **041 257 5111**. E: **info@unionlido.com**
alanrogers.com/**IT60200**

This amazing site is very large, offering everything a camper could wish for. It is extremely well organised and it has been said to set the standard that others follow. It lies right beside the sea with direct access to a long, broad sandy beach which shelves very gradually and provides very safe bathing (there are lifeguards). The site itself is regularly laid out with parallel access roads under a covering of poplars, pine and other trees providing good shade. There are 2,600 pitches for touring units, all with 6A electricity and 1,684 also have water and drainage. Because of the size of the site there is an internal road train and amenities are repeated through the site (cycling is not permitted and cars are parked away from the pitches). You really would not need to leave this site – everything is here, including a sophisticated Wellness centre. Overnight parking is provided outside the gate with electricity, toilets and showers for those arriving after 21.00 hrs. There are two aqua parks, one with fine sand beaches (a first in Europe) and both with swimming pools, lagoon pools for children, a heated whirlpool and a slow flowing 160 m. 'river'. A heated pool for hotel and apartment guests is open to others on payment. A huge selection of sports is offered, along with luxury amenities too numerous to list. Entertainment and fitness programmes are organised in season. The golf academy (with a professional) has a driving range, pitching green, putting green and practice bunker, and a diving centre offers lessons and open water diving. Union Lido is above all an orderly and clean site, which is achieved by reasonable regulations to ensure quiet, comfortable camping and by good management. Member of Leading Campings Group.

Facilities
Fifteen well kept, fully equipped toilet blocks which open and close progressively during the season. Eleven blocks have facilities for disabled people. Launderette. Gas supplies. Motorcaravan service points. Comprehensive shopping areas set around a pleasant piazza (all open until late). Eight restaurants each with a different style. Nine pleasant and lively bars. Impressive aquaparks (from 15/5). Tennis. Riding. Minigolf. Skating. Bicycle hire. Archery. Two fitness tracks in four ha. natural park with play area and supervised play for children. Golf academy. Diving centre and school. Windsurfing school in season. Boat excursions. Recreational events. Church service in English in July/Aug. Hairdressers. Internet cafés. ATM. Dogs are not accepted. Off site: Boat launching 3.5 km. Aqualandia (special rates).

Open: 30 April - 26 September, with all services.

Directions
From Venice - Trieste autostrada leave at exit for airport or Quarto d'Altino and follow signs first for Jesolo and then Punta Sabbioni, and site will be seen just after Cavallino on the left.
GPS: 45.46788, 12.53036

Charges guide
Per unit incl. 2 persons
and electricity	€ 25,40 - € 60,00
extra person	€ 6,60 - € 10,50
child (6-11yrs)	€ 5,20 - € 8,80
child (1-5 yrs)	€ 3,70 - € 7,10

Three different seasons: (i) high season 29/6-31/8; (ii) mid-season 18/5-29/6 and 31/8-14/9, and (iii) off-season, outside these dates.

Cavallino-Treporti
Italy Camping Village
Via Fausta 272, I-30013 Cavallino-Treporti (Veneto) T: **041 968 090**. E: **info@campingitaly.it**
alanrogers.com/**IT60210**

Italy Camping Village, under the same ownership as the better known Union Lido which it adjoins, is suggested for those who prefer a smaller site where less activities are available (although those at Union Lido may be used by guests here, charges applying). The 180 touring pitches are on either side of sand tracts off hard access roads under a cover of trees. All have 6A electricity connections and 70 are fully serviced. Being small (60-70 sq.m), they are impossible for large units, particularly in high season when cars are parked everywhere. There is direct access to a gently sloping sandy beach. A pleasant, heated, swimming pool has slides and a whirlpool at one end. Strict regulations regarding undue noise here make this a peaceful site and with lower charges than some in the area, this would be a good choice for families with young children where it is possible to book in advance.

Facilities
Two good quality, fully equipped sanitary blocks include facilities for disabled visitors. Washing machines. Shop. Restaurant. Bar beside beach. Heated swimming pool (17 x 7 m). Small playground, miniclub and children's disco. Weekly dance for adults. Bicycle hire. Barbecues are only permitted in a designated area. Dogs are not accepted. Off site: Use of facilites at IT60200 Union Lido. Sports centre 500 m. Golf or riding 500 m.

Open: 21 April - 22 September.

Directions
From Venice - Trieste A4 autostrada leave at exit for airport or Quarto d'Altino and follow signs for Jésolo and Punta Sabbioni. Site on left after Cavallino.
GPS: 45.46836, 12.53338

Charges guide
Per person	€ 4,80 - € 7,90
child (1-6 yrs)	free - € 6,10
pitch incl. electricity	€ 8,70 - € 19,30
pitch incl. electricity and water	€ 8,20 - € 20,80

Three charging seasons.

Check real time availability and at-the-gate prices...
www.**alanrogers**.com

UNION LIDO Vacanze

1955 2010

my holidays

PARK & RESORT
CAMPING • LODGING • HOTEL

55th Anniversary

FROM OCTOBER THE 1ST YOU MAY CHECK OUT WHAT'S NEW FOR NEXT YEAR ON
www.unionlido.com/55anniversary

New for 2010

- W10 Leisure Building, a new concept for sanitary blocks: inside pool, upstream swim, steam bath, Jacuzzi and ...more!
- 100 pitches measuring 100sqm
- 13 new luxury MV Tents
- 24 new Camping Home Roof (42sqm + veranda + roof terrace)

Union Lido Park&Resort is located on the Cavallino Riviera, a green peninsula between the splendid Venetian lagoon and the Adriatic Sea.

Open from 30th April to 26th September

BUNGALOWS, CAMPING HOMES, MOBILE HOMES, MAXICARAVAN PROVIDED WITH EVERY COMFORT.

Visit our website www.unionlido.com and get detailed information about the fantastic world of Union Lido, our packages and super-offers, both convenient and created to gratify every wish. Check the Last Minute...to find out the latest offers-not to be missed!latest offers-not to be missed!

30013 CAVALLINO
VENEZIA - ITALIA
Camping Park & Resort
Tel. Camping +39 0412575111
Tel. Art&Park Hotel +39 041968043
Telefax +39 0415370355
info@unionlido.com
booking@unionlido.com

Cavallino-Treporti
Camping Village Garden Paradiso

Via Baracca 55, I-30013 Cavallino-Treporti (Veneto) T: **041 968 075**. E: **info@gardenparadiso.it**
alanrogers.com/IT60400

There are many sites in this area and there is much competition in providing a range of facilities. Garden Paradiso is a good seaside site which also provides three excellent, centrally situated pools, a fitness centre, minigolf, a train to the market and other activities for children. Compared with other sites here, this one is of medium size with 776 pitches. All have electricity (4/6A), water and drainage points and all are marked and numbered with hard access roads, under a good cover of trees. Many flowers and shrubs give a pleasant and peaceful appearance and a new reception provides a professional welcome.

Facilities

Four brick, tiled toilet blocks are fully equipped with a mix of British and Turkish style toilets. Facilities for babies. Washing machines and dryers. Motorcaravan services. Shopping complex. Restaurant (23/4-30/9). Snack bar and takeaway. 'Aqualandia' pool complex (charged). Fitness centre. Tennis. Minigolf. Play area. Organised entertainment and excursions (high season). Bicycle hire. WiFi. Dogs are not accepted. Off site: Riding 2 km. Fishing 2.5 km.

Open: 23 April - 30 September.

Directions

Leave Venice - Trieste autostrada either by taking airport or Quarto d'Altino exit; follow signs to Jesolo and Punta Sabbioni. Take first road left after Cavallino roundabout and site is a little way on the right. GPS: 45.47897, 12.56359

Charges guide

Per unit incl. 2 persons,	
electricity, water and drainage	€ 20,10 - € 43,20
extra person	€ 4,80 - € 9,50
child (6-12 yrs) or senior (over 61 yrs)	€ 3,25 - € 7,30
child (3-5 yrs)	free - € 6,30

Less 10% for stays over 30 days (early), or 20 days (late) season.

Cavallino-Treporti
Camping Village Cavallino

Via delle Batterie 164, I-30013 Cavallino-Treporti (Veneto) T: **041 966 133**. E: **info@campingcavallino.com**
alanrogers.com/IT60320

This large, well ordered site is run by a friendly, experienced family who have other sites in this guide and offer tours between their sites. It lies beside the sea with direct access to a superb beach of fine sand, which is very safe and has lifeguards. The site is thoughtfully laid out with a large number of unusually large pitches shaded by olives and pines. All 400 touring pitches have 6-10A electricity and there is a 10% tour operator presence. The site has mobile homes to rent, most with air conditioning. For visiting Venice, there is a bus to the ferry at Punta Sabbioni which is 20 minutes away.

Facilities

The clean, modern toilet blocks (two with solar panels for hot water) are well spaced and can be heated. They provide a mixture of Turkish and British style WCs with facilities for disabled campers. Launderette. Motorcaravan services. Supermarket. Two restaurants, one with large terrace. Takeaway. Pizzeria. Swimming pools and whirlpool (May - Sept). Minigolf. Play area. Bicycle hire. Fishing. Ambitious entertainment programme aimed mostly at younger guests. ATM. WiFi area. Dogs are now accepted in certain areas. Mobile homes to rent. Off site: Golf 1 km. Riding 2 km. Tours to all attractions. Bus at gate.

Open: 25 March - 18 October.

Directions

From Venice - Trieste autostrada leave at exit for airport or Quarto and Altino. Follow signs, first for Jesolo, then Punta Sabbioni. Site signs will be seen just after Cavallino on the left. GPS: 45.45666, 12.50055

Charges guide

Per unit incl. 2 persons,	
water and electricity	€ 17,00 - € 42,00
extra person	€ 3,00 - € 10,50
child (3-9 yrs)	€ 2,00 - € 8,50
dog	€ 3,50 - € 8,50

Min. stay in high season I week.

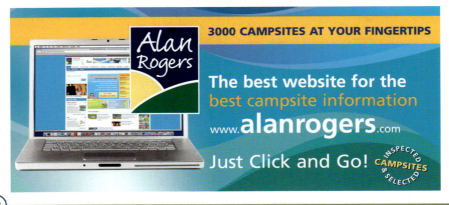
Check real time availability and at-the-gate prices...
www.**alanrogers**.com

Cavallino-Treporti

Camping Mediterraneo

Via delle Batterie 38, I-30010 Cavallino-Treporti (Veneto) T: 041 966 721. E: mediterraneo@vacanze-natura.it
alanrogers.com/IT60350

This large site has been considerably improved in recent years and is near Punta Sabbioni from where boats go to Venice. Mediterraneo is directly on the Adriatic Sea with a 480 metre long beach of fine sand which shelves gently and also two large pools and a whirlpool. The 750 touring pitches, of which 500 have electricity (from 4A), water and drainage, are partly in boxes with artificial shade, some larger without shade, with others in unmarked zones under natural woodland equipped with electric hook-ups where tents must go. Tour operators use 145 pitches. This is a well organised and efficient site.

Facilities

Eight good quality, modern sanitary blocks with British type WCs and free hot water. Laundry facilities. Motorcaravan services. Commercial centre with supermarket, shops, a restaurant, bars and a pizzeria near the pools. Swimming pool. Playground. Tennis. Bicycle hire. Programme of sports, games, excursions etc. Dancing or shows 3 times weekly in main season. Windsurfing and sailing schools. Dogs are not accepted. Off site: Riding and golf 3 km.

Open: 24 April - 27 September.

Directions

Site is well signed from Jesolo - Punta Sabbioni road near its end after Ca'Ballarin and before Ca'Savio. Follow site signs, not those for Treporti, which is some way from the site. GPS: 45.45413, 12.48173

Charges guide

Per unit incl. 2 persons	
and electricity	€ 16,10 - € 45,00
extra person	€ 4,10 - € 9,50
child (2-12 yrs)	free - € 8,50

Cavallino-Treporti

Sant'Angelo Village

Via F. Baracca 63, I-30013 Cavallino-Treporti (Veneto) T: 041 968 882. E: info@santangelo.it
alanrogers.com/IT60390

Sant' Angelo Village has a central square with an information centre and booking service for excursions, etc. The site is well planned and includes a beach bar servicing the sports areas and a fine sandy beach with lifeguards. There are 500 level pitches of good size and most are shaded by mature trees. Unusually a donation is paid to a UNICEF children's education programme for every child who stays at the campsite. This is a large site with a friendly atmosphere, ideal for families with young children and campers with mobility problems. The staff here are fluent in several languages including English.

Facilities

Five modern toilet blocks provide excellent facilities with mainly British toilets and very good facilities for disabled campers and babies. Washing machines. Restaurant and snack bar. Supermarket. Great pool complex with water slide, pool bar and fun pool. Aerobics. Fitness centre. Play areas. Games room. Tennis. Bicycle and boat hire. Small boat launching. Miniclub, entertainment and excursion service. Internet and WiFi. Fridge box hire. Dogs and other animals are not accepted. Accommodation to rent. Off site: Sailing 1.5 km. Golf or riding 5 km. Theme parks.

Open: 8 May - 20 September.

Directions

Leave autostrada A4 at San Doná Noventa exit and head for San Doná di Piave, Losolo and on to peninsula of Cavallino. Site is well signed shortly after town of Cavallino. GPS: 45.47681, 12.55509

Charges guide

Per unit incl. 2 persons,	
electricity and water	€ 17,40 - € 40,00
extra person	€ 4,70 - € 9,70
child (3-10 yrs)	free - € 7,40
senior (over 61 yrs)	€ 2,70 - € 7,40

Cavallino-Treporti

Camping Village Al Boschetto

Via della Batterie 18, Ca'Vio, I-30013 Cavallino-Treporti (Veneto) T: 041 966 145. E: info@alboschetto.it
alanrogers.com/IT60455

Al Boschetto is a really good, family owned, beachside site which prides itself in offering a sound service to its customers. When we visited, it had an open green and pleasant feel and everything was spotless. Of 335 pitches, 290 are offered to touring units and 218 of the flat, variably sized pitches (55-100 sq.m) are fully serviced. Book early for the largest pitches. This is a great site for families who do not want the razzamatazz of the bigger sites. All facilities are open the whole season.

Facilities

Three modern sanitary blocks have free hot water throughout. Mostly British style toilets and excellent facilities for disabled campers. Washing machines and dryers. Motorcaravan services. Well stocked supermarket. Restaurant with very smart section. Pizzeria and takeaway. Animation team in high season. Playground. Tennis. Beach. ATM. Gymnasium. Dogs are not accepted. Off site: Bicycle hire 1.5 km. Riding 5 km. Boat launching 5 km. Golf 13 km.

Open: 1 May - 15 September.

Directions

Leave A4 Venice - Trieste autostrada either by taking the airport exit or the Quarto d'Altino exit. Follow signs to Jesolo and Punta Sabbione. Site is well signed from here. GPS: 45.45186, 12.47631

Charges guide

Per unit incl. 2 persons	
and electricity	€ 18,30 - € 38,60
extra person	€ 5,00 - € 8,80
child (2-6 yrs) or senior (over 60 yrs)	€ 4,00 - € 7,50
No credit cards.	

99

Cavallino-Treporti

Camping Village Europa

Via Fausta 332, I-30013 Cavallino-Treporti (Veneto) T: **041 968 069**. E: **info@campingeuropa.com**

alanrogers.com/IT60410

F 258

Europa has a great position with direct access to a fine sandy beach with lifeguards. The site provides 411 touring pitches, all with 8A electricity, some with water, drainage and satellite TV connections. There is a separate area for campers with dogs and some smaller pitches are available for those with tents. The site is kept beautifully clean and neat and there is an impressive array of restaurants, bars, shops and leisure amenities. These are cleverly laid out along an avenue and include a jeweller's, a doctor's surgery, internet services and much more. Leisure facilities are arranged around the site. A professional team provides entertainment and regular themed 'summer parties'. Some restaurant tables have pleasant sea views. Venice is easily accessible by bus and then ferry from Punta Sabbioni.

Facilities

Three superb toilet blocks are kept pristine and have hot water throughout. Facilities for disabled visitors. Washing machines. Large supermarket and shopping centre. Bars, restaurants, cafés and pizzeria. New 'aqua park' with slide and spa centre planned. Tennis. Games room. Playground. Children's clubs. Entertainment programme. Internet access. Direct access to the beach. Windsurf and pedalo hire. Mobile homes and chalets for rent. Off site: Riding and boat launching 1 km. Golf and fishing 2 km. ATM 500 m. Walking and cycling trails. Excursions to Venice.

Open: 4 April - 30 September.

See advertisement opposite

Directions

From A4 autostrada (approaching from Milan) take Mestre exit and follow signs initially for Venice airport and then Jésolo. From Jesolo, follow signs to Cavallino from where site is well signed. GPS: 45.47380, 12.54903

Charges guide

Per person	€ 4,00 - € 7,90
child (2-5 yrs)	€ 3,00 - € 6,90
senior (over 60 yrs)	€ 3,40 - € 7,80
pitch	€ 8,20 - € 20,50
dog	€ 2,00 - € 4,50

No credit cards.

Cavallino-Treporti

Camping Ca'Pasquali

Via A. Poerio 33, I-30013 Cavallino-Treporti (Veneto) T: **041 966 110**. E: **info@capasquali.it**

alanrogers.com/IT60360

Situated on the attractive natural woodland coast of Cavallino with its wide, safe, sandy beach, Camping Ca'Pasquali is a good quality holiday resort with easy access to magnificent Venice. This is an ideal place for a holiday interspersed with excursions to Verona, Padova, the glassmakers of Murano, the local water park, pretty villages and many other cultural attractions. This is a large site affiliated with nos. IT60280 and IT60140. Detail is important here; there are superb pools, a fitness area, an arena for an ambitious entertainment programme and a beachside restaurant. The 400 pitches are shaded and flat (70-90 sq.m), and some have spectacular sea views.

Facilities

Three spotless modern units have excellent facilities with superb amenities for disabled campers and babies. Washing machines and dryers. Motorcaravan services. Restaurant. Pizzeria. Crêperie. Cocktail bar. Snack bar. Supermarket. Bazaar. Boutique. Superb pool complex with slides, fun pool and fountains. Fitness centre. Play areas. Bicycle hire. Canoe hire and lessons. Excellent entertainment. Amphitheatre. Miniclub. Internet access. Excursion service. Caravan storage. Dogs and other animals are not accepted. Off site: Golf and riding 5 km. Sailing 20 km. Fishing.

Open: 14 April - 30 September.

Directions

Leave autostrada A4 at Noventa exit in San Donà di Piave and head towards Jesolo and to Cavallino - Treporti. Site is well signed shortly after town of Cavallino. GPS: 45.45237, 12.48905

Charges guide

Per unit incl. 2 persons and electricity	€ 17,20 - € 43,50
extra person	€ 4,30 - € 9,50
child (1-10 yrs)	free - € 9,50

See advertisement on page 91

Cavallino-Treporti

Camping Scarpiland

Via A. Poerio 14, I-30010 Cavallino-Treporti (Veneto) T: 041 966 488. E: info@scarpiland.com

alanrogers.com/IT60470

Scarpiland faces the Adriatic and has a fine sandy beach. This campsite is a most peculiar shape in that it is dissected by rows of accommodation to rent belonging to the site with long separating fences. This forces campers in the touring area to have long walks to the single beach access. It is a large site with the informal touring pitches under the shade of mature pines. Pitches vary in size (70-90 sq.m) with 6A electricity. The irregular tree placing will challenge some units and large units are not suitable here. The site has an attractive woodland setting but there is a very long walk to the two sanitary blocks. The first very small block is unisex and has all Turkish toilets, we envisage problems here at peak periods. The larger block is even further away but has British style toilets and hot showers. The only chemical disposal site is in this block. Few activities are on offer but much is available outside the site. An entertainment team organises activities for the children in a small staged area. All other amenities are worryingly situated on the main road which serves the site. All are open fronted and the games area and some shops are across the road so children must be carefully supervised.

Facilities

Two sanitary blocks one large one very small with Turkish style toilets only. Dated facilities for babies in the large block and one unit for disabled visitors. Restaurant/pizzeria. Ice cream parlour. Newsagent. Supermarket. Butcher. Souvenir shop. Greengrocer and local produce (all on the main road). Bicycle hire. Internet. Off site: Golf 3.4 km. Riding 3.4 km. Boat launching 5 km.

Open: 24 April - 18 September.

Directions

From Milan, take A4 autostrada to Venice and continue towards Trieste as far as the A27 intersection, then follow signs to the airport. At the end of the bypass, follow signs to San Doná and Jesolo. At Jesolo, follow directions to Lido del Cavallino and Punta Sabbioni. From here the site is clearly signed. GPS: 45.45507, 12.48874

Charges 2010

Per unit incl. 2 persons and electricity	€ 15,60 - € 32,40

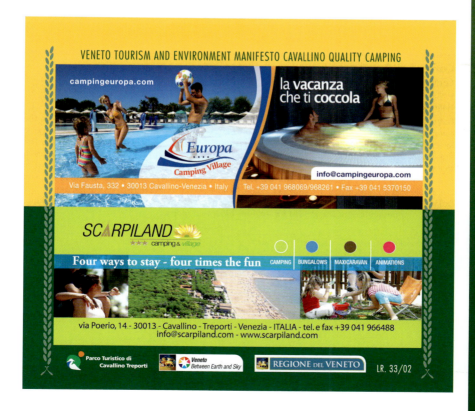

Check real time availability and at-the-gate prices...

www.alanrogers.com

Cavallino-Treporti

Camping Miramare

Punta Sabbioni, I-30010 Cavallino-Treporti (Veneto) T: 041 966 150. E: info@camping-miramare.it

alanrogers.com/IT60460

This family owned site is well located, being one of the closest sites to the Punta Sabbione ferry and offering a free bus service to the ferry and the local beach. It has an unusually long season compared with others in the area. Miramare is ideally located for exploring Venice and its islands, as well as the Lido di Venezia. There are 130 level pitches here, all with 6A electricity. They intend to increase the numbers by 50% this year. The shop is superb for a small site and the restaurant, 50 metres outside of the gate, is renowned for its excellent regional meals. An internet terminal is also here. Unusually, the site runs a free cycle loan scheme. The site is kept clean and most pitches have shade from mature trees and are level. Ask about the campsite logo – the 'Venetian iron' – very interesting, and the secret of the local flamingoes!

Facilities

Two toilet blocks (one heated in low season) with facilities for disabled people and babies. Motorcaravan service point. Excellent supermarket/shop. Bar, restaurant and pizzas from the oven in the restaurant. Takeaway. Play area. Internet point. Free bicycle hire. Dogs are not accepted. Free shuttle bus to Punta Sabbioni square (departure point for trips to Venice and the islands) and to the nearest beach on the Adriatic Coast. Off site: Fishing 2 km. Boat launching 1.5 km. Beach 1.8 km. Golf 8 km. Riding 8 km.

Open: 27 March - 23 Octobber.

Directions

Leave the A4 autostrada at exit for Venezia Mestre and follow signs to Noventa/San Dona
GPS: 45.44035, 12.42110

Charges guide

Per person	€ 4,70 - € 7,20
child (1-10 yrs)	€ 3,10 - € 5,40
pitch	€ 10,10 - € 17,00

Cortina d'Ampezzo

Camping International Dolomiti

Via Campo di Sotto, I-32043 Cortina d'Ampezzo (Veneto) T: 043 624 85. E: campeggiodolomiti@tin.it

alanrogers.com/IT62050

Cortina is a pleasant provincial town with many interesting shops and restaurants. A bus runs from the campsite gate to the town centre. The strength of this site is its beautiful mountain scenery and quiet location in a grassy meadow beside a fast flowing river (with a steep embankment but no fences). The site is dedicated to tourers with 390 good sized pitches, all with electricity (2A) and about half with shade. The site does not take reservations so arrive early in the day in the first three weeks of August to improve your chance of obtaining a pitch. There is a heated swimming pool on site, but otherwise this is a simple and uncomplicated site with fairly basic facilities which makes a good centre for touring the Dolomites. There are, of course, numerous opportunities for more energetic pursuits such as walking, cycling or mountain-biking, and indeed for extreme mountain sports.

Facilities

The large central toilet block (only open in high season) is quite old but should now be refurbished. All WCs are now British style. Washbasins have hot water sprinkler taps. A smaller heated block is open all season and is well equipped and kept very clean. Facilities for disabled visitors. Washing machines and ironing board. Gas supplies. Coffee and drinks bar and shop (restricted hours in low season). Heated swimming pool (5/7-25/8). Playground (hard base). Off site: Restaurant 600 m. Supermarket 1 km. Fishing 1 km. Golf 2 km. Bicycle hire and riding 3 km.

Open: 1 June - 20 September.

Directions

Cortina is 60 km. north of Belluno. Site is 3 km. south of town off the SS51 from Toblach/Dobbiaco to Belluno and Veneto. Follow signs to site, turning right towards Campo from north or left in Zuel from south.
GPS: 46.51623, 12.13600

Charges guide

Per person	€ 7,00 - € 9,30
child (under 6 yrs)	€ 5,00 - € 7,00
pitch incl. electricity	€ 9,00 - € 13,50

Eraclea Mare

Camping Village Portofelice

Viale dei Fiori 15, I-30020 Eraclea Mare (Veneto) T: **042 166 411**. E: **info@portofelice.it**
alanrogers.com/IT60220

Portofelice is an efficient and attractive coastal site with a sandy beach and plenty of well organised activity. There were many happy customers when we visited. It is unusual in being separated from the sea by a protected pine wood with a gravel path between the two. It is of medium size for this part of Italy with 427 touring pitches and 250 occupied by static caravans, bungalows and tour operators' accommodation. The pitches are arranged in rectangular blocks or zones in regular rows, separated by hedges from hard access roads and with either natural or artificial shade. Cars are parked separately. All pitches have electricity and 79 also have water, drainage and TV sockets. The social life of the site is centred around the stunning pool complex where the shops, pizzeria, bar, café and restaurant are also located. A wide range of entertainment and activities are organised for adults and children. If you can drag yourself away from the holiday village, you can explore the region by car with Venice, the Dolomites and the Italian Lakes within easy reach.

Facilities

Two modern sanitary blocks with slightly more Turkish style toilets than British. Baby room and special children's block (0-12 yrs). Facilities for disabled people. Supermarket. Pizzeria and takeaway. Restaurant (most tables on a covered terrace with waiter service). Three superb pools, waterfalls, slides and an area specifically for disabled guests. Hydro-massage and sunbathing. Playgrounds. Go-kart track. Pedaloes. Tennis. Sandy beach. Bicycle hire. ATM. Activity and entertainment programmes. Equipment repair and rental. WiFi. New arcade, supermarket-bazaar and internet room. No dogs accepted. Off site: Riding 200 m. Golf 6 km.

Open: 8 May - 15 September.

Directions

From A4 Venice - Trieste motorway take exit for 'San Dona/Noventa' and go south through San Dona di Piave and Eraclea to Eraclea Mare where site is signed. GPS: 45.55357, 12.76752

Charges 2010

Per person	€ 3,70 - € 10,20
child (6-10 yrs)	
or senior (over 60 yrs)	€ 3,40 - € 8,90
child (2-5 yrs)	free - € 7,40
pitch depending on type	€ 8,00 - € 24,00

Visit our website:
www.portofelice.it
info@portofelice.it ®

PORTOFELICE
CAMPING VILLAGE CENTRO VACANZE

Viale dei Fiori, 15
I - 30020 Eraclea Mare (VE)
Tel. +39. 0421. 66411
Fax +39. 0421. 66021

Bungalows - Mobile homes
2 whirlpools (20 seats)
Swimming pools
2 waterslides for children
Bar - Restaurant - Pizzeria
Ice cream parlour - Wine bar
Supermarket - Bazar
Internet point - Wi.Fi.
Cash dispenser - Sports centre
Playground - Entertainment
Pitches with electricity,
water and waste disposal
Booking pitches accepted
Ideal for families and children

PRICES AND SPECIAL OFFERS IN LOW SEASON

Farra d'Alpago

Camping Sarathei

Lago di Santa Croce, Via al Lago 13, I-32016 Farra d'Alpago (Veneto) T: **043 745 6996**. E: **info@sarathei.it**
alanrogers.com/IT61700

Camping Sarathei is a family-owned site on the banks of Santa Croce lake. It is very popular with windsurfers as the afternoon steady blows, combined with flat water, and is renowned in windsurfing circles. Below the surrounding mountains there are 236 pitches for touring units, all with 5/7A electricity. There are many (50) private wooden bungalows dotted around the site. Some pitches are formally marked, others informally aimed at groups. Some are shaded, all are flat and views of the lakes are possible. This is a 'no frills' site catering mainly for those interested in outside pursuits.

Facilities

One sanitary block has free hot showers and hot water for laundry, the remaining taps are cold only. A mixture of British and Turkish style toilets. One dated separate facility for disabled campers. Two washing machines. Motorcaravan services (€6 charge). Restaurant with terrace also sells basics (bread, milk). Pizzeria. Takeaway. Basic playground. Tennis. Bicycle hire. Watersports. Windsurfer and kite-surfer hire. Off site: ATM 200 m. Riding 5 km. Boat launching 5 km.

Open: 1 April - 30 September.

Directions

Leave A4 Venice - Padova autostrada and take the A27 Belluno road. Then take exit for Farra d'Alpago. Site is at the eastern end of the lake and signed. GPS: 46.1190, 12.3534

Charges guide

Per person	€ 3,50 - € 6,00
pitch	€ 9,00
No credit cards.	

Fusina

Camping Fusina

Via Moranzani 79, I-30030 Fusina (Veneto) T: **041 547 0055**. E: **info@camping-fusina.com**

alanrogers.com/IT60530

This is one of those sites that take one by surprise. This is old fashioned camping, but what fun, and we met English speaking people who have been coming here for 30 years. Choose from 500 well shaded, flat and grassy informal pitches or a position with views over the lagoon to the towers in Saint Mark's Square. With water on three sides there are welcoming cool breezes and fortunately many trees hide the industrial area close by. Those who don't wish to be disturbed by the lively bar can choose from the many superb informal waterside pitches on the far end of the site. The site owns a large ferry car park and a 700-boat marina which accepts and launches all manner of craft. A deep water channel carries huge ships close by and the water views are never boring. Fusina offers a very easy and comfortable, 20 minute ferry connection to the cultural heart of Venice, Accademia. Several site buildings, including some of the showers and toilets, were designed by the famous modern architect Scarpa.

Facilities

Modern, well equipped facilities include units for disabled visitors, along with some existing older units. Many washing machines and dryers. Motorcaravan service point. Shop (15/3-31/10). Charming restaurant (no credit cards). Pizzeria and beer garden. Very lively bar entertainment. TV with satellite. Playground. Boat hire. Marina with cranes, moorings, and maintenance facilities. Air-conditioned London Cyber bus (really!) and another 'Info bus' for information and ticket sales. WiFi. Bicycle hire. ATM. Torches useful. Off site: Excellent public transport and ferry connections to Venice and Alberono beach.

Open: All year.

Directions

From SSII Padua - Venice road follow site signs on road east of Mira, turning right as signed. Site is in Fusina at end of peninsula and is well signed (also as 'Fusina parking'). With the road system undergoing much modernisation, keep a keen watch for brown camping signs for Fusina and Serenisima. GPS: 45.4195, 12.2563

Charges guide

Per unit incl. 2 persons	
and electricity	€ 31,00 - € 33,00
extra person	€ 8,50 - € 9,50
child (5-12 yrs)	€ 4,50

CAMPING FUSINA VILLAGE - Venezia

Via Moranzani, 93 - I-30030 Fusina (VENICE)
Tel. 0039 041 5470055 - Fax 0039 041 5470050
www.camping-fusina.com - info@camping-fusina.com

★★★

Camping Fusina is the oldest and closest Tourist Village to Venice, it faces Venice and is located just a short 20 minute ferry ride across the lagoon. It lies on hectares of lush, landscaped parkland, offering a green gateway to the wonders of the Venetian Islands and the Palladian Villas of the Riviera del Brenta. Originally designed by world famous architect Carlo Scarpa, Camping Fusina has everything you need to make your holiday in Venice full of fun and fantastic memories!

Camping Fusina offers 500 beds in fully equipped bungalows and maxi-caravan as well as bar, restaurant, supermarket, gym, internet point and Wi-Fi, wide-screen satellite TV and booking office for Greece, Croatia and Slovenia. In the summer months Camping Fusina is linked with a regular ferry service to Lido Beach. Also available is a Marina, with cranes, moorings and slipway. **OPEN THROUGHOUT THE YEAR.**

For your holiday in Rome we recommend:
I-00188 Roma (Prima Porta)
Via Tiberina - Km. 1,5
Tel. +39 0633610733 - Fax +39 0633612314
www.campingtiber.com
info@campingtiber.com

tiber roma

Isolaverde

Villaggio Turistico Isamar

Isolaverde, via Isamar 9, I-30010 Chioggia (Veneto) T: **041 553 5811**

E: **info@villaggioisamar.com** alanrogers.com/IT60550

Improvements continue at this busy, well-managed site. The camping area, which may feel a little cramped at busy times, is under pine trees and grouped around the pool complex and covered entertainment centre. The pool complex comprises an Olympic size, saltwater pool, a paddling pool and several new leisure pools. The pitches are arranged on either side of hard access roads and vary in size (80-110 sq.m), all with electrical connections. There are many other areas containing well constructed chalets and holiday bungalows. The site is right beside the sea, with its own sandy beach.

Facilities

Four large modern sanitary blocks, are arranged carefully around the main camping area. Fully equipped and of good quality, with facilities for children and disabled visitors. Laundry. Motorcaravan services. Gas supplies. Hairdresser. Supermarket and general shopping centre. Large bar/pizzeria and self-service restaurant. Swimming pools. Tennis. Playground. Disco. Games room. Riding. Bicycle hire. Extensive entertainment and fitness programme. Dogs are not accepted. Off site: Fishing 500 m.

Open: 8 May - 14 September.

Directions

Turn off the main 309 road towards sea just south of Adige river about 10 km. south of Chioggia, and proceed 5 km. to site. GPS: 45.16516, 12.31992

Charges guide

Per unit incl. 2 persons	
and electricity	€ 14,00 - € 40,00
extra person	€ 3,00 - € 10,00
child (2-12 yrs)	free - € 10,00

Lido di Jesolo
Villaggio Turistico Malibu Beach

Viale Oriente 78, I-30016 Lido di Jesolo (Veneto) T: **042 136 2212**. E: **info@campingmalibubeach.com**
alanrogers.com/IT60330

This is a family site, twinned with Camping Wakiki nearby which has direct access to a beach. Malibu Beach has 407 pitches with 150 for touring units, all with 6A electricity. The touring pitches are set back from the beach, with the pitches in between used for mobile homes and chalets. All are well shaded by pine trees and there are some fully serviced pitches with electricity and water. The beach is of soft sand, shelves gently and has lifeguards and the usual Italian sunshades and loungers for hire. The central complex incorporates a bright, cheery bar/restaurant and a well-stocked supermarket. Other amenities include a large swimming pool, plus a paddling pool with slide and fountains. Everything on this site was clean and tidy and visitors we spoke to were happy. A professional team provides entertainment all season. Jesolo is nearby, along with seaside entertainment, and the possibility of excursions to Venice.

Facilities

Three clean blocks provide good facilities, including for disabled visitors and children. Bar, restaurant and pizzeria. Shop. Games room. Fitness centre. Hairdresser. Massage. Swimming pool and paddling pool (hats compulsory). Playground. Children's club. Entertainment programme. Direct access to the beach. Fridge box hire. WiFi (in restaurant). Dogs are not accepted. Mobile homes and chalets for rent. Off site: Lido de Jesolo, excursions to Venice. Riding. Golf. Walking and cycling trails.

Open: 15 May - 13 September.

Directions

From A4 autostrada (from Milan) take Mestre exit and follow signs initially for Venice airport and then Jesolo. From Jesolo, follow signs to Jesolo Pineta and site is well signed. GPS: 45.52385, 12.70015

Charges guide

Per person	€ 4,95 - € 8,10
child (2-7 yrs) and seniors (over 65)	€ 3,50 - € 6,55
pitch incl. electricity	€ 8,60 - € 22,00

No credit cards.
Minimum stay 2 nights.

Lido di Jesolo
Camping Waikiki

Viale Oriente 144, I-30016 Lido di Jesolo (Veneto) T: **042 198 0186**. E: **info@campingwaikiki.com**
alanrogers.com/IT60340

Waikiki is twinned with IT60330 Malibu Beach which is close by. This site also has direct access to a broad, soft sandy beach across a 300 m. grass area which has a boarded walkway. The beach shelves slowly so swimming is safe for children, there are sunshades and loungers to hire and lifeguards on the beach. The touring pitches here are shaded by pines and other trees, some close to the beach fence, but others with sea views. Relatively flat, all have 6A electricity and some have water. On site amenities include an attractive swimming pool and paddling pool, both with lifeguards. An attractive restaurant/pizzeria with a very large terrace offers a good choice of reasonably priced food and there is a well stocked supermarket. Entertainment is provided daily. A regular bus service runs from the campsite to Jesolo, where there is an excellent selection of shops, bars and restaurants.

Facilities

Three good toilet blocks are smart and clean. Facilities for disabled visitors and children. Shop and bazaar. Bar. Restaurant/pizzeria. Swimming and paddling pools (hats compulsory). Games room. Fitness centre. Playground. Children's club. Entertainment programme. Direct access to the beach. Dogs are not accepted. Mobile homes and chalets for rent. Off site: Lido de Jesolo, excursions to Venice, Vicenza and Padova. Riding. Golf.

Open: 10 May - 11 September.

Directions

From A4 autostrada (approaching from Milan) take Mestre exit and follow signs initially for Venice airport and then Jesolo. From Jesolo, follow signs to Jesolo Pineta and site is well signed. GPS: 45.53125, 12.72213

Charges 2010

Per unit incl. 2 persons and electricity	€ 16,50 - € 33,50
extra person	€ 3,75 - € 7,20
child (2-7 yrs)	€ 2,90 - € 5,00

Credit cards now accepted.
Minimum stay 2 nights.

Lido di Jesolo

Camping Jesolo International

Viale A. da Giussano, I-30016 Lido di Jesolo (Veneto) T: **042 197 1826**. E: **info@jesolointernational.it**

alanrogers.com/IT60370

At this brilliant family resort-style site with a focus on sporting activities, you can plan the cost of your holiday with confidence. The amazing array of on-site activities is included in the price and there are large discounts for some off-site attractions. Jesolo International is located on a beautiful promontory with 700 m. of uncrowded white sandy beach and slowly shelving waters for safe swimming. As the site is narrow, all the pitches are close to the sea. There is a choice of three types of pitch, all flat, well shaded and with 10-20A electricity, water and drainage. Most also have a satellite TV connection. Solar panels on the excellent shalet accommodation provide more than enough electricity for the entire site. The superb pool complex, where an excellent entertainment programme is presented each night, is centrally located and very spacious. The dynamic director Sergio Comino works long hours to maintain and improve this high quality family orientated site, to combine a unique holiday experience for guests, with real value for money. As the site is community owned, profits are returned to the guests in the form of facilities, sporting opportunities and entertainment. Cleanliness and security are high priorities, as are environmental issues. Electronic tags are given to guests to gain entrance and exit to the beach gates and this, combined with video surveillance of these key locations, allows guests to feel secure. Children's passes exclude them from accessing the beach or the hydro massage whirlpools reserved for adults alone. A ferry service to Venice leaves from the marina adjoining the campsite and takes just 40 minutes to reach St Mark's Square in the heart of the city.

Facilities

Sanitary facilities include 72 modern, continually cleaned bathroom units (shower, toilet and basin), private bathrooms (extra cost) and baby rooms. Washing machines and dryers. Fridge boxes. Motorcaravan service point. Supermarket. Family-style restaurant. Beach bar with snacks. Pool bar serving light lunches. Sports centre. Children's club. Indoor gym. Tennis courts and lessons (with equipment). Golf (lessons and fees all free). Sailing with tuition. Introductory scuba dive lesson. Pedaloes. Language courses. Large grass play area with adventure style equipment. Free internet. Dogs are not accepted. Off site: Golf 2 km. (free lesson and use of 18-hole course). Aqualandia 1.5 km. (free). Ferry to Venice and Murano 200 m. Jesolo promenade with shops, restaurants and bars 500 m.

Open: 1 May - 30 September.

Directions

From A4 Venice - Trieste autostrada take Dona di Piave exit and follow signs to Jesolo then Punta Sabbioni. Turn off to Lido di Jesolo just before the Cavallino bridge where the site is well signed.
GPS: 45.48395, 12.58763

Charges guide

Per unit incl. 2 persons	
and electricity	€ 25,00 - € 70,00
extra person	€ 5,50 - € 11,00
child (1-5 yrs)	free - € 4,50

Mestre

Camping Alba d'Oro

Via Triestina SS14 km 10, Ca'Noghera, I-30030 Mestre (Veneto) T: **041 541 5102**. E: **albadoro@tin.it**

alanrogers.com/IT60420

This well managed site is ideal for visiting Venice and the site's bus service takes you directly to the bus station on the west side of the city. There is always room here and on arrival you can select your own pitch. There is a separate area for backpackers and yet another for families. The 140 pitches, all with electricity, are of reasonable size and separated. The good sized pool is especially welcome after a hot day spent visiting Venice. The site is close to the airport and loud aircraft noise will be heard on some pitches especially to the east. Flights can arrive as late as 23.00 during the summer season.

Facilities

The four modern sanitary blocks are kept very clean. One block has facilities for disabled campers. Launderette. Motorcaravan services. Supermarket. Restaurant with pleasant terrace overlooking the pool and serving good food at reasonable prices. Part of the same complex, is a lively bar with entertainment in season. Pizzerias. Bicycle hire. Marina. Bus service April-Oct. Shuttle bus to Verona.

Open: All year.

Directions

From Venice - Trieste autostrada leave at exit for airport and follow signs for Jesolo on the SS14. Site is on right at 10 km. marker. GPS: 45.51660, 12.35470

Charges guide

Per unit incl. 2 persons	
and electricity	€ 26,00 - € 31,50
extra person	€ 7,00 - € 8,80
child (3-10 yrs)	€ 4,50 - € 5,00

A premium camping facility in the best position of the Adriatic coast, overlooking the longest shopping area of Europe and next to the boat connection to Venice. Unbeatable value for money because of countless free services: Wi-fi all over the place, Banana boat, loungers and umbrellas on the beach and at the pool, unlimited use of Aqualandia, the best italian water-park, and of Adventure Minigolf, 18-holes green fees and group golf lessons at Jesolo Golf Club, diving, pedal boats, canoes, catamaran, horse and pony riding, warm whirlpools, tennis, pirate boat, clay target shooting, archery, go-kart racing at the race track of Jesolo, top fitness centre, children entertainment, animation, medical service. Extraordinary environmental surveillance system. Exemplary environmental concept, the only "CO2 neutral" campsite in Europe.

Rented Accomodations Award 2008 & Unique Campsite Award 2006. Luxury mobile-homes with top-notch equipment and super service.

C O 2   N E U T R A L   Rented Accomodation   Unique Campsite

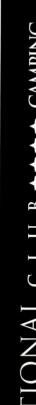

JESOLO INTERNATIONAL C L U B ★★★★ CAMPING

www.jesolointernational.it / info@jesolointernational.it / IMMEDIATE TELEPHONE RESERVATIONS 0039 0421 971826

Veneto

Punta Sabbioni
Camping Marina di Venezia
Via Montello 6, I-30013 Punta Sabbioni (Veneto) T: **041 530 2511**. E: **camping@marinadivenezia.it**
alanrogers.com/IT60450

This is a very large site (2,862 pitches) with much the same atmosphere as many other large sites along this appealing stretch of coastline. Marina di Venezia, however, has the advantage of being within walking distance of the ferry to Venice. It will appeal particularly to those who enjoy an extensive range of entertainment and activities, and a lively atmosphere. Individual pitches are marked out on sandy ground, most separated by trees or hedges. They are of an average size for the region (around 80 sq.m) and all are equipped with electricity and water. The site's excellent sandy beach is one of the widest along this stretch of coast and has a pleasant beach bar. The main pool is Olympic size and there is also a very large children's pool adjacent. The magnificent Aqua Marina Park swimming pool complex is now open and offers amazing amenities (free to all campers). This is a well run site with committed management and staff.

Facilities
Ten modern toilet blocks are maintained to a high standard with good hot showers and a reasonable proportion of British style toilets. Good provision for disabled visitors. Washing machines and dryers. Range of shops. Several bars, restaurants and takeaways. Swimming pool complex with slides and flumes. Several play areas. Tennis. Windsurf and catamaran hire. Kite hire. Wide range of organised entertainment. WiFi internet access in all bars and cafés. Church. Special area and facilities for dog owners.

Open: 25 April - 30 September.

Directions
From A4 motorway, take Jesolo exit. After Jesolo continue towards Punta Sabbioni. Site is clearly signed to the left towards the end of this road, close to the Venice ferries. GPS: 45.43750, 12.43805

Charges guide
Per unit incl. 2 persons and electricity	€ 19,80 - € 45,20
extra person	€ 9,20 - € 6,90
child or senior (2-5 yrs and 60+)	€ 3,70 - € 7,40
dog	€ 1,10 - € 2,90

Rocca di Arsiè
Camping Al Lago
Via Campagna 14, I-32030 Rocca di Arsiè (Veneto) T: **043 958 540**. E: **campingallago@libero.it**
alanrogers.com/IT61500

This simple lakeside site is located at the southern edge of the Dolomites and only 110 km. from Venice and the Adriatic. It is a peaceful spot, with views over the lake to the tree-clad slopes beyond, and is ideal as a stopover site or for a few days spent relaxing in the countryside. The main area slopes gently down to the lake and with plenty of shade; it has around 70 touring pitches, with 30 seasonal caravans along either side. There is also a large open field catering for both tents and caravans. Electricity (3A) is available to most parts, although long leads may be required.

Facilities
Central toilet block has controllable showers and a mixture of Turkish and British style toilets. Washbasins (open style) and sinks (under cover) have only cold water, but there are taps from which to collect hot water. Washing machines. Motorcaravan service point. Facilities for disabled visitors. Bar (with Sky TV). Restaurant/pizzeria with takeaway.

Open: 1 April - 4 October.

Directions
Arsiè is 45 km.southwest of Belluno and 65 km. east of Trento on the SS50/SS50bis linking Belluno to the SS47 Padua - Trento road. Site is in Rocca and signed to the south off the SS47. GPS: 45.96386, 11.7593

Charges guide
Per unit incl. 2 persons	€ 20,00 - € 23,00
extra person	€ 6,00 - € 7,00

Oriago
Camping Della Serenissima
Via Padana 334/a, I-30034 Oriago (Veneto) T: **041 921 850**. E: **info@campingserenissima.it**
alanrogers.com/IT60500

This is a delightful little site of some 155 pitches (all with 16A electricity) where one could stay for a number of days whilst visiting Venice (12 km), Padova (24 km), Lake Garda (135 km) or the Dolomites. There is a good service by bus to Venice and the site is situated on the Riviera del Brenta, a section of a river with some very large old villas. A long, narrow and flat site, numbered pitches are on each side of a central road. There is good shade in most parts with many trees, plants and grass. The management are friendly and good English is spoken.

Facilities
Sanitary facilities are of a good standard with all facilities in private cabins. Facilities for disabled visitors. Motorcaravan services. Gas supplies. Shop (all season). Bar. Restaurant and takeaway (1/6-31/10). Play area. Fishing. Bicycle hire. Reduced price bus ticket to Venice if staying for 3 days. No organised entertainment but local markets, etc. all well publicised. Off site: Golf or riding 3 km.

Open: Easter - 10 November.

Directions
Approaching Venice on the A4 take exite for Oriago-Mira then signs for Ravenna, Padova (SS11) to Oriago. A new road system is being tested and requires care. GPS: 45.451769, 12.183784

Charges guide
Per unit incl. 2 persons	€ 27,00 - € 30,00
extra person	€ 7,00 - € 8,00

Check real time availability and at-the-gate prices...

 www.**alanrogers**.com

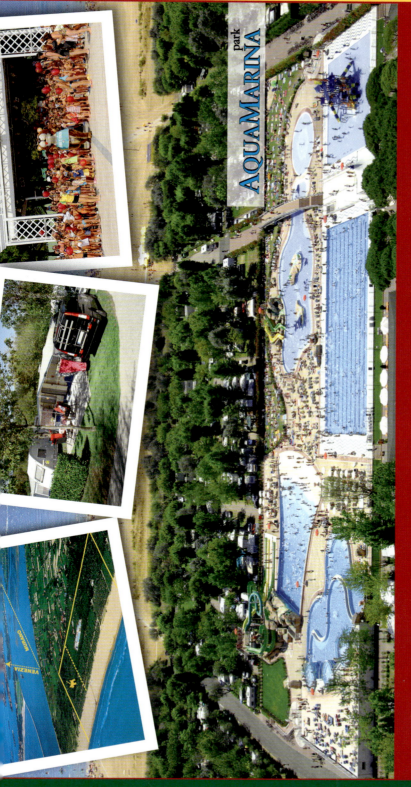

park
AQUAMARINA

Via Montello, 6 • Loc. Punta Sabbioni
30013 Cavallino-Treporti VE
Tel. +39 041 5302511 Fax +39 041 966036
camping@marinadivenezia.it
www.marinadivenezia.it

camping
Marina di Venezia
★ ★ ★

Parco Turistico di
Cavallino Treporti

Veneto
Between Earth and Sky

REGIONE DEL VENETO

LR. 33/02

Sottomarina

Kawan Village Oasi

Via A. Barbarigo 147, I-30019 Sottomarina (Veneto) T: 041 554 1145. E: info@campingoasi.com

alanrogers.com/IT60540

Camping Oasi is a traditional, friendly, family site where many Italian families return for the summer – you could certainly practise your Italian language skills here. An excellent marina is just outside the site gates. The flat, grass pitches for tourers are in separate areas from the permanent units. Varying in size (65-80 sq.m) with a choice of shade or sun, all have 6A electricity, 100 have water and drainage. Some overlook the pleasant pools, others have views over the harbour wall to the sea beyond. Through a rear gate there is a harbour wall walk to a soft sand beach where a thatched bar provides drinks and snacks.

Facilities

One sanitary block has been renovated (2007) and has mostly British style toilets and free hot showers. The second block is in the permanent area and has limited facilities for disabled campers and facilities for children and babies. They are both some way from the furthest touring pitches. Pleasant swimming pool and paddling pool with flumes. Adventure play area. Multisport pitch. Tennis. Bicycle hire. Riding. Watersports. Fishing. Free WiFi. Communal barbecue area. Off site: Historical city of Chioggia. ATM 2 km.

Open: 22 March - 30 September.

Directions

Site is off the S309 south of Chioggia. Follow signs to Sottomaria, crossing Laguna del Lusenzo, then look for site signs. Site off this road (Viale Mediterranneo) to the right. Site is last along this narrow road. GPS: 45.18148, 12.30755

Charges guide

Per person	€ 4,70 - € 7,70
child (1-5 yrs)	€ 2,30 - € 4,10
pitch	€ 8,00 - € 17,00

Camping Cheques accepted.

Sottomarina

Camping Miramare

259

Via Barbarigo 103, I-30015 Sottomarina di Chioggia (Veneto) T: 041 490 610. E: camping@tin.it

alanrogers.com/IT60560

Camping Miramare sits on both sides of the road leading to it. Reception and most of the amenities are on the beach side, the other side is very peaceful with just sports amenities and a sanitary block. The touring pitches are separate from the permanent units. All have 6A electricity, some have water and drainage, some have land views and others have shade. The beach is of soft sand with very safe bathing and a lifeguard. You can hire sunshades and loungers. The restaurant offers traditional food and a plethora of pizzas which can be enjoyed on the terraces. Some of these overlook the large safe paddling pool.

Facilities

Three identical, modern, clean blocks, one of which is in the area of the permanent campers. Pushbutton hot showers and primarily Turkish style toilets. Facilities for disabled guests. Baby room. Laundry rooms. Motorcaravan service point. Pleasant bar. Restaurant. Pizzeria and takeaway. Smart shop. Excellent swimming pool and separate paddling pool. Several great play areas. Multisport court. Entertainment and children's activities in high season. Mobile homes to rent. Dogs are not accepted. Off site: Bicycle hire 1 km. Fishing 1 km. Sailing 1 km. Riding 6 km. Golf 20 km. Visits to Chioggia. Excursions to Venice and other cities.

Open: 1 April - 20 September.

Directions

Site is off the S309 south of Chioggia. Follow signs to Sottomaria, crossing the Laguna del Lusenzo, then look for site signs. Site is off Viale Mediterranneo road to the right. Site is the second of many along this narrow road. GPS: 45.19018, 12.30341

Charges guide

Per person	€ 4,50 - € 7,50
child (under 6 yrs)	€ 2,25 - € 3,80
pitch	€ 9,50 - € 16,50

Via A. Barbarigo, 103
I-30019 Sottomarina Lido (VE)
Tel. and Fax 0039 041 490610
Tel. in winter: 0039 041 490193
E-mail: campmir@tin.it
www.miramarecamping.com

CAMPING ★★
MIRAMARE

The Boscolos will be pleased to welcome you to their family-run seaside campsite. It offers the latest sanitary fittings, bar, restaurant, mini-market, swimming pool with water games and other facilities for fun and relax, both for adults and children. Spacious well-equipped beach. Daily excursions to Venice and the islands. Modern comfort for holidays like in the good old days. NEW "BÜRSTNER" MAXI-CARAVANS.

Once two regions, Emilia-Romagna stretches from the Adriatic coast almost to the shores of the Mediterranean. A prosperous area with historical cities and thriving industry, it is also home to two of Italy's most famous food exports: Parma ham and parmesan cheese.

EMILIA-ROMAGNA COMPRISES NINE PROVINCES: BOLOGNA, FERRARA, FORLI, MODENA, PARMA, PIACENZA, RAVENNA, REGGIO EMILIA AND RIMINI

One of the richest regions of Italy, Emilia and Romagna only became united in 1947. Its landscape is varied, with the flat fields of the northern plain giving way to the forest covered Apennine mountains in the south. Carving a route through the heart of the region is the Via Emilia, a Roman military road built in 187 BC that linked the garrison town of Piacenza to Rimini on the coast. Most of the major towns lie along this route including Bologna, the region's capital. The historic city boasts a rich cultural heritage with its famous porticoes, old university buildings and medieval palaces clustered around bustling town squares. North of Bologna, Ferrara is one of the most important Renaissance centres in Italy, while further inland Modena and Parma are home to some of the regions finest architecture. Parma also boasts one of the country's top opera houses. In the east, Ravenna is renowned for the Byzantine mosaics that decorate its churches and mausoleums, and along the Adriatic coast lie various beaches and the seaside resorts of Cervia, Cesenatico and Rimini. A popular summer destination, Rimini has sandy beaches, a lively nightlife, an abundance of bars and restaurants.

Places of interest

Faenza: home of faience ceramic-ware.

Ferrara: walled town with impressive medieval castello.

Modena: the home of fast cars, both Ferrari and Maserati have factories on the outskirts.

Montese: wild black cherry festival in July, medieval singing, dancing and classical concerts in August.

Piacenza: historic Roman town, medieval and Renaissance architecture.

Valli di Comacchi: a wetland area, good for bird watching.

Vignola: best known for its cherries and cherry-blossom, spring festival, 15th-16th-century castle.

Cuisine of the region

Bologna is regarded as the gastronomic capital of Italy. Famous regional specialities include parmesan cheese (*parmigiano-reggiano*), egg pasta, Parma ham (*prosciutto di Parma*) and balsamic vinegar. Local dishes include lasagne, tortellini stuffed with ricotta and spinach, *bollito misto* (boiled meats), *zampone* (stuffed pig's trotter). Fish is also popular along the coast of Romagna.

Cannelloni: large pasta tubes stuffed with meat or cheese and spinach, covered in tomato or cheese sauce.

Ciacci: chestnut-flour pancakes filled with ricotta cheese and sugar.

Spaghetti al Ragù: pasta with beef and tomato sauce.

Torta di Limone: tart made with lemon and fresh cream.

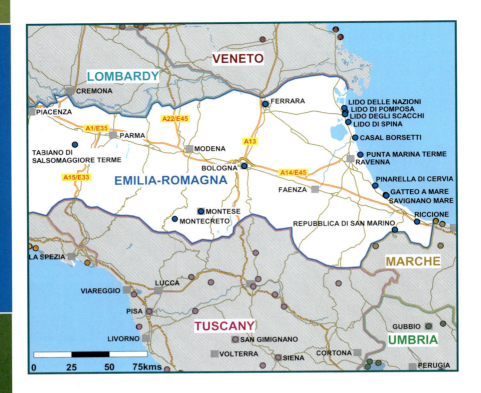

Map labels:
VENETO
LOMBARDY
CREMONA
PIACENZA
A1/E35
PARMA
A22/E45
FERRARA
LIDO DELLE NAZIONI
LIDO DI POMPOSA
LIDO DEGLI SCACCHI
LIDO DI SPINA
CASAL BORSETTI
TABIANO DI SALSOMAGGIORE TERME
MODENA
A13
PUNTA MARINA TERME
RAVENNA
BOLOGNA
A14/E45
PINARELLA DI CERVIA
A15/E33
EMILIA-ROMAGNA
FAENZA
GATTEO A MARE
SAVIGNANO MARE
MONTESE
MONTECRETO
REPUBBLICA DI SAN MARINO
RICCIONE
LA SPEZIA
MARCHE
LUCCA
VIAREGGIO
PISA
TUSCANY
GUBBIO
UMBRIA
LIVORNO
SAN GIMIGNANO
VOLTERRA
SIENA
CORTONA
PERUGIA
0   25   50   75kms

Bologna

Camping Hotel Cittá di Bologna

Via Romita 12-4A, I-40127 Bologna (Emília-Romagna) T: 051 325 016. E: info@hotelcamping.com

alanrogers.com/IT66020

This spacious site was established in 1993 on the edge of the Trade Fair Centre of this ancient and historic city and is very clean and modern. The 120 pitches are numbered and marked out by trees giving some shade. On level grass with hardstandings (open fretwork of concrete through which grass can grow) in two areas, there are electrical connections in all areas. You will always find space here as there is huge over capacity. Recent improvements include the closure of the poorly used caravan storage area allowing a potential increase to 300 pitches with associated facilities planned.

Facilities

Modern sanitary blocks include excellent provision for disabled visitors (some British style WCs with free showers and a arms connected to reception). Washing machines. Motorcaravan services. Smart bar with adjoining terrace where snacks are offered. Superb new heated and supervised swimming pool (free). Small play area. Minigolf. Internet access. Off site: Bicycle hire 5 km. Fishing 10 km. Bus service to city centre from site. Shops and restaurant 500 m.

Open: 10 January - 20 December.

Directions

Site is well signed from Bologna Fiera exit on the autostrada on the northeast of the city.
GPS: 44.52050, 11.37083

Charges guide

Per person	€ 5,50 - € 8,50
child (5-9 yrs)	€ 3,50 - € 5,00
pitch incl. electricity	€ 9,00 - € 13,00
single person and tent	€ 10,00 - € 15,00
dog	€ 2,00

Camping Cheques accepted.

Check real time availability and at-the-gate prices...

www.alanrogers.com

Casal Borsetti

Camping Village Adria

Via Spallazzi 30, I-48010 Casal Borsetti (Emilia-Romagna) T: 054 444 5217. E: adria@camping.it
alanrogers.com/IT60790

Adria is a modest site at first glance, however one soon realises this is a real gem. Unusually for the Adriatic, the setting is tranquil as there is no road or rail noise. Alongside the pretty beach, the site is surrounded by fields and a nature reserve. The pitches (80-100 sq.m.) are level and have 10A electricity. Well shaded in the older area, the trees in the new area will provide shade in the future. The beach has fine sand and gently shelves into the water. This family oriented site really does give value for money. When we visited, the entertainment team was excellent and the children were enjoying themselves.

Facilities

Six toilet blocks, four with showers. Facilities for disabled visitors in every block. Very good facilities for children. Washing machines. Three bars including a beach bar, restaurant, separate snack bar and pizzeria with large terrace. Swimming pool (hats obligatory). Excellent entertainment programme in season. Miniclub. Three excellent play areas. Archery. Boules. Multisport courts. Watersports. Off site: Beach 180 m. Bicycle hire 1 km. ATM 1 km. Riding 3 km. Golf 40 km.

Open: 23 April - 15 September.

Directions

Site is north of Ravenna. From the A13 take the Ferrara road towards the coast at Comacchio and then south on the S309 towards Ravenna. Continue to town of Casal Borsetti and site is well signed. GPS: 44.55910, 12.27965

Charges guide

Per person	€ 4,00 - € 7,90
child (2-9 yrs)	free - € 5,50
pitch incl. electricity	€ 8,00 - € 13,50
dog	€ 2,50 - € 4,00

Camping Cheques accepted.

Ferrara

Camping Communale Estense

Via Gramicia 76, I-44100 Ferrara (Emilia-Romagna) T: 053 275 2396. E: campeggio.estense@freeinternet.it
alanrogers.com/IT60600

Ferrara is an interesting and historic city, well worth a short visit. This pretty municipal campsite on the northern outskirts offers comfortable facilities for all types of units and includes 50 fairly large, grass pitches, with numerous electrical connections. Trees are used to provide shade and to screen the site. Unusual concrete portals are covered in roses, shrubs and other flowers giving a cheerful atmosphere. On-site facilities are limited, with machines for snacks and cold drinks, but there is an excellent trattoria within walking distance (1 km) and a wide choice of other eating places in the city itself.

Facilities

Two acceptable, adjacent toilet blocks are fully equipped, one heated with British and Turkish style toilets. Separate facilities for disabled visitors. Drinks and snacks machines. Torches required in places. Off site: Restaurant close by. Golf 100 m. Fishing 500 m. Riding 3 km.

Open: 25 February - 15 January.

Directions

Site is well signed from the city and is on the northern side of the ring road. GPS: 44.85217, 11.63417

Charges guide

Per unit incl. 2 persons and electricity	€ 21,50
extra person	€ 5,00
child (5-10 yrs)	€ 3,50 - € 5,00

No credit cards.

Gatteo a Mare

Villaggio Camping Delle Rose

Via Adriatica 29, I-47043 Gatteo a Mare (Emilia-Romagna) T: 054 786 213. E: info@villaggiorose.com
alanrogers.com/IT66210

On the Cesenatico coastline of Emilia Romagna, this site is unusually located in a shaded park area just a short distance from the beach. First impressions may be that it is a poor cousin to some of the more highly graded sites in the area, although very shortly after arrival it is clear that this family run site is both efficiently managed and well provisioned for the 300 touring pitches, as well as its permanent and chalet based campers. There is a large swimming pool on site which is very well maintained and a smaller one at the private beach about 450 m. walk away.

Facilities

Modern facilities are clean and well spaced around this fairly large site. Restaurant, pizzeria and snack bar with takeaway. Supermarket. Swimming pool with pool bar. Paddling pool. Playground. Games room. TV room. Children's club and entertainment programme (11/6-3/9). Sports field. Off site: Romagna retail centre including supermarkets nearby. Beach 1 km. Mirabillandia water park 5 km. Rimini 16 km. Ravenna 35 km. Gradara castle 14 km.

Open: 1 May - 26 September.

Directions

Take the Cesena exit from the A14 Bologna - Ancona motorway. Head east to join the SS16, and then south to Gatteo a Mare. Site is clearly signed. GPS: 44.16597, 12.43196

Charges guide

Per unit incl. 2 persons	€ 23,00 - € 47,00
extra person	€ 5,00 - € 9,00
child (4-10 yrs)	free - € 7,00
dog	€ 3,00 - € 8,10

113

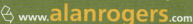

Lido degli Scacchi

Kawan Village Florenz

Viale Alpi Centrali 199, I-44020 Lido degli Scacchi (Emília-Romagna) T: 053 338 0193
E: info@campingflorenz.com alanrogers.com/IT60750

Popular with Italian families for over 30 years, Camping Florenz has many loyal campers who stay for the whole season. The area which is most sought after by tourers is over the sand dunes along the seafront where there are good sized, shaded and level pitches with views of the water. The gently shelving beach has fine grey sand and lots of chairs and umbrellas. Away from the beach area there is heavy shade cover from pine trees. The pitches are mostly a mixture of sand and grass, of a good size and level, all with electricity (3A). A large restaurant with a terrace area overlooks the lively entertainment area where lots of families were enjoying the entertainment when we visited.

Facilities

Six mixed mostly old sanitary blocks with half British, half Turkish style toilets and preset showers. Some unisex showers at beach. Good facilities for disabled people. Motorcaravan service point. Good supermarket. Restaurant and bar with TV. Large outdoor pool. Activities and children's club in season. Good play area. Excellent beach for swimming and boat launching. Beach bar. Bicycle hire. WiFi. Off site: Small town with restaurants and shops 1 km.

Open: 4 April - 27 September.

Directions

Site is at Lido degli Scacchi just off the S309 running between Chioggia and Ravenna. Both Lido degli Scacchi and site are well signed from the S309. GPS: 44.70111, 12.23806

Charges guide

Per person	€ 4,40 - € 9,00
child (3-10 yrs)	free - € 5,60
pitch	€ 10,00 - € 25,60
Camping Cheques accepted.	

Lido di Pomposa

Camping Vigna sul Mar

Via Capanno Garibaldi 20, I-44020 Lido di Pomposa (Emília-Romagna) T: 053 338 0216
E: info@campingvignasulmar.it alanrogers.com/IT60700

This quietly situated site is about 8 km. north of Ravenna and has many attractive amenities for a family holiday. Tall, mature trees determine pitches and give excellent shade in all parts. Some 640 pitches have 6A electricity and satellite TV connections. The beach is about 200 m. from the site entrance. The campsite's reserved section of the beach has a bar with snacks and beach equipment for hire. The site also has an excellent swimming pool and many sports and recreational facilities, including a small theatre with nightly entertainment of films and dancing. There is a 'nature track' amongst the trees on one side of the site. A nearby sailing centre has windsurfing boards and boats for hire. Trips are organised to famous towns and nearby beauty spots.

Facilities

Five toilet blocks are fairly old but tiled and clean. British and Turkish style WCs and hot water to some washbasins, showers and sinks. Facilities for disabled people. Washing machines. Motorcaravan services. Supermarket, greengrocer, ice cream parlour, tobacconist and newsagent. Bar, restaurant, pizzeria and snack bar by pool. Swimming pool (23/5-5/9). Play area. Minigolf. Jogging track. Bicycle hire. Canoe and pedalo hire. Entertainment and excursions (high season). Off site: Fishing 4 km. Riding 5 km.

Open: 21 April - 16 September.

Directions

From SS309 Ravenna - Venice road, follow signs to Lido Adriano and site signs from there. Many advertising boards some distance away are best ignored. GPS: 44.72117, 12.23700

Charges guide

Per person	€ 4,70 - € 9,00
child (2-10 yrs)	free - € 5,80
pitch	€ 10,50 - € 17,40
dog	free - € 5,80

Lido delle Nazioni

Camping Bungalow Park Tahiti Village

Viale Libia 133, I-44020 Lido delle Nazioni (Emilia-Romagna) T: **053 337 9500**. E: **info@campingtahiti.com**
alanrogers.com/IT60650

Tahiti is an excellent, extremely well-run site, thoughtfully laid out less than 1 km. from the sea (a continuous, small, fun, road-train link is provided). Flowers, shrubs, ponds and attractive wooded structures enhance its appearance and, unlike many campsites of this size, it is family owned and run. The 469 pitches are of varying size, back to back from hard roads and defined by trees with shade in most areas. There are 30 pitches with a private unit containing a WC and washbasin. Electricity is available throughout and 100 pitches also have water and drainage. Several languages, including English, are spoken by the friendly management team, although the British have not yet really discovered this site, which is popular with other European campers. The site is very busy in season with much coming and going, but all is always under control – it is superb, especially for families with children. It is also keen on recycling and even has a facility for exhausted batteries. They have thought of everything here and the manager Stefano is a dynamo who seems to be everywhere, ensuring the impressive standards are maintained. The staff are smart and attentive. As well as the 25 x 12 m. swimming pool, there is 'Atoll Beach' a Caribbean style water-play fun area with palms, plus a jacuzzi, bar and terrace (small extra charge for 'wet' activities). A new 'Thermal Oasis' offers health and beauty treatments and there are special spa break arrangements.

Facilities

All toilet blocks are of a very high standard. British and Turkish style WCs. Baby room. Large supermarket. Two waiter service restaurants. Bar. Pizzeria. Takeaway. Swimming pools. Fitness and beauty centre. Several playgrounds and miniclub. Gym. Tennis. Floodlit sports area. Minigolf. Bicycle hire. Entertainment and excursions (high season). 'Disco-pub'. ATM. Internet. Free transport to the beach. Torches needed in some areas. Dogs are not accepted. Off site: Fishing 300 m. Riding 500 m.

Open: 18 April - 23 September.

Directions

Turn off SS309 35 km. north of Ravenna to Lido delle Nazioni (north of Lido di Pomposa) and follow site signs. GPS: 44.73179, 12.22718

Charges guide

Per unit incl. 2 persons and electricity	€ 21,70 - € 49,70
extra person	€ 5,90 - € 9,90
child (2-8 yrs)	free - € 7,60

Lido di Pomposa

International Camping Tre Moschettieri

Via Capanno Garibaldi 22, I-44020 Lido di Pomposa (Emilia-Romagna) T: **053 338 0376**
E: **info@tremoschettieri.com** **alanrogers.com/IT60760**

Tre Moschettieri (three musketeers) is a compact, attractive site alongside the sea at Lido di Pomposa. The sandy beach, all decked out with its colourful umbrellas, is delightful. The slowly shelving beach is ideal for swimming and enjoying fun with the family. The site is in a garden setting and has many trees providing excellent shade for the 600 grass pitches (70-80 sq.m; 4A electricity). The roads are tarmac to reduce the dust and there are many water points around the site. The friendly management take care that campers are informed of programmed events and take an active interest in your enjoyment. There is an amazing range of entertainments on offer. The pools, bar, animation area and restaurant are of a uniformly high standard. This is an ideal site for excursions to places of interest in the area.

Facilities

Twelve refurbished toilet blocks placed around site. Facilities for disabled visitors. Washing machines. Bar, restaurant/pizzeria and takeaway with terrace. Swimming pools on elevated section. Tennis. Gym. Giant chess. Play areas. Entertainment programme in season. Excellent miniclub. Windsurfing school. Beach bar. Torches useful. ATM. Disco. Off site: Excursions. Bicycle hire 2 km.

Open: 8 April - 20 September.

Directions

Site is east of Ferrara. Take the road to the coast and Comaccio, then the S309 north to Lido de Pomposa. Site is well signed. GPS: 44.71666, 12.23333

Charges guide

Per unit incl. 2 persons and electricity	€ 20,00 - € 34,00
extra person	€ 5,00 - € 9,00
child (2-8 yrs)	€ 2,00 - € 6,00

Lido di Spina

Campéole Spina

Via del Campeggio 99, I-44024 Lido di Spina (Emilia-Romagna) T: 053 333 0179. E: nadine.ferran@atciat.com

alanrogers.com/IT60780

This new camping venture in the Adriatic Riveria is a real treat. Upon arrival it is clear that every effort is being made to provide a setting to ensure that campers have a pleasant time. There are lots of choices here – the fabulous beach or terrific pool, beach sports or games on the grassed areas within the campsite, for example. Pitches vary in size, services and setting, from park-like, open areas with rows of trees to heavily shaded pinewoods. The varied types of rental accommodations are also thoughtfully nestled within the site to provide maximum enjoyment for all.

Facilities

The three toilet blocks have been refurbished to a very high standard. Excellent facilities for disabled visitors. Good children's facilities. Washing machines. Supermarket. Bakery. Bar with restaurant and terrace. Miniclub. Play areas. Swimming pools (with lifeguard, caps required). Beach bar. Pool bar. Entertainment. Watersports. Torches useful. Off site: Fishing 700 m. Bicycle hire 2 km. Riding 20 km.

Open: 17 April - 19 September.

Directions

Site is north of Ravenna and east of Ferrara. Take road from Ferrara to the coast at Comacchio, then S309 south to Lido di Spina. Site is signed from here. GPS: 44.62806, 12.255

Charges guide

Per person	€ 3,50 - € 8,00
pitch incl. electricity	€ 8,00 - € 14,00

Montecreto

Campeggio Parco dei Castagni

Via del Parco 5, I-41025 Montecreto (Emilia-Romagna) T: 053 663 595. E: camping@parcodeicastagni.it

alanrogers.com/IT60980

This attractive, mountain site is well situated on the edge of a small village and is open all year round. It takes its name from the magnificent, centuries old chestnut trees. The owners here have completely cleared a former campsite and started afresh. The sanitary facilities are brand new and of top quality, the pool, bar and small restaurant are also very good. The pretty Swiss-style rental chalets and the pitches are on terraced ground and all 15 very small touring pitches have access to electricity (3A), water and drainage. This site extremely popular with people looking for a quiet site with good scenery.

Facilities

The new, purpose-built toilet block is heated, clean and provides very good facilities. Facilities for disabled visitors. Laundry with washing machines and dryers. Restaurant/bar (all year). Swimming pool (1/6-30/9). Play area. Bicycle hire. Barbecues are not permitted. Off site: Village with shops and restaurants 300 m. Chairlift 50 m. Fishing, golf and riding 6 km.

Open: All year.

Directions

Site is clearly signed from the centre of Montecreto, between Sestola and Pievepelago on the SS324. The site is best approached from Modena as the southern approach, from Pistioa or Lucca via Abetone, involves steep climbs and numerous hairpin bends. GPS: 44.24667, 10.71194

Charges 2010

Per unit incl. 2 persons and electricity	€ 21,00 - € 26,00
extra person	€ 4,00 - € 8,00

Montese

Camping Eco-chiocciola

Via Testa 80, Fraz. Maserno, I-41055 Montese (Emilia-Romagna) T: 059 980 065. E: info@ecochiocciola.com

alanrogers.com/IT66030

Tucked away in the Apennines in a small village, this interesting little campsite is open all year and has many surprises. Eco-chiocciola (named for the camper after the snail wearing his house on his back) is being developed by the owner Ottavio Mazzanti as a place to enjoy the natural geographic, geological, botanical and zoological features of the area. Comforts such as the swimming pool are designed to enhance the experience. The 74 small touring pitches, all with electrical connections (6A), are on level or gently sloping ground with some terraces, many enjoying superb views. This is a peaceful site with a distinctly rustic feel for people who enjoy natural settings.

Facilities

Two refurbished sanitary blocks have some British style WCs and coin-operated hot showers (a reader reports they do not always work well in high season). Solar panels have been installed. Facilities for disabled campers. Washing machine. Motorcaravan services. Restaurant. Bar. Large multipurpose room for entertainment. Swimming pool open afternoons and weekend mornings (19/5-1/9). Tennis and skating area as well as a tree house. Bicycle hire. Torches necessary. Off site: Riding trails, guided tours and mountain biking. Shop and bus stop in village 300 m. Riding 3 km.

Open: 4 April - 2 December, 19 December - 6 January.

Directions

From the A1 take Moderna South exit through Vignola, Montese, Sesta la Fanano, to Maserno di Montese. Site is 200 m. from the village, well signed. GPS: 44.25588, 10.93443

Charges 2010

Per unit incl. 2 persons and electricity	€ 20,00 - € 30,00
extra person	€ 4,00 - € 7,00

Show this guide and stay for 3 days, pay for 2. Also 7 days for 4 (low season).

Check real time availability and at-the-gate prices...
www.alanrogers.com

Pinarella di Cervia

Camping Adriatico

Via Pinarella 90, I-48015 Pinarella di Cervia (Emilia-Romagna) T: **054 471 537**. E: **info@campingadriatico.net**
alanrogers.com/IT66220

Adriatico, on the Italian Riviera, is owned and run by the pleasant Fabbri family. It is a busy seaside type of site popular with the Italians. English is spoken and all facilities are clean and well kept. As you would expect, there is some noise from the local resort (nearest disco is 200 m), and on the western side you will be serenaded by the voluble frogs in the adjacent allotment. On flat ground, the 190 touring pitches vary in size and are well shaded with lots of room to manoeuvre. The self service restaurant and bar complex is close to the entrance, as are the supervised pools.

Facilities

Four sanitary blocks, two large two small, have some British style WCs, individual washbasins with cold water and free hot showers. One hot tap in washing areas. Baby rooms. Washing machines and a dryer. Facilities for disabled campers. TV room. Restaurant/bar, snack bar and takeaway. Swimming pool (15/5-12/9; charged). Market. Play area. Excursions. Off site: Fishing, boat launching and bicycle hire within 1 km. Riding 3 km. Golf 4 km.

Open: 23 April - 12 September.

Directions

From A14 take Cesena or Ravenna exit and head for Cervia on SS16. Site is south of Cervia, well signed. Drive along the sea front and signs are between the 167/169 markers. GPS: 44.24763, 12.35910

Charges guide

Per unit incl. 2 persons and electricity	€ 21,00 - € 31,90
extra person	€ 5,50 - € 8,70
child (2-8 yrs)	€ 3,60 - € 5,70

Camping Cheques accepted.

Punta Marina Terme

Adriano Camping Village

Via dei Campeggi 7, I-48100 Punta Marina Terme (Emilia-Romagna) T: **054 443 7230**
E: **info@adrianocampingvillage.com** alanrogers.com/IT60620

Much has already been said about this area concerning sightseeing and excursions so there is very little to add. However, as far as camping goes, this site has to be one of the best. Despite the opportunities for excursions, there is so much to see and do on site that it would be quite believable if a visitor remained on site for the duration of their holiday. There are 380 touring pitches and the excellent facilities are well maintained and easily accessed. There are swimming pools, a sailing centre, bar, restaurants, shops, minigolf, an amusement arcade, bicycle hire and many sports facilities.

Facilities

Two acceptable, adjacent toilet blocks are fully equipped, one heated with British and Turkish style toilets. Separate facilities for disabled visitors. Drinks and snacks machines. Shop. Bar. Restaurant and takeaway. Swimming pools. Sailing. Sports facilities. Bicycle hire. Amusements. Torches required in places. Off site: Close by are the monuments of Ravenna, the Mirabilandia park and the Po Delta Regional Park. Beach 500 m. Fishing 1 km. Golf and riding 4 km.

Open: 9 April - 20 September.

Directions

Site is well signed from autostrada A14 (toll bridge). GPS: 44.43361, 12.29722

Charges guide

Per person	€ 5,50 - € 10,30
child (3-10 yrs) and seniors (over 65 yrs)	€ 4,00 - € 8,80
pitch	€ 7,50 - € 17,50

Camping Cheques accepted.

Repubblica di San Marino

Centro Vacanze San Marino

Strada San Michele 50, Cailungo, I-47893 Repubblica di San Marino (Emilia-Romagna) T: **054 990 3964**
E: **info@centrovacanzesanmarino.com** alanrogers.com/IT66230

Centro Vacanze San Marino, at 400 m. above sea level and spreading gently down a hillside, has lovely views across to the Adriatic. This excellent, modern site has a variety of well tended trees offering shade. On level terraces, the main grass pitches are roomy and accessed from tarmac or gravel roads. Separated by hedges, all have electricity, ten with satellite TV connections. Smaller pitches on lower terraces are for tents. There is a pleasant open feel to this site. Mobile homes and bungalows are available to rent and the site is used by a tour operator (30 pitches).

Facilities

Four high quality heated toilet blocks, kept very clean have British and Turkish style WCs. Motorcaravan services. Gas supplies. Shop (April-Sept). Campers' kitchen. TV room (satellite). Restaurant/pizzeria (all year). Swimming pool (20/5-31/8) with jacuzzi and solarium. Large enclosed play area. Games room with internet point. Tennis. Bicycle hire. Entertainment programme for children (high season). Bus service (timetable from reception).

Open: All year.

Directions

Leave autostrada A14 at exit Rimini-Sud (or SS16 where signed), follow SS72 west to San Marino. Site is signed from 15 km. GPS: 43.95957, 12.46126

Charges guide

Per person	€ 6,50 - € 9,50
child (2-9 yrs)	€ 3,00 - € 6,00
pitch and car	€ 6,50 - € 16,50
tent	€ 3,50 - € 8,50
dog	€ 1,00 - € 5,00

Camping Cheques accepted.

117

Riccione
Camping Alberello

Viale Torino 80, I-47838 Riccione (Emilia-Romagna) T: **054 161 5402**. E: **direzione@alberello.it**

alanrogers.com/IT60640

Camping Alberello is a small site on the Adriatic coast with direct access to the beach via a short underpass below the local road. The beach is wide with fine sand sloping gently into the sea. The friendly owners of Alberello have designed it with campers in the centre and sports facilities plus entertainment to the rear. The bar, restaurant and reception are at the front. This ensures that campers have the most tranquil pitches away from road and rail noise. The level, grass pitches are small and well shaded with tarmac access roads and regular water points.

Facilities

Three traditional and dated toilet blocks are brightly painted and kept very clean. British and Turkish style WCs. Facilities for disabled visitors. Washing machines. Supermarket. Bazaar. Bar, large restaurant with terrace. Pizzeria. TV room. WiFi. Very large play area. Limited entertainment programme in season. Miniclub. Watersports. Dogs are not accepted. Torches useful. Off site: Excursions arranged. Boat launching 4 km. ATM 500 m.

Open: 9 April - 28 September.

Directions

Site is southeast of Rimini. From A14 take Riccione exit and follow S16 towards town. Site is signed and is near the beach. GPS: 43.983333, 12.683333

Charges guide

Per person	€ 4,10 - € 8,80
child (2-8 yrs)	€ 3,45 - € 6,90
pitch	€ 9,15 - € 15,10
electricity	€ 2,50

Riccione
Camping Riccione

Via Marsala, I-47838 Riccione (Emilia-Romagna) T: **054 169 0160**. E: **info@campingriccione.it**

alanrogers.com/IT66200

Situated on the Adriatic coast, 400 metres from the beach, in high season Camping Riccione is a bustling, vibrant campsite with an Italian flavour and a carnival atmosphere. The pitches are of varying sizes, almost all have good shade and 75 are provided with water and drainage. Luigi Gobbi, who owns the site, takes pride in welcoming his guests and provides a very high standard of services proven by his high return custom figures. The noise from road and rail here is compensated for by the fine beaches nearby and when we visited all campers appeared to be having great fun.

Facilities

Five refurbished toilet blocks are bright, clean and cheerful. WCs are mixed British and Turkish style. Facilities for disabled visitors. Great facilities for children and babies. Washing machines. Two lively bars with TV. Restaurant and pizzeria with large terrace. Pool complex with waterfall. Play areas. Games room. Entertainment programme in season. Miniclub (5 yrs upwards). ATM. Dogs are not accepted in high season. Barbecues not permitted. Torches useful. Off site: Beach 400 m. Bicycle hire 1 km. Fishing 3 km. Riding 4 km. Golf 5 km.

Open: Easter - 15 September.

Directions

Site is in the village of Riccione, south of Rimini. From A14 take road to Riccione and then S16 southeast to Riccione. Site is well signed in the village. GPS: 43.98528, 12.67861

Charges guide

Per person	€ 4,30 - € 8,80
child (2-12 yrs)	€ 3,60 - € 6,90
pitch incl. electricity	€ 9,80 - € 45,90

Check real time availability and at-the-gate prices...
www.**alanrogers**.com

Savignano Mare

Camping Villaggio Rubicone

Via Matrice Destra 1, I-47039 Savignano Mare (Emilia-Romagna) T: 054 134 6377
E: info@campingrubicone.com alanrogers.com/IT66240

This is a sophisticated, professionally run site where the friendly owners, Sandro and Paolo Grotti are keen to fulfill your every need. Rubicone covers over 30 acres of thoughtfully landscaped, level ground by the sea. There is an amazing array of amenities on offer. The 520 touring pitches vary in size (up to 100 sq.m) and are arranged in back to back, double rows. In some areas the central pitches are a little tight for manoeuvring larger units. All the pitches are kept very neat with hedges and all have electricity, 40 with water and drainage and 20 with private sanitary facilities.

Facilities

Modern toilet blocks have hot water for showers and washbasins (half in private cabins), baby rooms and two excellent units for disabled visitors. Washing machines. Motorcaravan services. Bars. Restaurant, snack bar and excellent shop. Pizzeria. Swimming pools (caps mandatory). Games room with internet access. Tennis. Solarium. Jacuzzi. Beach. Sailing and windsurfing schools. Fishing. Dogs are not accepted. Off site: Bicycle hire 500 m. Riding 2 km.

Open: 15 May - 19 September.

Directions

Site is 15 km. northwest of Rimini. From Bologna exit the A14 at Rimini north and head for the S16 to Bellaria and San Mauro a Mare; site is well signed. GPS: 44.16301, 12.44330

Charges guide

Per unit incl. 2 persons and electricity	€ 22,90 - € 40,80
extra person	€ 5,20 - € 10,00
No credit cards.	

Tabiano di Salsomaggiore Terme

Camping Arizona

Via Tabiano 42/A, I-43039 Tabiano di Salsomaggiore Terme (Emilia-Romagna) T: 052 456 5648
E: info@camping-arizona.it alanrogers.com/IT60900

Tabiano and Salsomaggiore Terme are thermal springs dating back to the Roman era and the beneficial waters have given rise to attractive inland resort towns. The focus on water is developed within this family-run site. The complex of four large pools, long water slides, jacuzzi and play area are set in open landscaped grounds with good views and are also open to the public. Camping Arizona is a simple site set on steep slopes and is 500 m. from the town of Tabiano. Access is easy to the lower pitches for even the largest of units. The 350 level pitches vary from 50-90 sq.m. Those on terraces enjoy shade from mature trees, others have no shade. All have access to electricity (3A) and water points are within 30 m. On site traffic is kept to a minimum during the high season – with the exception of loading and unloading, vehicles must be parked in the large adjacent car park and golf trolleys are provided for use during your stay. Sporting facilities include the water park area, tennis, volleyball and basketball courts and a five-a-side football pitch on synthetic grass. Younger children will be entertained by the large, supervised play centre with bouncy castle, ball pool and other indoor and outdoor games.

Facilities

Sanitary facilities in two new blocks provide modern facilities including provision for disabled visitors. Washing machines and dryers. Small well stocked shop (all facilities from 1/4). Restaurant/bar with patio. Swimming pools, slides and jacuzzi (18/5-15/9, also open to the public but free for campers). Tennis. Boules. Play centre. Bicycle hire. Off site: Pub outside gate. Fidenza shopping village with designer outlets 8 km. Fishing 4 km. Golf 6 km.

Open: 20 March - 15 October.

Directions

From autostrada A1 take exit for Fidenza and follow signs for Tabiano. The site is on left 500 m. after Tabiano town centre. GPS: 44.79497, 10.01333

Charges guide

Per person	€ 6,00 - € 8,50
child (2-9 yrs)	€ 4,00 - € 6,50
pitch	€ 8,00 - € 13,50
dog	€ 2,00 - € 2,50
No credit cards.	

RELAX · SPORT · CULTURE

Camping Arizona
★★★★

Tabiano - Salsomaggiore Terme
Tel. 0039/0524565648
Fax 0039/0524567589
e-mail: info@camping-arizona.it
www.camping-arizona.it

New Sanitary Block

Imagine yourself in the wonderful countryside, with panoramic views. Tennis - 4 swimming pools - 2 waterslides - Football pitch - Basketball - Big playground. Restaurant with regional cooking - New Mobilhome with air conditioning - Cottage - Bungalows

Tuscany probably represents the most commonly perceived image of Italy, with its classic rolling green countryside, lush vineyard and olive groves with a backdr of medieval hilltowns and histori cities, where Renaissance art and beautiful churches abound.

Alan Rogers

TUSCANY IS COMPRISED OF THE FOLLOWING PROVINCES: AREZZO, FLORENCE, GROSSETO, LIVORNO, LUCCA, MASSA CARRARA, PISA, PISTOIA, PRATO AND SIENA

One of the most beautiful cities in Italy, much of Florence was rebuilt during the Renaissance, although there are parts which still retain a distinctly medieval feel. The city boasts a wealth of historical and cultural sights, including the Cathedral, the Baptistry, the Campanile, and the church of Santa Croce, to name but a few. It is also home to the Uffizi Gallery, which holds Italy's greatest art collection. Siena is another popular draw. At the heart of the city is the Piazza del Campo, one of the loveliest Italian squares, which plays host to the famous Palio, a bareback horse race which takes place twice a year in summer. Overlooking the piazza is the Gothic town hall of Palazzo Pubblico and bell tower, which is the second highest medieval tower ever built in Italy. Elsewhere in Tuscany, the medieval hilltown of San Gimignano is famed for its thirteen towers, built during the 12th and 13th centuries, which dominate the landscape. Lucca's old town is set inside a ring of Renaissance walls fronted by gardens. Another medieval hill town, Monteriggioni also has beautifully preserved walls, while Volterra is dramatically sited on a high plateau which offers fine views over the surrounding hills. And Pisa with its famous leaning tower needs no introduction.

Places of interest

Alpi Apuan Natural Park: protected area with hiking trails through wooded valleys.

Arezzo: 13th-century San Francesco churc houses famous frescoes by Piero della Francesca.

Bagni di Lucca: spa town.

Cortono: oldest hilltown in Tuscany with maze of old streets and medieval building

Elba: largest island off Tuscan coast with white sandy beaches and woodlands, goo for walking.

Fiesole: idyllic hilltop town offering super views of Florence.

Viareggio: coastal town boasting Art Nouveau architecture.

Vinci: birthplace of Leonardo da Vinci, with museum celebrating his works.

Cuisine of the region

Soups are very popular particularly *ribolli* (stew of vegetables, beans and chunks o bread) and the best place to try *cacciucc* (spiced fish and seafood soup) is in Livor the town of its birth. Meat is often grille and kept plain. Local cheeses include *pecorino*, made with sheep's milk, and *marzolino* from the Chianti region, whicl also renowned for producing some of th best wines in Italy. Tuscan desserts inclue *panforte* (a dense cake full of nuts and f and *cantuccini* (hard almond-flavoured biscuits), which are often served togethe with Vinsato, a traditional dessert wine.

Bistecca alla Fiorentina: rare char-grilled s

Pollo alla diavola: márinated chicken, gr with herbs.

Scottiglia di Cinghiale: wild boar chops.

Torta di Riso: rice cake with fruit.

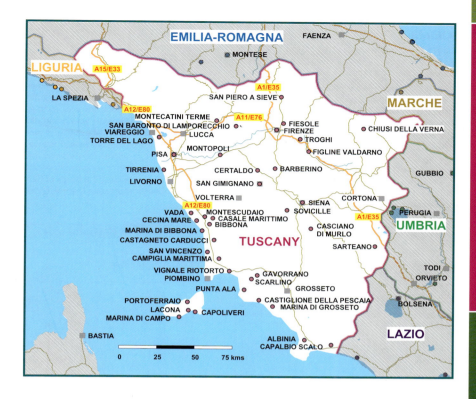

Albinia

Camping Voltoncino

SS1 Aurelia km 153, I-58010 Albinia (Tuscany) T: **056 487 0158**. E: **info@voltoncino.it**

alanrogers.com/IT66800

Set close to the beach with a boardwalk access path through tall pines, this is a traditional Italian site that shares its entertainment programme with a sister site next door. The busy SS1 road runs close to the boundary so expect traffic noise. We see this site as one for short visits rather than an extended stay. There are 284 pitches (with 3A electricity), many used by Italian seasonal visitors. The touring pitches are generally close to the entrance. On sand and well shaded, they are around 70 sq.m. and quite close together (you will have a chance to practise your Italian with the neighbours).

Facilities

Two traditional and clean toilet blocks are at each end of the site. Some WCs are Turkish style, showers are push button on payment. Facilities for disabled visitors. Baby rooms. Washing machines. Motorcaravan services. Shop. Restaurant, pizzeria and bar. Play area. Tennis. Shared entertainment programme. Miniclub (1-8 yrs). Barbecues only allowed on communal area. Internet and WiFi. Dogs not accepted. Off site: Public transport 2 km. Bicycle hire 2 km. Riding 10 km.

Open: Easter - mid September.

Directions

Site is south of Grosseto, northeast of Ortobello. From the SS1 (Aurelia) leave at the 153 km. marker towards Albinia. Site is well signed from here.
GPS: 42.51666, 11.18333

Charges guide

Per person	€ 5,80 - € 9,20
child (1-8 yrs)	€ 3,80 - € 5,00
pitch incl. electricity	€ 8,40 - € 13,20

Check real time availability and at-the-gate prices...
www.**alanrogers**.com

Albinia

Camping International Argentario

Localitá Torre Saline, I-58010 Albinia (Tuscany) T: 056 487 0302. E: info@argentariocampingvillage.com

alanrogers.com/IT66710

Argentario is really two separate campsites with a large holiday villa complex, all sharing the common facilities. The pools, entertainment area and bar area, like the villa complex are new and elegantly designed. The large irregularly shaped pool and smaller circular paddling pool are very inviting. Entertainment is organised daily by the team where there is something for everyone, young and old. The 806 pitches with 300 for tourers are small but mostly flat and on a surface of dark sand and pine needles, all are shaded by tall pines. The area is quite dusty and many of the pitches are a very long way from the amenities. Motorcaravans are parked in a large separate open square. Some campers may find the long walks trying, especially as the older style facilities are tired and stressed during peak periods. A basic restaurant and pizzeria is remote from the touring section and has no views. The beach of dark sand has attractive views across to the mountains. We see this site more for short stays than extended holidays and as unsuitable for disabled campers.

Facilities

Three mature blocks have mostly Turkish style toilets, a few cramped showers with hot water and cold water at the sinks (showers are very busy at peak periods). Facilities for disabled campers but the sand surface and remoteness of some facilities are unsuitable. Washing machines. Motorcaravan service point. Shop. Restaurant, bar and takeaway. Swimming pools. Tennis. Boat hire. Minigolf. ATM. Cars are parked in a separate car park in high season. Torches very useful. Dogs are not accepted. Off site: Bar and restaurant on the beach. Boat launching and riding 1 km. Golf 20 km.

Open: Easter/1 April - 30 September.

Directions

Site is south of Grosseto, off the SS1 at the 150 km. mark, signed Porto San Stefano. Ignore the first 'combined' campsite sign and proceed 300 m. to the main entrance. GPS: 42.49623, 11.19413

Charges guide

Per person	€ 7,00 - € 11,50
child (1-6 yrs)	€ 4,00 - € 7,00
pitch	€ 7,00 - € 11,50

Barberino

Camping Semifonte

Via Ugo Foscolo 4, I-50021 Barberino (Tuscany) T: 055 807 5454. E: semifonte@semifonte.it

alanrogers.com/IT66630

Barberino lies in the heart of Tuscany between Florence and Siena, an area rich in history and known for that special Italian wine Chianti. Camping Semifonte is a small basic, terraced site with fine views over the surrounding hills. The 60 pitches are on steep terraces, small and tight for manoeuvring. Each terrace has a tap and electricity connections. There is a very small shop selling basics. The site is unsuitable for disabled campers and infirm visitors. A good restaurant is 500 m. from the site with another in the small village a short walk away.

Facilities

Two small sanitary blocks have a mixture of British and Turkish toilets, showers and washbasins. Motorcaravan service point. Swimming pool. Children's supported pool with no safety fence – next to small play area. Off site: Regular bus route to/from Florence and Siena. Bicycle hire 500 m. Riding 1 km. Golf 15 km.

Open: Easter - 20 October.

Directions

From Florence - Siena autostrada take Tavarnelle exit to Barberino Val Elsa. Take first left on entering village and site is 500 m. at end of cul-de-sac. GPS: 43.54655, 11.17852

Charges guide

Per person	€ 7,50 - € 8,50
child (3-10 yrs)	€ 5,50 - € 6,50
pitch incl. electricity	€ 11,00 - € 13,00
tent	€ 7,50 - € 10,00

Toscana

Lazio

Coste della Maremma • Costa d'Argento

Pavilions • Bungalows • Caravans • Camping sites

Bibbona

Camping Le Capanne

Via Aurelia km 273, I-57020 Bibbona (Tuscany) T: 058 660 0064. E: info@campinglecapanne.it

alanrogers.com/IT66360

Marina di Bibbona is a relatively little-known resort situated a little to the south of Livorno and close to the better known resort of Cecina. The area retains much charm and a number of popular beaches are close at hand. There are 319 good sized pitches, 189 for tourers, most with electricity and 20 with water and drainage. They are nearly all well shaded by pine, olive and eucalyptus trees. A mobile home area has a sunnier, open setting with 75 mobile homes or chalets belonging to the site or to tour operators. Lagoon style pools with palm trees and extensive landscaped grass areas for sunbathing are a popular feature. The restaurant offers a good menu and there is also a new brasserie and gelateria.

Facilities

Three toilet blocks (in need of a clean when we visited) with plenty of hot water and toilets of British style. Washing machines. Shop and bazaar. Bar and popular restaurant away from camping area near site entrance specialising in Tuscan cuisine. Large swimming pool and large play area. Bicycle hire. Entertainment programme in high season. Minigolf. Off site: Beach 2 km. with bus from the site in high season. Riding 2 km. Fishing 2.5 km.

Open: 23 April - 26 September.

Directions

Site is south of Livorno. Take A12 autostrada (Livorno - Rosignano Marittimo) to its end and join Via Aurelia (S1) heading south. Exit at Bibbona and follow signs to site. GPS: 43.24077, 10.56949

Charges 2010

Per unit incl. 2 persons	
and electricity	€ 21,60 - € 51,00
extra person	€ 5,80 - € 11,00
child (1-10 yrs)	€ 4,20 - € 8,50
dog	€ 2,20 - € 8,50
No credit cards.	

Campiglia Marittima

Blucamp

Via Tuttiventi, I-57021 Campiglia Marittima (Tuscany) T: 056 583 8553. E: info@blucamp.it

alanrogers.com/IT66410

Blucamp is a simple site in a tranquil setting near the pretty village of Campiglia Marittima. The islands of Elba and Capraia can be sighted whilst checking in at the reception block, and there are fabulous views over green hills and the sea from some of the upper pitches. The 95 pitches (50-80 sq.m. and all with 4A electricity, six fully serviced) are terraced and on steep slopes; one area is for tents only and has the most amazing views. A tractor (free) will help you install your unit if required (this site is not really suitable for very large units).

Facilities

Two satisfactory toilet blocks have British and Turkish style WCs, individual washbasins with cold water and free hot showers. Six private sanitary units for hire. Washing machine. Small friendly restaurant/bar with a pretty terrace is run by a separate family and offers wonderful Tuscan cuisine specialising in fish. Attractive medium-sized swimming pool. Internet point and WiFi. Torches required in some areas. Off site: Riding 2 km. Fishing 8 km.

Open: 22 May - 12 September.

Directions

Site is northeast of Piombino. Take exit for San Vincenzo Sud off the main S1 road (Livorno to Follonica). Follow signs for Campiglia Marittima then camping signs from town. Site is 1 km. from the town. GPS: 43.0575, 10.6076

Charges guide

Per unit incl. 2 persons	
and electricity	€ 19,13 - € 41,51
Less 30% outside July/Aug.	

Check real time availability and at-the-gate prices...

www.**alanrogers**.com

Capalbio Scalo

Camping Capalbio

Strada Litoranea del Chiarone, Localitá Graticciaia, I-58010 Chiarone Scalo bei Capálbio (Tuscany)
T: 056 489 0101. E: mauro.ricci@ilcampeggiodicapalbio.it alanrogers.com/IT66810

This site has been recommended by our Italian agent and we plan to undertake a full inspection in 2010. Camping di Capalbio is a coastal site in southern Tuscany. The site is next to a wide sandy beach and has a good range of amenities, including a bar, restaurant and supermarket. There are 175 shady pitches here including a number of mobile homes. Various activities are organised on the beach including volleyball and a number of games and competitions. This is a lively site in peak season with evening entertainment based around the beachside bar and restaurant. This part of southern Tuscany is sometimes overlooked given the wealth of places of interest further north. However, the ancient village of Capalbio and the beautiful Lago di Burano are both well worth discovering.

Facilities

Supermarket. Bar. Restaurant. Beach bar. Takeaway food. Motorcaravan services. Entertainment and activities in peak season. Direct access to beach. Play area. Mobile homes and chalets for rent. Dogs are not accepted. Off site: Capalbio 12 km. Lago di Burano Nature Reserve 4 km. Saturnia hot springs and thermal spa 30 km. Walking and cycle trails.

Open: 30 March - 23 September.

Directions

Head south from Livorno and Pisa on the SS1 (Via Aurelia). Shortly after passing the Lago di Burano, ignore sign to Capalbio to the left, but take the next road to the right (signed Chiarone Scalo). Site is well signed from here. GPS: 42.4242, 11.388916

Charges guide

Per person	€ 6,00 - € 13,00
child (4-8 yrs)	€ 4,00 - € 8,00
pitch incl. electricity	€ 6,00 - € 15,00
Camping Cheques accepted.	

Capoliveri

Camping Lacona Pineta

Localitá Lacona, Capoliveri, I-57031 Isola d'Elba (Tuscany) T: 056 596 4322. E: info@campinglaconapineta.com
alanrogers.com/IT66860

Camping Lacona Pineta is a small terraced site that is constantly being improved and now includes an excellent large new heated swimming pool. With 180 pitches (150 for tourers) and just 50 m. from a sand and pebble beach it is well served by local bars, restaurants and shops in the small seaside town of Lacona. On the south coast of Elba this would make a good base for exploring the natural beauty of this sub-tropical paradise or for a beach holiday relaxing by the turquoise bay.

Facilities

Good sanitary facilities with free hot water. Laundry with iron and ironing board. Shop. Bar, pizzeria and restaurant. Heated swimming pool. Bicycle hire. Play area. Entertainment and activities for adults and children in high season. Off site: Beach. Walking routes. Lacona. Schools for diving, sailing and windsurfing. Riding. Tennis. Disco. Car, bicycle, motorbike and boat hire. Boat ramp.

Open: 1 April - 30 October.

Directions

From the port at Portoferraio follow the signs. GPS: 42.75978, 10.3133

Charges guide

Per person	€ 6,50 - € 14,00
child (3-10 yrs)	€ 4,00 - € 10,50
pitch	€ 5,00 - € 18,00
electricity	€ 1,50 - € 2,60

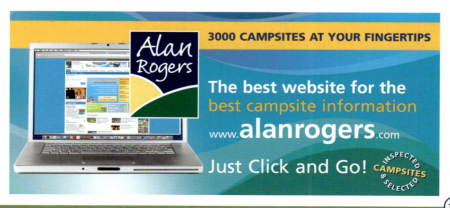

Capoliveri

Camping Le Calanchiole

Localitá Calanchiole, Capoliveri, I-57031 Isola d'Elba (Tuscany) T: 056 593 3488. E: info@lecalanchiole.it

alanrogers.com/IT66900

The super bay and beach to which this site has sole access is the strong card at this family-owned site. Back up on the site you have the choice of 274 terraced, flower lined pitches among the pine and gum trees (3/5A electricity). Most of the 80 sq.m. pitches have shade and some do have sea views, although the best are some cliff top (safely fenced) tent pitches. Cars are parked separately. In addition, there are 13 permanent pitches and eight bungalows to rent. The hub of the site is where you will find the amenities – the shop, bar/restaurant, pizzeria and takeaway and pleasant terraces are all here.

Facilities

Two traditional style sanitary blocks have a mixture of facilities. British and Turkish style toilets, cold water at washbasins, hot showers (token). Facilities for disabled visitors. Basic baby room. Laundry facilities. Motorcaravan services. Bar/restaurant, self service, takeaway and pizzeria. Shops. ATM. Boat launching and mooring. Sub-aqua club. Entertainment. Play area. Miniclub (high season). Torches useful. Off site: Village 3 km. Riding 1 km. Golf 1.5 km.

Open: Easter - 31 October.

Directions

From Elba head for Porto Azzuro. Site is west of town and well signed. It is on the road to Le Calanchiole on the coast. GPS: 42.74667, 10.37833

Charges guide

Per person	€ 6,00 - € 13,50
pitch	€ 1,00 - € 18,00
car	€ 2,60 - € 3,50
electricity	€ 2,20
Camping Cheques accepted.	

Casale Marittimo

Camping Valle Gaia

Via Cecinese 87, I-56040 Casale Marittimo (Tuscany) T: 058 668 1236. E: info@vallegaia.it

alanrogers.com/IT66320

Valle Gaia is a delightful family site with a friendly, laid-back atmosphere, in marked contrast to some of the busy sites on the coast; yet it is located just 9 km. from the sandy beaches at Cecina. This pretty site has two enticing pool complexes with a new 'Lagoon' pool, both with children's pools and generous sunbathing terraces. The 196 pitches are of a reasonable size (80-120 sq.m), well shaded by pine or cypress trees and surrounded by oleanders. Most have electrical connections. The bar and restaurant are both popular, the latter located in a splendidly converted farmhouse and specialising in local cuisine.

Facilities

Three toilet blocks of modern construction are maintained to a high standard with mainly British style toilets. Some washbasins in cubicles. Excellent facilities for children and baby bath. Washing machines. Bar. Restaurant. Pizzeria. Shop stocks a good range of provisions. Swimming pools. Tennis. Games room. Bicycle hire. Satellite TV. Internet access. Daily entertainment. Only gas barbecues permitted. Off site: Casale Marittimo 3.5 km. Riding 4 km. Beach 9 km.

Open: 1 week before Easter - 9 October.

Directions

From A12 take Rosignano Marittimo exit, follow SS1 signs towards Roma then take Cecina Centro exit and follow signs to Casale Marittimo. Site is clearly signed from here. GPS: 43.29999, 10.61664

Charges 2010

Per unit incl. 2 persons and electricity	€ 15,00 - € 31,90
extra person	€ 4,00 - € 8,50
child (2-10 yrs)	€ 3,00 - € 6,00

Casciano di Murlo

Camping Le Soline

Via delle Soline 51, I-53016 Casciano di Murlo (Tuscany) T: 057 781 7410. E: camping@lesoline.it

alanrogers.com/IT66650

Le Soline is a country hillside site with wonderful views of the Tuscan hills from its steep slopes. Just 20 km. south of Siena and 1 km. from the village of Casciano, it has 80 neat pitches for large units and 60 for tents on seven terraces, all with electricity. Many trees including olives provide shade for the pitches, most having views. There is a full entertainment programme in high season and some free guided tours of the area (includes a dip in the lake). The kind and attentive Broggini family spare no efforts in making your stay a pleasant memory and are extremely hard working to this end.

Facilities

A good quality, heated sanitary block is on the third terrace, providing mixed British and Turkish style WCs and showers on payment. Facilities for disabled campers. Motorcaravan services. Gas supplies. Laundry. Freezer. Restaurant. Pizzeria. Well stocked shop (15/3-15/10). Swimming pools (Easter-15/10). 12-person heated whirlpool. Playground. Excursions (June - Aug). Donkey and pony rides for children. Barbecue area (not allowed on pitches). WiFi (free). Mobile homes and bungalows to rent. Off site: Riding 600 m. Fishing 3 km. Bicycle hire 6 km. Golf 15 km.

Open: All year.

Directions

From Siena, turn off SS223 (Siena - Grosseto) left to Fontazzi (20 km) and keep right for Casciano, following signs. Alternatively, from Via Cassia SS2 turn at Lucignano d'Arbia for Murlo. GPS: 43.1552, 11.3323

Charges guide

Per person	€ 7,50
child (2-12 yrs)	€ 5,00
pitch and car	€ 7,00 - € 8,50
electricity	€ 2,00

Castagneto Carducci

Camping Le Pianacce

Via Bolgherese, I-57022 Castagneto Carducci (Tuscany) T: **056 576 3667**. E: **info@campinglepianacce.it**
alanrogers.com/IT66350

In a quiet situation in the Tuscan hills, six kilometres from the sea at Donoratico, this high quality site has an attractive medium-sized pool, overlooked by a restaurant/bar terrace that also has commanding views over the area. The site is on steeply rising ground and has 101 shaded pitches for touring units, all with electricity (3/6A) in tiered rows on fairly narrow terraces. Access to most is not easy because the limited space between the small dividing hedges and the high bank of the next terrace restricts manoeuvring so installation is sometimes made by the site's tractor.

Facilities

Three toilet blocks, including a small one at the top of the site, have British style WCs, individual washbasins with hot water and free hot showers. Baby room. Washing machines. Gas supplies. Motorcaravan services. Shop. Restaurant/bar/takeaway. Swimming pools with water games. Archery. Tennis. Minigolf. Bicycle hire. Playground. Internet point. Entertainment in season. Barbecues on a communal area only. Internet access. Free bus to beach. Torches required in some areas. Off site: Fishing and riding 6 km.

Open: One week before Easter - 30 September.

Directions

Site is south of Livorno. Turn off main S1 just north of Donoratico in hamlet of Il Bambolo to Castagneto Carducci. After 3 km. turn left at signs to Bolgheri and site. Follow signs to single track final approach. GPS: 43.16589, 10.6149

Charges 2010

Per person	€ 5,50 - € 10,50
child (0-10 yrs)	€ 4,00 - € 7,80
pitch	€ 9,00 - € 16,50

Some special offers in low season.

Castiglione della Pescaia

Camping Village Rocchette

Località Le Rocchette 62, I-58043 Castiglione della Pescaia (Tuscany) T: **056 494 1123**
E: **booking@rocchette.com** **alanrogers.com/IT66760**

Camping Village Rocchette can be found at the heart of the Maremma woods, 6 km. to the north of Castiglione della Pescaia. The well maintained site extends over 70,000 sq.m. of pinewood with a path leading to the sandy beach, just 300 m. away. Pitches are well shaded and of varying sizes, many with electrical connections. The site also offers 75 well equipped brick bungalows for rent. Good on-site amenities include a large swimming pool with spa baths and two pools for children, as well as a tennis court and sports field. This is a popular site in high season and bookings at this time must be for a minimum of 15 days.

Facilities

Sanitary facilities include private cubicles and facilities for disabled visitors. Laundry facilities. Supermarket and other shops. Bar. Restaurant. Swimming pool with spa baths. Two children's pools. Tennis. Sports field. Play area. Bicycle hire. WiFi (charged). Entertainment and activity programme. Direct access to beach 300 m. Bungalows for rent. Off site: Shops, restaurants and bars in Castiglione 6 km. Fishing and beach 300 m. Riding 10 km. Golf 15 km.

Open: 3 April - 23 October.

Directions

Approaching from the north, take Follonica Nord exit from the E80/S1 superstrada and head south to Castiglione on the S322. Before reaching Castiglione, turn right towards Roccamare and Rocchette. Site is well signed from here. GPS: 42.77926, 10.801234

Charges guide

Per unit incl. 2 persons and electricity	€ 20,00 - € 39,00
extra person	€ 6,00 - € 12,00
child (1-5 yrs)	€ 4,00 - € 8,00
dog	€ 6,00 - € 12,00

Castiglione della Pescaia

Camping Maremma Sans Souci

I-58043 Castiglione della Pescaia (Tuscany) T: 056 493 3765. E: info@maremmasanssouci.it

alanrogers.com/IT66600

This delightful seaside site is owned and run by the Perduca family and sits in natural woodland on the coast road between Follonica and Grosseto. The minimum amount of undergrowth has been cleared to provide 370 individually marked and hedged, flat pitches for camping enthusiasts. This offers considerable privacy in individual settings. Some pitches are small and cars may not remain with tents or caravans but must go to a shaded and secure car park near the entrance. There is a wide road for motorcaravans but other roads are mostly narrow and bordered by trees (this is a protected area, and they cannot fell the trees). Access to some parts is difficult so each pitch is earmarked either for caravans or for tents. There are electrical connections for all caravan and motorhome pitches. A positive feature of this site is that there are no seasonal pitches. Only 3 km. from Castiglione della Pescaia, a lively holiday town with an old walled village and castle at the centre, the site is on a small cliff overlooking a marina. An excellent sandy beach is less than 100 m. from one end of the site (400 m. from the other) and is used only by campers. Maremma Sans Souci has a welcoming and relaxing atmosphere. It is a most friendly site right by the sea which should appeal to many people who like a relaxed style of camping in a comfortable woodland setting with a real personal touch.

Facilities

Five small, very clean, mature toilet blocks are well situated around the site. Free showers, plus lots of little extras such as hair dryers and soap dispensers, etc. Three blocks have private cabins each with WC, basin and shower. Separate facilities for disabled campers. Motorcaravan services. Laundry. Shop. Excellent restaurant. Bar with snacks. Sailing school. Torches required in some areas. Dogs are not accepted 16/6-31/8. Off site: Excursions organised to Elba and Rome.

Open: 1 April - 31 October.

Directions

Site is 3 km. northwest of Castiglione on road to Follonica on the S322. GPS: 42.77343, 10.84392

Charges guide

Per person	€ 7,00 - € 11,00
child (2-6 yrs)	€ 5,00 - € 8,00
pitch and car	€ 9,00 - € 15,00

Castiglione della Pescaia

Camping Village Baia Azzurra

Le Rocchette, I-58043 Castiglione della Pescaia (Tuscany) T: 056 494 1092. E: info@baiaazzurra.it

alanrogers.com/IT66690

Encircled by hills, Baia Azzurra is a cool green site with lots of trees. There are 260 pitches with 200 average-sized, grassy pitches for touring units. These are flat, shaded by tall trees and artificial shade and have electricity (3A). The site has fairly basic amenities including the restaurant and bar near the entrance. The high spot of the site is the new pool and entertainment complex. The new lagoon shaped pool has a pretty bridge feature and lots of loungers. Also within the fenced pool complex is an entertainment area, a playground and small café. The lawn and garden here make it a pleasant place to relax. Cross a minor road and a 400 m. walk brings you to the fine yellow sand beach.

Facilities

Three refurbished sanitary blocks offer a slightly confusing range of unisex facilities with some British but mainly Turkish style toilets in one block only, plus units for disabled visitors in one block but otherwise the water is cold. Washing machines. Shop, restaurant, bar and pizzeria (all season). Swimming pools (May - Sept). Large play area. Bicycle hire. Evening entertainment and animation. Miniclub (high season). Barbecues are permitted. Off site: Beach 150 m. Riding 10 km. Golf 17 km.

Open: 1 April - 17 October.

Directions

From SS1 Livorna - Roma road take Grosseto exit on SS322. Follow SS322 north from Castiglione della Pescaia and turn left for Rocchette. Site is 3 km. on the right. GPS: 42.7778, 10.79392

Charges guide

Per person	€ 6,50 - € 12,50
child (under 6 yrs)	€ 5,00 - € 7,50
pitch	€ 10,00 - € 16,00
dog	€ 6,00

Camping Cheques accepted.

Check real time availability and at-the-gate prices...

www.alanrogers.com

Cecina Mare

Camping Mareblu

Localitá Mazzanta, I-57023 Cecina Mare (Tuscany) T: **058 662 9191**. E: **info@campingmareblu.com**

alanrogers.com/IT66310

Mareblu is a well equipped family site with an impressive range of amenities, including a large pool with an attractive terraced surround, and shopping complex incorporating a greengrocer, hairdressing salon, newsagent and internet centre. There is also a sandy beach 300 m. away, accessed through a pine wood. The pitches at Mareblu are well shaded and are all equipped with electrical connections (6A). Parking for all cars is in a dedicated area at the front of the site which ensures a pleasant traffic free ambience within the site. The site is close to Cecina Mare, a popular resort with easy access to some of Tuscany's great cities, and the island of Elba.

Facilities

Five modern toilet blocks include facilities for disabled visitors. Shopping centre. Bar, restaurant and self-service cafeteria, pizzeria and takeaway. Swimming and paddling pools. Play area. Games field. Boules. Bicycle hire. Entertainment. Miniclub. Internet access. Direct access to beach. Dogs are not accepted 4/7-29/8. Off site: Tennis. Riding. Watersports and diving. Excursions.

Open: 20 March - 16 October.

Directions

Site is south of Livorno. From north, take A12 to Rosignano and then join the E80 to Vada, then to La Mazzanta. From here site is well signed. GPS: 43.31848, 10.47407

Charges guide

Per person	€ 4,30 - € 8,10
child (0-10 yrs)	€ 3,20 - € 6,50
pitch incl. electricity	€ 5,50 - € 12,50
car	€ 1,70 - € 3,80

Camping Cheques accepted.

The "Mareblu Campsite" is to be found at Cecina Mare on the Tuscan coast, a short distance from artistic centres such as Florence, Pisa and Siena and from the islands of the Tuscan archipelago. It stretches out over an area of around 100,000 sqm of flat terrain, well-shaded by pine trees. The direct access to the beach crosses an age-old pinewood of around 300 metres wide, kept as a nature park. Spacious pitches with electricity supply, internal car park, 5 blocks of bathroom facilities, shop, supermarket, greengrocers', butcher, newsagent and tobacconist, bar, restaurant, self-service with pizzeria. Children's playground, volleyball, football pitch, hire of bicycles, table tennis, bowls, organised activities, swimming pool for adults and children. Nearby you'll find tennis, a diving

centre, a windsurfing school and horse riding. Mobile homes to rent. Dogs not allowed from 04.07. until 29.08.2010.

Loc. Mazzanta • I-57023
CECINA MARE (LIVORNO)
Tel. 0039/0586629191
Fax 0039/0586629192
info@campingmareblu.com
www.campingmareblu.com

NEW MOBILE HOMES

Certaldo

Camping Panorama del Chianti

Via Marcialla 349, Localitá Marcialla, I-50020 Certaldo (Tuscany) T: **057 166 9334**. E: **info@campingchianti.it**

alanrogers.com/IT66640

Gabriel Reali is developing this small country hillside site in Tuscany. Formerly named Toscana Colliverdi, it has space for 45 large units on deep terraces and two areas for tents. All the terrace pitches have electricity. There are panoramic views of the surrounding countryside. If you are content to be self-supporting and want assistance in exploring Tuscany along with the advantage of reasonable site fees, then this could be for you. A small bar with a tiny terrace offers welcoming cool drinks, excellent coffee and fresh bread in the mornings. Other supplies and good restaurants are available in the village of Marcialla 700 m. away.

Facilities

A small, clean toilet block is on the second terrace with British style toilets, showers and washbasins, plus dishwashing and laundry sinks, all with hot water. No facilities for disabled campers. Washing machine. Small bar and terrace (basic supplies on sale). Good size above ground pool (15/5-15/9). Off site: Restaurant, shop, butcher, greengrocer, post office 1 km.

Open: 1 April - 15 October.

Directions

From A1 autostrada Florence - Siena, take Tavarnelle exit and head for Tavarnelle. At the village follow signs for Marcialla. Site entrance is on the left 700 m. after village of Marcialla. GPS: 43.58235, 11.13828

Charges 2010

Per unit incl. 2 persons and electricity	€ 21,00 - € 29,50
extra person	€ 6,50 - € 8,50
child	€ 4,50 - € 5,50
dog	€ 2,00

Chiusi della Verna

Camping La Verna

Locatitá Vezzano, I-52010 Chiusi della Verna (Tuscany) T: **057 553 2121**. E: **info@campinglaverna.it**

alanrogers.com/IT66130

Camping La Verna is a rustic campsite, 850 m. above sea level, on the edge of the Casentino National Forest and close to the beautiful historic village of Chiusi della Verna which is widely known as an area of religious retreat and pilgrimage. Camping La Verna has basic facilities including a small pool, a bar and a restaurant/pizzeria. The shaded pitches of varying sizes are on terraces dotted throughout tall trees. Mostly level, all have 10A electricity and are on grass and sand. This is a peaceful and remote site suitable for campers who enjoy simple pleasures.

Facilities

One dated toilet block includes mixed Turkish and British style WCs and pushbutton showers. No facilities for disabled visitors. Washing machines. Bar, restaurant and pizzeria with small terrace. Communal Barbecue only. Torches very useful. Off site: Riding 1 km. Exploration of world famous religious/commercial centre. ATM 1 km.

Open: Easter - October.

Directions

Site is in village of Chiusi della Verna, north of Arezzo. From E45 (south or north) go to Pieve Sto Stefano. From here take P208 to Chiusi della Verna. Site is well signed in the village. Approaching from the west on the P208 be prepared for a long, hard, winding drive but with great views. GPS: 43.69780, 11.92351

Charges guide

Per person	€ 5,50 - € 7,00
pitch incl. electricity	€ 6,50 - € 8,50

Fiesole

Camping Panoramico Fiesole

Via Peramonda 1, I-50014 Fiesole (Tuscany) T: **055 599 069**. E: **panoramico@florencecamping.com**

alanrogers.com/IT66100

This is a mature but pleasant site in a fine hilltop situation offering wonderful views over Florence in the distance – on some evenings you can hear music from the nearby Roman amphitheatre famous for its classical entertainment in summer. It can become crowded in the main season and a very steep final access can be very difficult for larger units although the site will assist with a jeep. The 120 pitches, all with electricity (5A), are on terraces and steep walks to and from the various facilities could cause problems for people with mobility problems. There is shade in many parts.

Facilities

Two tastefully refurbished toilet blocks have mainly British style WCs, free hot water in washbasins and good showers. Washing machines and dryers. Fridges, irons and little cookers for campers' use. Shop (1/4-31/10) and restaurant (1/4-31/10). Swimming pool (1/6-30/9). Play area. Nursery. Torches required in some parts. English is spoken. Free shuttle service to Fiesole.

Open: All year.

See advertisement opposite

Directions

From A1 take Firenze-Sud exit follwing signs to Fiesole (NNE of central Firenze). From Fiesole centre follow SP54 and camping signs out of town for 1 km; the roads are very narrow through the town and the final steep access is difficult. Site is signed on right from Fiesole. Do not try to enter from the north as left turn is extremely difficult. GPS: 43.8065, 11.3051

Charges guide

Per unit incl. 2 persons and electricity	€ 30,00 - € 35,00
extra person	€ 4,00 - € 10,00

Figline Valdarno

Camping Norcenni Girasole Club

Via Norcenni 7, I-50063 Figline Valdarno (Tuscany) T: **055 915 141**. E: **girasole@ecvacanze.it**

alanrogers.com/IT66120

The Norcenni Girasole Club is a brilliant, busy and well run resort style site in a picturesque, secluded situation with great views of Tuscan landscapes 19 km. south of Florence. Owned by the dynamic Cardini-Vannucchi family, care has been taken in its development. There are 160 roomy pitches for touring, 136 with 6A electricity and 22 fully-serviced including 16A electricity. Most are shaded by well tended trees. The ground is hard and stony. Although on a fairly steep hillside, pitches are on level terraces. Tour operators and mobile homes occupy another 550 pitches. There are 20 permanent pitches.

Facilities

Sanitary facilities are very good with both British and Turkish style WCs. Family bathrooms to rent (book in advance). Facilities for disabled visitors. Laundry facilities. Supermarket and gift shops. Bar and 3 restaurants. Pizzeria. Gelateria. Swimming pools, one covered and heated (supervised; hats required). Pool bar, new pool with slide for children (under 6 yrs). Fitness centre. Soundproof disco. Minigolf. Bicycle hire. Internet access. ATM. Extensive entertainment programme. Off site: Riding 3 km. Fishing 5 km. Golf 30 km.

Open: 30 March - 18 October.

Directions

From Florence take Rome AI/E35 autostrada and take Incisa exit. Turn south on route 69 towards Arezzo. In Figline turn right for Greve and watch for Girasole signs - site is 4 km. up a twisting, climbing road. GPS: 43.61333, 11.44944

Charges guide

Per person	€ 7,20 - € 11,70
pitch	€ 10,00 - € 16,00
private sanitary facilities	€ 7,00 - € 10,50

Check real time availability and at-the-gate prices...

www.alanrogers.com

Firenze
Camping Internazionale
Via San Cristofano 2, Bottai, I-50029 Firenze (Tuscany) T: 055 237 4704
E: internazionale@florencecamping.com alanrogers.com/IT66090

Camping Internazionale is set in the hills about 5 km. south of Florence, and 8 km. from the Duomo with its wonderful dome by Brunelleschi. There is a 800 m. walk to a bus stop which will take you into Florence. This is a well shaded, terraced site with 240 touring pitches set around the top of a hill. These all have electricity with water obtained from the laundry and kitchen areas or the motorcaravan service point only. The site is often lively at night with young people from tour groups enjoying themselves, however this area is located well away from the touring pitches. Although it is a very green site, the camping area is somewhat more open with two electricity pylons at the top of the hill and some noise from the busy motorway which is below and next to the site. The two toilet blocks are clean and well equipped with many washing machines and dryers. Although showers are a little small they are fully adjustable with free hot water. There is a kitchen area stocked with pots, pans etc, gas hobs and free use of refrigerators. Two good sized pools, one for children, are fenced with a nice playground adjacent. The inviting restaurant with its open bar area has a good menu. This site offers an easily accessible location to explore Florence, and of the city sites is probably the most family friendly.

Facilities
Two toilet blocks include free hot showers. Laundry. Kitchen facilities. Motorcaravan service point. Shop. New bar and restaurant at the lower level. Evening entertainment. Two swimming pools. Playground. Off site: Florence 5 km.

Open: 1 April - 31 October.

Directions
From A1 take Firenza Certosa exit towards Florence. The turn to the site is just outside Bottai – turn left if coming from this direction (before Galluzzo). From Florence take Via Senese (S2) through Galluzzo, turn right at site sign just before entering Bottai. Continue 500 m. to site. GPS: 43.72187, 11.22058

Charges guide
Per unit incl. 2 persons and electricity	€ 29,00 - € 34,00
extra person	€ 4,00 - € 10,00

Firenze

Camping Michelangelo

Viale Michelangiolo 80, I-50125 Firenze (Tuscany) T: 055 681 1977. E: michelangelo@ecvacanze.it

alanrogers.com/IT66140

If you want to see Florence, this is the place, partly because the city is laid out like a tapestry 100 metres below and partly because it is easy to get into the city. A busy, bustling all year site with lots of backpackers, there are 240 flat pitches, half are for tourers. All have electricity (3A) and the pitches for motorcaravans and caravans are pleasant. The small bar (with takeaway) has a large terrace giving unrivalled views over the Duomo – what a backdrop for the entertainers who perform here regularly. The owners, the Cardini family, plan a continuous programme of improvements over the next few years.

Facilities

Three dated blocks struggle at peak periods and offer a mixture of Turkish and British style toilets with new facilities for disabled campers. Washing machines and dryers Motorcaravan service point. Supermarket. Gas. Takeaway. Play area. Bicycle hire. Electrical bicycle or electric car hire (allowed in the pedestrian area of city – good for the infirm). Bus service to city. Internet. ATM. Torches useful.

Open: All year.

Directions

Leave A1 heading for city centre. Site is south of river near Piazzale Michelangelo. Come to river 500 m. east of Ponte Vecchio, move east along the river bank until signs for Piazzale Michelangelo and camping. Site is off the main road down a steep incline. GPS: 43.7620, 11.2649

Charges 2010

Per unit incl. 2 persons and electricity	€ 31,10 - € 36,30
extra person	€ 4,60 - € 10,90

Gavorrano

Camping La Finoria

Via Monticello 66, I-58023 Gavorrano (Tuscany) T: 056 684 4381. E: info@campeggiolafinoria.it

alanrogers.com/IT66670

An unusual site, primarily for tents, La Finoria is set high in the mountains with incredible views. It is a rugged site with a focus on nature. Italian school children attend education programmes here. The three motorcaravan pitches are at the top of the site for those who enjoy a challenge, with a dozen caravan pitches on lower terraces accessed by a steep gravel track. Under huge chestnut trees there is a very pretty terraced area for tents. These have a private natural feel which some might say is what camping is all about. Electricity (3A) is available to all pitches, although long leads may be needed.

Facilities

Two blocks provide British and Turkish style toilets, hot showers and cold water at washbasins and sinks. Facilities for disabled campers. Washing machines and dryer. Quaint, small shop (closed Jan/Feb). Good restaurant and bar (closed Jan/Feb). Swimming pool (May-Sept). Tennis. Lessons on the environment. Excursions. Torches essential. Off site: Riding 2 km. Tennis 3 km. Village 3 km. Bicycle hire 6 km. Golf 8 km. Site's private beach for relaxing and fishing 12 km.

Open: All year.

Directions

From SS1 (Follonica - Grosseto) take Gavorrano exit, then the Finoria road. This is a steady, steep climb for 10 minutes. Start to descend and at junction (the only one), look left (difficult turn) downhill for a large white sign to site. Access to this site is only possible for small units. GPS: 42.92250, 10.91233

Charges guide

Per person	€ 3,00 - € 10,00
pitch	€ 4,00 - € 13,00

Check real time availability and at-the-gate prices...

www.alanrogers.com

Lacona

Camping Valle Santa Maria

Viale dei Golfi, Lacona, I-57031 Isola d'Elba (Tuscany) T: **056 596 4188**. E: **info@vsmaria.it**

alanrogers.com/IT66920

This small family site has smart paved roads and neat, clipped hedges and is proudly run by the experienced Rotellini family. Reception is a short walk from the entrance where English is spoken and there is also a bar. The 100 regular-sized pitches (with 4A electricity) are shaded by mature gum trees and some shade screens and access is gained over paved roads. Cars are parked off the pitches in a separate area. There are a few pitches by the beach boundary giving views over the attractive bay and the beach which is of soft sand.

Facilities

One smart, centrally located toilet block has hair dryers and other good fittings. Mixed Turkish and British style WCs. Facilities for children. Washing machines and dryers. Motorcaravan service point. Shop. Bar and restaurant. TV room. Play areas. Tennis. Entertainment programme in season and miniclub. Watersports on beach. Internet and WiFi. Off site: Public transport 100 m. Bicycle hire 300 m. Golf 8 km. Riding 10 km.

Open: 15 March - 1 November.

Directions

Site is on the south side of the island, in Lacona. From Portoferraio take the Lacona road and site is well signed as you approach the village. Do not take the first right turn signed to Lacona as this takes you cross country. GPS: 42.76080, 10.30221

Charges guide

Per person	€ 6,70 - € 12,50
child (under 8 yrs)	€ 5,00 - € 9,50
pitch	€ 13,00 - € 16,50
electricity	€ 1,50

Lacona

Camping Tallinucci

Lacona, I-57031 Isola d'Elba (Tuscany) T: **056 596 4069**. E: **info@campingtallinucci.it**

alanrogers.com/IT66940

Camping Tallinucci is a small family site which has a clean and pleasant feel. The roads are all paved and access is very easy to the 100 touring pitches. A few pitches are directly alongside the beach and have views over the pretty bay. Cars are parked off the pitches in a separate area. The pitches are on flat ground with 4A electricity and shade from mature trees and the site looks very green from hedges. This small site would be good for families who just wish to relax. It is ideal for disabled campers.

Facilities

One good, solar heated toilet block is centrally located. British and Turkish style WCs. Children's facilities and baby baths. Washing machines and dryers. Motorcaravan service point. Shop. Bar and restaurant/pizzeria on the beach. Tennis. Games room. Play areas. Guided walks in Spring and Autumn. Internet point. WiFi. Off site: Watersports on beach. Public transport 100 m. Bicycle hire 300 m. Golf 8 km. Riding 10 km. ATM 500 m.

Open: Easter - 31 October.

Directions

Site is on south side of the island in Lacona. From Portoferraio take the Lacona road site is well signed approaching the village. GPS: 42.76125, 10.30035

Charges guide

Per unit incl. 2 persons and electricity	€ 28,50 - € 47,50
extra person	€ 5,00 - € 13,00
dog	€ 6,00

Lacona

Camping Casa dei Prati

Lacona, Capoliveri, I-57031 Isola d'Elba (Tuscany) T: **056 596 4060**. E: **casadeiprati@elbalink.it**

alanrogers.com/IT66950

Casa dei Prati is a small family site on the southern side of the island of Elba, the largest in the Tuscan archipelago. The site is close to the pebble beach of Margidoreand is attractively laid out amongst almond, eucalyptus and pine trees. Pitches are well shaded and most have electrical connections. After unloading, parking is arranged in a separate area. There are also apartments and mobile homes here (available for rent). Leisure facilities include a swimming pool (and a separate pool for children) with fine views of the surrounding hills. There is a small bar serving snacks and a shop.

Facilities

Bar. Snack bar. Shop. Swimming and paddling pools. Games room. Play area. Tourist information. Mobile homes and chalets for rent. Off site: Beach at Margaride. Cycle and walking tracks. Excursions to Portoferraio, the island's largest town.

Open: 1 April - 31 October.

Directions

Site is close to the village of Lacona. From Portoferraio, head south on the SP26 and SP30 to Lacona, and follow signs to the site. GPS: 42.76583, 10.31411

Charges guide

Per unit incl. 2 persons and electricity	€ 27,80 - € 45,30
extra person	€ 6,50 - € 12,50
dog	€ 8,00

Marina di Bibbona

Camping Free Time

Via dei Cipressi, I-57020 Marina di Bibbona (Tuscany) T: 058 660 0934. E: info@freetimecamping.it

alanrogers.com/IT66330

Free Time is 700 m. from the beach and 500 m. from the little resort of Marina di Bibbona. The site is attractively landscaped with many flowers and trees provide welcome shade to most of the level grass pitches (80 sq.m) which have 10A electricity. Of the 124 pitches, 44 have their own thatched private facilities with toilet and shower, outside kitchen and patio. There is a bar/restaurant/pizzeria complex overlooking the lagoon style pool and paddling pool. There is also a superb thatched open air gymnasium and sauna by the fishing lake.

Facilities

Modern toilet blocks are well maintained. Facilities for disabled visitors. Some pitches have private sanitary facilities (extra charge). Motorcaravan service point. Fishing. Play area. Lively entertainment programme in peak season. Dogs are not accepted in high season. Internet access and WiFi. Off site: Beach 700 m. Cecina 5 km.

Open: Easter - 5 October.

Directions

Site is south of Livorno. From Livorno - Civitavecchia road (autostrada) take La California exit and follow signs to Marina di Bibbona. Site is well signed. GPS: 43.25235, 10.53090

Charges guide

Per unit incl. 2 persons and electricity	€ 24,50 - € 41,70
extra person	€ 4,20 - € 12,50
dog (not in high season)	€ 5,00

Marina di Bibbona

Camping Il Gineprino

Via dei Platani 56a.b.c, I-57020 Marina di Bibbona (Tuscany) T: 058 660 0550. E: info@ilgineprino.it

alanrogers.com/IT66370

This is a pleasant part of Tuscany with many interesting places within visiting distance. Il Gineprino, a small, family run site is on the edge of Bibbona but not directly on the coast. There are 194 pitches (10 with private sanitary facilities) on the main site plus 55 bungalows – watch for low branches if your unit is around 3.5 m. high. The 124 touring pitches are numbered and marked by trees at the corners and all have a water tap and electricity. A further area for 50 motorcaravans, with electricity and another toilet block, is directly across the quiet beach access road.

Facilities

Three dated sanitary blocks have British and Turkish style WCs, hot water in washbasins and showers, with cold for dishwashing and laundry. Family room (on payment). Facilities for disabled people. Motorcaravan services. Shop, restaurant with terrace. Swimming pool with paddling pool and aquagym. Games room. TV room. Bicycle hire. Some entertainment in high season. Excursions. Only small pets are accepted – contact site. Off site: Fishing 500 m. Riding 1 km.

Open: 1 April - 30 September.

Directions

Site is south of Livorno. Leave the SS1 coast road between La California and Marina di Bibbona. Follow signs to Marina di Bibbona where there are site signs. GPS: 43.23196, 10.53781

Charges guide

Per unit incl. 2 persons and electricity	€ 20,00 - € 34,00
extra person	€ 6,00 - € 10,00
child (1-8 yrs)	€ 4,00 - € 6,50
dog	€ 3,00 - € 5,00
No credit cards.	

Marina di Campo

Camping Ville degli Ulivi

Via della Foce, 89, Marina di Campo, I-57034 Isola d'Elba (Tuscany) T: 056 597 6098. E: info@villedegliulivi.it

alanrogers.com/IT66680

Camping Ville degli Ulivi is an impressive site with many quality activities for families. In a pleasant setting amongst pines and olives, it has access through a rear gate to a pretty sandy bay with a safe beach and all manner of watersports. Of the 285 pitches, about 50 are available for tourers. There is a very large contingent of tour operators and some bungalow and apartment accommodation. The touring pitches, scattered amongst the other pitches, are of reasonable size, flat and most have shade. All have electricity (6A), no cars are allowed to stay on site.

Facilities

Toilet facilities are good with hot showers, baby rooms and facilities for disabled visitors. Laundry facilities. Bar/restaurant. Pizzeria. Takeaway. Shop. Swimming pool. Play area. Bicycle and scooter hire. Diving centre. Multisport pitch. Internet access. Amusement arcade. Entertainment programme (May-Sept). Aquagym. Miniclub. Excursions. Off site: Village 1 km. Local markets. Watersports on the beach. Riding 3 km.

Open: 4 April - 24 October.

Directions

From Portoferraio ferry port follow signs for Procchio, then Marina di Campo. Before Marina di Campo village, turn left towards 'La Foce - Lacona'. In 800 m. turn right to site. GPS: 42.75190, 10.24502

Charges 2010

Per person	€ 6,50 - € 13,50
child (0-9 yrs)	€ 1,50 - € 10,00
pitch incl. car and electricity	€ 10,50 - € 20,50
pet	free - € 6,00

Marina di Grosseto

Camping Le Marze

Strada Provinciale 158, km 30,200, I-58046 Marina di Grosseto (Tuscany) T: **056 435 501**
E: **lemarze@boschettoholiday.it alanrogers.com/IT66620**

This natural site is four kilometres north of Marina di Grosseto and has 180 generously-sized pitches for touring units. Separated by hedges, all have electricity and most enjoy natural shade from mature pine trees. On sand and with easy access, there is a background noise of 'cicadas' (crickets) from the lofty pines and squirrels entertain high above. A private beach is across the main road. Bicycles are an asset and you could also enjoy a cycle ride to the town along a beach track. The beach is worth the walk as it is the strongest feature here, being soft sand which shelves slowly.

Facilities

The four toilet blocks are of a high standard, two of them new, with British style WCs. Facilities for disabled campers in the new blocks along with baby facilities and private bathrooms. Motorcaravan service point. Market and bazaar. Bar, restaurant, pizzeria and takeaway. Swimming pools. Aquarobics. Two play areas. Entertainment in season, excursions and activities. Barbecue areas. Bicycle hire. Internet point. Torches required in some areas.
Off site: Riding and boat launching 3 km. Golf 30 km.

Open: 1 April - 3 October.

Directions

Site is on the road between Castiglione delle Pescaia and Marina di Grosseto, known as the SS322 or SP158 in places. Site is well signed 3 km. from Marina di Grosseto. GPS: 42.74523, 10.94805

Charges 2010

Per unit incl. 2 persons	
and electricity	€ 17,40 - € 43,10
extra person	€ 5,70 - € 12,20
child (3-9 yrs)	€ 3,40 - € 6,90
dog	€ 4,00 - € 4,50

Marina di Grosseto

Camping Cieloverde

Via della Trappola 180, I-58100 Marina di Grosseto (Tuscany) T: **056 432 1611**. E: **info@cieloverde.it**
alanrogers.com/IT66750

Cieloverde Camping Village lies in the heart of the Tuscan Maremma, between Marina di Grosseto and Principina, bordering the Maremma Natural Park. The huge site lies deep in a long-established pinewood, looking out onto the Costa d'Argento where a sandy beach slopes gently down to the sea. The 1,000 touring pitches (all about 100 sq.m) are in circular zones around sanitary blocks and have 3A electricity and offer telephone connections. Parking is in designated areas away from the camping area. A wide range of entertainment is organized, including shows, dance events, open-air cinema and games.

Facilities

Modern toilet blocks. Shops, restaurant and takeaway. Pizzeria. Bars. Hairdresser. Play area. Games room. Archery. Cinema. Chapel. 'Tarzaland' adventure park. Transport to the beach. Dogs are not accepted in high season.
Off site: Watersports. Fishing (with licence). Marina di Grossetto. Riding 5 km. Golf 30 km.

Open: 9 May - 20 September.

Directions

Site is west of Grosseto on the coast. Take care here as Grosseto has only one way of crossing the railway for anything other than cars. Follow Grosseto signs from S1 (the Aurelia) and cross town following road to Castliglione della Pescaia until you connect with signs for Marina di Grosseto. Site signed. We stress this is the only way across town. GPS: 42.7131, 11.0075

Charges guide

Per person	€ 5,50 - € 14,00
child (2-5 yrs)	€ 3,90 - € 9,00
pitch	€ 5,90 - € 19,00
Camping Cheques accepted.	

Check real time availability and at-the-gate prices...
www.**alanrogers**.com

Montecatini Terme

Camping Belsito

Via delle Vigne, (Località Vico), I-51016 Montecatini Terme (Tuscany) T: **057 267 373**
E: **info@campingbelsito.it alanrogers.com/IT66010**

The owners of this site wish it to be for families and thus the emphasis is on peace and tranquillity. Whilst the towns below are blistering hot, the cool breezes here do make it as the name says 'Belsito' – a beautiful place. There are now 200 pitches of varying size, most with electricity and some with shade. It is very much a touring site with no permanent occupants and only two bungalows for hire. The views are excellent from most pitches, as they are from the modestly sized pool on the upper terrace and the new tent field. Unusually 64 pitches have a private sanitary unit for hire on the pitch.

Facilities

One clean and modern sanitary block plus 64 private units for hire. Hot water is provided throughout. Facilities for disabled visitors. Washing machines and dryer. Good shop, bar/restaurant/takeaway (all April-Sept). Swimming pool (no paddling pool). Play area. Book exchange. Some activities for children in high season. Communal freezer and barbecue area. Satellite TV. Off site: Bus 100 m. from gate to railway station. Town of Collodi – Pinnocchio's town!

Open: 1 April - 30 September.

Directions

From A11 Firenze - Mare autostrada take exit for Montecatini Terme. Follow signs for site and take Montecatini Alto road (do not use satellite navigation as you may end up in a very narrow village street). Site on the left in about 3 km. GPS: 43.90480, 10.78783

Charges guide

Per unit incl. 2 persons and electricity	€ 26,50 - € 32,50
extra person	€ 3,00 - € 8,50

Montescudaio

Camping Montescudaio

Via del Poggetto km 2, I-56040 Montescudaio (Tuscany) T: **058 668 3477**. E: **info@camping-montescudaio.it**
alanrogers.com/IT66300

This well developed site, south of Livorno, is fashioned out of a very extensive area of natural undulating woodland and (with low trees) famous for wild boar. The fact that the site is cleverly divided into separate areas for families and couples, including those in tourers, shows the owner's desire to reduce any possibility of noise for families on the site. There are 372 pitches for touring units in separate clearings with shade, most of a good size, plus 200 large caravans for rent along with ten bungalows. Electricity is available in all parts (long leads are required for some pitches).

Facilities

Top quality sanitary blocks are comprehensively appointed. Baby baths in the two main blocks. Motorcaravan services. Excellent laundry service. Shops. Bar. Restaurant and takeaway in main season. Open air pizzeria with bar and small dance floor (from mid June). Swimming pool. Tennis. Fitness field. Excursions and events (high season). Torches required in some areas. Dogs are not accepted.
Off site Beach 4 km. Bicycle hire 5 km. Riding 10 km.

Open: 15 May - 15 September.

Directions

From Genova - Livorno autostrada take Rosignano Marittimo exit. Take highway (Livorno - Grosseto) towards Roma and exit for Cecina. Follow signs for Guardistallo (important – not Montescudaio). Site is on Cecina - Guardistallo road, 2 km. from Cecina. GPS: 43.3161, 10.5547

Charges guide

Per person (any age)	€ 5,50 - € 7,50
pitch incl. electricity	€ 12,00 - € 24,50

Montopoli

Kawan Village Toscana Village

Via Fornoli 9, I-56020 Montopoli (Tuscany) T: **057 144 9032**. E: **info@toscanavillage.com**
alanrogers.com/IT66610

This area was once a forest surrounding the attractive medieval Tuscan village of Montopoli. Toscana Village has been thoughtfully carved out of the hillside under mature pines and it is ideal for a sightseeing holiday in this central area. The 150 level pitches (some large) are on shaded terraces and are carefully maintained. Some pitches have full drainage facilities and water, most with 6A electricity. The amenities are centrally located at the top of the hill in a pleasant modern building. English is spoken by the helpful reception staff who also organise a programme of vsits and events.

Facilities

Two modern toilet blocks have excellent facilities including British style toilets, hot water at all the stylish sinks, private cabins and two large en-suite cubicles which may be suitable for disabled campers. Washing machines and dryer. Motorcaravan services. Shop. Bread to order. Gas. Restaurant (limited menu, evenings only). Takeaway. Swimming pool. Play area. Bicycle hire. Organised activities. Torches useful. Off site: Montopoli village 1 km. Fishing 6 km. Golf and riding 7 km.

Open: All year.

Directions

From A12 autostrada (Genova - Florence) take Pisa Centro exit. Take F1,P1,L1 and then Montopoli exit. Follow signs to Montopoli village. Look for cemetery on right. Opposite is Via Masoria leading to Via Fornoli and site. Note: follow brown signs to site; do not use GPS as this will direct you through a prohibited area. GPS: 43.67611, 10.75277

Charges guide

Per person	€ 5,00 - € 8,00
pitch incl. electricity	€ 12,30 - € 15,50
Camping Cheques accepted.	

Pisa

Camping Torre Pendente

Viale delle Cascine 86, I-56122 Pisa (Tuscany) T: **050 561 704**. E: **info@campingtorrependente.it**
alanrogers.com/IT66080

Torre Pendente is a most friendly site, well run by the Signorini family who speak good English and make everyone feel welcome. It is amazingly close to the famous leaning tower of Pisa and obviously its position means it is busy throughout the main season. It is a medium sized site, on level, grassy ground with some shade from trees and lots of artificial shade. There are 220 touring pitches, all with electricity. All site facilities are near the entrance including a most pleasant swimming pool complex with pool bar and a large terrace. Here you can relax after hot days in the city and enjoy drinks and snacks or find more formal fare in the restaurant with á la carte menu. This is a very busy site in high season with many nationalities discovering the delights of Pisa. It is ideal for exploring the fascinating leaning tower and other attractions.

Facilities

Three new toilet blocks are clean and smart with British style toilets and good facilities for disabled campers. Private cabins for hire. Hot water at sinks. Washing machines. Motorcaravan services. New supermarket. New restaurant, bar and takeaway. Swimming pool with pool bar, paddling pool and spa. Playground. Boules. Entertainment in high season. Internet access. Accommodation. Off site: Bicycle hire. Riding 3 km. Fishing 10 km. Golf 15 km.

Open: 1 April - 15 October.

Directions

From A12, exit at Pisa Nord and follow for 5 km. to Pisa. Do not take first sign to town centre. Site is well signed at a later left turn (Viale delle Cascine). GPS: 43.7252, 10.3819

Charges guide

Per person	€ 8,00 - € 9,00
child (3-10 yrs)	€ 4,50 - € 5,00
pitch	€ 6,00 - € 15,00
dog	€ 1,60

GPS: N 43° 43' 27" - E 10° 22' 59"

The campsite is situated 800 meters far from the famous Leaning Tower and the historical city centre, but also only 2 kms far from the Natural Park of San Rossore, which is easily reachable on foot or by bike. We are very near to San Rossore railwaystation too: from there you can easily get to Florence and Lucca by train. Approximately 10 kms far from sea resorts Marina di Pisa and Tirrenia and 20 kms from the harbour of Livorno (ferryboats to the islands Corsica, Elba and Sardinia). Our campingplace develops itself on a flat grassy and shaded meadow and it is an ideal location for young families with children (animation throughout high season), for seniors but also for those people who enjoy active holidays! **Open from 01.04 till 15.10.2010.**

Min 3 Days 20% Discount only low season!

Via delle Cascine, 86 - I-56122 Pisa - Tel. 0039 050561704 - Fax 0039 050561734 www.campingtorrependente.com - info@campingtorrependente.com

Portoferraio

Camping Scaglieri

Localitá Scaglieri, Portoferraio, I-57037 Isola d'Elba (Tuscany) T: **056 596 9940**. E: **info@campingscaglieri.it**
alanrogers.com/IT66850

Camping Scaglieri is a small coastal site on a steep slope with a steep entrance. A small pool is directly alongside reception at the top of the site, as is the restaurant and bar, all enjoying great views. The 80 touring pitches are of varying sizes, all on terraces with 3A electricity and views over the bay, but the slopes are interesting! Some pitches have shade from attractive trees. The campsite is part of a group with two hotels and the facilities there may be used by camping guests. Due to the steep slopes this site is not recommended for disabled or infirm campers.

Facilities

One central toilet block is kept very clean with good fittings. WCs are mostly British style. Baby room. Washing machines. Motorcaravan service point. Bar, restaurant and takeaway. Gelateria and small shop. Swimming pool. Play areas. Bicycle hire. Entertainment programme in season. No barbecues allowed on pitches – communal area. Internet. Torches very useful. Off site: Golf 200 m. Sailing, windsurfing school and watersports 500 m. Beach 800 m. Riding 5 km. ATM 5 km. Hotel facilities may be used by camping guests. Public transport 20 m. in high season.

Open: Easter - 20 October.

Directions

Site is west of Portoferraio on the coast. From Portoferraio ferry take the Procchio road. After 5 km. and on a hilltop turn right towards Biodola and Scaglieri. Site entrance is on the right after 2 km. GPS: 42.80349, 10.27072

Charges guide

Per person	€ 7,80 - € 14,00
child (3-10 yrs)	€ 4,80 - € 12,00
pitch	€ 11,50 - € 23,50
electricity	€ 1,50 - € 3,00
dog	€ 5,00

Check real time availability and at-the-gate prices...

www.alanrogers.com

Portoferraio

Camping Rosselba Le Palme

Locális Ottone 3, Portoferraio, I-57037 Isola d'Elba (Tuscany) T: **056 593 3101**. E: **info@rosselbalepalme.it**

alanrogers.com/IT66880

Rosselba Le Palme is situated on Elba, Italy's third largest island. At this large resort style campsite there is a lot to explore; including the beach (500 m. down a private track and across a public road), the centrally located botanical gardens with the only blue palm found in Europe, the private bike track encircling the site or gaze up at the medieval castle on the hill above. Of the 280 pitches, 150 are available for touring units, all with electricity connections. The excellent toilet blocks are scattered throughout the site, but due to the landscape, may involve steep walking from some pitches.

Facilities

Eight modern, clean toilet blocks. Laundry with washing machines and ironing facilities. Supermarket. Restaurant, pizzeria, pool bar and café/bar. Large pool complex with swimming courses and aquarobics. Tennis with coaching. Volleyball. Archery. Five-a-side football. Basketball. Trampolines. Bicycle and motorcycle rental. Secure car park. Botanical gardens. WiFi. Off site: Beach with deck chairs, sun umbrellas, canoes and windsurfers. Scuba diving.

Open: 21 April - 30 September.

Directions

From ferry at Portoferraio follow signs for Porto Azzurro to begin. Then turn left towards Bagnaia and follow campsite signs, on the right, just after a fork to the left. GPS: 42.80146, 10.36488

Charges guide

Per person	€ 4,40 - € 14,30
child (3-8 yrs)	free - € 10,50
pitch	€ 5,40 - € 19,30

Punta Ala

PuntAla Camping Resort

Locális Punta Ala, Casta della Pescala, I-58043 Punta Ala (Tuscany) T: **056 492 2294**
E: **info@campingpuntala.it** alanrogers.com/IT66730

This very large site was established some 35 years ago. Some of the original infrastructure remains and some has been renovated. The pitches vary tremendously in size and position relative to the amenities. With the size of the site some serious distances have to be covered from some areas to the amenities, most of which are near the entrance. There are 450 pitches for touring units on sand on a mainly flat site. All have electricity (67 have water and drainage as well) and shade from very mature pines. Much hedging gives privacy and is quite extensive in parts.

Facilities

The nine blocks are a confusing mixture of facilities with some unisex facilities and many private cabins to hire. Two blocks have been rebuilt and these are popular (sometimes with long queues). The older blocks resemble old army blocks, and have mostly Turkish toilets. Unit for disabled campers. Laundry facilities. Motorcaravan services. Bars, restaurants and takeaway. Shop. Entertainment. Play areas. WiFi. Bicycle hire. Tennis. Beach with watersports. ATM. Communal barbecue areas (no barbecues on pitches). Excursions. Animals are not accepted. Torches essential. Off site: Bus service 800 m. Golf 14 km. Town 6 km.

Open: Easter - 30 October.

Directions

From E80/S1/Aurelia superstrada take Follonica Nord exit onto S322 for Punta Ala and Castiglione della Pescaia. Watch for district of Pian d'alma marked on maps – look for the Total petrol station on the right, go 450 m. past it to small white restaurant La Violina on the right. Site is now signed to the right along a narrow road. After 2 km. cross bridge and park on the left. GPS: 42.84143, 10.77960

Charges guide

Per person	€ 5,80 - € 18,10
pitch incl. electricity	€ 6,40 - € 22,60
with water and drainage	€ 10,40 - € 32,50

Punta Ala

Baia Verde International Camping

Via delle Collacchie, I-58040 Punta Ala (Tuscany) T: **056 492 2298**. E: **info@baiaverde.com**

alanrogers.com/IT66740

Baia Verde is a large, sprawling family site with direct access to a sandy private beach. The level pitches are shaded by mature pines and vary considerably in size. The site boasts a good range of amenities, notably a shopping and restaurant complex. This is a lively site in peak season with an extensive entertainment programme including a beach gym, various sports tournaments and evening discos. There is plenty to do on the beach – pedaloes and canoes are available for hire, along with loungers and parasols – and there's plenty to see in the area.

Facilities

Nine mature sanitary blocks provide a mixture of British and Turkish style toilets. Laundry. Motorcaravan service point. Shopping centre. Bar/restaurant. Pizzeria. Takeaway. Beach bar. Play area. Games room. Internet access. Bicycle hire. Boat and canoe hire. Direct access to beach. Evening entertainment in high season. Dogs are not accepted in high season. Off site: Various excursions. Free shuttle to ferry embarkation point. Riding 800 m.

Open: Easter - 14 October.

Directions

From the north, take E80 to Rosignano and join Via Aurelia (SS1) leaving at Follonica Sud exit. Follow signs to Punta Ala and site is well signed from here. GPS: 42.83446, 10.77988

Charges guide

Per person	€ 5,50 - € 11,50
child (2-7 yrs)	€ 3,70 - € 8,50
pitch incl. electricity	€ 8,00 - € 17,00

San Baronto di Lamporecchio

Camping Barco Reale

Via Nardini 11, I-51035 San Baronto di Lamporecchio (Tuscany) T: **057 388 332**. E: **info@barcoreale.com**
alanrogers.com/IT66000

Just 40 minutes from Florence and an hour from Pisa, this site is beautifully situated high in the Tuscan hills close to the fascinating town of Pistoia. Part of an old walled estate, there are impressive views of the surrounding countryside. It is a quiet site of 15 hectares with 250 pitches with good shade from mature pines and oaks. Some pitches are huge with great views and others are very private. Most are for tourers, but some have difficult access (site provides tractor assistance). All 187 touring pitches have electricity and 40 have water and drainage. Member of 'Leading Campings Group'.

Facilities

Three modern sanitary blocks are well positioned and kept very clean. Good facilities for disabled people (dedicated pitches close by). Baby room. Laundry facilities. Motorcaravan services. Dog shower. Shop. Restaurant. Bar. Supervised and enlarged swimming pool (caps required; 1/5-30/9). Ice cream shop (1/6-31/8). Playgrounds. Bowls. Bicycle hire. Internet point. WiFi. Disco. Entertainment. Cooking lessons for Tuscan style food. Excursions. Charcoal fires are not permitted. Off site: Village and shops 1 km. Fishing 8 km. Golf 15 km.

Open: 1 April - 30 September.

Directions

From Pistoia take Vinci - Empoli - Lamporecchio signs to San Baronto. From Empoli signs to Vinci and San Baronto. Final approach involves a sharp bend and a steep slope. GPS: 43.84190, 10.91130

Charges guide

Per unit incl. 2 persons	
and electricity	€ 24,20 - € 37,80
extra person	€ 7,10 - € 10,50
child (3-11 yrs)	€ 4,00 - € 6,50

Discounts for longer stays except in high season.

IN THE HEART OF TUSCANY

The campsite lies on a hill in a pine and oak wood with a lovely panorama. The house where Leonardo da Vinci was born and the famous towns of Tuscany are not far away, excursions by bus are organised. Barco Reale is an ideal site for a pleasant holiday from April to September owing to guided walks among the olive groves and wine country, the wonderful scenery, the local culture and the climate.

Via Nardini 11 • 51035 Lamporecchio (Pistoia)
www.barcoreale.it • info@barcoreale.com
tel. +39 0573 88332 • fax +39 0573 856003

San Gimignano

Camping Boschetto di Piemma

Localitá Santa Lucia 38/C, I-53037 San Gimignano (Tuscany) T: **057 794 0352**. E: **info@boschettodipiemma.it**
alanrogers.com/IT66270

The medieval Manhattan of San Gimignano is one of Tuscany's most popular sites. This new site lies just 2 km. from the town and there are 100 small pitches here, all with electrical connections (10A). The site is in a wood surrounded by olive groves and vineyards and has been developed with much care for the environment, using rain water for irrigation, for example. San Gimignano has been classified by UNESCO as a world heritage site and is best known for its towers, built by rival families, and which date back to the 11th century. An hourly bus service connects the site with the town.

Facilities

Excellent sanitary block and facilities for disabled visitors. Restaurant/pizzeria and bar. Shop (specialising in local produce). Swimming pool (15/5-15/9, small charge). Tennis (lessons available). Sports pitch. Playground. Entertainment and activity programme in high season. Apartments for rent. Off site: San Gimignano 2 km. Cycle and walking trails, riding, golf.

Open: All year.

Directions

Take the Poggibonsi Nord exit from the Florence - Siena superstrada. Then follow signs to San Gimignano. At first roundabout follow signs to Volterra and then take first road to the left, signed Santa Lucia. Site is located close to the sports area. GPS: 43.4533, 11.0536

Charges guide

Per unit incl. 2 persons	
and electricity	€ 20,30 - € 33,50
extra person	€ 6,70 - € 10,10
child (3-11 yrs)	€ 4,30 - € 5,40

San Piero a Sieve

Camping Mugello Verde

Via Massorondinaio 39, I-50037 San Piero a Sieve (Tuscany) T: **055 848 511**
E: **mugelloverde@florencecamping.com   alanrogers.com/IT66050**

Mugello Verde is a country hillside site with long curving terraces and one tarmac access road. Some pitches offer good views. English is spoken at reception where much tourist information is available – ask for the limited dates of the Ferrari team practices and the racing on the nearby international Mugello racing track! There are 200 good sized pitches for motorcaravans and caravans with smaller areas for tents. All pitches have electricity (6A) and mature trees provide shade. We met British campers who liked the site's charm and loved the proximity to the Ferrari race track, but found the facilities a little rustic and the pitches somewhat unkempt.

Facilities

Two toilet blocks on the terraces have been refurbished to a good standard and facilities are clean and relatively modern with mixed British and Turkish style WCs. Most washbasins have hot water. Comprehensive facilities for disabled campers. Laundry facilities. Shop. Restaurant/bar and pizzeria (all season). Swimming pool (15/6-15/9; no paddling pool). Play area. Tennis. Off site: Riding, golf, bicycle hire and fishing, all within 5 km.

Open: All year.

See advertisement on page 131

Directions

From A1 autostrada take Barberino del Mugello exit and follow SS65 towards San Piero a Sieve and before town, turn left and just past Tamoil garage turn right to site. GPS: 43.96148, 11.31030

Charges guide

Per unit incl. 2 persons	€ 22,00 - € 30,00
extra person	€ 6,00 - € 8,00
child (3-12 yrs)	€ 3,00 - € 5,50
Camping Cheques accepted.	

San Vincenzo

Campéole Park Albatros

Pineta di Torre Nuova, I-57027 San Vincenzo (Tuscany) T: **056 570 1018**. E: **nadine.ferran@atciat.com**
alanrogers.com/IT66380

Camping Albatros is another venture for the Cardini/Vanucchi families and is situated on the historic Costa Degli Etruschi where natural parks abound. A group of conical buildings form the hub of the original, somewhat dated, infrastructure of Albatros. This theme of circles is continued through the peaceful new development in the form of round buildings and the placing of mobile homes in curves. The 300 new touring pitches are in a separate area on flat ground of 110 sq.m. All have water, drainage, 10A electricity and some shade from newly planted trees.

Facilities

Two toilet blocks are on site. The new circular block is superb! All WCs are British style and the showers are really good, as are facilities for disabled visitors and children. Washing machines. Central area includes bar, restaurant and pizzeria with large terrace. Entertainment programme in season. Miniclub (4-12 yrs). Play areas. Lagoon pool complex. Bicycle hire. No barbecues allowed. Internet. Torches very useful. Off site: Beach 800 m. Riding 1 km. Vast choice of excursions and walks. Public transport at gate in high season.

Open: 9 April - 4 October.

Directions

Site is northwest of Grossetto and south of Livorno on the coast. From the SS1 take San Vincenzo exit. Site is well signed as you approach the village. GPS: 43.04972, 10.55861

Charges guide

Per unit incl. 2 persons and electricity	€ 1,50 - € 3,50
extra person	€ 8,50 - € 17,00
child (2-12 yrs)	€ 4,00 - € 9,00
dog	€ 6,00 - € 12,00

Sarteano

Parco Delle Piscine

Via del Bagno Santo 29, I-53047 Sarteano (Tuscany) T: **057 826 971**. E: **info@parcodellepiscine.it**
alanrogers.com/IT66450

On the spur of Monte Cetona, Sarteano is a spa, and this large, smart site utilises that spa in its very open environs. The site is well run with an excellent infrastructure and there is a friendly welcome from the English speaking staff. The 500 individual, flat pitches, are all 90 to 100 sq. m. with electricity (6/10A) and fully marked with high neat hedges giving real privacy. The novel feature here is the three unique swimming pools fed by the natural thermo-mineral springs. These springs have been known since antiquity as 'del Bagno Santo' which flows at a constant temperature of about 24 degrees.

Facilities

Two heated toilet blocks are of high quality with mainly British style WCs. Gas supplies. Motorcaravan services. Restaurant/pizzeria with bar. Takeaway. Coffee bar. Swimming pools (one all season). Satellite TV room and mini-cinema with 100 seats and very large screen. Tennis. Exchange facilities. Free guided cultural tours. Internet. Dogs are not accepted. Off site: Bicycle hire 100 m. Riding 3 km.

Open: 1 April - 30 September.

Directions

From autostrada A1 take Chiusi/Chianciano exit, from where Sarteano is well signed (6 km). In Sarteano follow camping/piscine signs to site (entrance sign reads Piscine di Sarteano). GPS: 42.9885, 11.8639

Charges 2010

Per unit incl. 2 persons	€ 32,00 - € 58,00
extra person	€ 9,00 - € 15,50
child (3-10 yrs)	€ 6,00 - € 10,00

Scarlino

Camping Baia dei Gabbiani

I-58020 Scarlino (Tuscany) T: **056 686 6158**. E: **info@baiadeigabbiani.com**

alanrogers.com/IT66770

Baia dei Gabbiani is a long and narrow site, situated between the busy S322 and the beach north of Puntino di Scarlino, 4 km. from the seaside resort of Follonica. The small pitches are on level ground and most have electrical connections. A range of amenities are on offer including a restaurant, bar and supermarket. The site has direct access to the beach and a lively activity programme is organised in peak season. Puntino is just 400 m. away and has a yachting harbour as well as a good selection of shops, bars and restaurants. The beach adjacent to the campsite has views towards Elba, and is popular for windsurfing, surfing and other water sports.

Facilities

The sanitary block is old and provides mainly Turkish style toilets, washbasins and token operated showers. Restaurant and bar. Shop. Playground. Entertainment and activity programme in high season. Direct beach access. Chalets for rent. Off site: Puntino 400 m. Follonica 4 km. Siena, Florence and Pisa are all within 2 hours drive.

Open: 26 May - 16 September.

Directions

From Livorno take the southbound Via Aurelia (S1). Leave at Follonica Nord exit. Head initially towards Follonica and then towards Grosseto. Site is signed to the right on the S322, just before the small town of Scarlino. GPS: 42.8933, 10.7859

Charges guide

Per person	€ 6,90 - € 11,70
child (3-7 yrs)	€ 5,20 - € 7,60
pitch incl. electricity	€ 9,70 - € 15,30

Scarlino

Camping Village Il Fontino

Localitá Il Fontino, Maremma Toscana, I-58020 Scarlino (Tuscany) T: **056 637 029**. E: **info@fontino.it**

alanrogers.com/IT66720

The name means 'Little Fountain' as springs provide all the drinking water here. The Maurizio family have worked hard to provide a most pleasant site for campers. There are 120 terraced pitches for tourers on a sloping site, all with 3/6A electricity and shade from mature olives. Once settled on the pitch cars are parked separately. The 25 metre pool with its separate paddling pool is the site's strength – it is stunning and free. As you swim you can enjoy the views over the town of Follonica below you, whilst in turn the village of Scarlino sits hundreds of metres above on the cliff top.

Facilities

Two dated sanitary blocks provide hot showers (2.5 minute timer). Mostly Turkish style toilets, cold water at washbasins. Single facility for disabled visitors. Washing machines and dryer. Bar/restaurant and takeaway. Shop. Swimming and paddling pools. Entertainment programme and miniclub (high season). Play area. Internet access. Bicycle hire. Free bus to beach with watersports. Off site: Town 2 km. Tennis 200 m. Beach 4 km. Golf, riding and boat launching 4 km.

Open: 24 April - 30 September.

Directions

From E80/S1 autostrada take Scarlino exit. Head for the hills and Scarlino. On approach to town look for site signs to right (towards Grosseto). Site is 1.4 km. on the left. GPS: 42.91101, 10.84347

Charges guide

Per unit incl. 2 persons and electricity	€ 20,00 - € 33,00
extra person	€ 5,50 - € 9,00
child (3-12 yrs)	€ 4,00 - € 6,40

Scarlino

Camping Butteri

I-58020 Scarlino (Tuscany) T: **056 654 006**. E: **info@riverbutteri.it**

alanrogers.com/IT66780

This is a sister site of Camping Baia dei Gabbiani (IT66770) and is closer to Follonica. The site is just 100 m. from the public beach and 15 minutes walk from the town centre. The 150 marked pitches are located beneath low trees and most have electrical connections. The site has a good range of leisure amenities including a restaurant, bar and supermarket. A varied activity and entertainment programme is organised in peak season, including activities for children. This is a suitable site for a reasonable overnight stay whilst travelling in the low season.

Facilities

Sanitary facilities include hot showers and provision for visitors with disabilities. Laundry facilities. Restaurant and bar. Shop and newsagent. Playground. Mountain bike hire. Entertainment and activity programme in high season. Miniclub. Chalets for rent. Off site: Nearest beach 100 m. Follonica 3 km. Siena, Florence and Pisa are all within 2 hours drive.

Open: 26 May - 25 August.

Directions

From Livorno take the southbound Via Aurelia (S1). Leave at Follonica Nord exit. Head initially towards Follonica and then towards Grosseto. Site is signed to left just as you begin to leave Follonica. GPS: 42.9111, 10.7736

Charges guide

Per person	€ 6,90 - € 11,70
child (3-7 yrs)	€ 5,20 - € 7,60
pitch incl. electricity	€ 9,70 - € 15,30

141

Siena

Camping Colleverde

Via Scacciapensieri 47, I-53100 Siena (Tuscany) T: 0577 332 545. E: info@campingcolleverde.com

alanrogers.com/IT66245

Camping Colleverde enjoys a panoramic setting overlooking the beautiful Tuscan city of Siena and the surrounding Chianti hills. The site re-opened in 2009 after a change of ownwership and extensive modernisation, and proprietor Andrea Sassolini and his family are on hand to ensure you have an enjoyable stay. Open for a long season, this is a good base for visiting Siena and the Chianti region. A bus stop is just 100 m. away and the railway station is 1.5 km. There are 221 pitches arranged on terraces, many with hardstanding and 97 with 10A electricity. On site facilities include a swimming pool, a pizzeria/restaurant, bar and a shop, all newly built in 2009. There are 25 mobile homes (which can be reserved for short stays). Siena needs little introduction and is undeniably one of Tuscany's finest medieval cities, famous for its Palio horse race and its fine cathedral. Colleverde is however also a good base for exploring other gems such as San Gimignano and other small towns such as Montepulciano and Montalcino. This is good country to explore on foot or by bike, and bike hire can be arranged by the site.

Facilities

Good sanitary units include facilities for disabled visitors. Laundry. Motorcaravan services. Shop. Bar. Restaurant and pizzeria. Swimming and paddling pools (June-Oct). Play area. WiFi (charged). Mobile homes for rent. Off site: City centre 2 km. Railway station 1.5 km. Chianti countryside. Cycle and walking tracks. Bicycle hire 3 km. Riding 10 km.

Open: 1 March - 31 December.

Directions

Site is north of the city. Approaching from the north, leave RA3 superstrada (Florence - Siena) at Siena Nord exit. Follow SR222 to Belverde and then turn right into the Toscana, then left into Via Nazareno Orlandi. Site is well signed and is the onoly campsite in Siena. GPS: 43.33771, 11.33048

Charges guide

Per unit incl. 2 persons	
and electricity	€ 30,20 - € 35,00
extra person	€ 9,50 - € 10,50
child (3-12 yrs)	€ 4,50 - € 5,50

Sovicille

Camping La Montagnola

Strada della Montagnola, I-53018 Sovicille (Tuscany) T: **057 731 4473**. E: **montagnolacamping@libero.it**
alanrogers.com/IT66250

An agreeable alternative to sites closer to the centre of Siena, La Montagnola is set in secluded woodland to the north of the village of Sovicille. The owners have worked hard to provide a good basic standard of amenities. There are 52 pitches which are of a good size (60-80 sq.m) and offer some privacy. Clearly marked and with shade, all are suitable for caravans and motorcaravans, all having electricity connections. However, there are just three water points on the site. There is a large wooded area and an overflow field for tents with no electricity and another field has a play area for children.

Facilities

A single toilet block provides free hot showers and mainly British style toilets – not luxurious, but adequate and clean. Small well stocked shop. Bar. Play area. Torches definitely required in tent areas. Off site: Large supermarket 6 km. (San Rocco a Pilli or Rosia), a small one 2 km. (Sovicille). Two restaurants in the village. Bus service to Siena.

Open: Easter - 30 September.

Directions

From north on Firenze - Siena motorway take Siena Ouest exit. Turn left on SS73 and at Malignano turn right towards Sovicille. Turn left just before mini roundabout. Site is 2 km. on the right. From south (Grosseto) take SS223 turn at crossroads to Rosia from where site is signed. GPS: 43.2811, 11.2199

Charges guide

Per person	€ 8,00
pitch incl. electricity	€ 8,00

Tirrenia

Camping Saint Michael

Via della Bigattiera 24, I-56018 Tirrenia (Tuscany) T: **050 33103**. E: **info@campingstmichael.com**
alanrogers.com/IT66085

Camping Saint Michael is quietly situated and lies in the middle of the Migliarino National Park and around 600 m. from a private sandy beach. Beneath the site's pine trees there are 160 pitches, mostly offering electrical connections. Separate areas have a range of accommodation to rent, including chalets and mobile homes. There is plenty to do here in high season with much activity focussed on the beach. There is also a children's club catering for different ages. Tirrenia is 2 km. distant and has all the amenities of a typical Italian resort. The Massaciuccoli National Park is very close and well worth a visit.

Facilities

Sanitary facilities are central and include British style WCs, open washbasins with cold water and controllable showers (charged). Facilities for disabled visitors and children. Laundry facilities. Shop for basics. Bar. Restaurant, pizzeria and takeaway meals. Play area. Multisport court. Children's club. Dogs are not accepted. Off site: Private beach 600 m. Swimming pool, tennis, riding, fishing and golf. Tirrenia 2 km. Cycle and walking trails.

Open: 1 June - 10 September.

Directions

Tirrenia is 12 km. north of Livorno. From the south, take SS224 to Tirrenia and continue towards Marina di Pisa. Site is 2 km. further north and is well signed. GPS: 43.64694, 10.295

Charges guide

Per person	€ 6,50 - € 8,00
child (3-12 yrs)	€ 5,50 - € 7,00
pitch incl. electricity	€ 9,50 - € 13,00

Torre del Lago

Camping Italia

Viale del Tigli 52, I-55048 Torre del Lago (Tuscany) T: **058 435 9828**. E: **info@campingitalia.net**
alanrogers.com/IT66260

This is a large site with a traditional Italian style that has benefited from the addition of a range of new facilities in 2009. There are 100 pitches for touring units which are set apart from 340 used by permanant units. The touring pitches are arranged informally with a degree of shade from mature trees and all pitches have a 5/10A electricity supply. There is some road noise to one side. The site has been owned by the Forti family since 1969 who have recently completed the construction of a modern restaurant and bar, a well-stocked small supermarket and new toilet facilities.

Facilities

One clean unisex toilet block is on the touring side supplemented by toilets in the new amenity block. All WCs are British style, showers are pushbutton on payment. Facilities for disabled visitors. Baby bath. Washing machines. Well stocked supermarket. Bar, restaurant with varied menu and pizzeria/takeaway. Swimming pool. Play area. TV in bar. Entertainment programme. Bicycle hire. Bungalows to rent. Site minibus to beach. Pets are only accepted in low season. Torches useful. Off site: Public transport 100 m. Riding and fishing 1 km. Golf 15 km.

Open: 20 April - 20 September.

Directions

Torre del Lago is on the west coast 15 km. north of Pisa. From A8 northbound leave at Viareggio exit, when heading south use Pisa North exit. Then take the S1 heading for Pisa. Continue towards the village of Torre del Lago where site is well signed. GPS: 43.81666, 10.26666

Charges guide

Per person	€ 4,50 - € 9,50
child (2-10 yrs)	€ 2,50 - € 5,00
pitch incl. electricity	€ 6,50 - € 11,50

143

Torre del Lago
Camping Europa
Viale dei Tigli, casella postale 115, I-55043 Torre del Lago Puccini (Tuscany) T: **058 435 0707**
E: **info@europacamp.it** **alanrogers.com/IT66060**

Europa is a large, flat, rectangular site with roads on all four sides of the site. There are 400 pitches in 17 rows, with the 136 touring pitches occupying six rows at the far end of the site. To reach these, you need to pass rows of very close together, well established permanent pitches and bungalows available for rent. The site's facilities including a bar, shop and air conditioned restaurant, are in rows five and six. The touring pitches are flat, very sandy and close together (55-70 sq.m). Some have shade from small trees or artificial cover and electricity (6A) is available. The pool (charged) and its separate paddling pool are near the site entrance and a jacuzzi is built into one end. The beach is a brisk 20 minute walk through a forest 1 km. away or a brisk 20 minute walk via a forest trail. A bicycle would be useful. However, there is a site minibus service to the beach and once there the sand is soft and the beach shelves gently into the water. Europa is conveniently situated for visiting many of the interesting places around such as Lucca, Pisa, Florence and the wealth of Puccini related historical items. The site has been owned by the Morescalchi family since 1967 and they are very keen that you have an enjoyable stay.

Facilities
Two sanitary blocks provide hot and cold showers (€ 0.40 token from reception). Toilets are mixed Turkish and British style. Facilities for disabled visitors. Laundry facilities. Cleaning goes on non-stop here. Motorcaravan service point outside gate. Bar/restaurant (air conditioned). Small shop. Good swimming pool (caps required). Large play area. Entertainment. Miniclub. Bicycle hire. Satellite TV. Internet access. Dogs are not accepted 3/7-24/8. Torches useful. Off site: Beach 1 km. Fishing. Golf 17 km. Riding 2 km.

Open: 4 April - 10 October.

Directions
From A11-12 to Pisa Nord take Viareggio exit. Turn south on Via Aurelia towards Pisa and then towards the sea for Marina di Torre Lago Puccini. Follow clear signs for site. GPS: 43.83083, 10.27055

Charges guide
Per person	€ 4,00 - € 8,50
child (2-10 yrs)	€ 2,50 - € 4,50
pitch	€ 8,50 - € 17,00
car	€ 4,00 - € 8,00
dog	€ 2,00

Troghi
Camping Il Poggetto
Via Il Poggetto 143, I-50067 Troghi (Tuscany) T: **055 830 7323**. E: **info@campingilpoggetto.com**
alanrogers.com/IT66110

This superb site has a lot to offer. It benefits from a wonderful panorama of the Colli Fiorentini hills with acres of the Zecchi family vineyards to the east adding to its appeal and is just 15 km. from Florence. The charming and hard working owners, Marcello and Daniella, come from a wine-producing background and you can purchase their fine wines at the site's shop. Their aim is to provide an enjoyable and peaceful atmosphere for families. All 106 pitches are of a good size and have electricity and larger units are welcome. On arrival you are escorted to view available pitches then assisted in taking up your chosen pitch. The restaurant offers excellent Tuscan fare including pizzas, pastas and delicate 'cucina casalinga' (home cooking). The locals also come here to eat. An attractive flower-bedecked terrace overlooks the two pools. Enjoy the typically Tuscan views and revel in the choice of Chianti from the region. A regular bus service runs directly from the site to the city. English is spoken at this delightful family site.

Facilities
Two spotless sanitary blocks with a mix of British and Turkish style WCs are a pleasure to use. Three private sanitary units for hire. Five very well equipped units for disabled campers. Separate facilities for children and baby room. Laundry facilities. Motorcaravan services. Gas supplies. Shop. Bar. Restaurant. Takeaway. Swimming pools and jacuzzi (1/5-30/9). Fitness room. Bicycle and scooter hire. Playground and entertainment for children all season. Excursions and organised trekking. Internet point. Off site: Tennis 100 m. Fishing 2 km. Golf 12 km. Bus service to the centre of Florence.

Open: 1 April - 15 October.

Directions
Exit A1 at Incisa southeast of Florence and turn right onto the SS69. After about 4 km. turn left following 'Pian dell Isola'. At next crossing turn right towards Firenze and follow the site signs. Do not use satellite navigation here as you may be taken into the steep and narrow streets of the nearby village. GPS: 43.7020, 11.41411

Charges 2010
Per unit incl. 2 persons and electricity	€ 28,50 - € 38,00
extra person	€ 7,50 - € 9,50
child (2-10 yrs)	€ 5,00 - € 6,50
dog	€ 2,00 - € 2,20

Vada

Camping Tripesce

Via Cavalleggeri 88, I-57016 Vada (Tuscany) T: **058 678 8167**. E: info@campingtripesce.it

alanrogers.com/IT66290

Neat and tidy, this family owned and run site has the great advantage of direct beach access through three gates (CCTV). The beach is of fine sand with very gentle shelving – super for children, with watersports and a lifeguard in season. This great beach makes up for the lack of a pool on the site and the fairly small size of the 230 pitches. All have 4A electricity and 60 are serviced with water and drainage with some shade provided by young trees and artificial shade. The site is contained within a rectangle and bungalows for rent are discreetly placed near reception. A pleasant bar with a terrace is alongside the small restaurant (limited but very reasonable menu), and just across the road is a well stocked shop. The play area is modern and pleasant but the slides end on gravel or concrete so children will need supervision. There is a small range of activities and a miniclub. Everything is kept spotlessly clean. The site has many German guests as demonstrated in the German language notices around the site. If you are a beach enthusiast this could be for you, especially the beachside pitches. This is a relaxing site without the razzmatazz of the larger sites along the coast and principally car-free.

Facilities

Three clean, fresh toilet blocks provide hot and cold showers (water is solar heated and free). British and Turkish style toilets. Facility for disabled visitors. Washing machines. Motorcaravan service points. Bar/restaurant and takeaway. Shop. Excellent beach. Aquarobics and aerobics (high season). Play area (supervision required). Miniclub (high season). Internet and WiFi. Fishing. Dogs are not accepted May - Sept. Off site: Bus service 300 m. Seaside town 1 km. Riding 5 km. ATM 1 km.

Open: 1 April - 17 October.

Directions

From S1 autostrada (free) between Livorno and Grosetto head south and take Vada exit. Site is well signed along with lots of others as you approach the town. GPS: 43.34301, 10.45825

Charges guide

Per person	€ 5,00 - € 8,00
child (0-7 yrs)	€ 3,00 - € 5,00
pitch incl. car and electricity	€ 10,00 - € 20,00
No credit cards.	

Check real time availability and at-the-gate prices...
www.alanrogers.com
145

Vada

Camping Baia del Marinaio

Via Cavalleggeri, 177, 57018 Vada (Tuscany) T: **058 677 0164**. E: **info@baiadelmarinaio.it**

alanrogers.com/IT66280

This well-run, family-owned site provides an inclusive holiday experience where all of your requirements are catered for without needing to set foot outside the campsite. The resident owner has overseen the development of the site to a high standard and first class leisure facilities are provided close to the magnificent pool complex. The site is split into sections with the 200 touring pitches positioned away from sections of 200 bungalows (50 of them are available to rent). Most of the fairly small pitches (60-70 sq.m) have good shade and 6A electricity is provided.

Facilities

Six toilet blocks, fitted out to a good standard, provide British style WCs, hot showers and washbasins. Laundry with washing machines. Good facilities for disabled visitors. Shop. Bar and restaurant. Large swimming pool complex with 30 m. water slide. Multisport court. Tennis courts. Bicycle hire. WiFi (charged). Bungalows for rent. Off site: Beach and beach fishing 500 m. Riding 2 km. Boat launching 5 km. Public transport from Vada 3 km.

Open: 25 April - 12 October.

Directions

From the S1/E80 take Cecina exit and follow road towards Vada. Site id well signed and is on the left side of the road towards Marina di Cecina. GPS: 43.33512, 10.461114

Charges guide

Per unit incl. 2 persons and electricity	€ 20,00 - € 37,00
extra person	€ 6,00 - € 10,00

Vada

Camping Molino a Fuoco

Via Cavalleggeri 32, I-57018 Vada (Tuscany) T: **058 677 0150**. E: **info@campingmolinoafuoco.com**

alanrogers.com/IT66420

This is a relatively small and quiet site with an attractively light and open feel. The 123 touring pitches are light and airy, with some natural shade. Motorcaravans are placed in pairs on very large 170 sq.m. shaded plots. Cars are parked away from the pitches in designated areas. Pleasant permanent pitches do not encroach on the touring units. This family owned site is part of the 'Tuscan For You' group and the Storace family will make you feel very welcome (they speak excellent English). The site is pristine and everything is spotlessly clean and smart. This is a great site for families.

Facilities

Three very clean toilet blocks provide British style WCs and good hot showers. Excellent facilities for disabled visitors. Baby bath and block for children with pretty showers and toilets. Washing machines. Bar, restaurant and pizzeria all with terraces. Swimming pool. Good play area. Bicycle hire. Watersports. Fishing. Entertainment programme in season. Miniclub. ATM. WiFi. Torches very useful. Dogs are not accepted 28/6-23/8. Bungalows to rent. Off site: Public transport 300 m. Riding and boat launching 2 km.

Open: 2 April - 16 October.

Directions

Site is south of Livorno and Vada. From the SS1 take Cecina exit and the site is well signed from here towards Marina di Cecina. GPS: 43.33201, 10.46062

Charges guide

Per unit incl. 2 persons and electricity	€ 19,30 - € 38,00
extra person	€ 4,90 - € 8,00
child (0-10 yrs)	€ 3,50 - € 5,50
dog (excl. 28/6-23/8)	€ 2,00

Vignale Riotorto

Camping Pappasole

Carbonifera 14, I-57025 Vignale Riotorto (Tuscany) T: **056 520 420**. E: **info@pappasole.it**

alanrogers.com/IT66400

This lively site offers an amazing array of services and activities and is located 250 metres from its own sandy beach facing the island of Elba. It is a large site on flat, fairly open ground offering 477 pitches, of which 427 are for touring units. The pitches are 90 sq.m. with electricity and water. They are separated by bushes with shade from mature trees and artificial shade in other areas. Some pitches have their own cosy individual sanitary facility and next to these a compartment with four burner gas stove, fridge and sink (extra cost for this about £5 per night). There may be some road or rail noise in certain parts. The excellent swimming pools in an open garden setting are a strong feature (the children's pool is huge).

Facilities

Four modern sanitary blocks have free hot water for washbasins and showers and British style WCs. Laundry facilities. Motorcaravan services. Gas supplies. Fridge hire. Supermarket. Hairdresser. Restaurant. Snacks. Bar. Swimming pools (23/5-17/10). Play area. Tennis. Bowls. Football. Watersports. Minigolf. Bicycle hire. Fishing. Medical services. Safety deposit boxes. Off site: Riding 5 km. Excursion programme (26/5-8/9).

Open: 3 April - 16 October.

Directions

Site is north of Follonica. From SS1 motorway take Follonica Nord exit onto SS322 and follow signs toward Piombino, not Follonica. After 1 km. turn east towards Torre Mozza. Site is 1.5 km. down this road to the north. GPS: 42.94893, 10.68630

Charges 2010

Per unit incl. 2 persons	€ 20,00 - € 56,50
extra person	€ 5,00 - € 13,00
child (3-9 yrs)	€ 3,50 - € 8,50

Check real time availability and at-the-gate prices...

www.alanrogers.com

Known as the 'Green Heart of Italy', Umbria is a beautiful region of rolling hills, woods, streams and valleys that gives way to high mountain wilderness. It is well known for the beauty and profusion of its medieval hilltowns.

UMBRIA HAS TWO PROVINCES: PERUGIA AND TERNI

Umbria's main attraction is the Vale of Spoleto and the hill towns of Spoleto and Assisi. The birthplace of Saint Francis, Assisi attracts vast numbers of art lovers and pilgrims throughout the year who visit his burial place, the Basilica di San Francesco, built in 1228 two years after his death. With a scenic woodland setting, Spoleto was once an important Roman colony. The town has the remains of a Roman amphitheatre, reputedly where ten thousand Christian martyrs were slaughtered, and a variety of Romanesque churches. It also boasts an impressive 14th-century aqueduct. Near Perugia, the regional capital, is Lake Trasimeno, the fourth largest lake in Italy. It has plenty of opportunities for fishing, swimming and watersports. The lakeside town of Castiglione del Lago is a good place to relax and unwind on the small sandy beaches; from here boats make regular trips to the Isola Maggiore, one of the lake's three islands. Further north is Gubbio, the most thoroughly medieval of all the Umbrian towns. A charming place full of twisting streets with soft-pink stone houses and terracotta-tiled rooftops, its beauty is enhanced by the forest-clad Apennines mountains looming up behind.

Places of interest

Deruta: town renowned for its ceramics.

Monte Cucco Regional Park: offers organised trails and outdoor activities.

Monti Sibillini: national park with good walking trails.

Norcia: mountain town, birthplace of St Benedict.

Orvieto: boasts one of the greatest Gothic churches in Italy.

Spello: renowned for frescoes in the 12th-13th-century church of Santa Maria Maggiore, Roman ruins.

Todi: striking hilltown, 13th century church and palaces.

Cuisine of the region

Simple pastas and roast meats are popular, especially pork and *la porchetta* (whole suckling pig stuffed with rosemary or sage, roasted on a spit). Truffles can be found in abundance, particularly in Noria, which also produces some of the country's best hams, sausages and salamis. The rivers yield fish such as eel, pike, trout and crayfish. Locally grown vegetables include lentils, beans, celery and cardoons. Good quality olive oil is readily available. Orvieto is a popular Umbrian white wine.

Agnello alla cacciatora: lamb with a sauce of anchovies, garlic and rosemary.

Crescionda: rich traditional cake prepared with almond biscuits, lemon rind and bitter chocolate.

Fichi: candied figs with almonds and cocoa.

Tartufo nero: black truffles.

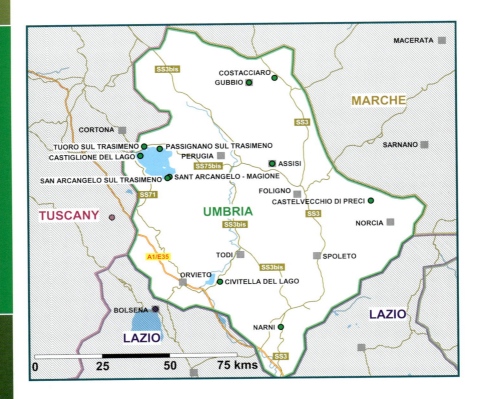

Assisi

Camping Village Assisi

San Giovanni in Campiglione 110, I-06081 Assisi (Umbria) T: **075 813 710**. E: **info@campingassisi.it**

alanrogers.com/IT66550

Camping Village Assisi is situated on the west side of Assisi and has high grade facilities which provide tourers with a good base to visit both Saint Francis' city and nearby Perugia and Lake Trasimeno. The 175 pitches are large and clearly marked on flat grass, all with electricity. There is shade as it can be very hot in this part of Italy, and a welcome relief is the site's pleasant, large pool. The city is lit up in the evenings to provide a beautiful backdrop from some areas in the site. The site is pleasantly out of the city bustle and heat and offers a regular shuttle bus service. The excellent restaurant has a large terrace which can be completely enclosed serving reasonably priced meals, ranging from pizzas to local Umbrian dishes. Finish off with a drink in the enjoyable bar which stays open a little later. Assisi boasts one of the finest cathedrals in Christendom, among many other attractions, and a stay in this area should not be cut too short. The site organises many tours in the area for individuals and groups, including artistic, religious, wine, food, archaeological and nature. In terms of value for money this is one of the cheapest sites we have seen in Northern Italy.

Facilities

The well appointed and clean toilet block has free hot showers, mainly Turkish style WCs (only four British style in each block) and facilities for disabled people. Washing machine. Gas supplies. Motorcaravan services. Campers' kitchen Restaurant/pizzeria with self-service section (closed Wednesdays). Bar with snacks. Shop. Swimming pool, jacuzzi and circular paddling pool (caps mandatory). Bicycle hire. Tennis. Off site: Riding 2 km. Fishing 3 km. Excursions to Assisi centre. Bus service to city three times daily from outside the site (one on Sundays except Easter).

Open: 1 April - 31 October.

Directions

Site is on the south side of the SS147, which branches left off SS75 Perugia - Foligno road. Follow Assisi signs and look for un-named camping sign going off left (downhill) as you enter the city. Site is 4 km. from the city. At Violi, just before Assisi, there is a warning of a low bridge of 3.3 m. – it is much higher at the centre of the curved bridge and even the highest units will pass through. GPS: 43.07510, 12.57440

Charges 2010

Per unit incl. 2 persons and electricity	€ 22,00 - € 38,00
extra person	€ 7,00 - € 10,00
child (3-9 yrs)	€ 4,00 - € 5,00
dog	€ 1,50 - € 2,00

Credit cards accepted for min. € 50.

Castelvecchio di Preci
Camping Il Collaccio

I-06047 Castelvecchio di Preci (Umbria) T: **074 393 9005**. E: **info@ilcollaccio.com**
alanrogers.com/IT66560

Castelvecchio di Preci is tucked away in the tranquil depths of the Umbrian countryside. The natural beauty of the Monti Sibillini National Park is nearby and there are walking and cycling opportunities with many marked paths. The camping area here has been carved out of the hillside and forms a natural amphitheatre with splendid views. At first sight the narrow, steep entrance seems daunting (the owner will assist) and the road leading down to the rather steep camping terraces takes one to the exit. The 114 large pitches are on level terraces with stunning views. Electricity (6A) is available – long leads useful.

Facilities
Three modern sanitary blocks spaced through the site have British and Turkish style WCs, cold water in washbasins and hot, pre-mixed water in showers and sinks. Facilities for disabled visitors. Washing machine. Motorcaravan services. Bar, restaurant and takeaway. Shop (basics, 1/6-20/9). Two swimming pools (20/5-30/9). Play area. Tennis. Boules. Entertainment in high season. Excursions. Off site: Cycling and walking. Canoeing and rafting 2 km. Fishing 10 km.

Open: 1 April - 30 September.

Directions
From SS77 Foligno-Civitonova Marche road turn south at Muccia for Visso from where Preci is signed. There is a direct route through a new tunnel, if the site is approached north of Eggi which is 10 km. north of Spoleto. The tunnel exit is at Sant Anatolia di Narco SS209, where a left turn is to Preci.
GPS: 42.888, 13.01464

Charges guide
Per person	€ 5,50 - € 8,50
caravan or motorcaravan	€ 6,50 - € 10,00
car	€ 2,00 - € 4,00

Castiglione del Lago
Camping Listro

Via Lungolago, I-06061 Castiglione del Lago (Umbria) T: **075 951 193**. E: **listro@listro.it**
alanrogers.com/IT66530

This is a simple, pleasant, flat site with the best beach on Lake Trasimeno. Listro provides 110 pitches all with electricity with 70% of the pitches enjoying the shade of mature trees. Younger campers are in a separate area of the site, ensuring no noise disturbance and some motorcaravan pitches are right on the lakeside giving stunning views out of your windows. Facilities are fairly limited with a small shop, bar and snack bar, and there is no organised entertainment. English is spoken and British guests are particularly welcome. If you enjoy the simple life and peace and quiet in camping terms then this site is for you. The campsite's beach is private and the lake has very gradually sloping beaches making it very safe for children to play and swim. This also results in very warm water, which is kept clean as fishing and tourism are the major industries hereabouts. Camping Listro is a few hundred yards north of the historic town of Castiglione and the attractive town can be seen rising up the hillside from the site.

Facilities
Two screened sanitary facilities are very clean with British and Turkish style WCs. Facilities for disabled visitors. Washing machine. Motorcaravan services. Bar. Shop. Snack bar. Play area. Fishing. Bicycle hire. Private beach. Off site: Town 800 m. Bars and restaurants nearby. Good swimming pool and tennis courts (discounts using the campsite card).

Open: 1 April - 30 September.

Directions
From A1/E35 Florence - Rome autostrada take Val di Chiana exit and join the Perugia (75 bis) superstrada. After 24 km. take Castiglione exit and follow town signs. Site is clearly signed just before the town.
GPS: 43.13333, 12.03983

Charges guide
Per person (over 3 yrs)	€ 4,10 - € 4,90
pitch	€ 4,10 - € 4,90
motorcycle or car	€ 1,10 - € 2,00
Less 10% for stays over 8 days in low season.	

Check real time availability and at-the-gate prices...
www.alanrogers.com

Castiglione del Lago

Camping Lido Trasimeno

Via Trasimeno 1, Piana, I-06061 Castiglione del Lago (Umbria) T: 075 965 9359. E: info@lidotrasimeno.com

alanrogers.com/IT66495

This small, quiet site is owned and run by a friendly Dutch family. It is located in the heart of the Trasimeno National Park on the banks of the Trasimeno lake. It offers 80 pitches (55 for touring units) under tall trees, some with views over Italy's fourth largest lake with its tranquil but melancholy beauty. A new small site with direct access to the sandy beach and the lake is planned to complement the existing site and its facilities should now be completed. The site is just five kilometres from the town of Castiglione del Lago, which juts out on a fortified promontory.

Facilities

A single clean, renovated sanitary block provides WCs, washbasins and showers. Facilities for disabled visitors. Washing machine and dryer. Bar and restaurant with internet access (WiFi planned). Swimming pool with sun deck with lake views, next to a small sandy beach. Bicycle hire. Umbrian cuisine workshop and live music in high season. Off site: Fishing, boating and riding. Golf 4 km. Castiglione del Lago.

Open: Easter - 30 September.

Directions

Site is north of Castiglione del Lago on the SS71 (Orvieto - Arrezo) close to the 106.3 km.marker and is between the road and the lake. From autostrada A1 take Val de Chiana exit and follow signs to Perugia then Castiglione del Lago. GPS: 43.14928, 12.02565

Charges guide

Per person	€ 6,00 - € 7,00
child	€ 5,00 - € 6,00
caravan and car or motorcaravan	€ 7,50 - € 9,50

Castiglione del Lago

Camping Badiaccia

Via Pratovecchio 1, I-06061 Castiglione del Lago (Umbria) T: 075 965 9097. E: info@badiaccia.com

alanrogers.com/IT66540

A lakeside site, Camping Badiaccia has excellent views of the surrounding hills and the islands of the lake. Being directly on the lake gives an almost seaside atmosphere – unusually they use a birdcage as the postbox! The 150 numbered pitches vary in size, some large, others smaller than average but there is good shade in most parts. All have electricity and are separated by trees and bushes in rows from hard access roads. Well tended and maintained, Badiaccia has a pleasant appearance enhanced by a variety of plants and flowers and English is spoken by the friendly staff. A very pleasant, large pool is by the restaurant and a children's pool is in the beach area.

Facilities

The two central sanitary blocks can be heated and are fully equipped. Washing machines and dryer. Motorcaravan services. Gas supplies. Restaurant, snack bar and shop. Fitness room. Health and well-being centre. Swimming pool and paddling pool (1/6-30/9). Play areas. Tennis. Boules. Minigolf. Watersports. Fishing. Boat hire. Entertainment and excursions in high season. Torches required in places. Boat trips around the lake. Off site: Riding 3 km. Golf 20 km.

Open: 1 April - 30 September.

Directions

From A1 (Milan - Rome) take Val di Chiana exit and turn east towards Perugia on SS75bis. At Castiglione exit take SS71 towards Castiglione. Site well signed 5 km. north of town. GPS: 43.18028, 12.01630

Charges guide

Per unit incl. 2 persons and electricity	€ 17,50 - € 24,50
extra person	€ 4.00 - € 7,50

Civitella del Lago

Camping Il Falcone

Località Vallonganino 2/a, I-05020 Civitella del Lago (Umbria) T: 074 495 0249. E: info@campingilfalcone.com

alanrogers.com/IT66485

This small 'eco-friendly' site provides just 36 pitches (half for motorcaravans and caravans) in a sloping olive grove with magnificent views across the valley below. The hilltop village of Civitella del Lago can be seen for miles around and is just 1 km. from the site. The friendly Valeri family will do all they can to make your stay peaceful and enjoyable. The terrace of the small bar is an ideal spot from which to watch the magnificent sunsets across Lago di Corbara and the countryside beyond. This is an excellent base from which to explore the Tuscany, Umbria and the Lazio regions.

Facilities

The single, well maintained sanitary block provides toilets, washbasins and showers and a separate room with sinks for clothes and dishwashing. Bar, shop and social room (with TV) are next to reception. Off site: Orveito, Civitella del Lago and the Lago di Corbara.

Open: 1 April - 30 September.

Directions

From Orvieto take the SR205 then the SS448 towards Todi. Just past 4 km. marker on the SS448 turn right on the S90 up towards the hilltop town of Civitella del Lago. Go past the village, about 6 km. up the hill, and bear right. Site is about 1 km. further along on the right. GPS: 42.70417, 12.28833

Charges guide

Per person	€ 5,10 - € 6,20
child (3-10 yrs)	€ 4,10 - € 5,20
pitch with vehicle	€ 7,00 - € 9,20

Check real time availability and at-the-gate prices...

www.alanrogers.com

Costacciaro

Camping Rio Verde

SS3 Flaminia km 206.5, I-06021 Costacciaro (Umbria) T: 075 917 0138. E: info@campingrioverde.it

alanrogers.com/IT66470

This is a quiet, simple campsite located in a wooded valley with plenty of shade during the day. There are 50 informally arranged pitches with 6A electricity possible. Some pitches are a little uneven and the site slopes in parts. Amenities include a small, fenced swimming pool (with lifeguard) and a restaurant serving simple food from the region. This site is ideal for outdoor activity enthusiasts. Siglio hosts the World Hang-gliding and Parascending Championships in July each year and there are permanent launch sites at the top of nearby Monte Cucco and facilities for getting to the top in the village.

Facilities

A large, recently built toilet block is a short walk. Facilities include British and Turkish style toilets and free showers. Facilities for disabled visitors (key from reception). Small shop. Restaurant. Swimming pool (5 x 15 m). Games room. Play areas. Wooden chalets for rent. Off site: Riding nearby.

Open: 25 April - 30 September.

Directions

From Via Flaminia SS3, follow brown camping signs which can be seen in all surrounding towns.
GPS: 43.35026, 12.68398

Charges guide

Per person	€ 5,00 - € 7,50
child (1-12 yrs)	€ 3,50 - € 5,00
pitch incl. car	€ 5,00 - € 10,00

Gubbio

Camping Villa Ortoguidone – Citta di Gubbio

Fraz. Cipolleto, 49 - Ortoguidone, I-06024 Gubbio (Umbria) T: 075 927 2037. E: info@gubbiocamping.com

alanrogers.com/IT66570

This is a site with a difference, just 3 km. from the walls of the fabulous old city of Gubbio. Surrounded by fields of sunflowers and corn, it has been constructed on an old farm. The family have owned the farm for over 135 years and the old villa is now used for guest accommodation. There are 14 excellent large pitches in the grounds of the villa (book ahead for these) and 100 serviced pitches in a new, flat area where young trees are beginning to provide some shade. This is an environmentally aware site where campers are encouraged to use free solar heated water.

Facilities

Two cane covered prefabricated units (in sympathy with the surroundings) provide excellent sanitary facilities with British and Turkish style toilets and facilities for disabled campers. Solar heating throughout. Washing machines. Motorcaravan service point. Snack bar. Swimming pools, paddling pool and spa (July/Aug). Fitness area by the pool. Basic play area. Tennis. Off site: River fishing 500 m. Restaurants, bars and shops 3 km. Riding 5 km. Golf 30 km.

Open: 1 April - 19 September.

Directions

From A1 take Orte exit and the E45 towards Perugia and Cesena, then Bosco Gubbio exit. Take SS298 to Gubbio and follow camping signs (site signs change from brown to white with 'Agriclub Villa Ortoguidon').
GPS: 43.3217, 12.5683

Charges guide

Per person	€ 6,50 - € 9,50
child (2-8 yrs)	€ 5,50 - € 7,00
pitch	€ 7,00 - € 11,00
electricity	€ 3,00

Narni

Camping Monti del Sole

Strada di Borgaria 22, Borgaria, I-05035 Narni (Umbria) T: 074 479 6336. E: info@campingmontidelsole.it

alanrogers.com/IT66480

Monti del Sole is a very friendly site situated in woodland, just 5 km. from the medieval town of Narni. Alfredo Petrini and his daughter will give you a very warm welcome. There are 85 medium-sized pitches, all of which have electrical connections (6A). Most are well shaded and grassy and a number are on slight terraces. A small shop sells basics and a bar/restaurant offers local cuisine. The attractive swimming pools are kept in very good condition. Prices here are reasonable but the facilities are fairly limited. Narni has much of interest, not least the underground rooms beneath the old monastery of San Domenico which include a cell used by the Inquisition and decorated with prisoners' graffiti.

Facilities

The modern sanitary block has a mixture of British and Turkish style toilets, and is well maintained. Motorcaravan service point. Small bar/restaurant (1/6-30/8). Swimming pool and adjacent paddling pool (1/6-30/8). Play area. Tennis court. Games field. Woodland walks. Off site: Riding 1 km. Fishing 4 km. Narni 5 km. Marmore falls and Piediluco lake both 20 km. Assisi, Perugia and Rome all around 80 km.

Open: 1 April - 30 September.

Directions

From the A1 (Rome - Florence - Milan) autostrada take Magliano Sabina exit. Follow signs to Narni. Site is on Borgaria road, 800 m. off the SS3.
GPS: 42.48306, 12.50389

Charges guide

Per person	€ 6,50 - € 7,50
child	€ 3,50 - € 4,50
pitch including electricity	€ 5,50 - € 7,50

Passignano sul Trasimeno
Camping Kursaal Hotel

Via Europa 24, I-06065 Passignano sul Trasimeno (Umbria) T: 075 828 085. E: info@campingkursaal.it

alanrogers.com/IT66500

Opened in 1965, Camping Kursaal is the oldest campsite at Lago Trasimeno. Located directly beside the lake, it is a small site with 65 touring pitches. The campsite forms part of grounds of a good quality hotel and camping visitors may use the hotel amenities including the bar, lounge and the excellent restaurant. Attractively laid out under tall pines (said to be about 80 years old) the pitches are fairly small (70-90 sq.m) but all have 6A electricity and shade from shrubs and the trees. Many have good views over the lake and our suggestion is to try to book one of these lakeside pitches!

Facilities

Two toilet blocks have showers and toilets in separate areas are very clean and well maintained. One is built around an old pine tree which avoided it having to be felled. Bar. Restaurant. Shop. Swimming and paddling pools. Whirlpool. Private beach with free hot showers. New swimming pool with area for children. Jacuzzi. Internet point. Off site: Passignano 1 km.

Open: 1 April - 31 October.

Directions

On the A1 (Firenze - Rome)take exit at Valdichiana - Bettolle). Follow until Passignano Est exit (30 km. from the A1 exit) and turn right and site is 200 m. on the left. GPS: 43.18354, 12.15063

Charges guide

Per unit incl. 2 persons	€ 20,00 - € 26,00
child (4-10 yrs)	€ 5,00 - € 6,00
child (0-4 yrs)	€ 2,00
electricity	€ 2,00

Passignano sul Trasimeno
Camping Village Europa

Localitá San Donato 8, I-06065 Passignano sul Trasimeno (Umbria) T: 075 827 405. E: info@camping-europa.it

alanrogers.com/IT66430

The shores of Lake Trasimeno are dotted with a large number of campsites but we feel that Camping Village Europa has something different to offer. This is a high quality friendly site which, with just 100 pitches, is relatively small but which still manages to offer a wide range of amenities. The pitches are separated into four groups by clusters of mature trees, although shade on the pitches is quite limited. All the pitches offer 6A electrical connections. A regular bus service links the site with the nearby town of Passignano and its railway station. On-site amenities include a small pool, bar, restaurant, pizzeria and well-stocked shop.

Facilities

The three toilet blocks include facilities for disabled users. Washing machines and dryers. Shop. Bar, restaurant, pizzeria and takeaway. Small pool. Play area. Children's club. Evening entertainment. Sports pitch. Direct access to lake and beach. Bicycle hire. Off site: Passignano 2 km. Perugia 30 km. Assisi 45 km. Riding, tennis, watersports.

Open: Easter - 10 October.

Directions

From Passignano take the road towards Perugia. Turn off this road after 1 km. and the site is clearly signed. GPS: 43.181695, 12.165384

Charges 2010

Per unit incl. 2 persons and electricity	€ 17,50 - € 23,70
extra person	€ 5,50 - € 6,70
child (3-10 yrs)	€ 4,30 - € 5,30

Check real time availability and at-the-gate prices...

www.alanrogers.com

Passignano sul Trasimeno

Camping La Spiaggia

Via Europa 22, I-06065 Passignano sul Trasimeno (Umbria) T: **075 827 246**. E: **info@campinglaspiaggia.it**
alanrogers.com/IT66460

This recently opened site has its own beach and is pleasantly covered with pine and oak trees to provide lots of shade. The 50 spacious pitches are clearly defined and separated by dwarf hedges with 6A electricity available. This is an attractive, compact site which is well managed and cared for. A small café/restaurant has a terrace overlooking the lake and a small shop provides fresh bread to order. All sorts of activities are possible on the lake including canoeing, sailing and windsurfing and there are numerous possibilities for hiking or mountain biking in the surrounding hills.

Facilities

The new toilet block is very clean and modern with free hot water, It includes facilities for disabled visitors and a baby room. Separate laundry room. Small shop. Bar/restaurant with terrace. Lake swimming. Play area. Bicycle hire. Off site: Restaurant in front of camping. New swimming pool 100 metres with discount for campers.

Open: 22 March - 11 October.

Directions

From A1 (Firenze - Roma) take Beltolle exit towards Perugia (S326). Follow this to Passignano exit (30 km. from the A1). Take the exit and go towards town (site signed). GPS: 43.188883, 12.149717

Charges guide

Per person	€ 6,00 - € 7,00
child (3-10 yrs)	€ 4,00 - € 5,50
pitch	€ 6,00 - € 9,00
car	€ 2,50

San Arcangelo sul Trasimeno

Kawan Village de Polvese

I-06060 San Arcangelo sul Trasimeno (Umbria) T: **075 848 078**. E: **cpolvese@interfree.it**
alanrogers.com/IT66510

Beside the lake, Polvese takes its name from the island which can be seen clearly from the site. The 80 tourist pitches (all with 6/10A electricity) are in two areas, generally separated from the very permanent pitches rented by Italian and German guests. We see this as a site for short visits rather than extended stays. On flat ground, the older pitches are reasonably sized, with some by the lake. Mature trees provide good shade. Children have a shallow pool in which to play and the adult pool is clean and pleasant. The restaurant, which is run as a separate business, has lake views and a pleasant terrace.

Facilities

Modernised sanitary block with free hot showers. British and Turkish style toilets and cold water at all the sinks. Facilities for disabled campers. Washing machine. Motorcaravan service point. Restaurant (not owned by site). Basic bar which doubles as shop. TV. Outdoor cinema (basic). Swimming pool. Bicycle hire. Miniclub. Barbecue area. Torches required. Off site: Riding 2 km. Golf (8-hole) 5 km.

Open: 1 April - 1 October.

Directions

Site is on south side of Lake Trasimino. From Florence - Rome autostrada take Magione exit and lakeside road south to San Arcangelo. Site is well signed. GPS: 43.08145, 12.14314

Charges guide

Per person	€ 5,00 - € 6,00
child (3-10 yrs)	€ 3,50 - € 4,50
pitch and car	€ 6,00 - € 8,00
animal	€ 2,00
Camping Cheques accepted.	

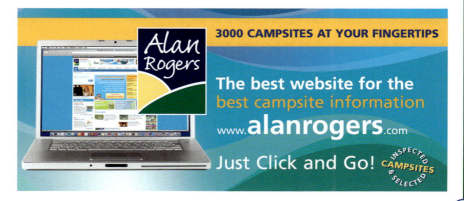

Sant Arcangelo – Magione

Camping Villaggio Italgest

Via Martiri di Cefalonia, I-06063 Sant Arcangelo - Magione (Umbria) T: **075 848 238**
E: **camping@italgest.com alanrogers.com/IT66520**

Directly on the shore on the south side of Lake Trasimeno, which is almost midway between the Mediterranean and the Adriatic, Sant Arcangelo is ideally placed for exploring Umbria and Tuscany. The area around the lake is fairly flat but has views of the distant hills and can become very hot during summer. Villaggio Italgest is a pleasant site with 208 touring pitches on level grass and, except for the area next to the lake, under a cover of tall trees. All pitches have electricity and cars are parked away from the pitches. The site offers a wide variety of activities and daily tours. There is entertainment in high season, including Italian language and civilisation courses. The bar/disco remains open until 02.00 hrs. There is a good sized swimming pool area, one pool with slides, a smaller paddling pool and a whirlpool. The site has a marina for boats with a crane. Whether you wish to use this site as a base for exploration or as a place to relax, you will find this a most pleasant place to stay. English is spoken.

Facilities

The one large and two smaller sanitary blocks have mainly British style WCs and free hot water in the washbasins and showers. Facilities for disabled people. Motorcaravan services. Washing machines and dryers. Kitchen. Bar, restaurant, pizzeria and takeaway (all season). Shop. Recently enlarged Swimming pool. Tennis. Play area. TV (satellite) and games rooms. Disco. Films. Watersports, motorboat hire and lake swimming. Fishing. Mountain bike and scooter hire. Internet point. Wide range of activities, entertainment and excursions. Off site: Golf, parachuting, riding, canoeing and sailing close.

Open: 1 April - 30 September.

Directions

Site is on the southern shore of Lake Trasimeno. From the Perugia spur of the Florence - Rome autostrada, take Magione exit and proceed southwest round lake to Sant Arcangelo where site is signed. GPS: 43.08633, 12.15383

Charges guide

Per unit incl. 2 persons	
and electricity	€ 18,00 - € 28,50
extra person	€ 6,00 - € 8,50
child (3-9 yrs)	€ 4,00 - € 6,50
dog	€ 2,00 - € 2,50

Camping Cheques accepted.

Camping & Village ★★★★
VILLAGGIO ITALGEST
LAKE TRASIMENO
camping@italgest.com • www.italgest.com
GPS: Latit. 43°05'18" Longit. 12°09'23"

PETS ADMITTED
MOBILE HOMES WITH AIR-COND
NEW SWIMMINGPOOL

At the shores of Lake Trasimeno, immersed in the green heart of typical Mediterranean trees, in front of the biggest of the 3 islands of the lake and on the border of the naturalistic oasis "La Valle" rises Camping Villaggio Italgest. At 500 m of the inhabited center of Sant'Arcangelo, the turistic complex, with it's facilities with lake stars classification, extends an area of 55.000 sqm. De campsite is located directly at the lake, **on the border between Umbria and Tuscany**, within the Lake Trasimeno Nature Park. Comfort, convenience and fun make it ideal for family vacations. Its geographic location makes it an excellent base for trips to art cities such as Rome, Florence, Siena, Perugia, Assisi and Orvieto, as nature areas and places in Umbria and Tuscany known for their food and wines. During activities and games are offered in English, with kids'club (also during Pentecost).

Tuoro sul Trasimeno

Camping Punta Navaccia

I-06069 Tuoro sul Trasimeno (Umbria) T: **075 826 357**. E: **navaccia@camping.it**
alanrogers.com/IT66490

Situated on the north side of Lake Trasimeno and run by friendly and welcoming owners, this is a large site with over 70,000 sq.m. and 400 touring pitches (200 with 4A electricity) and all with shade. The campsite has a long (stony) beach with facilities for mooring and launching your boat. There are 60 mobile homes with air conditioning for rent. The site is ideally located for exploring Umbria and its famous cities, such as Assisi and Perugia. Tuscany and its cities of Siena and Florence are also within easy reach and it is even possible to visit Rome for a day trip.

Facilities

Sanitary block with British style WCs, showers and some private cabins. Washing machine and dryer. Motorcaravan service point. Heated swimming and paddling pools. Shop. Restaurant and takeaway (April-Oct). Play area. Tennis. Covered amphitheatre. Disco. Cinema screen. Miniclub. Entertainment is organised in high season. Boat launching. Daily boat trip around island (free). Off site: Sandy beach 200 m. Windsurfing, sailing and canoeing 200 m.

Open: 15 March - 31 October.

Directions

Going south on the A1 (Florence/Firenze - Rome), take exit for Val di Chiana to Perugia near Bettolle. After 15 km. take Tuoro sul Trasimeno exit. Site is well signed. GPS: 43.19191, 12.07665

Charges guide

Per unit incl. 2 persons	
	€ 19,00 - € 26,00
extra person	€ 6,00 - € 8,50
child (2-9 yrs)	€ 4,00 - € 6,00

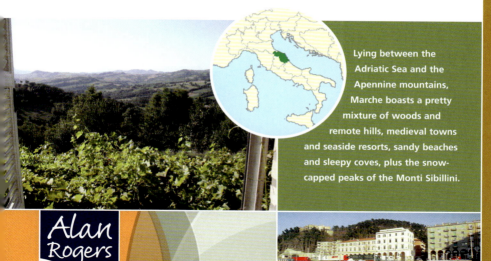

Lying between the Adriatic Sea and the Apennine mountains, Marche boasts a pretty mixture of woods and remote hills, medieval towns and seaside resorts, sandy beaches and sleepy coves, plus the snow-capped peaks of the Monti Sibillini.

THERE ARE FOUR PROVINCES IN MARCHE: ANCONA, ASCOLI PICENO, MACERATA AND PESARO E URBINO

Marche is not as well known or publicised as other regions but despite that it has plenty to offer. The medieval town of Urbino with its spectacular Renaissance palace is one of the highlights, as is Ascoli Piceno, which also boasts a medieval heritage, various churches and an enchanting town square. The dramatic fortress at San Leo is considered to be one of the best, while nearby San Marino is Europe's oldest republic. A tiny area with no customs regulations, its borders are just seven miles apart at its widest point. The republic has its own mint, an army and produces its own postage stamps. South of Ancona, the regional capital, and overlooked by the dramatic white cliffs of Monte Cónero is the Cónero Riviera, an impressive stretch of coast with small beaches, coves and picturesque little resorts, including Portonovo, Sirolo and Numana. Along the coast is Loreto, one of Italy's most popular pilgrimage destinations, and more beaches can be found at San Benedetto del Tronto. Further inland near the Verdicchio wine-producing hilltop villages around Jesi, is the Grotte di Frasassi, one of Europe's largest accessible cave networks. And the mountainous region of Monti Sibillini in the south offers good walking trails and stunning views.

Places of interest

Ancona: regional capital and Adriatic's largest port.

Fano: beach resort with old centre and historic monuments.

Jesi: medieval town walls, Renaissance and Baroque palaces.

Macerata: university town surrounded by lovely countryside, famous for its annual outdoor opera and ballet festival.

Numana: seaside resort on Córnero peninsula, boat trips to the offshore islets of Due Sorelle.

Sarnano: spa town.

Urbania: palace with art gallery and museum.

Ússita: winter sports resort.

Cuisine of the region

The food is a mix of seafood along the coastline and country cooking inland, involving locally grown produce – tomatoes, fennel and mushrooms. Typical seafood dishes include *zuppa di pesce* (fish soup with saffron) and *brodetto* (fish broths). Rabbit and lamb is popular plus *porchetta* (roast suckling pig). The region is best known for its Verdicchio wine although it does produce a variety of others.

Coniglio in porchetta: rabbit cooked with fennel.

Cicercchiata: balls of pasta fried and covered in honey.

Olive ascolane: olives stuffed with meat and herbs, served with *crema fritta*, little squares of fried cream.

Vincisgrassi: baked pasta dish with ham and truffles.

155

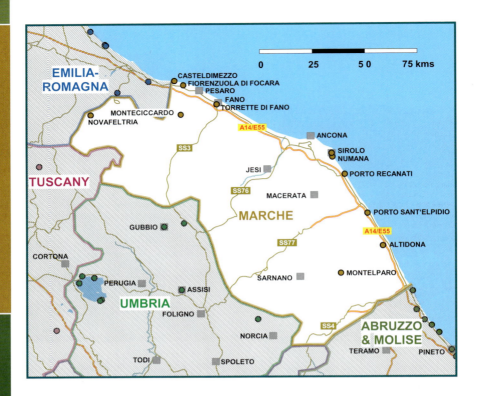

Altidona

Centro Vacanze Riva Verde

Via Aprutina 75, I-63017 Altidona (Marche) T: **073 493 2012**. E: **rivaverde@camping.it**

alanrogers.com/IT65240

An extremely well run site, Riva Verde offers everything a camper could require. The site stretches 1.5 km. beside the Adriatic with a shuttle bus service to combat the steep terraced roads. There are 450 small pitches with 420 for touring (electricity 6A), shaded by mature trees and with views over the Adriatic. Many have private bath facilities. A large aqua park provides slides, swimming pools and children's pools, all surrounded by a sunbathing area. All the pitches are terraced above the road and railway thus reducing ambient noise. Access to the site is via a tunnel, so difficult for large units.

Facilities

Eight well equipped and maintained toilet blocks with all necessary facilities including for those with disabilities. Pitches available with private washbasin or bathroom. Bar, restaurant, takeaway, pizzeria. Shops. Swimming pool complex (fee charged). Solarium. Disco. Games/TV room. Tennis. Minigolf. Dogs and other animals are not accepted. Off site Fishing 1 km. Bicycle hire 2 km. Sailing, boat launching 5 km. Riding 10 km. Golf 12 km. Pedaso 2 km. Porto San Giorgio 6 km.

Open: 22 May - 11 September.

Directions

From A14 exit Fermo and Porto San Giorgio follow A16 Adriatico south to Molinetto. Site is signed from Molinetto and is on the right.
GPS: 43.12389, 13.82944

Charges guide

Per person	€ 3,00 - € 10,00
child (2-6 yrs)	€ 2,50 - € 5,00
pitch	€ 6,00 - € 25,00
electricity (6A)	€ 3,00
Long stay low season offers.	

Casteldimezzo
Camping Paradiso
Via Rive del Faro 2, I-61010 Casteldimezzo (Marche) T: 072 120 8579. E: info@campingparadiso.it
alanrogers.com/IT65060

Camping Paradiso is quite close to Pesaro, home of Rossini (annual concerts held in August). The site is quite simple but well maintained and is a tranquil base to avoid August's beach crowds, although with easy access to some of the region's best beaches and the nightlife in nearby Gabicce Mare. The site is located on a hilltop in San Bartolo Natural Park. There are 100 touring pitches (most with electrical connections) which are of a good size and well shaded with a fine variety of different trees. The site also has a number of wooden chalets to rent.

Facilities
Centrally located toilet block. Motorcaravan services. Bar, snack bar. Play area. Tourist information. Off site: Nearest town is Gabicce Mare 6 km. with bars, shops and restaurants. Supermarket 13 km. Mountain biking and walking. Excursions to Pesaro 13 km. Rimini 26 km. Urbino 35 km.

Open: 1 March - 31 December.

Directions
Take the Cattolica exit from the A14 motorway (Bologna - Taranto) and join SS16 southbound towards Gabicce Mare. Here join the coast road (Strada Panoramica) towards Casteldimezzo and you will reach the site beyond Gabbice Monte and before reaching Casteldimezzo. GPS: 43.959733, 12.803883

Charges guide
Per person	€ 5,00 - € 8,50
pitch	€ 7,00 - € 11,50
electricity	€ 2,20

Fiorenzuola di Focara
Camping Panorama
Strand Panorama, I-61010 Fiorenzuola di Focara (Marche) T: 072 120 8145. E: info@campingpanorama.it
alanrogers.com/IT65070

Camping Panorama is a peaceful site located on a scenic coastal drive within a small national park (Parco del San Bartolo) and quite close to the delightful town of Pesaro. The site lies 100 metres above the sea and a pleasant path leads to the beach below. There are 150 pitches ranging in size from 45-100 sq.m. Most have electrical connections (6A) and all are well shaded. Leisure amenities include an attractive swimming pool (with smaller children's pool) and a sports court. This is a largely undeveloped area and has many opportunities for walking and mountain biking.

Facilities
Centrally located toilet block. Swimming pool and children's pool. Bar, pizzeria. TV room. Play area. Sports court. Tourist information. Off site: Nearest village is Fiorenzuola di Focara 2 km, a pretty village perched over the sea with bars, shops and restaurants. Pesaro 6 km. San Marino 42 km. Urbino 50 km. Mountain biking and walking. Riding 10 km. Golf 8 km. Fishing 0.5 km. Bicycle hire 6 km.

Open: 21 April - 30 September.

Directions
From A14 (Bologna - Taranto) take Cattolica exit and join SS16 southbound towards Siligata. Here join the coast road (Strad Panoramico) towards Fionenzuola. Site is beyond this town and Fiorenzuola di Focara and before reaching Pesaro. GPS: 43.941683, 12.84585

Charges guide
Per unit incl. 2 persons and electricity	€ 25,00 - € 35,00
extra person	€ 4,00 - € 9,00
No credit cards.	

Monteciccardo
Camping Podere Sei Poorte
Via Petricci 14, I-61020 Monteciccardo (Marche) T: 072 191 0286. E: info@podereseipoorte.it
alanrogers.com/IT65080

Podere Sei Poorte is run by a friendly Dutch family who promise 'a combination of culture, nature and simple enjoyment'. Hans and Sietske Poorte are experienced campsite owners and understand how to create the perfect environment for their guests. On arrival you will be welcomed with a drink on the comfortable terrace and the restaurant offers good, Italian style food. The site is laid out on two terraces so everyone has good views. With 80 large pitches (70 for touring units), the spacious pitches are almost flat on good grass, with or without shade. To reach the sanitary block a little uphill or downhill walking is required.

Facilities
One main block near the house and 8 smaller ones around the site are modern and tiled with free hot water. Facilities for disabled visitors. Motorcaravan service point. Shop. Bar and restaurant. Swimming pool (8 x 16 m; 1/5-15/10). Play area. Off site: Beach 25 minutes by car.

Open: April - 31 October.

Directions
From St Angelo in Lizzola (inland from Pesaro and the A14) follow the SP26 to Mombaroccio. Turn at Villa Ugolini (Fraz. di Monteciccardo) into Via Petricci. Site is 1.4 km. on the right. GPS: 43.8009, 12.82113

Charges guide
Per unit incl. 2 persons and electricity	€ 23,00 - € 33,00
extra person	€ 5,00 - € 8,00

Montelparo
Agricamp PicoBello
Contrada Cortaglie 24, I-63020 Montelparo (Marche) T: 073 478 9012. E: info@agricamppicobello.com
alanrogers.com/IT65260

Situated only 28 km. inland from the Adriatic coast at Pedaso, this very small site caters for campers who like to go back to basics. Catering only for tents, the site offers up to 18 pitches, some with shade. There is a hammock house in the central area where campers rig their hammocks in a shady and peaceful spot. Rob and his wife are keen outdoor people and are very enthusiastic about keeping the spirit of true camping aflame. Rob will be your guide for hiking tours to the Sibillini mountains. A relaxing campsite for the purist camper away from the hectic atmosphere of some of the coastal sites.

Facilities
The central toilet block is well maintained and very clean. Small bar. Small kitchen and social area for preparing light meals with fridge space. Dogs are not accepted. Off site: Lively little village with shops, bars, café, supermarket 3.5 km. Riding 5 km. Fishing 15 km.

Open: 1 April - 15 October.

Directions
From the A14 take exit for Pedaso. Follow the SS443 towards Amandola, just after Oretezzano follow signs to the right to site (well signed). GPS: 43.02730, 13.55643

Charges guide
Per person	€ 5,50 - € 6,50
child (up to 12 yrs)	€ 3,00 - € 4,00
pitch	€ 7,50 - € 9,00
Electricity by arrangement (3A).	

Numana
Numana Blu Camping Village
Via Costaverde 37, I-60026 Numana (Marche) T: 071 739 0993. E: info@numanablu.it
alanrogers.com/IT66190

Numana Blu lies on the Conero Riviera, south of Ancona, just 300 m. from the sea, and close to the town of Marcelli. Beneath the site's 12,000 trees there are 380 shady pitches, most offering electrical connections. Separate areas have a range of rentable accommodation, including chalets and bungalows. There's plenty to do here but the site retains a relaxed atmosphere. In peak season there are several children's clubs catering for different ages. The site also boasts an impressive array of leisure amenities including a large swimming pool, a restaurant/pizzeria and supermarket. This is a friendly site with multilingual reception staff. The beach is a short walk and offers private facilities. Numana is less than a kilometre away and has all the amenities of a typical Italian resort. The Sirolo National Park is very close and well worth a visit.

Facilities
Supermarket. Bar, restaurant/pizzeria and takeaway meals. Swimming pool and children's pool. Playground. Bicycle hire. Football pitch. Tennis. Children's clubs. Entertainment programme in high season. Off site: Beach 300 m. Conero Riviera, Monte Conero (at 572 m. the highest peak in the area) and Ancona. Riding 1 km. Cycle and walking trails. Golf 6 km.

Open: 24 April - 30 September.

Directions
From the A14 autostrada take the Loreto Porto Recanati exit and follow signs to Numana. Site is south of Numana, 1.5 km. from the small town of Marcelli. GPS: 43.49806, 13.62306

Charges guide
Per unit incl. 2 persons and electricity	€ 22,50 - € 45,40
extra person	€ 4,50 - € 9,50
child (under 7 yrs)	€ 2,80 - € 6,90
dog	€ 2,00

Check real time availability and at-the-gate prices...
www.alanrogers.com

Novafeltria
Camping Perticara
Via Serra Masini 10/d, Perticara, I-61015 Novafeltria (Marche) T: 054 192 7602
E: info@campingperticara.com alanrogers.com/IT66170

High in the Marche hills, not far from San Marino, Ravenna and Rimini, is Camping Perticara, a brand new, purpose-built camping site with glorious views across a valley to the mountains and the nearby traditional village of Perticara. Its 80 pitches have water and drainage and are very large, all arranged on terraces to take advantage of the fabulous scenery. Good sized trees have been planted to provide shade in the future. The shop, bar and restaurant area is attractively presented, with a terrace overlooking the swimming pool which shares the incredible vistas.

Facilities
Two immaculate modern units provide really excellent facilities with all the extras. Facilities are all in large luxury cabins with shower, toilet and basin. Units for disabled campers are of the same standard. Washing machine and dryers. Gas. Small shop. Restaurant (limited menu but good value). Snack bar. Swimming and paddling pools. Small play areas. Animation (miniclub) in high season. Torches useful. Off site: Fishing 10 km. Golf 25 km.

Open: 8 May - 20 September.

Directions
After Bologna on the A1 take A14 towards Ancona and exit for Rimini Nord. After 200 m. turn right (San Leo), over five roundabouts (San Leo and Montefeltro). At traffic lights turn right to Novafeltria (32 km). At Novafeltria, 400 m. after lights, turn right towards Perticara. Climb for 7 km. (under 12%) and at top turn left towards Santa Agata Feltria. After 400 m. turn right to site. GPS: 43.88350, 12.28340

Charges 2010
Per unit incl. 2 persons	
and electricity	€ 22,00 - € 34,00
extra person	€ 5,50 - € 9,00
child (4-12 yrs)	€ 3,50 - € 6,00

Porto Recanati
Camping Bellamare
Lungomare Scarfiotti 13, I-62017 Porto Recanati (Marche) T: 071 976 628. E: info@bellamare.it
alanrogers.com/IT65180

Situated on the Conero Riviera, just south of the river Musone, this site is ideal for campers who enjoy a well ordered and efficiently run site. The grounds are maintained to a meticulous standard. Unlike most sites along the 'Lungomare Adriatico', it does not suffer from either train or motorway noise. There are 400 flat, grassy pitches which are separated by maturing trees offering some shade in an area separate from the static units, some being quite small. Most beach holiday activities are provided on site or within easy walking distance.

Facilities
Large very clean central toilet block with two smaller blocks having mainly Turkish style toilets. Free cold showers, hot showers need electronic key supplied on registration. Shop, bar, restaurant, takeaway. Swimming and paddling pools (1/6-1/9). TV/games room. Play areas. Football. Bicycle hire. Organised family activities (high season). Dogs are not accepted. Off site: Fishing, sailing 2 km. Riding 3 km. Golf 5 km.

Open: 25 April - 30 September.

Directions
From A14 take exit for Porto Recanati. Follow beach road (Recanati - Porto Recanati) towards Numana. Site is well signed in both directions. GPS: 43.47095, 13.6412

Charges guide
Per person	€ 4,50 - € 12,00
child (under 4 yrs)	free
pitch	€ 6,50 - € 16,00
electricity (6A)	€ 3,00

Porto Sant' Elpidio
Villaggio Turistico Le Mimose
Via Faleria 15, I-63018 Porto Sant' Elpidio (Marche) T: 073 490 0604. E: info@villaggiolemimose.it
alanrogers.com/IT65200

Le Mimose is a quiet site in the centre of the town, surrounded by a three metre wall and tall holiday flats. There are 260 grassy or sandy pitches with 128 for touring, all with electricity (6A). The touring pitches, scattered around the holiday apartments, are surrounded by hedges and mature trees giving good shade, but which may be a little claustrophobic. The short walk to the sandy beach is very pleasant. There is a small market and bazaar, May to September, and a bar and restaurant open all season.

Facilities
Two central toilets blocks with all necessary facilities, including those for campers with disabilities. Swimming and paddling pools (June - Sept). Organised activities (June - Sept). Wellness centre. Sports facilities. Beach adjacent. ATM in reception. Off site: Tennis adjacent. Bicycle hire, boat ramp 1 km. Fishing 3 km. Golf 10 km. Riding 15 km.

Open: 23 March - 30 September.

Directions
From SS16 Adriatico in Porto Sant' Elpidio follow well marked signs to site. Access through town difficult for large outfits. GPS: 43.23768, 13.77365

Charges guide
Per person	€ 4,50 - € 8,50
child (2-6 yrs)	€ 2,00 - € 5,00
pitch	€ 8,00 - € 20,00
electricity (6A)	€ 2,50

Check real time availability and at-the-gate prices...

www.alanrogers.com

Sirolo

Camping Internazionale

Via Sa Michele 10, I-60020 Sirolo (Marche) T: **071 933 0884**. E: **campinginternazionale@tin.it**

alanrogers.com/IT65150

This is a high quality site with a particularly attractive location within the Parco del Conero, and is the only site on the Sirolo coast. Pitches are on steep terraces shelving down towards two bays. Most pitches have fine sea views and all have artificial shade and electrical connections. The terrain is steep and large caravans or motorhomes may find this site unsuitable. However, the site is efficiently run and well maintained with a good range of leisure amenities. The site restaurant and bar are very popular, thanks, no doubt to their magnificent views and good local cuisine.

Facilities

Bar and restaurant/pizzeria. Supermarket. Takeaway. Swimming pool. Play area. Children's club (high season). Gym. Football pitch. Tennis. Entertainment programme in high season. Internet access. Chalets and mobile homes for rent. Dogs are not accepted. Off site: Beach adjacent, Conero Riviera, Ancona, Urbino. Riding. Cycle and walking trails. Golf.

Open: 18 May - 18 September.

Directions

From A14 autostrada take Loreto Porto Recanati exit and follow signs to Numana and Sirolo. Site is by the town of Sirolo. GPS: 43.523706, 13.620472

Charges guide

Per person	€ 5,00 - € 10,00
child (1-6 yrs)	€ 2,00 - € 7,00
pitch incl. car	€ 12,00 - € 25,00
electricity	€ 3,00

Sirolo

Camping Village Green Garden

Via Peschiera 3, I-60020 Sirolo (Marche) T: **071 933 1317**. E: **greengarden@camping.it**

alanrogers.com/IT65160

Green Garden is a pleasant, well maintained site on the Conero Riviera, close to the attractive village of Sirolo. There are 200 shady pitches here, all with electrical connections (6A). The terrain is somewhat undulating and pitches are on terraces. Access could be difficult for larger units. There are a number of good facilities on site including the swimming pools. A shuttle bus operates to the beach and the sister site, both of which are ten minutes away. The caves at Frasassi are worth seeing and excursions to Urbino and Ancona are also popular.

Facilities

Bar, restaurant and takeaway meals. Motorcaravan service point. Swimming pool. Playground. Children's club (high season). Entertainment programme in high season. Internet access. Accommodation to rent. Dogs are not accepted. Off site: Private beach nearby (10 minutes by shuttle bus). Conero Riviera, Ancona, Urbino. Riding, cycle and walking trails, golf.

Open: 1 April - 30 September.

Directions

From A14 autostrada take Loreto Porto Recanati exit and follow signs to Numana and Sirolo. Site is by the town of Sirolo. GPS: 43.518883, 13.617517

Charges guide

Per person	€ 5,00 - € 10,50
child (under 3 yrs)	€ 4,00 - € 5,50
pitch	€ 10,00 - € 22,50
electricity	€ 2,00

Torrette di Fano

Camping Stella Maris

Via A. Cappellini 5, I-61032 Torrette di Fano (Marche) T: **072 188 4231**. E: **stellamaris@camping.it**

alanrogers.com/IT66180

This clean, modern Adriatic coast site is, in our opinion, the best in the area. The owner, Francesco Mantoni, is friendly, enthusiastic and proud of his site. The pitches are of a good size with some for touring units. In this informal setting touring pitches, permanent sites and cabins are blended together but the mixture works. For swimming and relaxing there is the choice of an excellent long fine soft sand beach or an excellent pool complex with loungers, umbrellas, jacuzzi and paddling pool. Alongside the pool is a most attractive restaurant with table service, a varied menu and good selection of wine.

Facilities

Clean, modern sanitary blocks are nicely decorated with a separate ladies room including hair dryers. Facilities for disabled campers. Laundry facilities. Motorcaravan services. Excellent large supermarket. Restaurant/bar. Snacks. Large swimming pool. Games room. TV room. Hard court with arena style seating used for organised games. Children's activities day and evening in season. Entertainment. Beach. Dogs or other animals are not accepted.

Open: 1 April - 30 September.

Directions

Site is between Fano and Falconara. From autostrada take Pesaro exit and follow signs on the SS16 for Ancona, site is 3 km. past Fano on waters edge. GPS: 43.79826, 13.09547

Charges guide

Per person	€ 6,50 - € 9,40
child (2-6 yrs)	€ 4,00 - € 7,00
pitch incl. electricity	€ 12,50 - € 16,50

Lazio lies between the Apennines and the Tyrrhenian Sea, with the Pontine marshes in the south and wooded hills the north. Home to the his city of Rome it also has numer lakes and coastal resorts which provide the perfect antidote to the heat of the city and its crowds.

LAZIO HAS FIVE PROVINCES: FROSINONE, LATINA, RIETI, ROMA AND VITERBO

Rome, the capital city of Italy, is crammed full of history, boasting a dazzling array of architectural and artistic masterpieces of the ancient world. Within Rome lies the Vatican City, the world capital of Catholicism, ruled by the Pope, Europe's only absolute monarch. It's also the world's smallest state, occupying 43 hectares within high walls watched over by guards. More historical sites can be found just outside Rome, including the ruins of Villa Adriana, just outside the hilltown of Tivoli. Once a favoured resort of the ancient Romans, the town is also home to the 16th century Villa d'Este, renowned for its beautiful gardens. Nearby Ostia Antica boasts one of the finest of Roman sites. For 600 years it was the busy, main port of Rome, and the site is well preserved, while Viterbo, in the north, is a medieval town with grand palaces, medieval churches enclosed by a preserved set of medieval walls. For recreation, there are numerous lakes including Lakes Bolsena, Bracciano, Vico and Albano. These lakes were created by volcanic activity which also left Lazio with hot springs, most notably those around Tivoli and Fiuggi. Popular coastal resorts include Sperlonga, Anzio and Nettuno, with some of the best beaches lying between Gaeta and Sabaudia.

Places of interest

Anguillara: pretty medieval lake town on the shore of Lake Bracciano.

Bolsena: lakeside beach resort on Lake Bolsena with medieval castle.

Caprarola: medieval village 4 km. from Lake Vico, with grandiose Renaissance villa

Fiuggi: spa town.

Rome: Colosseum, Forum, Palatine Hill, Pantheon, Trevi Fountain, the list is endless

Sermoneta: pretty hilltown overlooking the Pontine Plains, with medieval houses, palaces and churches.

Tarquinia: archeology museum, frescoed tombs of the necropolis.

Vatican City: St Peter's church, Sistine Chapel with famous painted ceiling by Michelangelo, museums.

Cuisine of the region

Pasta is eaten with a variety of sauces including *aglio e olio* (oil and garlic), *cacio e pepe* (percorino cheese and black pepper) and *alle vongole* (with baby clams). The w known dish *spaghetti alla carbonara* was first devised in Rome. Fish and offal is popular. Mushrooms and, in particular, artichokes (*carciofi*) are used in a variety of dishes, and rosemary, sage and garlic is us a lot for seasoning. Local wines include Frascati and Torre Ercolana, one of the fev red wines produced in Lazio. Fresh drinkir water is freely available in the numerous fountains scattered around Rome.

Risotto all Romana: rice with sauce of live sweetbreads and Marsala.

Saltimbocca: veal with ham and sage.

Torta di Ricotta: cheesecake made with ricotta, Marsala and lemon.

Bolsena

Lido Camping Village

Via Cassia km 111, I-01023 Bolsena (Lazio) T: **076 179 9258**. E: **lidocamping@bolsenacamping.it**

alanrogers.com/IT67680

Lido Camping Village is located on the edge of Lake Bolsena, 1.5 km. south of the fascinating town of Bolsena. The area is rich in the history of the ancient Etruscan civilization and major historical sites such as Tarquinia Vulci and Tuscania are close by. This beautifully landscaped, immaculate site has all new facilities, or so they appear. There are 600 flat, shaded and grassy pitches of an average size with some for larger units and some with lake views. A modern attractive restaurant, bar, pizzeria and terrace are located on the edge of the lake and have wonderful views.

Facilities

Excellent facilities include new showers (hot water by token) and facilities for disabled visitors and children; expect all facilities to be under pressure in high season. Supermarket, bar, restaurant and pizzeria (all open all season). Swimming pools. Dance area, cinema and music area. Tennis. Windsurfing and water skiing. Lake swimming and boat launching. Animation in high season. Dogs are not accepted. Off site: Bolsena 1.5 km.

Open: 24 April - 30 September.

Directions

Site is located on Lake Bolsena south of the town of Bolsena off the S2 (Via Cassia). It is well signed. GPS: 42.62716, 11.99524

Charges 2010

Per unit incl. 2 persons and electricity	€ 21,50 - € 29,00
extra person	€ 6,00 - € 8,00
child (3-10 yrs)	€ 2,70 - € 5,30

Camping Cheques accepted.

Check real time availability and at-the-gate prices...

www.**alanrogers**.com

Bolsena

Camping Internazionale Il Lago

Viale Cadorna 6, I-01023 Bolsena (Lazio) T: **076 179 9191**. E: **anna.bruti@libero.it**

alanrogers.com/IT67700

Camping Internazionale Il Lago is enchanting. A simple rustic site with only 34 pitches, it is in a garden setting on the lake shores of Bolsena, only 500 m. from the centre of town. The pitches, all for tourers and spread along the lake, are flat and grassy. There is shade from many trees, good hedging and two gravel roads. The same family has owned the campsite for over 50 years and some English is spoken. A small bar and café offers snacks, with restaurants within 100 m. of the campsite and more in town.

Facilities

The single well cared for sanitary block is clean and has good showers. Excellent facilities for disabled visitors. Drinks and snack bar with TV room. Fishing. Lake swimming. Boat launching. Off site: Restaurants near. Bicycle hire 500 m. Riding 3 km. Sailing.

Open: Easter - 30 September.

Directions

Site is located on Lake Bolsena in the southeast area of the town of Bolsena. In town follow lake and camping signs and site is easy to locate. GPS: 42.63833, 11.98472

Charges guide

Per person	€ 4,70 - € 5,50
child (3-6 yrs)	€ 3,20 - € 3,50
pitch	€ 7,70 - € 9,50
No credit cards.	

Bracciano

Camping Roma Flash

Via Settevene Palo km 19,800, I-00062 Bracciano (Lazio) T: **069 980 5458**. E: **info@romaflash.it**

alanrogers.com/IT68120

This excellent site is in a superb location with magnificent views over Lake Bracciano, the source of Rome's drinking water. When we visited, although it was busy, it was still peaceful and relaxing. There are 275 pitches in total and facilities include a restaurant with a large terrace and small indoor area both overlooking the lake where you can enjoy a good menu. The owners Elide and Eduardo speak excellent English and happily go out of their way to ensure guests enjoy their holiday. Many visitors return year after year and some stay for eight to 12 weeks at a time, enjoying all that the Lazio region has to offer.

Facilities

Two new large toilet blocks are very well appointed. Free hot water throughout and fully adjustable showers. Facilities for disabled visitors and children. Laundry facilities. Gas supplies. Bar/pizzeria. Small shop. Swimming pool (caps compulsory). Play area. Watersports. Games room. Entertainment for children in high season. Excursions. Private bus daily to Roma S. Pietro and return. New sports area. Off site: Rome (40 minutes).

Open: 1 April - 30 September.

Directions

From E35/E45 north of Rome, take Settebagni exit. Follow GRA orbital road west to Cassia exit. Follow sign for Lago Bracciano to town of Bracciano. Site is well signed southeast of town on the SP4A. GPS: 42.130113, 12.173527

Charges guide

Per unit incl. 2 persons and electricity	€ 16,00 - € 32,00
extra person	€ 3,50 - € 8,00
Camping Cheques accepted.	

Bracciano

Camping Porticciolo

Via Porticciolo, I-00062 Bracciano (Lazio) T: **069 980 3060**. E: **info@porticciolo.it**

alanrogers.com/IT68130

This small family run site, useful for visiting Rome, has its own private beach on the southwest side of Lake Bracciano. A pleasant feature is that the site is overlooked by the impressive castle in the village of Bracciano. There are 170 pitches (160 for tourers) split into two sections, some with lake views and 120 having electricity. Pitches are average-sized and shaded by very green trees that are continuously watered in summer by a neat overhead watering system. The friendly bar has two large terraces, shared by the trattoria which opens for lunch and the pizzeria with its wood fired oven in the evenings.

Facilities

Three somewhat rustic, but clean, sanitary units with children's toilet and showers. Hot showers (by token). Laundry facilities. Motorcaravan services. Gas supplies. Shop (basics). Bar. Trattoria/pizzeria (15/5-5/9). Tennis. Play area. Bicycle hire. Fishing. Internet point and free WiFi. Torches required in some areas. Excursions 'Rome By Night' and nearby nature parks. Off site: Bus service from outside the gate runs to central Rome. Air conditioned train service from Bracciano (1.5 km) into the city - the site runs a connecting bus (09.00 daily). Riding 2 km.

Open: 1 April - 30 September.

Directions

From Rome ring road (GRA) northwest side take Cassia exit to Bracciano S493 (not Cassia bis). 2 km. before Bracciano village, just after going under a bridge follow site signs and turn along the lake away from Anguillara. Site is 1 km. on the SP1f and has a steep entrance. GPS: 42.10582, 12.18928

Charges guide

Per person	€ 5,00 - € 7,00
child (3-10 yrs)	€ 3,50 - € 6,00
pitch incl. electricity	€ 5,00 - € 8,00
car	€ 2,50 - € 4,00

Lido di Ostia

Camping Internazionale Castelfusano

Via Litoranea, 132, I-00122 Lido di Ostia (Lazio) T: **056 488 7026**

alanrogers.com/IT67790

For a beach holiday this site is ideally situated with easy access across the road to a lovely long sandy beach. It is a rustically attractive site with 65 pitches interspersed on undulating ground among mature trees. Although they offer plenty of shade, there are many low hanging branches (they are protected) and, as a result, some pitches are small and inappropriate for larger units. However, tents and smaller units can tuck themselves away in interesting nooks and crannies. The soil is sandy but the access roads are mostly tarmac and gravel. Most of the pitches have 3A electricity. Reception is a pleasant wooden building near a large flat area that can accommodate larger units.

Facilities

Three toilet blocks with functional facilities including hot showers but only cold water for dishwashing and laundry. No facilities for disabled visitors (except a couple of toilet/washbasin cubicles). Washing machine and dryer. Well stocked shop (March-Oct). Bar/restaurant (closed January and November) with terrace. Live music (high season). Playground. Games area. Entertainment for children twice a week (July/Aug). Internet access and information in reception. Off site: Beach 300 m. Ostia 3 km. Roman excavations 10 km. Rome 25 km. (1 hour bus and subway).

Open: All year.

Directions

Site is southwest of Rome. From GRA exit 26 or 27 (depending on direction) onto Via Cristofer Coloumbo heading towards Flumicino. Site is signed. Continue on Via Cr. Coloumbo to the end (beach). Keeping in left lane, follow road to right then immediately left and left again in about 100 m. Turn right in 150 m. and site is 1.5 km. on right. GPS: 41.705833, 12.34

Charges guide

Per unit incl. 2 persons and electricity	€ 20,50 - € 33,50
extra person	€ 4,00 - € 9,50

Marina di Montalto di Castro

Camping Pionier Etrusco

Via Vulsinia snc, I-01014 Marina di Montalto di Castro (Lazio) T: **076 680 2807**. E: **meleute@tin.it**

alanrogers.com/IT68165

This family run site has 250 pitches, just under half of which are used for static units. On sandy ground, all the pitches are under tall pine trees resulting in good shade. In fact, few see any direct sun for long during the day. Oriented towards families, this site in a small seaside town would make a good base for touring the local Etruscan ruins or perhaps for a short stop en route. The beach is about 100 m. away and is of dark volcanic sand. It clearly provides a popular resort for the population of Rome.

Facilities

Two old, but well maintained sanitary blocks provide toilets (some Turkish style), washbasins and unisex hot showers. Motorcaravan service point. Bar. Restaurant (self-service). Pizzeria. Bungalows to rent. Off site: Bars, shops, beach and everything you would find at a busy seaside resort. Montalto di Castro 8 km.

Open: 1 March - 30 September.

Directions

Leave the SS1 at exit for Marfina di Montalto di Castro and head towards the coast. At roundabout turn left, then right and at T-junction turn right again. Site is off to the left and is clearly signed. GPS: 42.32706, 11.58155

Charges guide

Per unit incl. 2 persons and electricity	€ 17,00 - € 36,00
extra person	€ 3,00 - € 10,50

Marina di Montalto

California International Camping Village

SS1 Aurelia km 105,500, I-01014 Marina di Montalto (Lazio) T: **076 680 2848**

E: **info@californiacampingvillage.com** **alanrogers.com/IT68160**

The first vision of California Camping on the approach is the excellent lagoon style, pool complex with its bridges and large fountain surrounded by palms. A smart bar, pizzeria and restaurant complex are in an octagonal building overlooking the pools. The cheerful restaurant with its bright décor boasts a fine menu at good prices. The 420 pitches for touring units are rather big, arranged in close level rows under tall pines, which give excellent shade. Pitches are a little dusty from the combination of the pine needles and fine dark sand. Electricity is provided and cars are parked separately in high season.

Facilities

Nine refurbished blocks contain varying facilities. These include facilities for disabled campers. Hot water for showers but only cold at sinks. Showers are concentrated in one block (therefore a walk for some). Supermarket. Excellent restaurant, bar and takeaway. Large lagoon pool complex. Minigolf. Amphitheatre. Tennis. Discos. Play areas. Entertainment. Miniclub. Boat hire. Dogs are not accepted. Off site: Town close by with all usual amenities. Fishing. Sailing 1 km. Riding 2 km. Bicycle hire 3 km. Golf 10 km.

Open: 1 May - 20 September.

Directions

Site is 100 km. north of Rome off the SS1 between Ortobello and Civitavecchia. At Montalto di Castro take minor road to the coast and Montalto Marina. On approach to town, site is clearly signed. GPS: 42.30550, 11.62333

Charges guide

Per person	€ 6,00 - € 10,00
child (1-6 yrs)	€ 4,00 - € 6,00
pitch	€ 6,00 - € 10,00

165

Roma

I Pini Camping

Via delle Sassete 1/A, Fiano Romano, I-00065 Roma (Lazio) T: 076 545 3349. E: ipini@ecvacanze.it

alanrogers.com/IT68110

Built only a few years ago by experienced campers, all members of the family are involved in the operation of this site to make your stay enjoyable. The 117 pitches here are set on shaded grassy terraces with views of the nearby hills. Access is easy for all units via tarmac roads and everything is here, including a well stocked and reasonable supermarket. The beautifully designed restaurant is typical of the thought that has gone into making I Pini a place where you can relax. We recommend sampling the excellent menu, especially the traditionally cooked pizzas on the large terrace where there is entertainment in high season.

Facilities

The single excellent sanitary block is spotless and hot water is free. Two well equipped units for disabled visitors and separate child's shower. Washing machines and dryers. Motorcaravan services. Bar. Restaurant. Snack bar and pizza oven. Pleasant market. Swimming pool (with lifeguard). Tennis. Play area. Entertainment (1/6-30/8). Free internet access and WiFi in bar area. Torches required in some areas. Air conditioned buses to Rome daily. Off site: Fishing 3 km. Golf and riding 20 km.

Open: 30 March - 2 November.

Directions

From Rome ring road (GRA) take A1 exit to Fiano Romano. As you enter the town turn right along via Belvedere opposite an IP petrol station and follow camping signs (there is only the one site).
GPS: 42.1558, 12.5732

Charges guide

Per person	€ 9,00 - € 10,80
child (2-12 yrs)	€ 5,80 - € 7,10
pitch incl. electricity	€ 10,50 - € 12,30
dog	€ 1,50
Electricity included.	

Roma

Fabulous Camping Village

Via Cristoforo Colombo Km 18, I-00125 Roma (Lazio) T: 065 259 354. E: fabulous@ecvacanze.it

alanrogers.com/IT67780

Fabulous Camping Village is another venture in the Cardini/Vannucchi family group of campsites. Purchased only a few years ago, developments are still in progress to create a superb family campsite on top of a hill, midway between Rome and the sea. The site is attractively located under tall pine trees which give plenty of shade. Pitches are of varying size, all with 6/10A electricity and access is by tarmac and hardcore roads. They are frequently positioned close to the access routes so it can be quite noisy. The wonderful pools, tennis courts and activity amenities are at the far end of the site where there are superb views toward Rome.

Facilities

Three blocks, two in traditional style in the permanent area and one new for the tourers. This block is excellent. Facilities for disabled visitors. Baby rooms. Washing machines. Motorcaravan services. Excellent supermarket (1/5-31/10). Restaurant/pizzeria and bar. Three swimming pools, one for paddling, with lifeguards. Play area. Tennis. Miniclub (5 yrs plus) and teenage activities. Entertainment programme for all ages. Internet. Torches useful. Off site: Riding and golf 2 km. Public transport 2 km. Ostia and the coast 10 km.

Open: All year.

Directions

Site is southwest of Rome. It is on the GRA (Rome's M25 equivalent ring road). Take exit 27 or 26 depending on your approach of direction. Site is signed as 'camping' on a small yellow marker. Follow larger camping signs once off the GRA.
GPS: 41.77817, 12.39678

Charges guide

Per person	€ 8,00 - € 10,00
child (2-11 yrs)	€ 5,50 - € 7,30
pitch	€ 9,00 - € 14,00

Roma

Camping Tiber

Via Tiberina km 1,400, I-00188 Roma (Lazio) T: 063 361 0733. E: info@campingtiber.com

alanrogers.com/IT68090

An excellent city site with extensive facilities which also cater for backpackers. Although a lively site, the thoughtful layout and the division of different areas with flowering shrubs makes it surprisingly peaceful. It is ideally located for visiting Rome with a free shuttle bus every 30 minutes to the station and then an easy train service to Rome (20 minutes), with trams operating late at night. The 350 touring pitches (with electricity) are mostly shaded under very tall trees and many have very pleasant views over the river Tiber. This mighty river winds around two sides of the site boundary (safely fenced) providing a cooling effect for campers. There is a new section with some shade, and bungalows to rent are in a separate area. A small but pleasant outdoor pool with a bar awaits after a busy day in the city. The excellent main bar, beer garden and restaurant all have terraces and, along with the takeaway, give good value. The site is extremely well run with friendly and helpful staff and especially good for campers with disabilities. Visiting the delights of Rome is easy from here.

Facilities

Fully equipped, very smart sanitary facilities include hot water everywhere, private cabins, a baby room and very good facilities for disabled campers. Laundry facilities. Motorcaravan service point. Shop. Bar, restaurant, pizzeria and takeaway. Swimming pool (hat required) and bar. Play area. Fishing. Internet access. Free shuttle bus to the underground station every 15 or 30 minutes according to season. Torches useful. WiFi. Off site: Local bars, restaurants and shops. Golf or riding 20 km.

Open: March (Easter) - 31 October.

Directions

From Florence, exit at Rome Nord Fiano on A1 and turn south onto Via Tiberina and site is signed. From other directions on Rome ring road (GRA) take exit 6 northbound on S3 Via Flaminia following signs to Tiberina. GPS: 42.00950, 12.50233

Charges guide

Per person	€ 9,50 - € 11,00
child (3-12 yrs)	€ 6,50 - € 8,00
motorcaravan	€ 10,50 - € 12,60
caravan and car	€ 12,00 - € 14,30

camping **tiber roma**

When you're in Rome you definitely have to make an overnight at Camping Tiber because from here you can reach the entire city very easily. We can offer you fix places and places for caravans and tents. Furthermore free at your disposal there's a swimming pool, bar, restaurant, supermarket and internet-point. The campsite is located at the bank of the river Tiber. The most important thing: from the subway stop Prima Porta, you can reach the city centre of Rome within 15 min. From exit Nord from the A1 follow directions for Roma Nord. Follow the G.R.A. and take exit 6 (Prima Porta). Turn to via Tiberina . At the campsite we have parking places for busses, on request not for free.

First class washroom facilities

WiFi AREA

GPS N 42°00'37" E 12°30'14"

For your visit in Venice we recommend:

CAMPING FUSINA VILLAGE - Venezia

Via Moranzani, 79 - I-30030 Fusina (VE)
Tel. 0039 0415470055 - Fax 0039 0415470050
www.camping-fusina.com
info@camping-fusina.com

Booking Online
www.campingtiber.com

METRO 15 MINUTES

The best access to the city center

I-00188 Roma (Prima Porta)
Via Tiberina km 1,5
Tel. 0039 06 33610733
Fax 0039 06 33612314
info@campingtiber.com

Check real time availability and at-the-gate prices...

www.**alanrogers**.com

Roma

Camping Village Roma

Via Aurelia 831, I-00165 Roma (Lazio) T: **066 623 018**. E: **campingroma@ecvacanze.it**

alanrogers.com/IT67800

Perched high on a hilltop on the edge of Rome this is another venture by the Cardini/Vanucchi family, who have other quality city sites in Italy: IT60420, IT66140 and IT66120. Camping Village Roma has been brilliantly re-developed over the past three years into possibly the best city campsite in Europe. The diverse range of facilities are designed in particular to meet the needs of young travellers and the aim here is to provide a friendly helpful service all year round. There are 150 pitches of varying sizes on level terraces. Motorcaravans are mostly placed in a separate area where 80 pitches are fully serviced. There is some shade and most have attractive views.

Facilities

Two superb toilet blocks with British style WCs and showers. Good facilities for disabled visitors and children. Baby baths. Washing machines. Motorcaravan service point. New supermarket. Large restaurant/late night bar with DJ plus pizzeria with terrace and poolside bar. Swimming pool and jacuzzi. Huge TV screen. Evening entertainment/disco and regular themed parties. Play area. Internet. Travel information. Off site: Public transport at gate. Golf 500 m.

Open: All year.

Directions

From A1 autostrada take Roma North exit towards the airport Fuimcino. Take the GRA and exit 1 'Aurelia' towards San Pietro-Citta del Vaticano-Centro. At the 831 km. marker the site is well signed. On exit at dual carriageway continue straight on and site is 50 m. on the right. GPS: 41.8877, 12.4042

Charges guide

Per person	€ 9,60 - € 11,00
pitch	€ 10,80 - € 13,50

Roma

Camping Seven Hills Village

Via Cassia 1216, I-00189 Roma (Lazio) T: **063 031 0826**. E: **info@sevenhills.it**

alanrogers.com/IT68100

Close to Rome, this site provides a quieter, garden setting in some areas, but has a very lively, busy atmosphere in others. It is situated in a delightful valley, flanked by two of the seven hills of Rome and is just off the autostrada ring road (GRA) to the north of the city. The site runs a bus shuttle service every 30 minutes in the mornings to the local station and one return bus to Rome each day (08.00-12.00 and 16.30-20.30). The 250 touring pitches (3A electricity to some) are unmarked, but the management supervise in busy periods. Arranged in two sections, the top half, near the entrance, restaurant and shop consists of small, flat, grass terraces with two to four pitches on each, with smaller terraces for tents. Access to some pitches may be tricky. The flat section at the lower part of the site is reserved mainly for ready erected tents and cabins used by international tour operators who bring guests by coach. These tend to be younger people and the site, along with its often busy pool, has a distinctly youthful feel. Consequently there may be a little extra noise, so choose your pitch carefully.

Facilities

Three soundly constructed sanitary blocks are well situated around the site, with open plan washbasins, and hot water in the average sized showers. Facilities for disabled campers. Well stocked shop. Bar/restaurant and terrace. Money exchange. Swimming pool at the bottom of the site with bar/snack bar and a room where the younger element tends to congregate (separate pool charge). Disco. Excursions. Bungalows to rent. WiFi. Off site: Golf 4 km.

Open: 15 March - 1 November.

Directions

From autostrada ring road exit 3 take Via Cassia (signed SS2 Viterbo, NOT Via Cassia Bis) and look for site signs. Turn right after 1 km. and follow small road, Via Italo Piccagli for 1 km. to site. This narrow twisting road is heavily parked on during the day so access can be interesting. GPS: 41.99300, 12.41685

Charges guide

Per unit incl. 2 persons	€ 15,00 - € 17,00
extra person	€ 6,50 - € 8,00
child (5-12 yrs)	€ 5,00 - € 6,50

Roma

Flaminio Village Camping Bungalow Park

Via Flaminia Nuova 821, I-00189 Roma (Lazio) T: **063 332 604**. E: **info@villageflaminio.com**
alanrogers.com/IT68140

We were impressed with Camping Flaminio. It is an attractive campsite with many flowers, shrubs and trees giving some shade. Being 400 metres from the main road it is protected from traffic noise. Although it is quite a large site there are only 300 pitches all with 6A electricity which are approached by 'environmentally approved' brick access roads. There is reasonable space allocated to touring units and the majority of these pitches in the lower areas are of average size. Pitches are situated away from the main facilities so there is quite a walk between the two. There are 120 well equipped bungalows attractively arranged in a village-style setting on the slopes.

Facilities

The sanitary facilities are of a high quality including provision for disabled visitors and a very good baby room. Bar/pizzeria and restaurant. Shop. Swimming pool (hats required), pool bar and solarium (15/6-5/9). Bicycle hire. Internet access. Bus service. Torches useful. Pick-up service to and from Ciampino airport. Off site: Shops, service station, bank and access to cycle route alongside river into the City. Buses and trains outside the gate. Fishing 3 km.

Open: All year.

Directions

From the ring road north of the city take Via Flaminia exit 6 south towards the city centre. After 3 km. follow Flaminia signs and bear left where roads split in order to avoid tunnel. Warning: site entrance comes up suddenly on the right as the central barrier ends 150 m. after passing tunnel entrance.
GPS: 41.95618, 12.48240

Charges guide

Per person	€ 9,50 - € 13,30
child (under 12 yrs)	€ 6,10 - € 8,70
carvan or motorcaravan	€ 10,50 - € 16,00
tent	€ 4,50 - € 7,30
Camping Cheques accepted.	

Salto di Fondi

Camping Villaggio Settebello

Via Flacca km 3,6, I-04020 Salto di Fondi (Lazio) T: **077 159 9132**. E: **settebello@settebellocamping.com**
alanrogers.com/IT68190

The SS213 hugs this beautiful coast line for many miles, running between small towns and villages and alongside the pine forests that are directly behind the beach. Camping Settebello, an attractive and well managed site, is in a rural area but unfortunately the site straddles this busy road and inevitably there is traffic noise. The touring pitches are all on the beach side of the site in a wooded area. The ground rises before the beach and this is where many of the bungalows for rent have been built. With a total of 600 pitches about 260 are available for touring units.

Facilities

Five toilet blocks include showers, WCs (Turkish and British style) and washbasins. Facilities for disabled visitors. Motorcaravan service point. Small shop. Bar and restaurant (1/6-10/9). Swimming pool and children's pool (1/6-30/8). Skating. Tennis. Minigolf. Entertainment and children's club. Disco. Amphitheatre and cinema. Dogs (or cats) are not accepted. Bungalows and mobile homes to rent. Bicycle hire. Off site: Narrow public beach. Fondi 10 km. Riding 20 km. Watersports.

Open: 1 April - 30 September.

Directions

The Via Flacca is a comparatively short stretch of the SS213 between Sperlonga and Terracina. The site straddles this road at km. 3.6 which is close to Terracina. Turn towards the beach to find reception.
GPS: 41.29028, 13.33111

Charges guide

Per unit incl. 2 persons	€ 20,00 - € 62,00
extra person	€ 7,00 - € 15,00
child (3-12 yrs)	
or senior (over 65 yrs)	€ 6,00 - € 12,00

Trevignano Romano
Camping Internazionale Lago di Bracciano

Via del Pianoro 4, I-00069 Trevignano Romano (Lazio) T: 069 985 032. E: camping.village@gmail.com

alanrogers.com/IT67850

Lago di Bracciano, just 45 km. north of Rome, is of a size that provides excellent opportunities for watersports and is inevitably very popular with windsurfers. With some pitches alongside a little beach, the site provides 110 pitches of which about 50 are for tourers. Our pitch had a full view of the lake and the gentle breeze made the temperature at the end of June quite bearable. Some shade is provided by large trees. A bar and restaurant near the entrance are behind the site's small swimming pool and play area. The local bus has a regular service to Rome. There are various opportunities for excursions that the site owners will be pleased to tell you about. This site would be a good choice for long or short stays, especially in low season.

Facilities

The single toilet block is well equipped. Facilities for disabled visitors. Washing machine. Motorcaravan service point. Small shop. Bar and restaurant/pizzeria. Small swimming pool (15/5-15/9). Play area. Barbecue area (not allowed on pitches). WiFi and Internet access. Mobile homes and bungalows to rent. Off site: Lago di Bracciano.

Open: 1 April - 30 September.

Directions

From the Rome GRA take exit 5 on SS2 towards Cassia. Turn left at Trevignano exit (km. 35) and follow SP4a towards the lake where you will find the site on the left. The access road and gate are max. 2.6 m. wide. GPS: 42.144717, 12.26865

Charges 2010

Per unit incl. 2 persons and electricity	€ 23,00 - € 28,00
extra person	€ 6,00 - € 7,00
child (3-10 yrs)	€ 4,50 - € 5,50
dog	€ 3,20 - € 3,70

170
Check real time availability and at-the-gate prices...
www.alanrogers.com

Until 1963 Abruzzo and Molise was just one combined region known as Abruzzi. With some of the wildest terrain in Italy, Abruzzo is bordered by the Apennine mountain range with vast tracts of forest while Molise has a gentler countryside with high plains, soft peaks and valleys.

THE REGIONS ARE DIVIDED INTO THE FOLLOWING PROVINCES: ABRUZZO: CHIETI, L'AQUILA, PESCARA AND TERAMO MOLISE: CAMPOBASSO AND ISERNIA

A popular attraction in Abruzzo is the medieval hilltown of Scanno. Surrounded by high peaks looming above, the town hosts a range of activities in the summer including riding, boating and a classical music festival. Close by is Italy's third largest national park. With mountains, rivers, lakes and forests it is an important wildlife refuge, home to bears, wolves and the golden eagle. It also offers good walking, with an extensive network of paths, plus riding, skiing and canoeing. Around Scanno are the historic mountain towns of L'Aquila and Sulmona, and the village of Cocullo, where the bizarre Festival of Snakes takes place in May; a statue of a local saint is draped with live snakes and paraded through the streets. Along the Abruzzo coast is Pescara, the main resort, which has a 16 km. long beach. Ferries to Croatia and the Dalmatian islands depart from here. Nearby are the small hilltowns of Atri, Penne, and Loreto Apruntino, one of the regions most important market towns. In Molise, the city of Isernia is where traces of a million-year-old village were unearthed in 1979, the most ancient signs of human life ever found in Europe. And the quiet resort and fishing port of Térmoli, from where Italian and Central European time is set, is a good place to relax.

Places of interest

Alba Adriatica: most northern of Abruzzo's coastal resorts.

Atri: 13th-century cathedral, archaeology and ethnography museums.

Celano: pretty village with turreted castle.

Lanciano: historic town.

Larino: medieval town centre, cathedral, amphitheatre.

Pineto: coastal resort.

Saepinum: ruined Roman town.

Téramo: remains of Roman amphitheatre, theatre and baths.

Cuisine of the region

As sheep-farming dominates the regions, lamb is popular: *abbacchio* (roasted baby lamb), and *castratro* (castrated lamb) is used to make *intingolo di castrato*, a casserole prepared with tomatoes, wine, onion and celery. Chilli is another favourite ingredient, known locally as *pepdinie* (*peperoncino* elsewhere in Italy). Abruzzo is famous for *maccheroni all chitarra*, pasta made by pressing sheets over a wooden frame, and other local pastas include *stengozze* and *maltagliati*, usually served with a lamb sauce.

Ceci e Castagne: chickpeas and chestnuts.

Coniglio all zafferano: rabbit with saffron.

Linguine d'Ovidio: pasta with pancetta and truffles.

MARCHE

MARTINSICURO

TORTORETO LIDO
GIULIANOVA LIDO
COLOGNA SPIAGGIA
ROSETO DEGLI ABRUZZI

TERAMO

PINETO
SILVI

PESCARA

A24

A25/E80

A14/E55

CASALBORDINO LIDO

L'AQUILA

MARINA DI VASTO

A24

A14/E55 TERMOLI

ABRUZZO & MOLISE

CELANO

SULMONA

A25/E80

AVEZZANO
VILLALAGO

PUGLIA

OPI

BARREA

CAMPOBASSO

LAZIO

FROSINONE

CAMPANIA

0   25   5 0   75 kms

Barrea

Camping La Genziana

SS83 Ctra Tre Croci, Parco Nazionale D, I-67030 Barrea (Abruzzo) T: 086 488 101. E: pasettanet@tiscali.it

alanrogers.com/IT68080

This is the place to get away from it all – situated in the middle of Italy, high in the Abruzzo mountains with views over Barrea lakes. It is an hour from Rome or Pescara, but the village of Barrea with the usual supplies is just 500 metres away. The ebullient owner Tomasso Pasetta and his family make everyone welcome to his site where he attempts to retain a 'natural' feel – this means that you shouldn't expect any luxuries. The facilities are adequate and the 110 informal pitches (100 have electricity) and 50 more for tents are embraced by wild flowers and grasses. Tomasso is an expert in Alpine walking and a great raconteur – ask him about 'calling wolves', he really does! If mountain walking is for you he will give sound advice and many tracks start from the site. The site has limited facilities but swimming, riding and fishing are all possible nearby. The site is suitable for disabled people.

Facilities

Single, basic but clean sanitary block with hot showers. British and Turkish style toilets. Laundry facilities. Motorcaravan services. Bar, coffee bar and small shop. Off site: Beach 3 km. Bicycle hire, fishing, sailing all within 3 km. Riding 7 km. Trekking and walking information.

Open: All year.

Directions

From A25 take route 83 from Celano and the site is signed 4 km. before Barrea. Alternatively take route 17 from Pratola/Sulmona through Castel di Sangro, then right to route 83 and site is 1 km. before Barrea. GPS: 41.74267, 13.98867

Charges guide

Per person	€ 7,20
child (under 9 yrs)	€ 4,00
pitch	€ 8,00
car	€ 4,00
pet	€ 3,00
No credit cards.	

Casalbordino Lido

Centro Vacanze Poker

Ctra Termini 27 Lungomare sud, I-66021 Casalbordino Lido (Abruzzo) T: **087 391 8321**
E: **info@centrovacanzepoker.it alanrogers.com/IT67960**

This has to be one of the most exclusive campsites in Italy. It is an integral part of a five-star hotel and has only 15 pitches set in beautifully landscaped gardens, each being provided with a personal bathroom. It is inevitably popular, with guests returning year after year. Although there is clearly no need to leave the site there are restaurants and bars in the nearby town. Sadly the adjoining beach is rocky but the extensive grass area for sunbathing near the swimming pool and jacuzzi amply makes up for this. The pitches are not generous, so large outfits may be disappointed.

Facilities

15 medium size pitches, each with a private bathroom nearby. Swimming pool and jacuzzi. Restaurant and bar. Entertainment. Off site: Casalbordino Lido.

Open: 1 June - 15 September.

Directions

Leave the A14 at Torino di Sangro and join the SS16 south. In Casalbordino Lido go under the railway (good headroom) and go south on the Lungomare. The complex is at the far end of the road. GPS: 42.19094, 14.64433

Charges guide

Per person	€ 10,00 - € 15,00
child (3-10 yrs)	€ 6,00 - € 8,00
pitch	€ 19,00 - € 26,00

Cologna Spiaggia

Camping Stork

Via del Mare 11, I-64020 Cologna Spiaggia (Abruzzo) T: **085 893 7076**. E: **stork@camping.it**
alanrogers.com/IT67860

This is a relaxed site set back from the SS16 Adriatica in a 21-acre park with plenty of space for larger caravans or motorcaravans. Pitches are well laid out and offer good shade. Some pitches are available adjacent to the beach, for a small supplement. There is direct access to a sandy beach with a range of amenities on offer, including a beach bar and beach volleyball. A lively entertainment programme is organised in peak season, including a children's club and aquagym. Leisure facilities are extensive and include a large swimming pool and separate children's pool.

Facilities

Two centrally located toilet blocks. Shop. Bazaar. Bar. Restaurant/pizzeria. Beach bar. Swimming pool. Children's pool (swimming lessons available). Tennis. Beach volleyball. Play area. TV room. Entertainment and children's activities (July/August). Chalets for rent. Off site: Mountain biking and walking in the Abruzzo national parks. Rafting and canoe trips. Excursions to Pescara and Ancona.

Open: 15 May - 15 September.

Directions

From A14 motorway (Bologna - Taranto) take Teramo - Giulianova exit and join SS80 towards Giulianova, and then continue towards Cologna Spiaggia. Site is well signed. GPS: 42.72119, 13.98901

Charges guide

Per person	€ 4,50 - € 10,00
child (3-7 yrs)	€ 3,50 - € 6,50
pitch incl. electricity	€ 7,00 - € 17,00
Camping Cheques accepted.	

Giulianova Lido

Camping Holiday

Lungomare Zara, I-64022 Giulianova Lido (Abruzzo) T: **085 800 0053**. E: **holiday@camping.it**
alanrogers.com/IT68010

A site for Italian families on the Adriatic coast, this site has a tropical atmosphere. It appears that some have been coming here for years and have developed imaginative 'homes away from home' using all the available space for their comforts. The 320 pitches are flat, reasonably sized and many are with shade, water and drainage. There is lively entertainment at night and music during the day and the site is generally buzzing with activity, the centre being under the palms near the huge pool, sun deck and bar. About a quarter of the area is devoted to mainly older style cabins and mobile homes.

Facilities

Three sanitary blocks have a mixture of adequate facilities although it will be busy at peak periods for showering. Units for disabled campers are in one. Laundry facilities. Supermarket. Bar. Self-service restaurant. Snack bar. Pizzeria. Very good, large swimming pool. Large play area. Tennis. Ambitious entertainment. Disco. Beach club and bar. Dogs not accepted in July/Aug. Off site: Sea fishing. Watersports.

Open: 1 June - 15 September.

Directions

Leave autostrada E14 north of Pescara and take SS80 to Giulianova Lido. Follow site signs (there are many). Providing you follow the signs, to end up at the north end of the town, you will find the bridge with a 3.6 m. clearance. All other bridges have 'car only' clearances. Site is 400 m. on left after the bridge. GPS: 42.7779, 13.955883

Charges guide

Per person	€ 4,50 - € 9,00
child	€ 2,50 - € 5,50
pitch	€ 10,00 - € 19,00

Giulianova Lido

Don Antonio Camping Residence

Via Padova s.n.c., I-64021 Giulianova Lido (Abruzzo) T: 085 800 8928. E: info@campingdonantonio.it

alanrogers.com/IT68020

Set alongside the beautiful Adriatic coast with its sandy beaches, Baviera is a small site with basic, older-style facilities. However, there is access to the facilities of its larger sister site Camping Holiday (IT68010) with its tempting pool, restaurant, games and supermarket. Many of the campers also pop 'next door' to join in and enjoy the organised entertainment. This quiet site may be subject to some noise during the evening and music in the daytime from the other camp sites in the immediate area. A lovely simple café and gelateria is at the front of the site near the beach where there is also a beach bar.

Facilities

Four traditional units provide a mixture of sanitary facilities which are clean but a little tired. The new units for disabled campers are of a high standard. Washing machine. Snack bar. Beach bar. Torches useful. Dogs and other animals are not accepted in July/Aug. Off site: Beach fishing. Bicycle hire 1 km. Golf 35 km. All resort facilities in town.

Open: 1 June - 15 September.

Directions

Leave autostrada E14 north of Pescara and take SS80 to Giulianova Lido. Follow site signs - there are many, many signs so travel slowly! Providing you follow the signs and end up at the north town you will find the bridge with a 3.6 m. clearance. All other bridges have 'car only' clearances. The site is 400 m. on left after the bridge. GPS: 42.777322, 13.951178

Charges guide

Per unit incl. 2 persons and electricity	€ 19,00 - € 42,00
extra person	€ 5,00 - € 12,00
child (3-8 yrs)	€ 2,00 - € 7,00

Marina di Vasto

Camping Villaggio Il Pioppeto

SS16 Sud km. 521, I-66055 Marina di Vasto (Abruzzo) T: 087 380 1466. E: infocampeggio@ilpioppeto.it

alanrogers.com/IT67970

Il Pioppeto lies to the south of Pescara and is a great choice for a low season holiday, notwithstanding its pitches which are a little small. However, in peak season the adjacent beach and main road (SS16) are both very busy and there is a lively entertainment programme. The site is well maintained and tidy with shady pitches on level ground (all with 3A electrical connections). The sandy beach is delightful and the site also boasts a good range of leisure amenities. The four toilet blocks are of a good standard although some washbasins have just cold water.

Facilities

Four well appointed toilet blocks. Motorcaravan services. Supermarket. Bar and snack bar. Restaurant. Play area. Games room. Entertainment and children's club in peak season. Adjacent beach. Chalets for rent. Off site: Riding centre (owned by site) 700 m. Disco. Tennis. Roller skating rink. Mountain biking and walking.

Open: 15 May - 15 September.

Directions

From the A14 motorway (Bologna - Taranto) take Vasto exit and join SS16 towards Vasto from where site is well signed. GPS: 42.08800, 14.73667

Charges guide

Per unit incl. 2 persons and electricity	€ 25,20 - € 35,90
extra person	€ 6,60 - € 8,30
child (2-8 yrs)	€ 4,40 - € 6,00
dog	€ 5,00

Martinsicuro

Camping Riva Nuova

Via dei Pioppi 6, I-64014 Martinsicuro (Abruzzo) T: 086 179 7515. E: emanuele.dionisi@rivanuova.it

alanrogers.com/IT67980

Situated at the south end of the small town of Martinsicuro on the Adriatic Coast, this excellent site offers a first class camping experience. Set in well landscaped gardens and well planned, you will find 129 bungalows to rent and 359 pitches for campers varying from 60 to 120 sq. m. with an increasing level of services. There are 114 pitches with water, drainage and electricity and a further 24 with a private bathroom on the pitch. Alongside is an extensive sandy beach with endless bars, pizzeria and restaurants. The town shops are nearby. This is a great site for low or high season.

Facilities

An exceptional, central sanitary block provides everything to the highest standard. Ample toilets, showers and washbasins. Laundry facilities. Children's bathroom. Facilities for disabled visitors. Private bathrooms to rent. Bar, restaurant and shop. Swimming pool and sunbathing area. Gym. Boules. Tennis. Entertainment in high season. ATM. Dogs are not accepted. Off site: Martinsicuro. Tremano.

Open: 1 May - 15 September.

Directions

Leave the A14 at San Benedetto and take SS16 to Martinsicuro. Turn onto the coast road and go south of the town to the site in via dei Pioppi (well signed). GPS: 42.88010, 13.9205

Charges guide

Per person	€ 3,50 - € 10,90
child	€ 2,00 - € 7,00
pitch	€ 8,90 - € 44,80

Opi

Camping Il Vecchio Mulino

S.R. Marsicana 83 km 52, I-67030 Opi (Abruzzo) T: **086 391 2232**. E: **ilvecchiomulino@tiscalinet.it**
alanrogers.com/IT67920

Il Vecchio Mulino enjoys a fine woodland setting on the slopes of Monte Marsicano at the heart of the Abruzzo National Park. The site is open all year and is popular for walking and cycling in the summer and is well located for the Pescasseroli and Macchiarvana ski resorts in the winter. The focal point of the site is the old mill and attractively restored farm buildings house a restaurant and B&B accommodation. The restaurant specialises in local Abruzzese cuisine and is open from May to September. The 200 pitches here are spacious and level and all are equipped with a wooden picnic table and electrical connection.

Facilities

Centrally located toilet block. Restaurant, snack bar. Small shop (local produce). Games room. Bar (in restaurant). Sports field. Play area. Games room. Barbecue area. Motorcaravan services. Tourist information. Off site: Village centre 1 km. Bus service from site entrance. Abruzzo National Park. Mountain biking and walking.

Open: All year.

Directions

Take Pescina exit from the A24/A25 Rome - Pescara motorway and join the SS83 through Passo del Diavolo to Pescasseroli from where the site is well signed (1 km. from Opi). GPS: 41.780017, 13.867767

Charges guide

Per person	€ 6,50 - € 7,00
electricity	€ 2,50
car	€ 3,00 - € 3,50

Camping Cheques accepted.

Pineto

Camping Heliopolis

Ctra Villa Fumosa 1, I-64025 Pineto (Abruzzo) T: **085 949 2720**. E: **info@heliopolis.it**
alanrogers.com/IT68050

Heliopolis is an attractive, well run site with a charming English speaking lady owner named Gigliola who is delighted to receive British customers at her site which is very popular with Italians. This is an unusual site for the Adriatic as most of the pitches have their own neat, clean and covered private units with shower/WC and washing facilities. The pitches are of average size arranged in rows at right angles to the beach, most with artificial shade provided and all with electricity. Cars may be parked elsewhere. The site opens directly onto a wide pleasant sand and shingle beach.

Facilities

Two excellent toilet blocks, one for men and one for women, include facilities for disabled campers. Individual units for 120 of the 160 pitches. Laundry facilities. Bar/coffee shop. Restaurant (weekends only until 1/6). Shops (from 1/6). Swimming pool (from 15/6). Tennis. Playground. Games room. Entertainment in high season. Torches required near beach areas. Off site: Trips to Rome, Napoli, Capri, San Marino and other local attractions can be organized.

Open: 1 April - 30 September.

Directions

Site is north of the town sharing an approach with Camping Pineto Beach; both sites are clearly signed from A14 road (exit Pineto) and SS16 (in town). GPS: 42.62630, 14.05370

Charges guide

Per person	€ 4,00 - € 8,50
child (3-12 yrs)	€ 3,50 - € 7,50
pitch incl. electricity	€ 9,50 - € 24,00
pitch with private facilities	€ 16,50 - € 30,00
small tent pitch	€ 4,00 - € 9,00

Pineto

International Camping

Ctra Torre Cerrano, I-64025 Pineto (Abruzzo) T: **085 930 639**. E: **into@internationalcamping.it**
alanrogers.com/IT68060

This small family run site, just north of Pescara and south of Pineto and is situated between the coastal railway line and a sandy beach. Inevitably there is some railway noise but it is not too intrusive. Access to the site is via a 4 m. high bridge followed by a sharp right hand turn, then through narrow gates to reception about 300 m. ahead. With 100 small pitches for touring units, all with electricity and ten mobile homes to rent, it is quieter than the larger sites that are the norm on this coast. During June to August it is a family site with entertainment and all sorts of fun and games on the beach.

Facilities

One sanitary block provides ample toilets (British and Turkish style) washbasins and hot showers. Shop (1/5-15/9). Bar, restaurant and takeaway. Beach. Internet point. Entertainment (high season). Excursions organised. Mobile homes and bungalows to rent. Dogs only accepted in May and Sept. Off site: Pineto.

Open: 1 May - 30 September.

Directions

On the SS16 at 431.2 km. marker just past the Cerrano tower, turn towards the beach and under the railway (4 m. bridge). Then turn immediately right site. GPS: 42.58124, 14.09294

Charges guide

Per unit incl. 2 persons and electricity	€ 21,00 - € 41,50
extra person	€ 8,50 - € 17,00
child (3-6 yrs)	€ 4,00 - € 9,50

No credit cards.

Roseto degli Abruzzi

260

Camping Village Eurcamping

Lungomare Trieste Sud, I-64026 Roseto degli Abruzzi (Abruzzo) T: 085 899 3179. E: **eurcamping@camping.it**

alanrogers.com/IT68040

Eurcamping is about 2 km. south of the small town of Roseto degli Abruzzi, on the small coastal road which runs parallel to the SS16. This is a quiet site, situated beside the sea, with a total of 265 small pitches (many under green screens) and all with electricity (3/6A). Accessing the site may be difficult for higher units as you have to pass under the coastal railway line and many of the bridges offer less than 2 m. headroom. There is some road noise but little noise from the railway. There are good facilities and some entertainment is provided for children in high season.

Facilities

Three sanitary blocks with free hot showers. Facilities for disabled people. Motorcaravan services. Laundry. Bar. Restaurant. Takeaway. Pizzeria. Shop. Swimming pools (hats must be worn) with solarium terrace. Play area and sports ground. Tennis. Bowling. Internet point. Bicycle hire. Entertainment in high season. Clubs for children and teenagers. Pets are allowed only on assigned pitches. Off site: Beach. Canoe and pedalo hire.

Open: 1 April - 31 October.

Directions

From north or south on A14 motorway, take exit for Roseto degli Abruzzi. Turn on SS150 to Roseto degli Abruzzi. From Rome and L'Aquila on A24 motorway take exit for Villa Vomano-Teramo, onto SS150 (Rose to degli Abruzzi). GPS: 42.6577, 14.0353

Charges guide

Per unit incl. 2 persons and electricity	€ 17,00 - € 38,50
extra person	€ 4,50 - € 10,00
child (3-8 yrs)	€ 3,00 - € 6,50
dog	free - € 5,00

Camping Cheques accepted.

DIRECT TO THE SEA

OPEN 01.04. - 31.10.

ITALIA Abruzzo

✔ Situated in a quiet area
✔ Possibility of booking pitches
✔ 265 grassy, numbered and good shaded pitches (60-110 sqm)
✔ Mobil Homes and Bungalows

camping village
Eurcamping

Lungomare Trieste Sud
I-64026 Roseto degli Abruzzi (Teramo)
Tel. +39.085.8993179 • Fax +39.085.8930552
www.eurcamping.it

Silvi

Camping Europe Garden

Via Belvedere 11, I-64028 Silvi (Abruzzo) T: 085 930 137. E: **info@europegarden.it**

alanrogers.com/IT68000

This site is 13 kilometres northwest of Pescara and, lying just back from the coast (2 km) up a very steep hill, it has pleasant views over the sea. The 204 pitches (40 for touring), all with electricity, are mainly on good terraces – access may be difficult on some pitches. However, if installation of caravans is a problem a tractor is available to help. When we visited the site was dry but we suspect life might become difficult on some pitches after heavy rain. Cars stand by units on over half of the pitches or in nearby parking spaces for the remainder, and most pitches are shaded.

Facilities

Two good toilet blocks are well cleaned and provide mixed British and Turkish style WCs. Washing machines. Restaurant. Bar. Swimming pool (hats compulsory; 300 sq.m), small paddling pool and jacuzzi. Tennis. Playground. Entertainment programme. Free weekly excursions (15/6-8/9). Free bus service (18/5-7/9) to beach. Dogs are not accepted.

Open: 27 April - 20 September.

Directions

Turn inland off S16 coast road at km. 433 for Silvi Alta and follow site signs. From autostrada A14 take Pineto exit from north or Pescara Nord exit from the south. GPS: 42.56738, 14.09247

Charges guide

Per person	€ 5,00 - € 10,00
child (0-3 yrs)	€ 4,00 - € 7,50
pitch	€ 10,00 - € 16,50
2 man tent	€ 6,00 - € 13,00
electricity	€ 2,50

Discounts for longer stays outside high season.

Check real time availability and at-the-gate prices...

www.**alanrogers**.com

Tortoreto Lido

Camping Village Del Salinello

Lungomare Sud, I-64018 Tortoreto Lido (Abruzzo) T: **086 772 31**. E: **info@salinello.com**

alanrogers.com/IT67990

This large, attractive site is at the southern extremity of Tortoreto Lido. It provides over 300 chalets and bungalows to rent and a further 250 small pitches for camping under trees. With an adjacent sandy beach alongside the turquoise Adriatic, the site has an excellent location and is close to both the SS16 and the A14 autostrada. However, access to the coast road, Lungomare is complicated by the necessity to go under the railway since many of the bridges have less than 2 m. headroom. Once you find a suitable crossing point (the site signs lead us to an impossible crossing) turn south.

Facilities

Two large sanitary blocks for campers' use have mainly Turkish toilets, showers in small cubicles and open plan washbasins. Facilities for disabled visitors. Private bathrooms to rent. Swimming complex (on payment). Bars. Restaurants. Commercial centre and cinema/theatre. Entertainment in high season. Tennis and 5-a-side pitches (on payment). ATM. Dogs are not accepted. Off site: Tortoreto Lido.

Open: 15 May - 15 September.

Directions

From the A14 join the SS16 via either the Valvibrata or the Teramo exits and head towards Tortoreto. In the town turn towards the coast having found a suitable point to cross the railway (watch the headroom signs). Then turn south on the Lungomare to the site which is in a cul-de-sac at the southern extremity of the town. GPS: 42.75222, 13.97583

Charges guide

Per person	€ 5,00 - € 10,00
child (2-6 yrs)	€ 4,00 - € 8,00
pitch	€ 8,50 - € 17,00

Villalago

Camping I Lupi

Riviera di Villalago, Lago di Scanno, I-67030 Villalago (Abruzzo) T: **086 474 0100**. E: **campingilupi@libero.it**

alanrogers.com/IT67930

I Lupi is a large, friendly, all year site in a beautiful location within the Abruzzo National Park. The site is located in a valley on the banks of the Lago di Scanno. Pitches are generally large and many have fine views of the surrounding mountain scenery. Around 500 pitches have electrical connections (10A) and some hardstandings are available. This is a large site and at night torches may be useful. Amenities on site are limited – there is a small shop and snack bar/takeaway but no restaurant. However, a number of restaurants are available within easy walking distance.

Facilities

Two well appointed toilet blocks with upgraded facilities including private cabins. Motorcaravan services. Bar, snack bar. Supermarket. Play area. Children's club in peak season. Tourist information. Games room. Sports field. Direct access to lake. Chalets for rent. Off site: Riding. Tennis. Mountain biking and walking throughout the National Park. Fishing.

Open: All year.

Directions

From A25 motorway (Rome - Pescara) take Cocullo exit and join the SP60 towards Anversa Degli Abruzzi. At this town, join the SR479 towards Scanno and you will reach the Lago di Scanno and the site shortly after passing Villalago. GPS: 41.92009, 13.859081

Charges guide

Per person	€ 6,00
child (2-6 yrs)	€ 5,80
pitch	€ 8,20 - € 10,20
electricity	€ 2,70

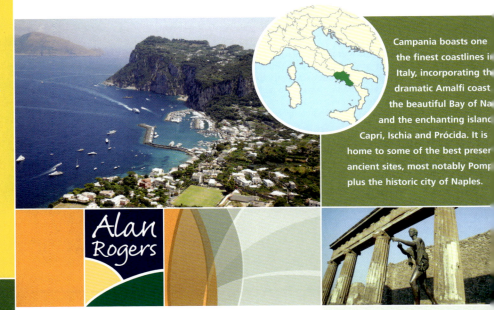

Campania

Campania boasts one
the finest coastlines i
Italy, incorporating th
dramatic Amalfi coast
the beautiful Bay of Na
and the enchanting island
Capri, Ischia and Prócida. It is
home to some of the best preser
ancient sites, most notably Pomp
plus the historic city of Naples.

Alan Rogers

**THE REGION HAS FIVE PROVINCES: AVELLINO,
BENEVENTO, CASERTA, NAPOLI AND SALERNO**

Filled with palaces, churches and convents,
the regional capital of Naples also boasts
an archaeology museum housing artefacts
excavated from the nearby Roman sites of
Pompeii and Herculaneum. Situated on the
Bay of Naples, these sites were buried after
Mount Vesuvius erupted in 79 AD, leaving
them frozen in time. Although still active
(the only one on mainland Europe) it is
possible to scale up the volcano. Not far
from Pompeii, is the popular holiday
destination of Sorrento and off the coast of
the bay are the islands of Ischia, Capri and
Prócida. The largest is Ischia, which along
with Capri, attracts vast numbers of
tourists; Prócida is the smallest and least
visited. All three can be explored on day
trips from the mainland. Further south is
the Amalfi coast, a spectacular stretch of
coastline littered with superb beaches and
resorts, including Positano, Amalfi and
Ravello. The busy port of Salerno is near to
the ancient Greek site of Paestum, with
temples dating back to the 6th century BC,
and the area known as the Cilento,
a mountainous region with a quiet
coastline. It has a number of seaside resorts
including Agropoli, Acciaroli and Palinuro
plus the inland villages of Castelcivita and
Pertosa, both of which have cave systems
open to the public.

Places of interest

Benevento: once an important Roman
settlement, monuments include the Arch
of Trajan and the Roman theatre.

Campi Flegri: area known as the Fiery Fie
with volcanic craters and hots springs.

Caserta: opulent royal palace with garde
open to the public.

Ravello: offers best view of the Amalfi co

Salerno: medieval old quarter, 11th centu
cathedral, annual fair in May.

San Marco: picturesque fishing village.

Santa Maria Capua Vetere: ruined Roma
amphitheatre with series of tunnels
beneath it.

Cuisine of the region

Naples is the home of pizza, pasta and
tomato sauce. Aubergines and courgette
are frequently used in pasta sauces. Seaf
is widely available along the coast includ
fresh squid, octopus, clams and mussels.
Cilento produces strawberries, artichoke
and mozzarella cheese. Made with buffa
milk, mozzarella is usually accompanied
tomatoes.

Calzone: stuffed fried pizza with ham ar
cheese.

Marinara: pizza topped with tomato, ga
and basil, no cheese.

Sfogliatella: flaky pastry case stuffed wit
ricotta and candied peel.

Zuppa di cozze: mussels with a hot pepp
sauce.

Zuppa Inglese: dessert made with spong
fingers, peaches, custard, brandy and e
whites.

Baia Domizia

Baia Domizia Villaggio Camping

I-81030 Baia Domizia (Campania) T: 082 393 0164. E: info@baiadomizia.it

alanrogers.com/IT68200

This large, beautifully-maintained seaside site is about 70 kilometres northwest of Naples, and is within a pinewood, cleverly left in its natural state. Although it does not feel like it, there are 750 touring pitches in clearings, either of grass and sand or on hardstanding, all with electricity. Finding a pitch may take time as there are so many good ones to choose from, but staff will help in season. Most pitches are well shaded, however there are some in the sun for cooler periods. The central complex is superb with well designed buildings providing for all needs (the site is some distance from the town). Member of Leading Campings Group. Restaurants, bars and a 'gelaterie' enjoy live entertainment and attractive water lily ponds surround the area. The entire site is attractive, with shrubs, flowers and huge green areas. Near the entrance is a new swimming pool complex complete with hydromassage points and a large sunbathing area. The supervised beach is of soft sand and a great attraction. A large grassy field overlooking the sea is ideal for picnics and sunbathing. A wide range of sports and other amenities are provided. The site is very well organised with particular regulations (e.g. no dogs or loud noise), so the general atmosphere is relaxing and peaceful. Although the site is big, there is never far to walk to the beach, and although it may be some 300 m. to the central shops and restaurant from the site boundaries, there is always a nearby toilet block. It is the ideal place to recover from the rigours of touring or to relax and allow the professionals to organise tours for you to Rome, Pompeii, Sorrento etc. Charges are undeniably high, but this site is well above average and most suitable for families with children.

Facilities

Seven new toilet blocks have hot water in washbasins (many cabins) and showers. Good access and facilities for disabled people. Washing machines, spin dryers. Motorcaravan services. Gas supplies. Supermarket and general shop. Large bar. Restaurants, pizzeria and takeaway. Ice cream parlour. Swimming pool complex. Playground. Tennis. Bicycle hire. Windsurfing hire and school. Disco. Excursions. Torches required in some areas. Dogs are not accepted. Off site: Fishing and riding 3 km.

Open: 30 April - 20 September.

Directions

The turn to Baia Domizia leads off the Formia - Naples road 23 km. from Formia. From Rome - Naples autostrada, take Cassino exit to Formia. Site is to the north of Baia Domizia and well signed. Site is off the coastal road that runs parallel to the SS7.
GPS: 41.19999, 13.79999

Charges guide

Per person	€ 5,10 - € 11,20
child (1-11 yrs)	€ 4,00 - € 8,50
pitch incl. electricity	€ 11,50 - € 23,00

Eboli Mare

Camping Village Paestum

Litoranea Localitá Foce Sele, I-84025 Eboli Mare (Campania) T: 082 869 1003. E: info@campingpaestum.it
alanrogers.com/IT68410

This site is near the important ancient Greek temples of ancient Poseidon, built by the Greeks in the sixth century BC and taken by the Romans and renamed in 273 BC. It fell into decline and was abandoned in the ninth century, was rediscovered in the 18th century and is well worth a visit today. Fast becoming a popular tourist resort, the town of Paestum is some way south of the site which enjoys a quiet, rural environment. With 480 pitches, 170 are for tourers and a special area is maintained for non-Italian guests on the basis that they prefer more peace and quiet.

Facilities

Five toilet blocks make up a good provision which includes Turkish and British style WCs. Facilities for disabled visitors. Motorcaravan service point. Washing machines. Small shop. Bar and restaurant. Swimming pool, children's pool and slide (swimming caps compulsory). Tennis. Entertainment and children's club. Disco. Shuttle bus to beach. Bungalows to rent. Pets are not accepted. Off site: Beach 300 m. Paestum archaeological site 10 km.

Open: 1 May - 15 September.

Directions

Site is north of Paestum Capaccio on the coast road (SP173). From Paestum go north along main coast road. At T-junction turn left, past military zone to site about 3 km. on right. From A3 near Salerno follow signs initially for Pontecagnano. Then keep south on coast road (SP173). GPS: 40.491167, 14.944583

Charges guide

Per person	€ 5,00 - € 8,00
pitch	€ 12,00 - € 20,00

Massa Lubrense

Camping Nettuno

Via A. Vespucci 39, Marina del Cantone, I-80061 Massa Lubrense (Campania) T: 081 808 1051
E: info@villaggionettuno.it alanrogers.com/IT68380

Camping Nettuno is owned and run by the friendly Mauro family who speak excellent English. Nestling the bay of Marina del Cantone, it is situated in the protected area of 'Punta Campanella', away from the busiest tourist spots, so the approach roads are difficult and narrow. This tiny campsite of only 42 pitches (4A) is spread over three levels above the pebbly beach. Up several steps and across the road are the amenities, reception, shop, and dive centre and then above this is a restaurant. The pitches, which are small and close together, are informally arranged, some with a fabulous sea view (extra charge).

Facilities

The central sanitary block includes facilities for disabled people (and access via a ramp to the beach). Washing machine. Basic motorcaravan service point. Gas supplies. Small shop. Delightful restaurant with sea views. Bar (lively at night). Dive centre. Excursions. TV in bar area. Small play area. Free tennis arranged at court next door. Off site: Small beach (pebbles) 5 m. from bottom of site. Excellent restaurant 100 m. Amalfi Coast, Capri, nature parks, walking etc.

Open: 1 March - 2 November.

Directions

From A3 (Naples - Salerno), take Castellamare di Stabia exit onto S145. Pass Castellamare, follow signs to Meta di Sorrento through Vico Equense bypass tunnel and turn off towards Positano in Meta. After 5 km. turn to Sant Agata dei due Golfi (6.5 km) then follow signs to Nerano and finally Marina del Cantone. Site entrance is 50 m. past the entrance to reception and dive centre. You will need to go on for 100 m. to turn round in order to enter site with its steep and narrow entrance. GPS: 40.58389, 14.35194

Charges guide

Per person	€ 6,50 - € 9,00
pitch incl. electricity	€ 11,50 - € 16,50
Camping Cheques accepted.	

Paestum

Camping Villaggio Athena

Via Ponte di Ferro, I-84063 Paestum (Campania) T: 082 885 1105. E: vathena@tiscalinet.it
alanrogers.com/IT68530

This level site, which has direct access to the beach, has most facilities to hand. Much of the site is in woodland, but sun worshipers will have no problem here. The access is easy and the staff are friendly. There are 150 pitches, of which only 20 are used for static units and these are unobtrusive. There is no disco, although cabaret shows are staged in July/Aug. The management, the Prearo brothers, aim for a pleasant and happy environment.

Facilities

Toilet facilities in three blocks have mixed British and Turkish style WCs, washbasins and showers. Dishwashing and laundry sinks. Toilets for disabled people. Shop. Bar and restaurant (1/5-30/9). Riding. Watersports. Dogs and barbecues are not permitted. Off site: Tennis 1 km. Hourly bus service. Greek temples nearby.

Open: 1 March - 30 October.

Directions

Take SS18 through Paestum and, at southern end of town before the antiquities, turn right as signed and follow to sea. At crossroads turn left and a little further, right. Site signed. GPS: 40.42061, 14.99608

Charges guide

Per person	€ 5,00 - € 8,50
pitch incl. electricity	€ 8,50 - € 14,00

Pompeii

Camping Zeus

Via Villa dei Misteri, I-80045 Pompeii (Campania) T: **081 861 5320**. E: **info@campingzeus.it**
alanrogers.com/IT68300

The naming of this site is obvious once you discover it is just 50 metres from the entrance to the fantastic ruins at Pompeii (closer than the car park). It is a reasonably priced, city type site perfect for visiting the famous Roman archaeological sites here. The site's 100 pitches, all for touring units, are on flat grass under mature trees that give shade. All have access to 10A electricity. Larger units use the tarmac parking area. This site provides a safe central location and is of a high standard for the area, albeit with none of the holidaying trimmings.

Facilities

The single sanitary block is clean and modernised, with British and Turkish type WCs. Showers have hot water with cold water in washbasins and dishwashing sinks. No facilities for disabled campers. Washing machines. Shop. Gas supplies. Bar/restaurant with good value daily menu at lunch times (evening in high season) with waiter service. Off site: Pompeii, Sorrento, Herculaneum, Amalfi coast.

Open: All year.

Directions

Leave Napoli - Salerno autostrada at the Pompeii Ovest exit. Turn left towards the ruins and go under the autostrada. A further 100 m. turn left towards Pompeii and the site. Site is straight ahead past the railway station. GPS: 40.74958, 14.47240

Charges guide

Per person	€ 5,00 - € 6,00
pitch	€ 5,00 - € 12,00
car	€ 4,00

Pozzuoli

Camping Il Vulcano Solfatara

Via Solfetara no. 163, I-80078 Pozzuoli (Campania) T: **081 526 7413**. E: **info@solfatara.it**
alanrogers.com/IT68250

This is truly a unique site situated within the crater of an active volcano. Solfatara is one of the many volcanoes that surround Naples, Vesuvius being the most widely known. Here you can camp in a pleasant wooded area with modern facilities, yet be just a couple of minutes from the barren moon-like landscape of the other side of the crater with its steaming fumaroles. This is a site and sight not to be missed. The one problem here is the access arch which is just 2.30 m. wide and the only way in – we got in by turning our wing mirrors in and getting help from the staff and it was a tight squeeze.

Facilities

The single sanitary block provides, toilets (British and Turkish style), hot showers and washbasins. Washing machine. Motorcaravan service point. Bar, restaurant and small shop. Small volcano museum. Off site: The Solfatara natural park and the living breathing volcano!

Open: 1 April - 4 November.

Directions

Take the Naples 'tangenziale' from the autostrada and exit at junction n11 (Agnano). Follow signs towards Pozzuoli and turn right at traffic lights at the top of the hill. Site is 3.5 km. along this road on the right. GPS: 40.82858, 14.13583

Charges guide

Per person	€ 7,60 - € 9,40
child	€ 3,80 - € 4,70
pitch	€ 4,50 - € 14,00

Sorrento

Camping Santa Fortunata

Via Capo 39 AB, I-80067 Sorrento (Campania) T: **081 807 3574**. E: **info@santafortunata.com**
alanrogers.com/IT68340

Camping Santa Fortunata is situated on the hillside just outside Sorrento among olive and lemon groves. There is plenty of shade but low hanging branches make some of the pitches unsuitable for larger units. There is a steep tarmac approach to some but the stunning views over the bay more than compensate. Pitches are of average size with several spaces for larger units and there is a feeling of spaciousness as many are separated by trees and shrubs intersected with wooden constructed walkways. Two small beaches can be reached via long steep inclines. A daily excursion to Capri (well worth taking) departs from one of the beaches.

Facilities

Five older-style refurbished sanitary blocks with adjustable hot showers. Hot water for dishwashing but not laundry sinks. Washing machine. Good restaurant/bar. Small well stocked shop. Swimming pool. Excursions. WiFi. Off site: Local bus to Sorrento. Boat trips to Capri. Amalfi, Naples, Pompeii and Positano are all within easy reach.

Open: 1 April - 19 October.

Directions

From the A3 (Naples - Salerno) follow signs to Pensisola Sorrentina. Exit at Castellammare di Stabia and on through Sorrento. Then take SS145 towards Massa Lubrense, running along Via Capo. Site is .5 km. past Sorrento. GPS: 40.62753, 14.35736

Charges guide

Per person	€ 6,00 - € 11,00
child (0-10 yrs)	free - € 6,00
pitch	€ 11,00 - € 16,50

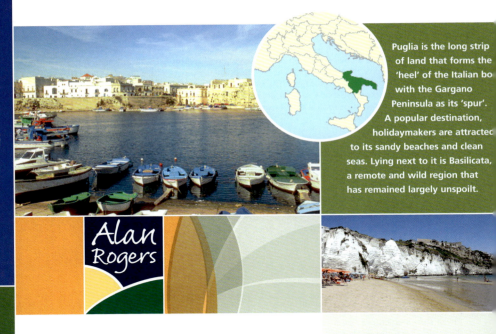

Puglia is the long strip of land that forms the 'heel' of the Italian bo with the Gargano Peninsula as its 'spur'. A popular destination, holidaymakers are attracted to its sandy beaches and clean seas. Lying next to it is Basilicata, a remote and wild region that has remained largely unspoilt.

PUGLIA HAS FIVE PROVINCES: BARI, BRINDISI, FOGGIA, LECCE AND TARANTO

BASILICATA HAS TWO: MATERA AND POTENZA

Made into a national park in 1991, the Gargano peninsula in Puglia boasts a diverse landscape of beaches, lagoons, forests and mountains. Up in the hills is the town of Monte Sant'Angelo. Home to one of the earliest Christian shrines in Europe, it attracts pilgrimages from all over the country. Further inland is the Forest of Shadows, an area covering 11,000 hectares with a variety of wildlife, ideal for walking. The seaside towns of Vieste, Rodi Garganico, Péshici and Manfredonia are popular with tourists, as are the Trémiti Islands – including San Nicola, San Domino and Capraia – off the Gargano coast. Heading south is Trani, one of the most important medieval ports with an ornate cathedral, and Bari. Ferries to Greece depart from Bari, as well as from Bríndisi. At the southern tip of Puglia is Lecce, renowned for its Baroque architecture, and the Salentine peninsula. Good beaches can be found along the western coast of the peninsula around Gallipoli. To the west Basilicata is mostly upland country, scattered with ruins. The brooding town of Melfi has a formidable Norman castle, while nearby Venosa was once the largest Roman colony. The town has an archaeology park with remains of Roman baths and an amphitheatre.

Places of interest

Alberobello: home to whitewashed circula buildings with conical roofs known as *trui* there are truilli restaurants, shops plus a cathedral.

Galatina: important wine-producing town famous for its tarantella dance performed on the feast day of Saints Peter and Paul in June.

Lucera: ruins of Roman amphitheatre, 13th-century castle with fortified walls and towers.

Matera: town perched on edge of a ravin

Mattinata: popular, small resort in Gargo

Metaponto: Roman ruins, museums.

Vieste: holiday capital of Puglia with excellent beaches.

Cuisine of the region

Puglia is the main source of Italy's fish. It also produces some of the country's best olives and is famous for its almonds, tomatoes, figs, melons and grapes. Lamb is commonly eaten, often roasted with rosemary and thyme, and as there is little poultry, beef or pork in the region, horsemeat is popular, particularly in the Salento area. Peppers and *zenzero* (ginge are widely used in dishes throughout Basilicata. Local cheeses include *ricotta*, *mozzarella*, *scamorza*, *burrata* (soft and creamy, made with cow's milk), and *capr* (small fresh goat's cheese preserved in olive oil).

Braciole di cavallo: horsemeat steaks coc in a rich tomato sauce.

Latte di mandorla: almond milk.

Panzarotti alla barese: pasta stuffed with meat sauce, egg and cheese, deep-fried olive oil.

Alberobello

Camping Dei Trulli

Via Castellana, I-70011 Alberobello (Puglia) T: **080 432 3699**. E: **info@campingdeitrulli.it**
alanrogers.com/IT68700

The UNESCO listed site at Alberobello is just 15 km. inland from the coast and offers the chance to see the unusual Trulli properties. It is a dry, almost arid, landscape which is covered with olive groves, orchards, vineyards and the trulli (strange circular buildings with conical roofs and domed within, built from local limestone without mortar). Camping Dei Trulli is a short stay site offering visitors a chance to explore the area. It has 120 small pitches all with 5A electricity. Bungalows and caravans are available to rent. The grottos of Castellana are not far away.

Facilities

The toilet block includes facilities for disabled visitors and also holds the washing machine and is used for emptying chemical toilets. Small shop. Bar. Restaurant (Aug. only). Swimming pool and children's pool (1/6-15/9). Pool table and electronic games. Indoor disco during the winter months. Off site: Alberobello (Trulli properties). The Grottos of Castellana.

Open: All year.

Directions

From E55 coast road south of Bari take Alberobello exit (SP113) and bear left then right. Site is 15 km. along this road. At crossroads go straight ahead towards Alberobello and the site is on the left 1.5 km. before the town. GPS: 40.801283, 17.251217

Charges 2010

Per person	€ 5,00 - € 8,00
child (3-8 yrs)	€ 4,00 - € 5,00
pitch	€ 6,00 - € 11,00
electricity	€ 2,50

Gallipoli

Centro Vacanze La Masseria

I-73014 Gallipoli (Puglia) T: 083 320 2296. E: info@lamasseria.net

alanrogers.com/IT68655

Located near the Torre Sabea and within an ancient farm, this site provides 300 pitches under pinewood. During the low seasons most pitches are unmarked in two large areas, but in high season the lines of marked pitches at the end of the site with their high net screens come into use. Gallipoli is just a short ride away and the site operates a shuttle bus in high season. The old town has much to offer and the fish market and restaurants near the port entrance are well worth a visit. The beach is just across the coastal road at the side of the site.

Facilities

Five sanitary blocks and 36 private bathrooms (to rent) provide ample toilets, showers and washbasins. Bar, restaurant and shop. Washing machines. Motorcaravan service point. Large swimming pool complex. Shuttle bus to Gallipoli in high season. Wine and oil tasting on site. Off site: Gallipoli.

Open: All year.

Directions

From the SS101 (Lecce - Gallipoli) road leave at km. 30 towards the Porto. Site is close by and is well signed. Reception is beyond the restaurant and pools. GPS: 40.07417, 18.00889

Charges guide

Per unit incl. up to 3 persons	€ 21,00 - € 38,00
extra person	€ 6,00 - € 10,00

Gallipoli

Camping Baia di Gallipoli

Litoranea per Santa Maria di Leuca, I-73014 Gallipoli (Puglia) T: 083 327 3210. E: info@baiadigallipoli.com

alanrogers.com/IT68660

The western shoreline of Puglia offers beaches of excellent quality, interspersed with small villages and some holiday complexes. The Baia of Gallipoli campsite is in a quiet rural area to the southwest of the town on a minor coast road. It offers 600 pitches, all with electricity, under pine and eucalyptus trees. Cars are parked in a separate area and access for vehicles is strictly controlled which gives the site a quiet, peaceful ambience. Although it is about 1 km. from the beach it has solved that problem in partnership with others by providing regular shuttle buses to the beach car park.

Facilities

Five toilet blocks include facilities for disabled visitors, both on the site and at the beach. Motorcaravan service point. Washing machines. Shop. Bar and restaurant (1/4-31/10). Swimming pool (1/6-30/9). Tennis. Shuttle bus to beach (1 km). Off site: Gallipoli.

Open: All year.

Directions

The SS101 motorway south of Bari heads first to Lecce, then turns southwest towards Gallipoli. Join the SS274 towards Santa Maria di Leuca and exit at Lido Pizzo. Follow the coast road (SP215) towards Gallipoli and site is on the right 4 km. before Gallipoli. GPS: 39.998317, 18.0265

Charges guide

Per person	€ 6,00 - € 18,00
child (3-8 yrs)	€ 3,00 - € 18,00
Camping Cheques accepted.	

Peschici

Centro Turistico San Nicola

I-71010 Peschici (Puglia) T: 088 496 3420. E: sannicola@sannicola.it

alanrogers.com/IT68450

This is a really splendid site occupying a hillside position, sloping down to a cove with a 500-metre beach of fine sand – a special feature is an attractive grotto at the eastern end. Hard access roads lead to spacious, well constructed, grassy pitches, under shade from mature trees. Scores of pitches are on the beach fringes (no extra charge) and there is a separate area for campers with animals. There are 800 pitches of varying sizes, all with electricity. Cars may have to be parked away from the pitches in high season. There are no static caravans, but some bungalows on site. Member of Leading Campings Group.

Facilities

Six modern toilet blocks, two in the beach part, the others around the site, are excellent with British and Turkish style toilets, hot water in the washbasins (some with toilets in private cabins) and showers. Laundry facilities. Supermarket. Two beach bars (from 1/5; some evening noise until 22.30 hrs). Large bar/restaurant with terraces and pizzeria. Tennis. Watersports. Playground. Organised activities and entertainment (July/Aug). Off site: Coach and boat excursions. Gargano National Park.

Open: 1 April - 15 October.

Directions

Leave autostrada A14 at exit for Poggio Imperiale, and proceed towards Peschici and Vieste. Just as you enter Peschici, follow Vieste signs. At T-junction turn left towards Peschici and at top of hill turn right towards San Nicola. It will take at least 1.5 hrs from the motorway. GPS: 41.94291, 16.03493

Charges guide

Per unit incl. 2 persons and electricity	€ 23,00 - € 45,00
extra person	€ 6,60 - € 12,50
child (3-7 yrs)	€ 3,80 - € 7,50

Check real time availability and at-the-gate prices...

www.alanrogers.com

Porto Cesareo
Camping Porto Cesareo
Via Torre Lapillo - Torre Columena km. 0,7, I-73010 Porto Cesareo (Puglia) T: **083 356 5312**
E: **info@portocesareocamping.it** **alanrogers.com/IT68705**

Porto Cesareo is a new site, attractively located in the Salento region of Puglia, to the north of Gallipoli. The site forms a part of Terrestre Palude park and is a short walk from the white sandy beaches of Torre Lapillo bay. The site is well equipped with a swimming pool, self service restaurant and sports field. There are 300 pitches here, 14 of which are occupied by mobile homes (available for rent). There is little natural shade yet and pitches are therefore equipped with artificial shade and vary in size from 60-90 sq.m.

Facilities
Sanitary facilities include those for disabled visitors. Washing Machine. Bar/restaurant and takeaway. Shop (1/7-20/9). Outdoor swimming pool. TV room. Sports field. Games room. Play area. Mobile homes for rent. Off site: Beach 400 m. Sailing 1 km. Porto Cesareo. Lecce. Gallipoli. Watersports. Fishing.

Open: 6 June - 20 September.

Directions
Approaching from the north (Taranto) head southeast on S7 as far as Manduria, and then continue on the S174 to Porto Cesareo. Site is clearly signed from here. GPS: 40.28996, 17.8272

Charges guide
Per unit incl. 2 persons	
and electricity	€ 22,10 - € 39,50
extra person	€ 2,90 - € 10,90
Camping Cheques accepted.	

Vieste
Camping Le Diomedee
CP 289, I-71019 Vieste (Puglia) T: **088 470 6472**. E: **info@lediomedee.com**
alanrogers.com/IT68460

This stretch of coast is a real holiday area with numerous campsites, holiday villages and hotels between the coast road and the sandy beach on this large bay northeast of Vieste. Situated at the far end of the Gargano peninsula and close to the Foresta Umbra, Camping Le Diomedee is part of a large chain of campsites and other holiday resorts. The site has 320 pitches, 170 used for touring units, the remainder occupied by bungalows or caravans for rent. The touring pitches are under high screens to provide some shade, so are between vertical metal poles. Some are directly in front of the beach. The beach-front restaurant/pizzeria seemed a little expensive, but that is perhaps the price you pay for its location. When we visited in June there was an active entertainment programme for children. English is spoken at reception but most signs are in Italian and German.

Facilities
The large central toilet block includes showers, WCs (mixed Turkish and British style) and washbasins. Washing machines. Motorcaravan service point. Shop and fruit stall. Bar. Restaurant/pizzeria. Large swimming pool with loud music. Windsurfing school and hire. Tennis. Children's entertainment (high season). Off site: Vieste and the Gargano park area.

Open: 1 April - 30 September.

Directions
Site is 5 km. from Vieste on the coast road towards Peschici which is about 15 km. away. GPS: 41.91195, 16.124083

Charges 2010
Per unit incl. 2 persons	
and electricity	€ 16,50 - € 53,00
extra person	€ 5,00 - € 15,00
child (3-12 yrs)	free - € 9,00

Check real time availability and at-the-gate prices...
www.alanrogers.com

Ugento

Camping Riva di Ugento

Litoranea Gallipoli, Santa Maria di Leuca, I-73059 Ugento (Puglia) T: **083 393 3600**. E: **info@rivadiugento.it**

alanrogers.com/IT68650

There are some campsites where you can be comfortable, have all the amenities at hand and still feel you are connecting with nature. Under the pine and eucalyptus trees of the Bay of Taranto foreshore is Camping Riva di Ugento. Its 900 pitches are nestled in and around the sand dunes and the foreshore area. They have space and trees around them and the sizes differ as the environment dictates the shape of most. The sea is only a short walk from most pitches and some are at the water's edge. The site buildings resemble huge wooden umbrellas and are in sympathy with the environment. There are swimming and paddling pools, although these are expensive to use in high season. A free cinema also shows special events via satellite TV near the main bar and restaurant area. The area is sandy but well shaded, and the sea breezes, scented with pine give the site a cool fresh feel. This site has an isolated, natural feel that defies its size. Cycling along the kilometre of beach, we enjoyed the tranquillity of the amazing pitches – shaded, private and inviting. We were sorry to leave the site which was by far the best we found in the area.

Facilities

Twenty toilet blocks all with WCs, showers and washbasins. New bathrooms. Bar. Restaurant and takeaway. Swimming and paddling pools. Tennis. Bicycle hire. Watersports incl. windsurfing school. Cinema. TV in bar. WiFi. Entertainment for children. Dogs are not accepted. New play area. Beach volleyball. Off site: Fishing. Riding 500 m. Boat launching 4 km. Golf 40 km.

Open: 15 May - 30 September.

Directions

From Bari take the Brindisi road to Lecce, then SS101 to Gallipoli, followed by the SR274 towards Sta Maria di Leuca, and exit at Ugento. Site is well signed and turn right at traffic lights on SS19. Bumpy approach road. GPS: 39.87321, 18.14347

Charges guide

Per unit incl. 2 persons and 1 child	€ 19,00 - € 41,00
extra person (over 2 yrs)	€ 5,00 - € 9,00
Camping Cheques accepted.	

Vieste

Punta Lunga Camping Village

CP 339, Località Defensola, I-71019 Vieste (Puglia) T: **088 470 6031**. E: **puntalunga@puntalunga.com**

alanrogers.com/IT68480

Punta Lunga is located in the spectacularly beautiful Gargano region, a huge National Park. The coast here has an ambience of its own; the scent of pines mingles with the cool Adriatic breezes inviting you to relax. This site nestles into a bay with easy access to a second beach in the next cove. The 320 pitches are flat on a mixture of sand and grass and of a reasonable size. Some are shaded by trees, others by artificial shade, and most are on steep terraces. Camping along the shore is less formal and in some cases less shaded, but some pitches have spectacular views.

Facilities

Two toilet blocks consist of a mixture of unisex showers and dedicated toilets. The facilities are clean and fresh. Single, good central unit for disabled campers. Laundry facilities. Hairdresser. Small shop. Gas. Excellent restaurant with pleasant views. Beach bar with snacks. Children's clubs (high season). Small play area. Bicycle hire. Windsurfing school. Dogs are not accepted. Off site: Restaurants, bars and shops. Boat launching 3 km. Riding 10 km.

Open: 28 April - 1 October.

Directions

From north take A14 exit for Poggio Imperiale, then to Vico Gargano and Vieste. From south take A14 exit Foggia, then towards Manfredonia, Mattinata and Vieste. GPS: 41.89798, 16.15047

Charges 2010

Per unit incl. 2 persons and electricity	€ 13,50 - € 43,00
extra person	€ 3,50 - € 12,00
child (2-8 yrs)	free - € 7,50

The 'toe' of the Italian boot, Calabria, like its neighbouring region, is a sparsely populated region with unspoilt countryside. The coastline boasts fine, sandy beaches, while the interior features the rugged Aspromonte and Sila mountains, which dominate the landscape.

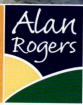

THERE ARE FIVE PROVINCES IN CALABRIA: CATANZARO, COSENZA, CROTONE, REGGIO DI CALABRIA AND VIBO VALENTIA

One of the main towns in the region is Cosenza, which is completely enclosed by mountains – the Sila to the east, the Catena Costiera to the west separating it from the sea. The Sila massif is divided into three parts: the Sila Greca, Sila Grande and the Sila Piccola. Lying in the Sila Greca are the villages of Santa Sofia, San Sosmo and Vaccarizzo, which come alive during annual festivals, held throughout the year. There are ski slopes in the Sila Granda plus numerous lakes, ideal for fishing. Camigliatello is one of the best-known resorts here offering winter-sports, riding and hiking. Lastly, Sila Piccola is the region's most densely forested section, which has been designated national park status. South of Cosenza along the Tyrrhenian coast is the picturesque town of Tropea, whose old town clings to the cliffside, offering superb views of the sea and beaches. There are more sandy beaches nearby at Capo Vaticano, while across on the Ionian coast is the popular resort of Rossano Scalo. Just inland from here is the attractive hilltown of Rossano while further south are the vineyards of Cirò. To the north of Rossano is Sibari, home to the world's largest archaeological site, covering 1000 hectares; excavations have revealed evidence of ancient Greek and Roman civilisations.

Places of interest

Aspromonte: scenic mountainous region in the southernmost tip of Italy's boot.

Capo Colanna: Greek ruins, nearby beaches.

Gerace: impressive cathedral, ruined castle.

Locri: Greek ruins.

Pizzo: picturesque town with small castle and beaches.

Reggio di Calabria: national museum.

Soverato: popular resort with good beaches.

Stilo: home to the 10th-century five-domed Cattolica.

Cuisine of the region

Food is largely influenced by Greek cuisine – aubergines, swordfish and sweets, using figs, almonds and honey. Many biscuits and cakes are made in honour of a religious festival or saint's day, which can be deep-fried in oil, soaked in honey or encrusted with almonds. Pasta is popular plus pork and cheeses such as mozzarella and perorino. Locally produced wines include the Greco di Bianco, a sweet white wine, and those from Cirò.

Briatico

Villaggio Camping Dolomiti sul Mare

SS522 per Tropea km 16,5, I-89817 Briatico (Calabria) T: 096 339 1355. E: info@dolomitisulmare.com

alanrogers.com/IT68900

Set high above the Gulf of Eufemia, a few hundred metres from the beach, Dolomiti is a large sprawling site where the focus is on bungalows. The pitches are informally laid out in a large, somewhat dusty olive grove where the ground slopes to the sea (chocks useful). Campers share the pool, bar, restaurant and entertainment with the other residents, but the high standards of the main complex make a stay worthwhile. It is popular with Italians and the village area within the resort is growing fast resulting in a little chaos at times, especially at reception and the restaurant. The site is probably unsuitable for disabled campers (rough terrain).

Facilities

One unit with mixed British and Turkish style toilets and hot showers provides adequate, clean facilities. Washing machines. Motorcaravan service point. Shop. Bar and terrace. Self service restaurant and snack bar. Swimming pool and spa. Play area. Amphitheatre with entertainment and miniclub. Dogs are accepted but contact site first. Torches useful. Off site: Riding and beach 500 m.

Open: 14 May - 16 September.

Directions

Take E45 Cosenza - Reggio road and leave at Serre exit. Head for Vibo Valentia, then take the coast road and Briatico - the site is well signed on the SS522 at the 165 km. marker. GPS: 38.7191, 16.0589

Charges guide

Per person	€ 6,00 - € 14,00
pitch	€ 7,00 - € 18,00
dog	€ 3,00 - € 6,00

Cariati Marina

Vascellero Villaggio Camping

I-87063 Cariati Marina (Calabria) T: **098 391 127**. E: **villaggio@vascellero.it**
alanrogers.com/IT68750

The superb, irregularly shaped pool with its bar and 'gelateria' are the hub of Vascellero. Signora Franca and her family aim to please their guests, whether it is for summer holidays or skiing in the winter. The camping area just inside the gate is modest, but there are 100 pitches of gravel and sand under artificial shade and giant poplars. The pool area is a delightful place to while away the day and the beach is equally tempting. Alongside the pool is the air-conditioned restaurant, which is beddecked with tasteful artefacts. A sophisticated beach bar serves food on terraces overlooking the sea.

Facilities

The single toilet block, kept clean at all times, provides mixed Turkish and British style toilets. Washing machines. Motorcaravan services. Pizzeria. Good swimming pool with pool bar (charged). Two good play areas. Hairdresser. Tennis. Bicycle hire. Miniclub, entertainment and aerobics. Beach 250 m. Beach restaurant. Watersports. Excursions. Dogs are not accepted in Aug. Off site: Riding 500 m. Sailing. Fishing. Boat launching 3.5 km.

Open: All year.

Directions

Take SS106 Taranto - Reggio road. At km. 299.2 marker in village of Cariati, turn towards beach at campsite signs. Site is well signed over the railway line. GPS: 39.4856, 16.9976

Charges guide

Per person	€ 5,00 - € 10,00
child (2-5 yrs)	€ 3,00 - € 7,00
pitch	€ 5,00 - € 12,00
electricity	€ 1,50 - € 3,00

Corigliano Cálabro

Camping Il Salice

Ctra Ricota Grande, I-87060 Corigliano Cálabro (Calabria) T: **098 385 1169**. E: **info@salicevacanze.it**
alanrogers.com/IT68580

The site's reception is inside the hotel which forms part of this holiday complex and this site is becoming increasingly popular with tour operators. The advantage is there are many choices here – to visit the hairdresser, have a massage, enjoy the warm Ionian sea or have a relaxing drink by the pool. The flat pitches are under tall pines and eucalyptus, many with views of the beach, some right alongside the sand. It is a real treat to stay here and enjoy the excellent facilities and we think it well worth the drive. In the distance the mountains of Pollino National Park can be seen.

Facilities

One large heated and two small unheated toilet blocks provide high quality facilities including excellent units for disabled campers. Laundry. Restaurant, pizzeria, takeaway and bar. Shop. Hairdresser. Massage. Very large outdoor pool (fairly hefty family charge in high season € 36 - € 62). Solarium. Tennis. Bicycle hire. Electronic games. Internet access. Amphitheatre and entertainment. Pedaloes. Windsurfing. Off site: Excursions. Fishing. Boat launching 4 km. Golf 20 km.

Open: All year.

Directions

From A3 Salerno - Reggio Calabria autostrada take Sibari exit, then SS106 road towards Crotone. Before km. 19 marker look for campsite sign and turn for Centro Vacanze Il Salice towards beach. Site is well signed through a small housing estate. GPS: 39.68140, 16.52165

Charges guide

Per person	€ 2,50 - € 13,00
child (3-6 yrs)	free - € 9,00
pitch incl. electricity (3-6A)	€ 6,00 - € 22,00

Cropani Marina

Camping Casa Vacanze Lungomare

Viale Venezia 40, I-88050 Cropani Marina (Calabria) T: **096 196 1167**. E: **info@campinglungomare.com**
alanrogers.com/IT68830

The Ionian coast of Calabria is a mixture of industrial areas (there is off-shore oil and gas), rural areas and large and small holiday resorts. Cropani Marina is definitely at the smaller end of the holiday spectrum and it is some considerable way south on a road that gets progressively slower as you travel. The site has 120 pitches in total but has mobile homes, static caravans and tent only areas. This means that there are perhaps only 40 pitches for touring caravans or motorhomes, all with 6A electricity. There are apartments opposite for rent and a bar/restaurant just outside the gates.

Facilities

Two toilet blocks include showers (tokens required), WCs (Turkish and British style). Facilities for disabled visitors (Portacabin style). Washing machine. Motorcaravan service point. Bar and restaurant/pizzeria. All weather tennis court/football pitch. Accommodation to rent. Off site: Sandy beach and local bars and restaurants.

Open: 1 April - 30 September.

Directions

Site is on main coast road (SS106) south of Crotone on the way to Catanzaro. Just south of the resort of Botricello you come to Cropani Marina. Site is well signed at the junction towards the beach and is about 500 m. on the right. GPS: 38.908917, 16.80945

Charges guide

Per person	€ 2,50 - € 8,50
pitch	€ 3,50 - € 8,50
electricity	€ 2,00

189

Diamante
Villaggio Turistico Mare Blu

Cirella di Diamante, I-87020 Diamante (Calabria) T: 098 586 097. E: mareblu.villaggio@libero.it

alanrogers.com/IT68950

Mare Blu is a large site with lots of watersports activities and an open feel to the it, and is aimed at Italian families spending their holidays by the sea. This is a good site for a short stay to get a taste of the Italian way of camping, or a transit site whilst passing as it is one of the best in the area with many amenities. The 100 touring pitches are flat with some grass, 40 have electricity and most enjoy shade from trees. There is beach access under the railway line and the fine sand provides a safe area for children.

Facilities
Two units provide mixed British and Turkish style toilets. Facilities are in separate blocks – showers from toilets, but are clean. Unit for disabled campers. Laundry facilities. Motorcaravan service point. Shop. Self-service restaurant. Bar and terrace. Snack bar. Play area. Minigolf. Tennis. Animation on the beach. Boat, mountain bike and bicycle hire. Evening animation programme. Disco. Miniclub. Beach (300 m). Windsurfing. Off site: Riding 5 km. Golf 40 km.

Open: May - September.

Directions
From E45 Salerno - Cosenza road take Cosenza Nord and SS107 to Paola. Then SS585 coast road north to Diamante. Site is well signed before reaching the village of Cirella. GPS: 39.7035, 15.8140

Charges guide
Per person	€ 9,00 - € 15,00

Marina di Caulonia
Camping Calypso

Via Nazionale, I-89040 Marina di Caulonia (Calabria) T: 096 482 028. E: info@calypso.st

alanrogers.com/IT68860

This site is at the southern end of the SS106 Taranto - Reggio road and it would take some hours to get there by this route. However, the road from Rosarno to Siderno (SS582) has been improved, with numerous tunnels, and the 36 kilometres across the toe of Italy can now be covered in as many minutes. This is likely to see an increase in tourist development in this arid, rural area, at mainland Italy's most southern point. Camping Calypso is a simple site providing 96 pitches for touring use with some shade offered by the olive and eucalyptus trees.

Facilities
The toilet block includes showers (charged), Turkish and British style WCs and open style washbasins. Washing machines. Motorcaravan service point. Bar and restaurant (high season only). Off site: Sandy beach 50 m. Supermarket 800 m.

Open: 1 April - 1 October.

Directions
From the north the easiest route is via the A3 leaving at Rosarno exit. Turn left on SS582 towards Siderno, then turn north along the SS106. Site is at 123.2 km. Turn sharp right turn down towards a railway bridge. The access road is poor, steep and bumpy. GPS: 38.354117, 16.484917

Charges guide
Per unit incl. 2 persons and electricity	€ 16,50 - € 32,00
extra person	€ 3,00 - € 7,50
No credit cards.	

San Nicolo di Ricadi
Villaggio Camping Costa Verde

Capo Vaticano di Ricadi, I-89865 San Nicolo di Ricadi (Calabria) T: 096 366 3090. E: tropea@costaverde.org

alanrogers.com/IT68890

The coast near Capo Vaticano is listed as one of the best 100 in the world and one of the top three in Italy. From our pitch the sandy beach was just five metres below, down a flight of steps, and we had an unobstructed view of the turquoise sea, the beach and beyond. What more can you ask for? Camping Costa Verde nestles in a small bay, almost hidden from the surrounding area. With its 80 shaded pitches, it offers all year round camping in a beautiful location. The nearby small town of Tropea is one of the most picturesque on the Tyrrhenian coast.

Facilities
The toilet block includes showers, WCs and washbasins. Washing machine. Small shop (1/5-30/10). Bar/coffee shop and restaurant (1/5-30/10). Good sandy beach. Excursions arranged. Children's club in high season. Disco. Apartments to rent. Dogs are not accepted in July/Aug. Barbecues not permitted. Off site: Tropea and Capo Vaticano.

Open: All year.

Directions
From A3 (Naples - Reggio) take Rosarno exit and go through town. Follow signs for Nicotera then Tropea. Before Tropea look for signs for Ricadi and at a large junction, for Costa Verde (railway viaduct means you have gone too far). Turn left here, then right for site. Last 400 m. is a narrow, steep and winding road, difficult for large outfits. GPS: 38.639067, 15.834267

Charges guide
Per person	€ 5,50 - € 11,00
pitch	€ 6,00 - € 11,00
car	€ 2,80 - € 5,50

Sellia Marina

Camping Costa Blu

Localitá Finocchiaro, I-88050 Sellia Marina (Calabria) T: **044 960 232**. E: **info@costabluresidence.it**
alanrogers.com/IT68850

This tiny campsite of just 50 clean, flat pitches has remarkable features for its size plus an attractive Italian ambience. This is a great site if you think small is beautiful and is a cut above the other sites in this area and the prices in low season are very favourable. The generously sized pitches (with electricity) are shaded by pines and eucalyptus. The clean beach is just 30 m. through a secure gate and it is excellent for relaxing and enjoying the tranquil atmosphere, to soak up the sun or swim in the cool Ionian sea.

Facilities

One block of sanitary facilities has mixed Turkish and British style toilets and unisex coin operated showers (20c). Washing machine. Motorcaravan service point. Pleasant small pool complex with a slide. Paddling pool. Play area. Beach volleyball. Small amphitheatre. Animation and miniclub. Off site: Watersports. Fishing. Restaurants, bars and shops.

Open: 15 June - 31 August.

Directions

Take SS106 Crotone - Reggio road. At km. 199.7 marker in village of Sellia Marina take a turn towards beach indicated by campsite signs. Site well signed over railway line. At tall eucalyptus trees, turn left then left again and right where indicated. Narrow turn into site. GPS: 38.8929, 16.7634

Charges guide

Per person	€ 5,00 - € 9,00
pitch	€ 6,00 - € 9,00
dog	€ 2,00 - € 3,00

Sibari

Camping Pineta di Sibari

Fuscolari, I-87070 Sibari (Calabria) T: **098 174 135**. E: **info@pinetadisibari.it**
alanrogers.com/IT68600

Calabria was immortalized in the drawings of Edward Lear who, travelling on a donkey in 1847, was transfixed by the landscape. Camping Pineta di Sibari is on the Ionian Sea coast and provides 500 touring pitches under pine and eucalyptus trees. Most are of average size and many have sea views. The large sandy beach stretches for miles in both directions and the backdrop is the mountains of the Pollino National Park. This is a rural area and is away from the industrial areas found further south along this coast. Karin Rudolph runs a happy site where peace and quiet are prime features.

Facilities

Five toilet blocks include showers, WCs (Turkish and British style) and open style washbasins. Facilities for disabled visitors. Motorcaravan service point. Bazaar and shop, bar and restaurant (all 1/5-16/9). Tennis. Sandy beach with sunbeds and shades (to rent). Mobile homes to rent. Off site: Ancient Sibari. Pollino National Park.

Open: 22 April - 16 September.

Directions

Take SS106 south towards Reggio Calabria. South of Trebisacce take Villapiana Salco exit (third Villapiana exit). Turn right along the coast road (SS106R), then left at sign for site and go over level crossing. To avoid narrow tunnel on this road (only 2.8 m. headroom), after level crossing turn right and go straight on as road bears left. Site is 700 m. down this road. GPS: 39.78100, 16.41932

Charges guide

Per person	€ 4,50 - € 9,50
child (3-6 yrs)	free - € 4,90
pitch incl. electricity	€ 9,00 - € 16,00
No credit cards.	

Check real time availability and at-the-gate prices...
www.**alanrogers**.com

The largest island in the Mediterranean, Sicily has seen a range of settlers come and go, from the early Greeks and Romans to the Arabs and Normans, French and Spanish. With its beach resorts, volcanic islands, ancient sites and varied cuisine, Siciliy is also home to Mount Etna.

SICILY IS COMPRISED OF THE FOLLOWING PROVINCES: AGRIGENTO, CALTANISSETTA, CATANIA, ENNA, MESSINA, PALERMO, RAGUSA, SIRACUSA AND TRAPANI

The capital of Sicily is the bustling city of Palermo. With its medieval streets and markets, it has the island's greatest concentration of sights, and architecture that boasts a range of styles from Arabic to Norman, Baroque and Art Nouveau. Boats depart from here to the tiny volcanic island of Ústica, renowned for its marine life and popular with divers. Along with Milazzo and Messina, the capital also provides connections to the Aeolian Islands, of which Lípari is the most popular. Outside the capital is Monte Pellegrino, which offers superb views of the city, plus the seaside resort of Mondello. Europe's highest volcano, Mount Etna is situated in the east. Still active, its lower reaches are accessible on foot or by public transport. The closest town to the summit is Randazzo, built entirely of lava, as is Catania, situated further down the Ionian coast. Engulfed by lava in 1669 followed by an earthquake in 1693, Catania has been rebuilt on a grand scale. The coastline also bears traces of ancient Greek cities, most notably at Megara Hyblaea and Siracusa. More Greek ruins can be found near Agrigento, on the south-west coast, while around to the west is Marsala, famous for its fortified wine, and the harbour town of Trápani, a jumping off point for the Egadi Islands.

Places of interest

Acireale: spa centre, hosts one of Sicily's best festivals in February.

Agrigento: nearby archaeological area known as the Valley of the Temples.

Enna: Sicily's highest town.

Erice: medieval town, cathedral.

Marsala: home of the famous wine, in production since the 18th century.

Segesta: ancient temple, nearby ruins of an ancient theatre where summer concerts are held.

Taormina: lively resort with sandy beaches, ancient Greek theatre and 13th-century cathedral.

Vulcano: Aeolian Island, with hot mud baths and fine black beaches.

Cuisine of the region

Given its location, Sicily has attracted an endless list of invaders which has impacted on its food, resulting in one of Italy's most varied cuisines. Fish is abundant, including anchovies, sardines, tuna and swordfish, often teamed with pasta, as in *spaghetti con le sarde*. Sicily is famous for its sweets, in particular *cannoli*, fried pastries stuffed with sweet ricotta. Made from sheep's milk ricotta is used in a variety of desserts, with percorino and provolone cheeses also widely available. Wines include Marsala, Corvo and Regaleali.

Maccheroni con le sarde: sardines cooked with fennel, raisins, pine nuts, breadcrumbs and saffron.

Pesce spada: swordfish steak, grilled or pan-fried with lemon and oregano.

Sicilin cassata: ice-cream made with ricotta, nuts, candied fruit and chocolate in a sponge cake.

Acireale

Panorama Village & Camping

Via Santa Caterina 55, I-95024 Acireale (Sicily) T: **095 763 4124**. E: **info@panoramavillage.it**
alanrogers.com/IT69220

Panorama is a site where the focus is on good apartments and accommodation and the supporting facilities for these are of a high standard. The campsite with 90 shady, flat pitches on the cliff top, shares these facilities making this a popular high season site. We are told that all the pitches are fully booked for July and August most years, so phone ahead during this period or choose to visit at other times. The major attraction here is the cliff top setting with the beautiful pool, bar, disco and entertainment area.

Facilities

One large block for men and another for women are clean, but in need of some repairs and probably under pressure in high season. Laundry facilities. Bar, pizzeria, restaurant and excellent large swimming pool (all 1/6-30/9). Entertainment area. Small play area in older style (supervision required). Boules. Off site: Site is on the outskirts of Acireale close to historical sites.

Open: All year.

Directions

From A18 take Acireale exit. Follow signs to the coast road SS114. On SS114 in the southern part of Acireale between km. 81 and 82 turn to S. Catrina from where site is just 50 m. and signed. You will need to pass under a 3 m. high bridge. GPS: 37.60603, 15.17001

Charges guide

Per person	€ 5,00 - € 10,00
pitch incl. car	€ 11,00 - € 18,00
electricity	€ 3,00

Agrigento

Camping Valle dei Templi

Viale Emporium, I-92100 Agrigento (Sicily) T: **922 411 115**. E: **info@campingvalledeitempli.com**
alanrogers.com/IT69175

This site shares its name with Sicily's premier attraction, the Unesco World Heritage listed complex of temples and old city walls of the ancient town of Akragas, although these are about 2.5 km. to the north. Built as a beacon for homecoming sailors, the five Doric temples built on a ridge are an impressive sight even at a distance. This site is therefore a good base from which to explore these ruins. With 195 unmarked pitches, about half are suitable for caravans and campers. Most have 6A electricity.

Facilities

The single sanitary block in the centre of the site provides good WCs, showers and washbasins. Facilities for disabled visitors. Motorcaravan service point. Washing machine. Bar and restaurant. Swimming pool. Off site: Fishing 1 km. Riding 2 km. Valle dei Templi and Agrigento.

Open: All year.

Directions

From the main SS115 raod or the SS640, follow signs to San Leone, just east of Agrigento. Site is on left just as you enter the town, about 700 m. before the coast. GPS: 37.26935, 13.5835

Charges guide

Per person	€ 5,50 - € 7,50
pitch incl. car	€ 6,50 - € 9,50
electricity	€ 2,50 - € 3,00

Check real time availability and at-the-gate prices...
www.**alanrogers**.com
193

Agrigento

Camping Internazionale Nettuno

Via Lacco Ameno N3, Santa Leone, I-92100 Agrigento (Sicily) T: **922 416 268**

alanrogers.com/IT69180

Internazionale Nettuno is a small site with about 50 pitches for tourers. It would be a good place to get an early start to see the amazing ruins before the heat of the day. Alternatively, it would make a quiet place to stay after touring the ruins as it is alongside a beautiful sandy beach. The pitches are on shady level terraces, some with their own beach access. There is a bar and a small shop. The sanitary facilities were clean when we visited (unisex as half were closed in early season), but required some maintenance as did the motorcaravan service area.

Facilities

One large central sanitary block (unisex in low season) provides adjustable hot showers and small cabins. Motorcaravan service area. Bar. Restaurant and pizzeria. Off site: Valley of the Temples 4 km. Bar, restaurants and excellent white sandy beach nearby.

Open: All year.

Directions

Site is located on the beach at San Leone about 5 km. south of the city of Agrigento on the south coast of Sicily. From S115 road follow signs to San Leone from where site is well signed some 2 km. east of the town. Access is a steep climb just after road leaves the coast. GPS: 37.24306, 13.61556

Charges guide

Per person	€ 6,00 - € 7,00
caravan and car	€ 11,00 - € 13,00
motorcaravan	€ 9,00 - € 10,00
tent	€ 5,00 - € 12,00

Avola

Camping Sabbiadoro

Ctra da Chivsa di Carlo, I-96012 Avola (Sicily) T: **093 156 0000**. E: **info@campeggiosabbiadoro.com**

alanrogers.com/IT69215

This is truly one of Sicily's hidden gems and the Alia family will ensure your stay is pleasant and peaceful at this delightful campsite with 100 pitches. With over 100 different species of trees and flowers around the site the whole site is awash with colour and good shade. A small sandy beach compliments the site's natural charm. When we arrived, a party was in progress to celebrate the natural products of the area and a huge copper pot was being used to make Ricotta cheese, which within an hour was being distributed, around the site, with local bread. It was delicious!

Facilities

Smal old, but clean and well maintained sanitary block has toilets (British and Turkish style), washbasins and unisex hot showers (token required). This block is to be demolished soon to make way for a new one. Motorcaravan service point. Shop. Bar. Restaurant and takeaway (1/6-30/9). Sandy beach. Off site: Avola with its unusual town planning.

Open: All year.

Directions

On the SS115 north of Avola the site is 400 m. down a narrow twisting lane. GPS: 36.93639, 15.17472

Charges guide

Per person	€ 8,00
pitch	€ 11,00 - € 14,00
electricity	€ 4,00

No credit cards.
Camping Cheques accepted.

Catania

Camping Jonio

Via Villini a Mare 2, Ognina, I-95126 Catania (Sicily) T: **095 491 139**. E: **info@campingjonio.com**

alanrogers.com/IT69230

This is a small, uncomplicated and tranquil city site with the advantage of being on top of the cliff at the waters edge. The 70 level touring pitches are on gravel with shade from some tall trees and artificial bamboo screens. There are some clean high quality sanitary facilities (also some private facilities for hire). There is no pool but the views of the water compensate and there are delightful rock pools in the sea just a few steps from the campsite. A new attractive restaurant offers food in the summer high season. Camping Jonio is ideal for a short stay to unwind.

Facilities

Sanitary facilities are modern and clean in two blocks, one small block for men and another for women. Laundry with roof top drying area. Motorcaravan services. Shop. Bar and restaurant. Basic old style playground (supervision recommended). Entertainment (high season). Diving school. Access to small gravel beach. Excursions. Dogs are not accepted in July/Aug. Off site: Large town of Catania, many historical sites and Mount Etna.

Open: All year.

Directions

From A18 Catania exit follow signs to the coast road (SS114) towards Ognina. Site is off the SS114 (signed) on the northeast outskirts of town. Access to site is off the small one way system and via the site's separate car park. GPS: 37.53232, 15.12012

Charges guide

Per person	€ 7,00 - € 10,00
pitch	€ 7,00 - € 14,00
car	€ 4,00 - € 6,00
electricity	€ 3,00

Check real time availability and at-the-gate prices...

www.**alanrogers**.com

Cefalu

Camping Costa Ponente

Ctra Ogliastrillo, SS113, I-90015 Cefalu (Sicily) T: **092 142 1354**. E: **info@camping-sizilia.de**
alanrogers.com/IT69360

The pleasant Costa Ponente site, with easy access from the A20 and SS113 roads, is located between the small coastal railway line and the beach. However, its layout does much to minimise the impact of the infrequent trains. There are 150 pitches, all with 3A electricity, of which 120 are used for touring units. Arranged on terraces and with over 25% having water and drainage on the pitch, the site has a good ambiance and views. An area for tents near the swimming pools caters for large groups travelling by coach. There is access to the beach, as well as sunbathing areas near the bar and pools.

Facilities

Four sanitary blocks provide good facilities with ample toilets (British and Turkish style), washbasins and hot showers. Facilities for disabled visitors. Washing machine. Motorcaravan services. Bar (high season). Shop. Swimming pools. Dogs are not accepted in August. Off site: Cefalu.

Open: 1 April - 31 October.

Directions

From the A20 Cefalu exit take the SS113 towards the town. Site is at the 190.2 km. marker on the left down a slope and across a level crossing. GPS: 38.02684, 13.9828

Charges guide

Per person	€ 6,00 - € 7,20
pitch incl. car	€ 6,50 - € 12,00
dog (excl. Aug)	€ 3,00 - € 3,50

Finale di Pollina

Camping Rais Gerbi

Ctra Rais Gerbi, SS113, km 172.9, I-90010 Finale di Pollina (Sicily) T: **092 142 6570**. E: **camping@raisgerbi.it**
alanrogers.com/IT69350

Rais Gerbi provides very good quality camping with excellent facilities on the beautiful Tyrrhenian coast not far from Cefalu. This attractive terraced campsite is shaded by well established trees and the good size pitches vary from informal areas under the trees near the sea to gravel terraces and hardstandings. Most have stunning views, many with their own sinks and with some artificial shade to supplement the trees. From the mobile homes to the unusual white igloos, everything here is being established to a high quality. The large pool with its entertainment area and the restaurant, like so much of the site, overlook the beautiful rocky coastline and aquamarine sea. Vincenzo Cerrito who speaks excellent English has been developing the site for many years and is continually upgrading and improving the resort style facilities. A frequently used rail line in a cutting, then a tunnel, divides part of the site. The cutting is well fenced and lined with trees but has some impact and one is unaware of the tunnel under the site. Budget airlines fly into a nearby airport and it is possible to rent tents or accommodation on the site. Packages are available to tour the island and use other campsites near major attractions in Sicily (the reception staff will advise). This is a central location from which to explore many of the island's attractions, although it may prove difficult to leave the glorious coastline. Try to visit in spring and autumn when the weather is usually perfect and the site is less busy.

Facilities

Excellent new sanitary blocks with British style toilets, free hot showers in generous cubicles. Small shop. Casual summer terrace and indoor (winter) restaurant. Entertainment area and pool near the sea. Tennis. High quality accommodation and tents for rent. Rocky beach at site. Off site: Small village of Finale 500 m. Larger historic town of Cefalu 12 km.

Open: All year.

Directions

Site is on SS113 running along the east - north coast of the island, km. 172.9 just west of the village of Finale (the turn into site is at end of the bridge on the outskirts of the village). It is 12 km. east of Cefalu and 11 km. north of Pollina. GPS: 38.02278, 14.15389

Charges guide

Per person	€ 5,00 - € 10,00
pitch	€ 5,00 - € 17,00
car	€ 3,00 - € 5,00
electricity	€ 4,00

Check real time availability and at-the-gate prices...
www.**alanrogers**.com

Letojanni
Camping Paradise

Via Nazionale 2, SS114 km 41, I-98037 Letojanni (Sicily) T: **094 236 306**
E: **campingparadise@campingparadise.it alanrogers.com/IT69260**

Camping Paradise is situated 40 km. south of the ferry port at Messina, on a long narrow strip along the sea with direct beach access. Most of the pitches have views over the crystal clear waters that are a delight to bathe in on a hot day. The level, grass and gravel pitches are fairly small with paved access roads and shade from well established, mainly olive trees. This site with a mountain backdrop is very popular so you may need to book ahead in high season. There is some noise from the local train service all along this coast.

Facilities

One large centrally located sanitary block has mainly Turkish style toilets, fully adjustable hot showers and facilities for disabled visitors. Small shop for essentials. Large bar/restaurant with views over the sea. Off site: Rich in history, the area has many antiquities. Good crystal clear beaches. Nearby town Letojanni is a popular seaside resort. Mount Etna within easy reach.

Open: May - October.

Directions

From the A18 motorway between Messina and Catania take Taormina exit and then turn north on S114 towards Letojanni. Site is on this road (S114) at 41 km. marker just north of the village of Letojanni. There is quite a sharp bend on entering the site and a 3.1 m. bridge. GPS: 37.89717, 15.32699

Charges guide

Per person	€ 6,00 - € 10,00
pitch	€ 6,00 - € 13,00
electricity	€ 3,00 - € 4,00
car	€ 4,00 - € 5,00

Mazara del Vallo

260

Sporting Club Village & Camping

Ctra Bocca Arena, I-91026 Mazara del Vallo (Sicily) T: **092 394 7230**. E: **info@sportingclubvillage.com**
alanrogers.com/IT69160

Mazara del Vallo can be found on Sicily's southwestern coast. As the crow flies, Tunisia is not far, and the town has a distinct Arabic influence in its winding streets. The site is 2.5 km. from Mazara and boasts some good amenities including a large swimming pool, surrounded by tall palm trees. Pitches here are grassy and generally well shaded. This is a lively site in high season with a wide range of activities and a regular entertainment programme. The nearest beach is 350 m. away and the site is also adjacent to a nature reserve. Sporting Club's focal point, however, is its restaurant with typical Sicilian dishes on offer, notably locally caught fish.

Facilities

Good sports club with swimming pool, gymnasium, floodlit football pitches, tennis and volleyball. Restaurant, bar and large reception/function room. Off site: Beach 350 m. Mazara 2.5 km. Various excursions organised by the site, for example to the acropolis at Selinunte (25 km) or the island of Mozia.

Open: 15 March - 15 October.

Directions

From the A29 take the Mazara del Vallo exit and head towards the town. Go straight over first roundabout and after about 1.5 km. turn right at the traffic lights toward the beach. At the roundabout exit left and go straight ahead to the site, not over the bridge. GPS: 37.63647, 12.61631

Charges guide

Per person	€ 4,50 - € 8,50
child (4-10 yrs)	€ 3,00 - € 6,00
pitch	€ 5,00 - € 15,00
car	€ 3,50 - € 6,00

Check real time availability and at-the-gate prices...
www.alanrogers.com

Messina

Nuovo Camping Dello Stretto

Via Circuito, Torre Faro, I-98614 Messina (Sicily) T: 090 322 3051. E: info@campingdellostretto.it

alanrogers.com/IT69255

This delightful campsite is just 15 minutes from the port of Messina. Having been closed for 22 years, it reopened in 2005 under the skilled management of Alberto Galleta. He is painstakingly restoring it to an exceptionally high standard. The restaurant alongside the two pools is one of the best we have seen in our travels. With 60 pitches for caravans and motorcaravans to the rear of the site, all with 3A electricity, this offers a peaceful resting place after the long journey south. The site's restaurant and pizzeria are set alongside the pools in a beautiful garden and are such that you will not want to walk to the other local establishments.

Facilities

Two sanitary blocks provide ample toilets, showers and washbasins. Facilities for disabled visitors (plus another in the restaurant). Motorcaravan service point. Exceptional restaurant and pizzeria. Two swimming pools with lifeguard. Miniclub (July/Aug). Off site: Messina and Taormina.

Open: All year.

Directions

Site is well signed from Messina Port. At the port exit turn right at traffic lights and head north along Viale della Liberta, then Consolare Pompea (SS113). Go through Ganzirri with the lake on your right. At first crossroads turn right again alongside the lake and at T-junction turn left. Site is on the left where the road forks. GPS: 38.26167, 15.63333

Charges guide

Per person	€ 5,00 - € 9,00
child (4-13 yrs)	€ 3,50 - € 6,50
pitch incl. electricity	€ 11,00 - € 16,00

Messina

Camping Il Peloritano

Ctra Tarantonio ss 113 dir., Rodia, I-98161 Messina (Sicily) T: 090 348 496. E: il_peloritano@yahoo.it

alanrogers.com/IT69250

Set in a 100-year-old olive grove which provides shade for 50 informally arranged pitches, Camping Il Peloritano is a quiet uncomplicated site, off the coast road, with excellent clean facilities. It is a 200 m. walk to the sandy beach and approximately 2 km. to the nearby village. The friendly owners, Patrizia Mowdello and Carlo Oteri, provide help and assistance to arrange excursions to the Aeolian Islands, Taormina and Mount Etna and will do everything to make your stay a pleasant one.

Facilities

Single refurbished toilet block provides hot showers (by token). Good facilities for disabled visitors. Washing machine. Motorcaravan service point. Small shop and bar. Meals can be ordered in from local restaurants. Excursions arranged. Sub-aqua school and diving with guide. Bowls. Bicycle hire. Off site: Sandy beach 200 m. Small seaside village 2 km. Riding 2 km.

Open: 1 March - 31 October.

Directions

From Messina on the A20 motorway take Villafranca exit then follow 'Messina dir' and Tarantonio for 2 km. From Palermo on the A20, take exit for Rometta and signs for Messina and Tarantonio for about 5 km. GPS: 38.25932, 15.46782

Charges guide

Per person	€ 5,00 - € 8,00
child (3-7 yrs)	€ 3,00 - € 5,00
pitch	€ 4,00 - € 8,00
car	€ 2,00 - € 4,00
electricity	€ 3,50

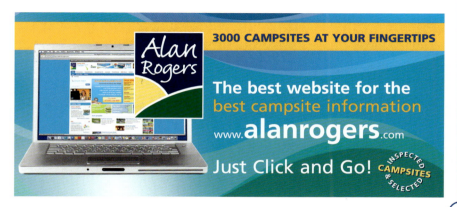

197
Check real time availability and at-the-gate prices...
www.alanrogers.com

Oliveri

Camping Villaggio Marinello

Via del Sol 17, I-98060 Oliveri (Sicily) T: 094 131 3000. E: marinello@camping.it

alanrogers.com/IT69300

Camping Marinello is located alongside the sea with direct access to a lovely uncrowded sandy beach with an informal marina at one end and natural pool areas with a spot of sand at the other. The 220 gravel touring pitches here are shaded by tall trees. We enjoyed a delicious traditional meal in the excellent terraced restaurant with its lovely sea views. Tours are arranged to major sightseeing destinations such as Mount Etna, Taormina and the nearby Aeolian Islands. The Greco family have been here for over 30 years and work hard to ensure that their guests enjoy a pleasant stay. There is some noise from the coastal rail line which runs along the length of the site. The nearby resort area town has lots of attractions for the tourist and the site is easily accessible from the ferry at Messina.

Facilities

Two sanitary blocks with free hot showers, one is not currently used and is awaiting a much-needed heating and refurbishment. Washing machines. Bazaar, market and supermarket. Bar with sea views. Restaurant and terraced eating area also with views. Electronic games. Piano bar in high season. Dogs are not accepted in July/Aug.
Off site: Seaside resort style town of Oliveri.

Open: All year.

Directions

From A20 motorway take Falcone exit and follow signs to Oliveri. At the town turn north towards the beach (site sign), then turn west along the beach and continue 1 km. to site. You will need to make a right turn just before a small narrow bridge (2.2 m. high and 2.5 m. wide). GPS: 38.13246, 15.05452

Charges guide

Per person (over 3 yrs)	€ 4,50 - € 9,00
pitch incl. electricity	€ 13,00 - € 21,00
tent	€ 4,50 - € 12,00
car	€ 3,00 - € 5,00

San Croce Camerina

260

Camping Scarabeo

I-97017 San Croce Camerina (Sicily) T: 093 291 8096. E: info@scarabeocamping.it

alanrogers.com/IT69190

Scarabeo is a beautiful site located in Punta Braccetto, a little fishing port in Sicily's southeastern corner. It is a perfect location with exceptional facilities to match. Split into two separate sites (just 50 m. apart) with a total of 80 pitches, it is being constantly improved with care by Angela di Modica. All pitches are well shaded, some naturally and others with an artificial cane roof and have 3/6A electricity. Scarabeo lies adjacent to a sandy beach and the little village is close by. The site layout resembles a Sicilian farm courtyard and is divided into four principal areas. The ancient Greek ruins of Kamerina and Caucana are just a few kilometres from the site and their ruins can be reached by bike. The Riserva Naturale at the mouth of the River Irminio is also a popular excursion.

Facilities

Exceptional sanitary blocks provide personal WC compartments (personal key access). Ample hot showers (free low season). Facilities for disabled visitors. Washing machine. Direct access to beach. Playground. Entertainment programme in high season. Mobile homes for rent.
Off site: Supermarket 4 km. Restaurant/café 500 m. Cycling and walking trails.

Open: All year.

Directions

Site is 20 km. southwest of Ragusa. From Catania, take S194 towards Ragusa and, at Comiso, follow signs to S. Croce Camerina, then Punta Braccetto, from where site is well signed. Use second entrance for reception. GPS: 36.81645, 14.46964

Charges guide

Per person	€ 4,00 - € 8,50
child (3-6 yrs)	€ 2,00 - € 5,00
pitch	€ 4,00 - € 11,00

Excellent long term discounts in low season.

San Vito Lo Capo

El Bahira Camping Village

Ctra da Makari - Localitá Salinella, I-91010 San Vito Lo Capo (Sicily) T: 092 397 2577. E: info@elbahira.it
alanrogers.com/IT6914

El Bahira is a popular site in quite a remote area overlooking the Gulf of Makari toward Monte Cofano. The views are outstanding and the location is good as it is near the sea, nature reserves and ancient cities such as Segtesta and Selinunte with their awe inspiring antiquities. Partners Maurizio, Maceri, Sugameli and Michele who speak good English have chosen this area to develop a campsite of a high standard. The 200 fairly small pitches are on sloping gravel (chocks required), most are shady and all have electricity. There are also numerous statics which unfortunately rather spoil the look of the site. There is a separate area for tents. The excellent restaurant, pizzeria and the pool all have views of the sea and there are very good entertainment and sporting facilities. Sanitary facilities with the exception of the showers are very good. The unisex showers are by timed token (outside the cabin), the cubicles are tiny and there are no hooks or places to keep clothing dry so go prepared in a towelling robe or swimsuit. Book ahead for this site in July and August as sites this good are few and far between in Sicily. Mothia with its prehistoric caves with early signs of man is also nearby, as is the enchanting Erice where time appears to have stood still and you can meander the ancient streets and enjoy the Norman castle and wonderful Duomo.

Facilities

Three well placed sanitary blocks. The showers are by token (€ 4 for 8 showers), these are unisex in tiny cabins. Motorcaravan service point. Supermarket. Restaurant and pizzeria. Swimming pool. Two entertainment areas. Tennis. Sub-aqua facilities. Boat launching at rocky beach on site. Off site: Popular resort village of San Vito Lo Capo 3 km.

Open: 1 April - 4 October.

Directions

From the east follow the A19 motorway and take the Castellammare del Golfo exit then follow the S187 towards Trapani. After about 16 km. turn right and follow signs to San Vito Lo Capo and site is well signed off the road approaching the town.
GPS: 38.150707, 12.73191

Charges guide

Per unit incl. 2 persons and electricity	€ 24,90 - € 35,40

Porto di Capo Passero

Camping Residence Capo Passero

Ctra da Vigne Vecchie, I-96010 Porto di Capo Passero (Sicily) T: **093 184 2333**. E: **info@italiaabc.com**

alanrogers.com/IT69210

Camping Residence Capo Passero is located on the southeast point of Sicily. There are often nice sea breezes at the campsite which has a clean and well maintained appearance, although when we visited the shade was patchy due to the Italian custom of trimming trees aggressively. The touring pitches are generally level and all have 6A electricity connections. The sandy beach only 50 m. walk away is inviting and there is a very good pool area with grassy areas to sunbathe. The nearby village is quite interesting for the region and has a number of restaurants and bars.

Facilities

Three older style toilet blocks, all clean when visited with washbasins but only cold showers. There are six warm showers near reception but tokens are required. Facilities for disabled visitors in one block. Attractive typical style restaurant and bar area. Excellent pool with grassy sunbathing area. Good play area. Disco area. Boules. Tennis. Good access to sandy slow shelving beach. Off site: Local town with bars, restaurants and marina within 1.5 km.

Open: Easter - 15 October.

Directions

From SS115 road follow signs to Pachino, then Portopalo di Capo Passero. Site is located west of the town on the beach and there are some signs from the village. Low bridges may cause problems on some routes. GPS: 36.6775, 15.1208

Charges guide

Per person	€ 6,50 - € 9,00
child (3-10 yrs)	€ 4,00 - € 6,00
pitch	€ 4,00 - € 15,00
car	€ 3,50

San Vito Lo Capo

261

Camping Village La Pineta

via de Secco, 88, I-91010 San Vito Lo Capo (Sicily) T: **0923 972 818**. E: **info@campinglapineta.it**

alanrogers.com/IT69145

La Pineta is attractively located on Sicily's north coast and is within easy access of Palermo and Trapani. The site enjoys easy access to a fine sandy beach (250 m). Pitches are well shaded and most are provided with electricity. La Pineta also has around 30 brick built bungalows available for rent, as well as a number of apartments. Leisure facilities include two good sized swimming pools (with a generous sunbathing terrace), tennis and volleyball. The Restaurant della Pineta is the site's focal point and specialises in Sicilian cuisine, making good use of local fish. This is a stunning coastline and there are some excellent local walks to enjoy. Off shore, the mini-archipelago of the Aegadian islands provides for a popular excursion. The islands have been inhabited since prehistoric times and are surrounded by wonderful crystal waters. Palermo is, of course, the island's capital and is a major Italian city (with a population of 1.2 million). There is a great deal to see here, including a fine cathedral and the Palazzo dei Normanni, one of Italy's most beautiful palaces.

Facilities

Swimming pools. Tennis. Volleyball. Restaurant. Dive school. Play area. Tourist information. Activity and entertainment programme. Chalets and apartments to rent. Off site: Nearest beach 250 m. Fishing. Windsurfing. Excursions to the Aegadian islands.

Open: All year excl. November.

Directions

Approaching from Palermo, leave the A29 autostrada at the exit for Castellamare del Golfo. Continue to Castellamare and then follow SS167 to Messina. Here, take the northbound SP46 to Custonaci and then to San Vito lo Capo. The campsite is clearly signed from here. GPS: 38.173905, 12.747939

Charges guide

Per unit incl. 2 persons and electricity	€ 23,60 - € 39,30
extra person	€ 5,00 - € 9,50

Check real time availability and at-the-gate prices...

www.alanrogers.com

With dramatic, rolling uplands covered with grassland, and a beautiful coastline boasting isolated coves, long sandy beaches and hidden caves, Sardinia offers more than just sunshine and clear waters: littered around the island are thousands of prehistoric nuraghic remains.

SARDINIA HAS FOUR PROVINCES: CAGLIARI, NUORO, ORISTANO AND SASSARI

The busy port of Cágliari is the island's capital. Attractions include the city walls, archaeology museum and cathedral plus an impressive Roman amphitheatre. More ruins can be found just outside the city at Nora, while some 7,000 or so nuraghi are dotted all around the island. Unique to Sardinia, these stone-built constructions are remnants of Sardinia's only significant native culture. The most famous of them is at Su Nuraxi, the oldest and largest nuraghic complex, dating from around 1500 BC. The island's second city, Sássari, is known for its spectacular Cavalcata festival on Ascension Day; festivities include traditional singing and dancing plus a horse race. Not far from Sássari is Alghero, a major fishing port and the island's oldest resort. Surrounded by walls and defensive towers the old town is full of narrow, cobbled streets with flamboyant churches and brightly-coloured houses. Boat or car trips can also be made to Neptune's Grotto, a spectacular, deep marine cave, around the point of Capo Caccia. Sardinia's best known resort is the Costa Smeralda, one of the Mediterranean's loveliest stretches of coast, a 10 km. strip between the gulfs of Cugnana and Arzachena. Beaches can be found at Capriccioli, Rena Bianca and Liscia Ruia.

Places of interest

Bosa: small, picturesque seaside town.

Cala Gonone: bustling seaside resort and fishing port, with good beaches, isolated coves and natural caves including the famous Grotta del Bue Marino.

Carloforte: an attractive town on the island of San Pietro.

Dorgali: in wine-growing region of Cannonau.

Maddalena Islands: popular tourist attraction, sandy and rocky beaches.

Oristano: nearby lagoon is home to one of the island's largest populations of flamingo.

Cuisine of the region

Fresh ingredients are widely used to create simple dishes: seafood, especially lobster, is grilled over open fires, as is suckling pig. Fish stews and pasta is popular. The island also produces a variety of breads. Cheeses tend to be made from ewe's milk, including percorino Sardo. Nougat is a sweet Sardinian speciality and pastries are often flavoured with almonds, lemons or orange. Vernaccia is the island's most famous wine.

Agnello arrosto: roast lamb, roasted on a spit or in casseroles with rosemary and thyme.

Bottarga: a version of caviar made with mullet eggs.

Culigiones: massive ravioli stuffed with cheese and egg.

Maloreddus: saffron flavoured pasta.

Map of Sardinia showing: PALAU, CANNIGIONE DI ARZACHENA, AGLIENTU, OLBIA, VALLEDORIA, LOIRI PORTO SAN PAOLO, PORTO TORRES, BUDONI, SS131, SASSARI, SS199, SANTA LUCIA DI SINISCOLA, SS131, ALGHERO, NUORO, CALA GONONE, BOSA, SARDINIA, SS131, LOTZORAI, TORTOLI, BARI SARDO, TORRE GRANDE, ORISTANO, ARBOREA, SS125, MURAVERA, SS131, SS125, SS130, CAGLIARA, CARLOFORTE, SANT'ANTIOCO, DOMUS DE MARIA

Aglientu

Camping Baia Blu La Tortuga

Pineta di Vignola Mare, I-07020 Aglientu (Sardinia) T: **079 602 200**. E: **info@baiablu.com**

alanrogers.com/IT69550

In the northeast of Sardinia and well situated for the Corsica ferry, Baia Blu is a large, professionally run campsite. The beach with its golden sand, brilliant blue sea and pretty rocky outcrops is warm and inviting. The site's 304 touring pitches, and almost as many mobile homes (most with air conditioning), are of fine sand and shaded by tall pines with banks of colourful oleanders and wide boulevards providing good access for units. Four exceptionally good toilet blocks provide a good ratio of excellent facilities to pitches including some combined private shower/washbasin cabins for rent. This is a busy, bustling site with lots to do and attractive restaurants.

Facilities

Four excellent blocks (two with solar panels for hot water) with free hot showers, WCs, bidets and washbasins. Facilities for disabled people. Washing machines and dryers. Motorcaravan services. Supermarket. Gas. Bazaar. New bar and restaurant. Beachside restaurant and bar. Self-service restaurant. Snack bar and takeaway. Gym. Hairdresser. Doctor's surgery. Playground. Tennis. Games and TV rooms. Windsurfing and diving schools. Internet point and WiFi area Massage centre. Entertainment and sports activities (mid May - Sept). Excursions. Barbecue area (not permitted on pitches). Off site: Disco 50 m. Riding 18 km.

Open: 1 April - 18 October.

Directions

Site is on north coast between towns of Costa Paradiso and San Teresa di Gallura (18 km) at Pineta di Vignola Mare and is well signed.
GPS: 41.12611, 9.06722

Charges guide

Per unit incl. 2 persons, water and electricity	€ 17,00 - € 49,00
tent pitch incl. electricity	€ 14,00 - € 39,00
extra person	€ 2,00 - € 12,00
junior (3-9 yrs)	€ 2,00 - € 9,50
dog	€ 3,50 - € 8,00

Alghero
Camping Torre del Porticciolo

Localitá Porticciolo- Parco di Porto Co, Sede lagale via G. Ferret 17, I-07041 Alghero (Sardinia)
T: **079 919 010**. E: **info@torredelporticciolo.it** **alanrogers.com/IT69950**

Torre del Porticciolo is set high on a peninsula with fabulous views over the sea and old fortifications. It is a friendly, family owned site with striking traditional old buildings, attractive landscaping and large pools. A really huge site in terms of area, the camping area is under pine trees and totally shaded. There are some pitches with views, although most are tucked in under the pine trees. A walk out of the site down a very steep slope with stunning views leads to the attractive beach and warm waters. The owner Marisa Carboni and her friendly staff speak a little English and are very helpful.

Facilities

Two clean toilet blocks have mainly Turkish style toilets and free showers. Washing machines. Motorcaravan service point. Large supermarket. Restaurant. Good supervised pool and paddling pool. Aerobics. Fitness centre. Play areas. Bicycle hire. Miniclub. Entertainment. Excursion service. Beach 100 m. down fairly steep slope. Excellent diving. Off site: Fishing. Sailing. Riding 1 km.

Open: 15 May - 10 October.

Directions

Take SS291 Sassari - Alghero road east, then the SS55 to Capo Caccia. Turn to Porticciolo town where site is well signed. GPS: 40.64230, 8.19060

Charges guide

Per person junior or senior	€ 7,00 - € 14,00
(under 12 or over 60 yrs)	€ 6,00 - € 13,00
pitch	€ 2,00 - € 14,00
dog	€ 2,00 - € 6,00
Camping Cheques accepted.	

Alghero
Camping Mariposa

Via Lido 22, I-07041 Alghero (Sardinia) T: **079 950 360**. E: **info@lamariposa.it**
alanrogers.com/IT69960

Mariposa is situated right by the sea with its own beach and the range of sports available here probably makes it best suited for active young visitors. Kite surfing, diving, windsurfing, sailing, surfing and paragliding courses are all available here on payment, whilst evening entertainment is provided free. Pitches range in size from 50-80 sq.m. so they are also better suited for tents, although they do all have 6A electrical connections and caravans and motorcaravans are welcome. However, there are few marked pitches and the land is undulating and may be unsuitable for units which tend to park beside roads. Cars must be parked away from the pitches. Alghero (1.5 km) still has a strong Catalan flavour from its 400 year occupation by the Spanish. There are many small coves and the Neptune caves are well worth a visit.

Facilities

The sanitary facilities are fairly basic, open plan, with cold washbasins and troughs, dishwashing and laundry sinks and an equal amount of warm (token needed) and cold showers. Washing machines and dryer. Motorcaravan service point. Shop, self-service restaurant and bar (all 10/6-30/9). Bicycle hire. Dogs are not accepted in July/Aug.

Open: 1 April - 31 October.

Directions

Alghero is on the northwest coast, about 35 km. southwest of Sassari. Mariposa is at the north of the town. Turn left at main traffic lights towards the Lido then left again at the T-junction, site is immediately on the right. GPS: 40.57885, 8.31253

Charges guide

Per person	€ 8,00 - € 11,00
child (3-12 yrs)	€ 4,00 - € 8,50
pitch	free - € 14,00
car	free - € 4,00
electricity	€ 2,50

07041 ALGHERO (SS)
Tel. +39 0799504800

E-mail: info@lamariposa.it
Http: www.lamariposa.it

la**M a r i p o s a** ★★★ camping con bungalows ▶ IS 110
il gioco, ritrovarsi

Camping La Mariposa is very well equipped with bar, grocer's, market and private beach. It is well-known because of its care and hospitality. The camping site provides equipped pitches for tents, caravans and motocaravans, but also duble rooms, 4 bedded bungalows, 2/4 bedded caravans and 4 bedded mini-villas. Camping La Mariposa is looking forward to welcoming you for a pleasant holiday from 1st April till 30th October with booking facilities avaiable all the year long.

Check real time availability and at-the-gate prices...
www.**alanrogers**.com

Arborea
Camping S'Ena Arrubia
Strada 29, I-09092 Arborea (Sardinia) T: **078 380 9011**. E: **info@senarrubia.it**
alanrogers.com/IT69890

S'Ena Arrubia can be found on Sardinia's west coast, close to the neo-gothic and art deco town of Arborea. This is a well equipped family site with grassy, well shaded pitches and a good range of leisure facilities. These include a swimming pool, tennis courts, football field and various activities on the adjacent sandy beach (including beach volleyball). Pitches are arranged beneath pine trees and all are equipped with electrical connections. There is a separate area for motorcaravans which offers special 'camper stop' rates. Alternatively, a number of caravans and mobile homes are available for rent.

Facilities

Shop. Bar. Snack bar. Swimming pool. Football pitch. Tennis. Games room. Direct access to beach. Diving school. Play area. Tourist information. Activity and entertainment programme. Mobile homes and caravans for rent. Off site: Cycle and walking tracks. Organised excursions. Nearby town of Arborea.

Open: 22 March - 30 September.

Directions

Approaching from the north (Sassari), head south on SS131 to Oristano then join the SP49 to Arborea, and follow signs to the site. GPS: 39.81697, 8.55637

Charges guide

Per unit incl. 2 persons and electricity	€ 17,00 - € 34,00

Camping Cheques accepted.

Bari Sardo
Camping l'Ultima Spiaggia
Localitá Planargia, I-08042 Bari Sardo (Sardinia) T: **078 229 363**. E: **info@campingultimaspiaggia.it**
alanrogers.com/IT69720

A great name for this campsite 'the ultimate beach' and the beach really is extremely good, along with the bright colourful decor and amenities. We think you will enjoy this clean and pleasant site, although little English is spoken. The 250 pitches are terraced on sand, some enjoy sea views and are located at the end of the site. New mobile homes occupy the top of the site which slopes towards the sea. The good entertainment programme can be enjoyed from the terrace of the friendly restaurant which offers a reasonably priced menu which includes the local seafood specialities.

Facilities

Two toilet units include mainly Turkish style toilets and good facilities for disabled campers. Washing machines. Motorcaravan service point. Small supermarket. Restaurant and snack bar. Play areas. Windsurfing. Aerobics. Riding. Tennis. Minigolf. Canoeing. Bicycle hire. Entertainment. Miniclub. Excursions. Torches useful. Off site: Restaurants, bars and shops. Fishing. Boat launching.

Open: 20 April - 30 September.

Directions

Site is on east coast of Sardinia, well signed from SS125 in village of Bari Sardo. Note that the roads are very winding from the north - allow lots of time. GPS: 39.81910, 9.67010

Charges guide

Per person	€ 6,50 - € 13,50
child (1-6 yrs)	€ 3,50 - € 6,50
pitch	€ 6,00 - € 14,50
electricity	€ 3,00

Budoni
Camping Pedra & Cupa
Via Nazionale, I-08020 Budoni (Sardinia) T: **078 484 4004**. E: **info@pedraecupa-camping.com**
alanrogers.com/IT69650

The modern and bustling tourist resort of Budoni lies on Sardinia's east coast, just north of Siniscola and this delightful site is just to the south. It is a modern and attractive site where thought has clearly gone into its planning. Modern bungalows (for rent) screen the camping area from the coastal road. The camping area benefits from being close to the white sands of the extensive clean beach and within the shade of the eucalyptus and pine trees that adjoin the coast. With additional net screening the site provides about 55 level grassy pitches, for campers and caravans, with tents filling in around the site.

Facilities

Twin sanitary blocks provide toilets (mainly Turkish style), open style washbasins and ample hot showers (token required). Motorcaravan service point. Restaurant. Bar. Shop. Swimming pool and sunbathing terrace (little shade). Tennis. Football. Off site: Riding. Walks and cycle routes.

Open: 15 May - 30 September.

Directions

From the SS131 take Budoni exit and follow the SS125 north for about 8 km. Site is on the right just after entering the town. GPS: 40.70583, 9.70083

Charges guide

Per person	€ 6,50 - € 14,50
child (2-11 yrs)	€ 3,50 - € 9,00
pitch	€ 7,00 - € 14,00
electricity	€ 2,50 - € 3,00

Special low season deals.

Check real time availability and at-the-gate prices...
www.alanrogers.com

Cannigione di Arzachena
Isuledda Holiday Centre
Localitá Laconia, I-07021 Cannigione di Arzachena (Sardinia) T: 078 986 003. E: info@isuledda.it
alanrogers.com/IT69630

This high quality, commercialised resort style operation has something for everyone, with an amazing choice of activities and entertainment. The central area buzzes with activity, although it is possible to find a quiet area to relax. There is a balance of activities for all age groups and a large range of pitch choice. The site is enormous with a variety of accommodation (flats, bungalows, mobile homes, caravans and tour operator tents) and in high season, very crowded. Cars must be parked in car parks outside the entrance. Most of the 600 good sized, gravel pitches have some shade from eucalyptus trees and are flat.

Facilities
Six toilet blocks include British and Turkish style toilets and good facilities for disabled campers. Showers. Washing machines. Motorcaravan service point. Large supermarket. Restaurant, pizzeria and snack bar. Aerobics. Play areas. Boat, car, bicycle and scooter hire. Windsurfing. Sailing. Sub-aqua. Marina. Miniclub and entertainment. Excursions. Disco and beer bar (can be noisy until late). Dogs are not accepted. Off site: Riding 10 km. Golf 15 km.

Open: 1 April - 30 October.

Directions
Site is on the Costa Smeralda in the northeast of Sardinia. From SS125 Olbia - Cannigione road, south of Arzachena, take road north towards Baia Sardinia. Then follow road north to Cannigione, go through town and further north for about 2 km. where you will find the site. GPS: 41.1302, 9.4387

Charges guide
Per unit incl. 2 persons and electricity	€ 20,00 - € 55,00
extra person	€ 5,00 - € 12,50
child (3-12 yrs)	€ 3,00 - € 7,00

Camping Cheques accepted.

Domus de Maria
Camping Torre Chia
Chia, I-09010 Domus de Maria (Sardinia) T: 070 923 0054. E: torre.chia@tiscalinet.it
alanrogers.com/IT69830

Torre Chia is set on a beautiful sandy beach in the Golfo di Cagliari – you have an hour's drive over good roads from Cagliari port or airport. The main buildings include a bar and large restaurant with a huge terrace area to enjoy the cool breezes. Good sized sandy pitches which are mostly level, are quite close together, and they are shaded by tall eucalyptus and pine trees. Access to the beach is via a 60 m. walk through tall pines where families enjoy picnics in the shade. A family oriented site, Torre Chia has a modest range of facilities, ideal for independent campers who like a simple site with good amenities.

Facilities
A single modern block has excellent, clean sanitary facilities with mainly British style toilets. Locked facilities for disabled campers. Showers are coin operated. Washing machine. Motorcaravan service point. Shop. Restaurant and snack bar. Play area. Tennis. Bicycle hire. Fishing. Windsurfing. Canoeing. Small boat launching. Excursions. Off site: Golf and riding 2 km. Sailing, sub-aqua diving and canoeing.

Open: 1 June - 30 September.

Directions
Site is south of Cagliari near San Margherita di Pula. Go to the village and the site is brightly signed towards the beach. GPS: 38.8968, 8.8851

Charges guide
Per person	€ 7,50 - € 8,50
child (1-10 yrs)	€ 6,00 - € 6,50
pitch	€ 5,50 - € 10,50
electricity	€ 2,00

Loiri Porto San Paolo
Camping Tavolara
SS125 km 300,300, I-07020 Loiri Porto San Paolo (Sardinia) T: 078 940 166. E: info@camping-tavolara.it
alanrogers.com/IT69640

This small site with just 200 pitches is located just south of Olbia and 30 minutes from the ferry port and airport. Just 500 m. inland from the beach, this is a great location near the Stagno di San Teodoro (good for observing ducks and herons) and opposite Isola Tavolara. This spectacular island, literally a mountain rising out of the sea, is famous for the legendary 'goats with golden teeth', a phenomenon caused by the grass they eat. The island and the area around are soon to become a marine reserve. The growing holiday town of Porto San Paolo is just 2 km. up the road.

Facilities
Two sanitary blocks provide toilets (mainly Turkish style), washbasins and showers. Facilities for disabled campers. Motorcaravan service point. Restaurant and bar. Pizzeria. Shop (all facilities open Easter-Sept). Diving school. Archery. Excursions and entertainment (high season). Caravans and mobile homes to rent. Off site: Isola Tavolara. Costa Smeralda. Olbia.

Open: 8 January - 10 December.

Directions
Site is at 300 km. marker on SS125 south of Olbia. From port follow signs for 'aeroporto' and pass the airport heading towards San Teodoro. Site is on left just past Porto San Paolo. GPS: 40.87556, 9.64222

Charges guide
Per person	€ 8,00 - € 11,00
child (4-12 yrs)	€ 4,50 - € 6,50
pitch	free - € 15,00
electricity	€ 2,50

Check real time availability and at-the-gate prices...
www.alanrogers.com
205

Sardinia (sidebar)

Lotzorai
Camping Le Cernie

Localitá Case Sparse, I-08040 Lotzorai (Sardinia) T: 078 266 9472. E: info@campinglecernie.com

alanrogers.com/IT69690

Le Cernie is situated in a remote area on the east coast of Sardinia and was originally a diving enterprise. Le Cernie has grown into a very modest campsite which is surprisingly expensive. It is somewhat chaotic in nature, although most amenities are here, including a popular restaurant. Life at Le Cernie seems to meander along at its own pace – it is somewhat rugged and would not suit campers without a sense of humour and patience. The site is accessed by a 900 m. long and very uneven track, which was waterlogged and muddy when we last visited.

Facilities

A single modern unit has a rather confusing mixture of clean sanitary facilities with a mix of Turkish and British style toilets and very good facilities for disabled campers and babies. Ample unisex hot showers and six private bathrooms for rent. Washing machines. Motorcaravan service point. Small shop. Restaurant and snack bar. Bicycle hire. Play area. Beach volleyball. Small boat launching. Sub-acua diving. Off site: Riding 10 km.

Open: All year (facilities open May - September).

Directions

Site is off the eastern coast road SS125. At Lotzorai village, north of Abratax, site is well signed, but the streets through the village are narrow, winding and subject to heavy parking. GPS: 39.9709, 9.6847

Charges guide

Per person	€ 7,00 - € 14,80
child (0-12 yrs)	free - € 9,70
pitch	€ 2,00 - € 8,80
'millennium' pitch	€ 3,00 - € 20,00

Muravera
Camping le Dune

Localitá Piscina Rei, I-09043 Muravera (Sardinia) T: 070 991 9057. E: info@campingledune.it

alanrogers.com/IT69740

The Costa Rei in southeast Sardinia is a popular seaside resort which has not as yet been over-developed. A white sandy bay and the turquoise sea make it a perfect location and Le Dune can be found at the northern edge of the bay. With 200 pitches in total, over half of which are occupied by mobile homes, the site is continually changing. When we visited around 40 pitches for caravans and motorcaravans, all under low trees, were located at the far end of the site near the beach access, with tents occupying the intervening spaces.

Facilities

The single sanitary block provides toilets, washbasins (open style) and showers. Restaurant. Bar. Shop. Swimming pool. Tennis and football. Off site: Costa Rei. Diving.

Open: 10 April - 30 September.

Directions

Site is in southeast corner of Sardinia in the north of the Costa Rei. From old coast road SS125 at San Priamo travel south to Villagio Capo Ferrato. Site is well signed from here. GPS: 39.2767, 9.5821

Charges guide

Per person	€ 6,00 - € 18,00
child (3-12 yrs)	€ 4,50 - € 10,00
pitch	€ 2,00 - € 6,00
electricity	€ 2,50

Muravera
Camping Villaggio Porto Pirastu

Capo Ferrato, I-09043 Muravera (Sardinia) T: 070 991 437. E: info@portopirastu.net

alanrogers.com/IT69750

This family site situated at Capo Ferrato has a wide range of facilities in a tranquil area alongside the beautiful Mar Tirreno with its warm turquoise water, rocky outcrops and long stretches of sandy beach. The 260 shaded, reasonably sized pitches are on gravel and sand, some having views of the water, but the site appears a little cluttered with static caravans. The traditional buildings lend atmosphere to the main square and the restaurant has a charming ambience with its arched ceilings. There are shaded terraces and sitting out areas where you can relax and enjoy the sea breezes whilst enjoying an aperitif or ice-cream.

Facilities

Three very pleasant blocks of sanitary facilities with mainly British style toilets. Facilities for disabled campers. Washing machine. Motorcaravan service point. Shop. Restaurant and snack bar. Play areas. Miniclub and entertainment in high season. Cinema. Tennis. Excursions. Water aerobics. Sub-aqua diving. Windsurfing school. Torches useful. Off site: Sailing 1.5 km. Bicycle hire 4 km. Golf or riding 5 km.

Open: 3 April - 30 October.

Directions

Site is in southeast corner of Sardinia in the north of the Costa Rei. From coast road SS125 at San Priamo travel south to Villaggio Capo Ferrato. Site is well signed from here. GPS: 39.2923, 9.5987

Charges guide

Per unit incl. 2 persons and electricity	€ 18,80 - € 48,40
extra person	€ 4,20 - € 13,50
child (3-9 yrs)	€ 3,20 - € 8,90
dog	€ 2,60 - € 4,30

Muravera-Castiadas

Camping Capo Ferrato

Localitá Costa Rei, I-09040 Muravera-Castiadas (Sardinia) T: **070 991 012**. E: **info@campingcapoferrato.it**
alanrogers.com/IT69770

Situated at the southern end of the magnificent Costa Rei, this small, friendly and well managed site has 80 touring pitches, many with sea views. Managed by the same family since 1965, the campsite was one of the first in Sardinia. Close to the hamlet of Costa Rei, it benefits from close proximity to the shops and restaurants, yet enjoys the tranquillity of its semi-rural location with direct beach access. In low season educational sessions are organised entitled 'Discovering a bit about Sardinia' with a cultural and gastronomic entertainment programme.

Facilities

Two sanitary blocks include toilets, washbasins and free hot showers. No facilities for disabled visitors. Washing machine. Baby room. Motorcaravan service point. Bar. Restaurant. Pizzeria. Well stocked shop. TV room. Bicycle hire. Tennis. Minigolf. Football and basketball pitch. Children's play area. Bungalows to rent. Off site: Boat launching 200 m. Riding 3 km. Golf 20 km. Costa Rei - Castiadas, Muravera.

Open: Easter - 2 November.

Directions

From Cagliari travel along the coast road towards Villasimus (SP17) as far as Solanas (until km. 26.500), turn left and follow signs to Costa Rei. From Arbatax drive along SS125 until exit Olia Speciosa, then follow signs to Costa Rei. NB: Campsite is in Costa Rei (loc. Monte Nai) and not on the promonotory of Capo Ferrato. GPS: 39.24297, 9.56941

Charges guide

Per person	€ 5,30 - € 12,40
pitch	€ 4,70 - € 17,40
electricity	€ 2,10 - € 3,40
Camping Cheques accepted.	

Nuoro

Camping Agritourism Costiolou

SS389, I-08100 Nuoro (Sardinia) T: **078 426 0088**. E: **info@agriturismocostiolu.com**
alanrogers.com/IT69670

Costiolou is a 100 hectare, organic farm high in the hills above Nuoro, with fantastic views in almost every direction. This is a most unusual campsite, located on the working farm run by Giovanni di Costa. It provides simple amenities and a place to be close to nature. Breeding horses (which are available to ride) and growing simple crops including cereals and olives, the site provides just nine pitches on a flat and level field behind the farmhouse. Eagles circle overhead and the sheep and sheepdog sleep under trees along the access track. The site is open all year although in winter 2006 the snow was a metre deep.

Facilities

Toilets and showers are provided in a restored farm building alongside the pitches. Bar. Restaurant (by arrangement). Rooms to rent. Riding. Dogs are not accepted. Off site: Wild Sardinian countryside.

Open: All year.

Directions

From the Nuoro exit on the SS131dcn follow signs for Bitti. After 8 km. you reach a track on the right signed to the farm 900 m. GPS: 40.36740, 9.29658

Charges guide

Per person	€ 6,00 - € 10,00
child	€ 3,00 - € 5,00
pitch	€ 7,00 - € 10,00
Cash only.	

Palau

Camping Capo d'Orso

Localitá Saline, I-07020 Palau (Sardinia) T: **078 970 2007**. E: **info@capodorso.it**
alanrogers.com/IT69600

Capo d'Orso is some 4.5 km. from the village of Palau in northern Sardinia. It is an attractive terraced site with views of the Maddalena Archipelago. Set into a hillside that slopes down to the sea, the 350 terraced pitches (40-80 sq.m) are of gravel, grass and sand, some with views over the sea and some others set alongside the beach. Access to the pitches is quite good despite the rocky terrain. Cars are parked away from the pitches in high season. The very Italian (self-service) restaurant serves delicious meals which can be eaten on a small terrace with sea views.

Facilities

Three toilet blocks provide adequate facilities, including hot showers and mainly Turkish, but with some British style WCs. Shop. Bar/restaurant. Pizzeria. Takeaway. Scuba diving, windsurfing, sailing school, boat excursions, boat hire and moorings (all main season). Tennis. Underground disco. Entertainment programmes for children and adults. Excursions arranged in high season. Off site: Scuba diving. Windsurfing. Sailing.

Open: 1 May - 30 September.

Directions

Site is 5 km. from Palau, in the northeast of Sardinia. On the SS133 Porto Pozzo - Cannigione road. It is well signed towards the beach. GPS: 41.16117, 9.40300

Charges guide

Per person	€ 5,00 - € 8,00
child (6-12 yrs)	€ 3,00 - € 6,00
small tent (2 persons)	€ 4,00 - € 16,00
pitch incl. electricity	€ 9,00 - € 30,00
car or motorcycle	€ 2,00 - € 4,00

Sant' Antioco

Camping Tonnara

CP 83, I-09017 Sant' Antioco (Sardinia) T: **078 180 9058**. E: **tonnaracamping@tiscalinet.it**

alanrogers.com/IT69860

A small and beautiful campsite, Tonnara is situated on the west side of Sant' Antioco island in the southwest corner of Sardinia. Access to the island is via a causeway and Tonnara is located 12 km. away in the pretty Cala Sapone inlet with its delightful sandy beach and rocky outcrops. The 60 sandy pitches are on terraces with small trees and some artificial shade. Some are very close to the beach and most enjoy views of the inlet. The drinking water supply is delivered by tanker, so we would recommend that you arrive with a full tank of your own or use bottled water.

Facilities

The single sanitary block has toilets (both Turkish and British style), washbasins and hot showers but no facilities for disabled campers. Washing machine. Motorcaravan service point. Neat little shop (15/6-15/9). Restaurant and snack bar (all season). Small play area. Bicycle hire. Tennis. Bocce. Sandy beach. Sub-aqua diving arranged. Excursions. Off site: Sailing 1 km. Nearest town 12 km. Riding 20 km.

Open: 20 April - 30 September.

Directions

Site is on island of Sant' Antioco on southwest coast of Sardinia. Go over causeway and immediately at end, turn left and left again at T-junction towards Cala Sapone (site signed). When road forks, look carefully for yellow campsite sign (straight ahead) to cross to western side for site. GPS: 39.0053, 8.3873

Charges guide

Per person	€ 8,50 - € 11,30
pitch	free - € 19,00
electricity	€ 2,20 - € 3,00

Torre Grande

Campeggio-Villaggio Spinnaker

Strada Provinciale, Oristano, I-09170 Torre Grande (Sardinia) T: **078 322 074**. E: **info@spinnakervacanze.com**

alanrogers.com/IT69900

Set on the undulating foreshore under tall pines, with beach frontage to the camping area, Spinnaker Village is a purpose-built, modern beach site. The 100 pitches are sandy and the majority are for tents, however, about 40 are suitable for caravans and motorhomes. All have electricity and there are plenty of water taps. Tent pitches are large and clearly marked, each with a tree to provide shade. All cars must be parked in a car park outside the site. The restaurant, a café and the swimming pool are set around a large square where activities for families take place. The pool is very inviting, surrounded by sunshades and with a shallow end for children (it is unfenced and alongside the play area, so supervise little ones). Whilst there are no views of the sea from the pitches, it is an easy 60 metre stroll to the beach of fine white sand where there are free sun loungers and parasols. It is an easy walk along the beach to the resort of Marina Torre Grande. Excursions from the site could include a visit to the marine reserve of 'Sinis Isola di Maladentre' or the ruins of Tharros and San Christina – a 'Nuraghe village'.

Facilities

Toilet blocks are modern and clean with British style toilets and facilities for disabled campers. Showers are coin operated (€ 0.50) and there are few for the number of pitches so expect to wait in busy periods. Washing machine. Motorcaravan service point (on payment). Small shop. Restaurant and small snack bar. Swimming pool (unfenced). Good play area. Bicycle hire. Small boat launching. Miniclub and animation in high season. Excursions. Torches essential. Off site: Riding 2 km. Golf 23 km.

Open: All year.

Directions

Take SS131 Cagliari - Oristano road then minor road to Cabras and Torre Grande. Just before Torre Grande village by large water tower take angled left turn back on yourself to site (signed). GPS: 39.90300, 8.53010

Charges guide

Per person	€ 7,50 - € 20,00
child (3-12 yrs)	€ 4,50 - € 12,00
pitch	€ 4,00 - € 6,00
electricity	€ 2,00 - € 2,50
Camping Cheques accepted.	

VILLAGE CAMPING

SPINNAKER ★★★★

Strada Oristano-Torregrande • tel. 0039 0783 22074 | 0039 0783 22071
www.spinnakervacanze.com • info@spinnakervacanze.com

Santa Lucia di Siniscola

Selema Camping

Tiria Seliana, I-08029 Santa Lucia di Siniscola (Sardinia) T: 079 953 761. E: info@selemacamping.com

alanrogers.com/IT69660

Selema is a pretty site with a tropical feel. There is considerable shade from pine and eucalyptus, although access to many pitches is restricted by tall, bending trees. Flowers and cacti have been used to provide landscaping features and unusually there are grassy areas. There are 170 large pitches of grass and sand, well shaded with shallow terracing. The site runs along the Pineta coast with its long white sandy beaches and vibrant blue water, and has a wide river flowing along the other side. Some pitches are near the beach and a few have views of the distant mountains. The helpful staff speak some English.

Facilities

Two sanitary blocks have good facilities with a mixture of British and Turkish toilets. Good hot showers. Facilities for disabled campers. Washing machine. Motorcaravan service point. Pleasant shop. Restaurant and snack bar. Play areas. Tennis. Bocce. Large screen TV. Electronic games. Bicycle hire. Windsurfing. Small boat launching. Excursions. Off site: Fishing. Riding 500 m. Sailing 4 km. Golf 40 km.

Open: 1 May - 15 October.

Directions

Site is on the SS125, about 30 km. north of Orosei. Turn towards the coast, near the 254 km. marker to Santa Lucia. Site is well signed. GPS: 40.5785, 9.7730

Charges guide

Per person	€ 5,50 - € 12,50
pitch	€ 4,50 - € 17,00
electricity	€ 3,00

Tortoli

Camping Cigno Bianco

Lido di Orri, I-08048 Tortoli (Sardinia) T: 078 262 4927. E: info@cignobianco.it

alanrogers.com/IT69700

The small town of Tortoli is just 5 km. inland from the busy port of Arbatax with its regular ferry services to and from the mainland. With its white swan sign, this site is just to the south, in the rural area of Lido di Orri. Here the Pinna family run a quiet and restful site with good facilities and direct beach access. The unmarked pitches have good shade from the tall eucalyptus and pine trees which cover most of the site. Not far to the north is the magnificent Gennargentu National Park with spectacular, wild mountain scenery and wildlife.

Facilities

Two adjacent sanitary blocks provide toilets (some are Turkish style), washbasins and showers (token required). Motorcaravan service point. Restaurant, bar and small shop. Tennis court and multisport pitch. Flats and mobile homes to rent. Off site: Gennargentu National Park. Cala Sisine.

Open: 1 May - 30 September.

Directions

Site is just off the SS125, south of Tortoli. From large roundabout head towards the coast and Lido d'Orri. Turn right where signed and site is just over a narrow bridge. GPS: 39.91686, 9.68433

Charges guide

Per person	€ 7,50 - € 10,50
child (3-10 yrs)	€ 5,00 - € 8,50
pitch incl. electricity	free - € 9,00

Valledoria

Camping La Foce

Via Ampurias 1 c.s, I-07039 Valledoria (Sardinia) T: 079 582 109. E: info@lafoce.eu

alanrogers.com/IT69500

English speaking Stefano Lamparti is the enthusiastic owner of La Foce which is a large sprawling site in the Golfo del Asinara. A river flows through the site into the sea and there is a motorboat to ferry campers to a secluded area of the coast on the other side of the river where they can enjoy the golden sand dunes and have a refreshing swim away from other beachgoers. The 300 sandy pitches vary in size and are informally arranged under tall shady eucalyptus trees stretching along the length of the site, some close to the river.

Facilities

Four mature toilet blocks house good facilities with British and Turkish style toilets but no facilities for disabled campers. Hot water is available 24 hours. Washing machine. Motorcaravan service point. Supermarket. Restaurant and snack bar. Two pools and sun deck. Play areas. Tennis. Bocce. Excursions. Beaches – some by free punt. Boat launching. Windsurfing. Canoeing. Sub-aqua diving. Off site: Fishing. Sailing 1.5 km. Riding 2 km.

Open: 1 May - 30 September.

Directions

From Sassari take coast road go east to Castelsardo and Valledoria. As you arrive at the village watch for campsite signs towards beach. GPS: 40.9265, 8.8157

Charges 2010

Per unit incl. 2 persons and electricity	€ 18,00 - € 35,00
extra person	€ 5,00 - € 9,70
child (1-4 yrs)	€ 3,00 - € 8,00
dog	€ 3,00

Camping Cheques accepted.

The world famous Postojna caves are well worth a visit. Guided tours by special cave trains take you through extensive and marvellous rock formations.

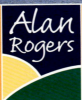

With its snow capped Julian Alps and the picturesque Triglav National park that include the beautiful lakes of Bled and Bohinj, and the peaceful Soca River, it is no wonder that the northwest region of Slovenia is so popular. Stretching from the Alps down to the Adriatic coast is the picturesque Karst region, with pretty olive groves and thousands of spectacular underground caves, including the Postojna and Skocjan caves. Although small, the Adriatic coast has several bustling beach towns such as the Italianised Koper resort and the historic port of Piran, with many opportunities for watersports and sunbathing. The capital Ljubljana is centrally located; with Renaissance, Baroque and Art Nouveau architecture, you will find most points of interest are along the Ljubljana river. Heading eastwards the landscape becomes gently rolling hills, and is largely given over to vines (home of Lutomer Riesling). Savinja with its spectacular Alps is the main area for producing wine.

Population
2 million

Capital
Ljubljana

Climate
Warm summers, cold winters with sno
in the Alps.

Language
Slovene, with German often spoken i
the north and Italian in the west.

Telephone
The country code is 386.

Currency
The Euro (€).

Banks
Mon-Fri 08.30-16.30 with a lunch br
12.30-14.00, plus Saturday mornings
08.30-11.30.

Shops
Shops usually open by 08.00, someti
07.00. Closing times vary widely.

WHAT SLOVENIA LACKS IN SIZE IT MAKES UP FOR IN EXCEPTIONAL BEAUTY. SITUATED BETWEEN ITALY, AUSTRIA, HUNGARY AND CROATIA, IT HAS A DIVERSE LANDSCAPE WITH STUNNING ALPS, RIVERS, FORESTS AND THE WARM ADRIATIC COAST.

Public Holidays

New Year 1, 2 Jan; Preseren Day 8 Feb; Easter Monday; Resistance Day 27 Apr; Labour Day 1-2 May; National Day 25 Jun; Assumption; Reformation Day 31 Oct; All Saint's Day; Christmas Day; Independence Day 26 Dec.

Motoring

A small, but expanding network of motorways radiates from Ljubijana. A 'vignette' system for motorway travel is in place. The cost is around € 35 (for a six-month vignette) and they can be purchased at petrol stations and DARS offices in Slovenia and neighbouring countries near the border. Failure to display a vignette will lead to fines of up to € 300. For more information: www.cestnina.si. Winter driving equipment (winter tyres or snow chains) is mandatory between 15 Nov and 15 March. By law, you must have your headlights on **at all times**, while driving in Slovenia. You are also required to carry a reflective jacket, a warning triangle and a first aid kit in the vehicle. Do not drink and drive – any trace of alcohol in your system will lead to prosecution.

Tourist Office

Slovenian Tourist Office
South Marlands, Itchingfield
Horsham RH13 0NN
Tel: 0870 225 5305
E-mail: slovenia.tourism@virgin.net
Internet: www.slovenia.info

British Embassy

4th Floor Trg Republike 3
1000 Ljubljana
Tel: (386) (1) 200 3910

Places of interest

Adriatic Coast: Venetian Gothic architecture can be found at Piran, the best beach along the coast is at Fiesa.

Julian Alps: Mt Triglav is the country's highest peak, Bled's Castle, Bled Island has a 15th-century belfry with a 'bell of wishes', Lake Bohinij.

Ljubljana: Municipal Museum, National Museum, Museum of Modern Art all along the banks of the Ljubljana River, Tivoli Park with bowling alleys, tennis courts, swimming pools and a roller-skating rink.

Skocjan Caves: filled with stalactites and stalagmites and housing 250 plant varieties and five types of bats.

Cuisine of the region

Traditionally the cuisine mainly consists of venison and fish, but there are Austrian, Italian and Hungarian influences.

Dunajski zrezek: wiener schnitzel

Golaz: goulash

Klobasa: sausage

Njoki: potato dumplings

Paprikas: chicken or beef stew

Struklji: cheese dumplings

Zavitek: strudel

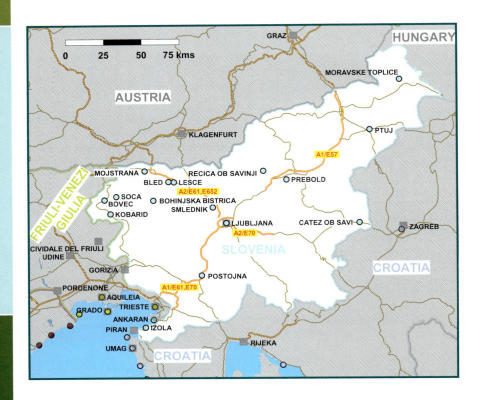

Ankaran

Camping Adria

Jadranska Cesta 25, SLO-6280 Ankaran T: 056 637 350. E: adria.tp@siol.net

alanrogers.com/SV4310

Camping Adria is on the south side of the Milje/Muggia peninsula, right on the shore of the Adriatic Sea and just beyond the large shipyard and oil storage depot. It has a concrete promenade with access to the sea, complemented by an Olympic size pool with children's pool, both filled with sea water. The site has 500 pitches (250 for tourers), all with 10A electricity, set up on one side of the site close to sea. Pitches are off tarmac access roads, running down to sea and most are between 80 and 90 sq.m. There are six fully-serviced pitches for motorcaravans with electricity, water and waste water.

Facilities

Five modern toilet blocks with British and Turkish style toilets, open style washbasins (cold water only) and preset showers (on payment). Facilities for disabled visitors. Laundry room. Fridge box hire. Supermarket. Beach shop. Newspaper kiosk. Bar/restaurant with terrace. Swimming pool (40 x 15 m.) with large slide. Playground on gravel. Playing field. Tennis. Minigolf. Fishing. Jetty for mooring boats. Boat launching. Canoe hire. Disco and bowling club. Off site: Historic towns of Koper, Izola, Piran and Portoroz are close.

Open: 1 May - 30 September.

Directions

From Koper drive north to Ankaran. Site is immediately on the left after entering Ankaran.
GPS: 45.57797, 13.73633

Charges guide

Per person	€ 4,10 - € 8,40
child (2-8 yrs)	€ 3,40 - € 6,60
pitch	€ 8,95 - € 14,40
electricity	€ 2,85
dog	€ 2,60
Camping Cheques accepted.	

Bled
Camping Bled
Kidriceva 10c Sl, SLO-4260 Bled T: 045 752 000. E: info@camping.bled.com
alanrogers.com/SV4200

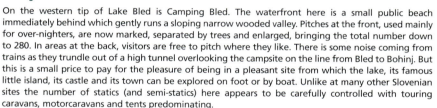

On the western tip of Lake Bled is Camping Bled. The waterfront here is a small public beach immediately behind which gently runs a sloping narrow wooded valley. Pitches at the front, used mainly for over-nighters, are now marked, separated by trees and enlarged, bringing the total number down to 280. In areas at the back, visitors are free to pitch where they like. There is some noise coming from trains as they trundle out of a high tunnel overlooking the campsite on the line from Bled to Bohinj. But this is a small price to pay for the pleasure of being in a pleasant site from which the lake, its famous little island, its castle and its town can be explored on foot or by boat. Unlike at many other Slovenian sites the number of statics (and semi-statics) here appears to be carefully controlled with touring caravans, motorcaravans and tents predominating.

Facilities
Toilet facilities in five blocks are of a high standard (with free hot showers). Two blocks are heated. Solar energy used. Washing machines and dryers. Motorcaravan services. Gas supplies. Fridge hire. Supermarket. Restaurant. Play area and children's zoo. Games hall. Trampolines. Organised activities in July/August including children's club, excursions and sporting activities. Mountain bike tours. Live entertainment. Fishing. Bicycle hire. Internet access and WiFi. Off site: Riding 3 km. Golf 5 km. Within walking distance of waterfront and town. Restaurants near.

Open: 1 April - 15 October.

Directions
From the town of Bled drive along south shore of lake to its western extremity (some 2 km) to the site. GPS: 46.36155, 14.08075

Charges 2010
Per person	€ 8,50 - € 12,50
child (7-13 yrs)	€ 5,95 - € 8,75
electricity	€ 3,50
dog	€ 1,50 - € 2,50

Less 10% for stays over 6 days.

Camping Bled

Camping Bled
Kidričeva 10 c, 4260 Bled, Slovenia
tel.: +386 (0)4 / 575 20 00
fax: +386 (0)4 / 575 20 02
e-mail: info@camping-bled.com

www.camping-bled.com

Bohinjska Bistrica
Camping Danica Bohinj
Triglavska 60, SLO-4264 Bohinjska Bistrica T: 045 721 702. E: info@camp-danica.si
alanrogers.com/SV4250

For those wanting to visit the famous Bohinj valley, which stretches like a fjord right into the heart of the Julian Alps, an ideal site is Danica Bohinj which lies in the valley 3 km. downstream of the lake. Danica occupies a rural site that stretches from the main road leading into Bohinj from Bled (25 km. away), to the bank of the newly formed Sava river. It is basically flat meadow, broken up by lines of natural woodland. This excellent site has 165 pitches, 145 for touring units, all with 10A electricity and forms an ideal base for the many sporting activities the area has to offer.

Facilities
Two good toilet blocks with open plan washbasins and hot showers. Facilities for disabled visitors. Laundry facilities (expensive). Motorcaravan service point. Small shop. Bar (also used by locals, open until 01.00 and can be noisy). Café. Tennis. Fishing. Bicycle hire. Excursions in the Triglavski National Park. Off site: Riding 6 km. Canoeing, kayaking, rafting and numerous walking and mountain bike trails.

Open: May - September.

Directions
Driving from Bled to Bohinj, the well signed site lies just behind the village of Bohinjska Bistrica on the right-hand (north) side of the road. GPS: 46.27335, 13.94868

Charges guide
Per person	€ 7,60 - € 11,00
child (7-14 yrs)	€ 6,10 - € 9,00
electricity	€ 3,50
dog	€ 2,50

Less 10% for stays over 7 days.

Bovec

Camping Polovnik

Ledina 8, SLO-5230 Bovec T: 053 896 007. E: kamp.polovnik@siol.net

alanrogers.com/SV4280

The Polovnik site is little more than a large, circular field, with trees in the centre that provide useful shade, and an open part to one side. There are 50 unmarked pitches (45 for tourers) all with 16A electricity, off a circular, gravel access road. To the back of the site is a separate field for groups. All pitches have good views of the surrounding mountains. This site is useful as a stopover on your way to the Postojna Caves, the Slovenian Riviera or Italy and for touring the local area with kayaking, rafting and canoeing possible.

Facilities

One traditional style toilet block with British style toilets, open style washbasins with cold water only and preset hot showers (€ 0,50 token). Washing machine. Off site: Restaurant at entrance. Fishing 1 km. Bovec town.

Open: 1 April - 16 October.

Directions

Bovec is on main road (54) from the Italian/Slovenian border to Postojna. Site is just outside Bovec next to a church. GPS: 46.33622, 13.55837

Charges guide

Per person	€ 5,00 - € 7,00
child (7-14 yrs)	€ 3,75 - € 5,25
pitch	€ 3,00
electricity	€ 2,50

Catez ob Savi

Camping Terme Catez

Topliska cesta 35, SLO-8251 Catez ob Savi T: 074 936 723. E: camp@terme-catez.si

alanrogers.com/SV4415

Terme Catez is part of the modern Catez thermal spa, renowned for its medical programmes to treat rheumatism and for a wide range of programmes to improve or maintain your health. The campsite has 590 pitches, with 190 places for tourers, the remainder being taken by privately owned mobile homes and cottages. One large, open field, with some young trees – a real sun trap – provides level, grass pitches which are numbered by markings on the tarmac access roads. All have 10A electricity connections. It would be a very useful stopover on a journey to Croatia in the low season or for an active family holiday.

Facilities

Two modern toilet blocks with British and Turkish style toilets, open style washbasins and controllable hot showers. Child size washbasins. Facilities for disabled visitors. Laundry facilities. Motorcaravan service point. Supermarket. Kiosks for fruit, newspapers, souvenirs and tobacco. Restaurants. Bar with terrace. Several large indoor and outdoor pools (free, max. two entries per day per person). Go karts. Pedaloes. Rowing boats. Jogging track. Fishing. Golf. Bicycle hire. Sauna. Solarium. Riding. Magic shows. Dance nights. Fashion shows. Casino. Video games. Off site: Golf 7 km.

Open: All year.

Directions

From Ljubljana take no. 1 road southeast towards Zagreb and follow signs for Terme Catez (close to Brezice). GPS: 45.89137, 15.62598

Charges guide

Per person	€ 14,50 - € 15,80
child (4-12 yrs)	€ 7,25 - € 7,90
electricity	€ 3,60
dog	€ 3,20

Izola

Hotel-Camping Belvedere

Dobrava 1A, SLO-6310 Izola T: 056 605 100. E: belve@siol.net

alanrogers.com/SV4300

Under the management of Hotel Belvedere, this site has developed into a massive leisure complex of which camping is a small part. It may be suitable for a short stay but is not recommended for a beach holiday. There are 280 pitches, with 200 for touring units. All have 6A electricity, but pitching is haphazard and that may make it difficult to find a place in high season. The site is divided into five different areas, divided by a narrow public road which has to be crossed to reach the toilet facilities (watch out for local drivers).

Facilities

Two identical toilet blocks provide modern fittings but cleaning is under pressure in high season. Very comprehensive leisure facilities, including a huge swimming pool, restaurant, night club (can be very noisy late into the night) and hotel. Kiosk for basics (25/6-1/9). Beach shop. Torch useful. Off site: Historic town of Izola is close. Beach 500 m. Riding and bicycle hire 5 km.

Open: April - September.

Directions

Follow the main A2 coast road west just beyond the Izola by-pass; the site is clearly signed but the exit is on a rather confusing summit road junction that the original entrance and exit have been closed so access is not easy). GPS: 45.53095, 13.63328

Charges 2010

Per unit incl. 2 persons and electricity	€ 22,00 - € 28,00
extra person	€ 6,00 - € 12,00
dog	€ 3,00

Kobarid

Lazar Kamp

Gregorciceva, SLO-5222 Kobarid T: 053 885 333. E: edi.lazar@siol.net
alanrogers.com/SV4265

This new campsite high above the Soca river has a good location. However, the road to the site from the Napoleon Bridge is narrow, twisting and unmade and is not really suitable for most modern motorcaravans or larger caravans, although the owner of the site does insist that it is possible. With a large overhanging cliff face on the left and a low stone wall, or rusting railings on the right (before the 100 foot drop into the river) it is not for the fainthearted. The site is very suitable for tents and those with small outfits and offers 50 pitches (all with electricity) and good facilities.

Facilities

The sanitary block is of a good standard and includes facilities for disabled visitors. Washing machine. Fridge. Bar. Crêperie and grill with terrace area. Internet access. Ranch style clubroom. Excursions and lots of local sporting activities.

Open: 1 April - 31 October.

Directions

Site is on a side road leading east out of Kobarid towards Bosec, just beyond the so-called Napoleon's Bridge. It is not well signed but follow Kamp Koren signs to the bridge then the site is straight on down the narrow unmade road. GPS: 46.25513, 13.58626

Charges guide

Per person	€ 8,00 - € 10,00
child (7-14 yrs)	€ 4,00 - € 5,00
electricity	€ 2,00

Kobarid

Kamp Koren Kobarid

Drenzniske Ravne 33, SLO-5222 Kobarid T: 053 891 311. E: info@kamp-koren.si
alanrogers.com/SV4270

The campsite, run to perfection by Lidija Koren, occupies a flat, tree-lined meadow on a wide ledge which drops down sharply to the Soca river and a new, terraced area behind reception. A small, site with just 60 pitches, it is deservedly very popular with those interested in outdoor sports, including paragliding, canoeing, canyoning, rafting and fishing. Equally, a pleasant atmosphere is generated for those seeking a quiet and relaxing break. New additions in 2009 were wooden bungalows (sleeping two and four). The Julian Alps and in particular the Triglav National Park is a wonderful and under-explored part of Slovenia that has much to offer.

Facilities

Two attractive log-built toilet blocks are of a standard worthy of a high class private sports club. Facilities for disabled visitors. Laundry facilities. Motorcaravan services. Shop (March-Nov). Café dispenses light meals, snacks and drinks apparently without much regard to closing hours. Sauna. Play area. Bowling. Fishing. Bicycle hire. Canoe hire. Climbing walls for adults. Off site: Town within walking distance. Riding 5 km. Golf 20 km. Guided tours.

Open: All year.

Directions

Site is on a side road that leads east out of Kobarid towards Bovec, just beyond so-called Napoleon's Bridge, well signed on left. GPS: 46.25075, 13.58658

Charges guide

Per person	€ 9,50 - € 11,00
child (7-13 yrs)	€ 4,75 - € 5,50
electricity	€ 4,00
dog	€ 2,00

Lesce

Camping Sobec

Sobceva cesta 25, SLO-4248 Lesce T: 045 353 700. E: sobec@siol.net
alanrogers.com/SV4210

Sobec is situated in a valley between the Julian Alps and the Karavanke Mountains, in a pine grove between the Sava Dolinka river and a small lake. It is only 3 km. from Bled and 20 km. from the Karavanke Tunnel. There are 500 unmarked pitches on level, grassy fields off tarmac access roads (450 for touring units), all with 16A electricity. Shade is provided by mature pine trees and younger trees separate some pitches. Camping Sobec is surrounded by water – the Sava river borders it on three sides and on the fourth is a small, artificial lake with grassy fields for sunbathing.

Facilities

Three traditional style toilet blocks (all now refurbished) with mainly British style toilets, washbasins in cabins and controllable hot showers. Child size toilets and basins. Well equipped baby room. Facilities for disabled visitors. Laundry facilities. Motorcaravan service point. Supermarket, bar/restaurant with stage for live performances. Playgrounds. Rafting, canyoning and kayaking organised. Miniclub. Tours to Bled and the Triglav National Park organised. Off site: Golf and riding 2 km.

Open: 21 April - 30 September.

Directions

Site is off the main road from Lesce to Bled and is well signed just outside Lesce. GPS: 46.35607, 14.14992

Charges 2010

Per unit incl. 2 persons and electricity	€ 24,80 - € 29,00
extra person	€ 10,70 - € 12,80
child (7-14 yrs)	€ 8,00 - € 9,60
dog	€ 3,50

215

Ljubljana

Camping Ljubljana Resort

Dunajska Cesta 270, SLO-1000 Ljubljana T: **015 683 913**. E: **ljubljana.resort@gpl.si**

alanrogers.com/SV4340

Located only five kilometres north of central Ljubljana on the relatively quiet bank of the river Sava, Ljubljana Resort is an ideal city campsite. This relaxed site is attached to – but effectively separated from – the sparkingly modern Laguna swimming pool complex (open 1/6-15/9). The site has 220 pitches, largely situated between mature trees and all with electricity connections (16A). A modern toilet block is operational in summer while a smaller heated block is opened in winter. The main building and pool complex provide several bars, restaurants and takeaways for the campsite guests and day visitors.

Facilities

The modern toilet block includes facilities for disabled people, a baby room and children's toilet and shower. Motorcaravan service point. Laundry service. Internet access. Airport transfer service. Bicycle hire. New children's play area. Animation for children in July and August. Off site: Ljubljana centre 5 km.

Open: All year.

Directions

From either direction on the northern city ring road, take exit for Ljubljana-Jezica north towards Crnuce for a little over 1 km. (through Dunajska cesta). Site is signed (blue sign) on right just before railway crossing and bridge over river. GPS: 46.09752, 14.5187

Charges 2010

Per unit incl. 2 persons and electricity	€ 18,50 - € 30,50
extra person	€ 7,00 - € 13,00
child (3-12 yrs)	€ 5,25 - € 9,75
dog	€ 3,50

Camping Cheques accepted.

Mojstrana

Camping Kamne

Dovje 9, SLO-4281 Mojstrana T: **045 891 105**. E: **info@campingkamne.com**

alanrogers.com/SV4150

For visitors proceeding down the 202 road, from Italy or the Wurzen Pass, towards the prime attractions of the twin lakes of Bled and Bohinj, a delightfully informal little site is to be found just outside the village of Mojstrana. For those arriving via the Karavanke Tunnel the diversion along the 202 is very well worth it. Owner Franc Voga opened the site in 1988, on a small terraced orchard. He has steadily developed the facilities, adding a small pool, two tennis courts and improved all other facilities. The little reception doubles as a bar.

Facilities

The small excellent sanitary block is of a high quality and well maintained. New facilities for babies and disabled visitors. Reception/bar. Small swimming pool. Two tennis courts. TV room. Mountain bike hire. Franc's English is good and his daughter Anna is fluent. Twice weekly excursions to the mountains (free) in July and August. Two new apartments and bungalows now available to rent. Off site: Walking trails.

Open: All year.

Directions

Site is well marked on north side of the 202, 4 km. from Jesenice, just to west of exit for Mojstrana. Site is 4 km. from the Karawanken tunnel. GPS: 46.46453, 13.95787

Charges guide

Per unit incl. 2 persons and electricity	€ 17,50 - € 19,50
child (5-17 yrs)	€ 4,50 - € 5,00
dog	€ 2,00

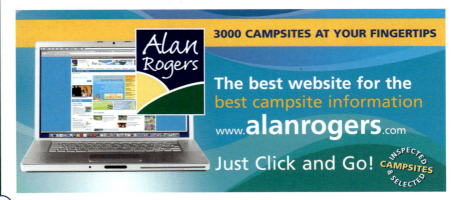

Moravske Toplice

Camping Moravske Toplice

Kranjceva ulica 12, SLO-9226 Moravske Toplice T: **025 121 200**. E: **info@terme3000.si**
alanrogers.com/**SV4410**

Moravske Toplice is a large site with 450 pitches. There are 250 places for touring units (all with 10A electricity), the remaining pitches being taken by seasonal campers. On a grass and gravel surface (hard tent pegs may be needed), the level, numbered pitches are of 50-80 sq.m. There are hardstandings available in the newer area of the site. While there are a few activities on the site, it is only 200 metres from the enormous thermal spa and fun pool complex under the same name. Here there are over 5,000 sq.m. of water activities – swimming, jet streams, water falls, water massages, four water slides (the longest is 170 m) and thermal baths. The complex also provides bars and restaurants and a large golf course. Access to the pool complex and sauna is free for campsite guests. Once you have had enough of the 22 indoor and outdoor pools, you could go walking or cycling through the surrounding woods and fields or try the delicious wines of the Goricko region.

Facilities

Modern and clean toilet facilities provide British style toilets, open washbasins and controllable, free hot showers. Laundry facilities. Football field. Tennis. Archery. Gymnastics. Daily activity programme for children. Off site: Large water complex with shop, bars, restaurants and takeaway. Golf.

Open: All year.

Directions

From Maribor, go east to Murska Sobota. From there go north towards Martjanci and then east towards Moravske Toplice. Access to the site is on the right before the bridge. GPS: 46.67888, 16.22165

Charges 2010

Per unit incl. 2 persons and electricity	€ 39,00

Postojna

Camping Pivka Jama

Veliki Otok 50, SLO-6230 Postojna T: **057 203 993**. E: **autokamp.pivka.jama@siol.net**
alanrogers.com/**SV4330**

Postojna is renowned for its extraordinary limestone caves which form one of Slovenia's prime tourist attractions. Pivka Jama is a most convenient site for the visitor, being midway between Ljubljana and Piran and only about an hour's pleasant drive from either. The 300 pitches are not clustered together but nicely segregated under trees and in small clearings, all connected by a neat network of paths and slip roads. Some level, gravel hardstandings are provided. The facilities are both excellent and extensive and run with obvious pride by enthusiastic staff. This good site is deep in what appears to be primeval forest, cleverly cleared to take advantage of the broken limestone forest bedrock. It even has its own local caves (the Pivka Jama) which can spare its visitors the commercialisation of Postojna.

Facilities

Two toilet blocks with very good facilities. Washing machines. Motorcaravan service point. Campers' kitchen with hobs. Supermarket. Bar/restaurant. Swimming pool and paddling pool. Tennis. Bicycle hire. Daytrips to Postojna Caves and other excursions organised. Off site: Fishing 5 km. Riding or skiing 10 km. Golf 30 km.

Open: March - October.

Directions

Site is 5 km. from Postojna. Take the road leading east from Postojna and then northwest towards the Postojna Cave. Site is well signed 4 km. further along this road. GPS: 45.80533, 14.20457

Charges guide

Per person	€ 9,90
child (7-14 yrs)	€ 7,90
electricity	€ 3,50

Prebold

Camp Dolina Prebold

Vozlic Tomaz Dolenja vas 147, SLO-3312 Prebold T: **035 724 378**. E: **camp@dolina.si**
alanrogers.com/**SV4400**

Prebold is a quiet village about 15 kilometres west of the large historic town of Celje. It is only a few kilometres from the remarkable Roman necropolis at Sempeter. Dolina is an exceptional little site and more than the garden of the house, taking 50 touring units, 25 with 10A electricity. It belongs to Tomaz and Manja Vozlic who look after the site and its guests with loving care. It has been in existence for 40 years and is one of the first private enterprises in the former Yugoslavia.

Facilities

The small, heated toilet block would certainly qualify for Slovenia's 'best loo' award. Washing machine and dryer. Reception with bar in the old stable. Small swimming pool (heated, 1/5-30/9). Sauna. Bicycle hire. WiFi. Off site: Good supermarket and restaurant 200 m. Tennis and indoor pool within 1 km. Fishing 1.5 km.

Open: All year.

Directions

Site is well signed in a small side street by turning right in centre of Prebold. Best reached via signed exit on Ljubljana - Celje motorway. GPS: 46.24392, 15.09108

Charges 2010

Per unit incl. 2 persons and electricity	€ 20,00
extra person	€ 6,25
dog	€ 2,00
No credit cards.	

Prebold

Camping Park Plevcak

Latkova vas 227, SLO-3312 Prebold T: **037 001 986**. E: **info@campingpark.si**

alanrogers.com/SV4402

Park Plevcak is situated on a grassy field directly beside the Savinja river, close to the Sempeter/Prebold motorway junction, and is just seven years old. It provides 30 pitches (all for tourers) and is attractively landscaped with young trees. Pitching is haphazard on one large field, with some shade provided by mature trees and the high hedge surrounding the site. Pitches are not separated, but when it is quiet you can take as much space as you need. There are 18 electricity connections. Tennis courts and a riding centre are just 1 km. It is possible to fish and swim in the Savinja river (an outdoor swimming pool is only 2 km). The site organises excursions to the nearby Pekel Cave in Sempeter, the Roman Nekropolis, the Lasko, Dobrna and Topolsica health resorts, and to the castles in Celje and Velenje.

Facilities

One traditional style toilet block with modern fittings with toilets, open plan washbasins and controllable hot showers. Laundry facilities. Fridge boxes (free). Fishing. Large barbecue area. Torch useful. Dogs by arrangement only. Off site: Riding 1 km. Golf 20 km.

Open: 1 April - 30 October.

Directions

Follow E57 northeast from Ljubljana towards Celje and leave at the Sempeter/Prebold exit. Site is 250 m. from the motorway exit first turn right and then left. GPS: 46.25588, 15.09917

Charges guide

Per person	€ 7,50
electricity	€ 3,50

Ptuj

Camping Terme Ptuj

Pot v toplice 9, SLO-2251 Ptuj T: **027 494 100**. E: **info@terme-ptuj.si**

alanrogers.com/SV4440

Camping Terme Ptuj is close to the river, just outside the interesting town of Ptuj. It is a small site with only 100 level pitches, all for tourers and all with 10A electricity. In two areas, the pitches to the left are on part grass and part gravel hardstanding and are mainly used for motorcaravans. The pitches on the right hand side are on grass under mature trees, off a circular, gravel access road. In this area a promising new toilet block was being built when we visited. The main attraction of this site is clearly the adjacent thermal spa and fun pool complex that also attracts many local visitors. It has several slides and fun pools, as well as a sauna, solarium and spa bath. The swimming pools are free for campsite guests. This site would also be a useful stopover en-route to Croatia and the beautiful historic towns of Ptuj and Maribor are well worth a visit.

Facilities

Modern toilet block with British and Turkish style toilets, open washbasins and controllable, hot showers (free). En-suite facilities for disabled visitors with toilet and basin. Two washing machines. Football field. Torch useful. Off site: Large thermal spa 100 m. Bar/restaurant and snack bar 100 m.

Open: All year.

Directions

From Maribor go southeast towards Ptuj and follow the site signs. Site is on the left before you cross the river and not very well signed. GPS: 46.422683, 15.85495

Charges guide

Per person	€ 12,50 - € 15,50
child (7-14 yrs)	€ 8,75 - € 10,85
child (4-7 yrs)	€ 6,25 - € 7,75
electricity	€ 3,50
dog	€ 3,00
Camping Cheques accepted.	

Recica ob Savinji
Camping Menina

Varpolje 105, SLO-3332 Recica ob Savinji T: **035 835 027**. E: **info@campingmenina.com**
alanrogers.com/SV4405

Menina Camping is in the heart of the 35 km. long Upper Savinja Valley, surrounded by 2,500 m. high mountains and unspoilt nature. It is being improved every year by the young, enthusiastic owner, Jurij Kolenc and has 200 pitches, all for touring units, on grassy fields under mature trees and with access from gravel roads. All have 6-10A electricity. The Savinja river runs along one side of the site, but if its water is too cold for swimming, the site also has a lake which can be used for swimming as well. This site is a perfect base for walking or mountain biking in the mountains.

Facilities

Two toilet blocks (one new) have modern fittings with toilets, open plan washbasins and controllable hot showers. Motorcaravan service point. Bar/restaurant with open air terrace (evenings only) and open air kitchen. Sauna. Playing field. Play area. Fishing. Mountain bike hire. Giant chess. Russian bowling. Excursions (52). Live music and gatherings around the camp fire. Indian village. Hostel. Skiing in winter. Kayaking. Mobile homes to rent. Off site: Fishing 2 km. Recica and other villages with much culture and folklore are close. Indian sauna at Coze.

Open: 1 April - 15 November.

Directions

From Ljubljana take A1 towards Celje. Exit at Sentupert and turn north towards Mozirje. Follow signs Recica ob Savinj from there. Continue through Recica to Nizka and follow site signs. GPS: 46.31168, 14.90913

Charges 2010

Per unit incl. 2 persons and electricity	€ 19,00 - € 22,00
extra person (over 16 yrs)	€ 8,00 - € 9,50

Smlednik
Camp Smlednik

Dragocajna 14a, SLO-1216 Smlednik T: **013 627 002**. E: **camp@dm-campsmlednik.si**
alanrogers.com/SV4360

Camp Smlednik is relatively close to the capital, Ljubljana, yet within striking distance of Lake Bled, the Karawanke mountains and the Julian Alps. It provides a good touring base, set above the river Sava, and also provides a small, separate enclosure for those who enjoy naturism. Situated beside the peaceful tiny village of Dragocajni, in attractive countryside, the site provides 190 places for touring units, each with electricity (6/10A). Although terraced, it is probably better described as a large plateau with tall pines and deciduous trees providing some shade. A small naturist area accommodates 15 units adjacent to the river (INF card not required) and measures only 30 x 100 m.

Facilities

Three fully equipped sanitary blocks of varying standards, but with adequate and clean provision. In the main camping area a fairly new, solar-powered block has free hot showers, the lower half for use within the naturist area. Normally heated showers in the old block are also free. Laundry facilities. Toilet for disabled visitors. Supermarket at entrance. Bar (all year), food from 1/5-30/9. Two good quality clay tennis courts (charged). Swings for children. River swimming and fishing. WiFi.

Open: 1 May - 15 October.

Directions

Travelling on road no.1, both Smlednik and the site are well signed. From E61 motorway, Smlednik and site are again well signed at the Vodiice exit. GPS: 46.17425, 14.41628

Charges guide

Per person	€ 7,00 - € 8,00
child (7-14 yrs)	€ 3,50 - € 4,00
electricity (6-10A)	€ 3,00 - € 4,00

Soca
Kamp Klin

Lepena 1, SLO-5232 Soca T: **053 889 513**. E: **kampklin@volja.net**
alanrogers.com/SV4235

Kamp Klin is next to the confluence of the Soca and Lepenca rivers and is surrounded by mountains. Being next to two rivers, the site is also a suitable base for fishing, kayaking and rafting. The campsite has only 50 pitches, all for tourers and with electricity, on one large, grassy field, connected by a circular, gravel access road. It is attractively landscaped with flowers and young trees, but this also means there is not much shade. Some pitches are right on the bank of the river (unfenced) and there are beautiful views of the river and the mountains.

Facilities

One modern toilet block and a portacabin style unit with toilets and controllable showers. Laundry with sinks. Bar/restaurant. Play field. Fishing (permit required). Torch useful. Off site: Riding 500 m. Bicycle hire 10 km.

Open: March - October.

Directions

Site is on main Kranjska Gora - Bovec road and is well signed in Soca. Access is via a sharp turn from the main road and over a small bridge that may be difficult for larger units. GPS: 46.33007, 13.644

Charges guide

Per person	€ 5,50 - € 7,20
child (7-12 yrs)	€ 2,80 - € 3,60
electricity	€ 2,40

With its warm seas, crystal-clear waters and over one thousand islands to explore, Croatia is an ideal place to try scuba diving. Diving centres can be found at the larger resorts.

The heart-shaped peninsula of Istria, located in the north, is among the most developed tourist regions in Croatia. Here you can visit the preserved Roman amphitheatre in Pula, the beautiful town of Rovinj with its cobbled streets and wooded hills, and the resort of Umag, well-known for its recreational activities, most notably tennis. Islands are studded all around the coast, making it ideal for sailing and diving enthusiasts. Istria also has the highest concentration of campsites.

Further south, in the province of Dalmatia, Split is the largest city on the Adriatic coast and home to the impressive Diolectian's Palace. From here the islands of Brac, Hvar, Vis and Korcula, renowned for their lively fishing villages and pristine beaches, are easily accessible by ferry. The old walled city of Dubrovnik is 150 km south. At over 2 km. long and 25 m. high, with 16 towers, a walk along the city walls affords spectacular views.

Population
4.5 million

Capital
Zagreb

Climate
Predominantly warm and hot in summer with temperatures of up to 40°C.

Language
Croatian, but English and German are widely spoken.

Telephone
The country code is 00 385

Currency
Kuna

Banks
Mon-Fri 08.00 - 19.00

Shops
Mainly Mon-Sat 08.00-20.00, although some close on Monday and Sundays.

CROATIA HAS THROWN OFF OLD COMMUNIST ATTITUDES AND BLOSSOMED INTO A LIVELY AND FRIENDLY PLACE TO VISIT. A COUNTRY STEEPED IN HISTORY, IT BOASTS SOME OF THE FINEST ROMAN RUINS IN EUROPE AND YOU'LL FIND PLENTY OF TRADITIONAL COASTAL TOWNS, CLUSTERS OF TINY ISLANDS AND MEDIEVAL VILLAGES TO EXPLORE.

Public Holidays

New Year's Day; Epiphany 6 Jan; Good Friday; Easter Monday; Labour Day 1 May; Parliament Day 30 May; Day of Anti-Fascist Victory 22 June; Statehood Day 25 june; Thanksgiving Day 5 Aug; Assumption 15 Aug; Independence Day 8 Oct; All Saints 1 Nov; Christmas 25, 26 Dec.

Motoring

Croatia is proceeding with a vast road improvement programme. There are still some roads which leave a lot to be desired but things have improved dramatically. Roads along the coast can become heavily congested in summer and queues are possible at border crossings. Drive carefully especially at night - roads are usually unlit and have sharp bends. Tolls: some motorways, bridges and tunnels. Cars towing a caravan or trailer must carry two warning triangles. It is illegal to overtake military convoys.

Remember - if you travel to Croatia via Slovenian motorways, you now require a vignette (see Slovenia introduction).

Tourist Office

Croatian National Tourist Office
2 The Lanchesters
162-164 Fulham Palace Road
London W6 9ER
Tel: 020 8563 7979 Fax: 0208 563 2616
Email: info@cnto.freeserve.co.uk
Internet: www.croatia.hr

British Embassy

Ivana Lucica 4, Zagreb
Tel: (385)(1) 6009 100

Places of interest

Dubrovnik: particularly appealing is the old town Stari Grad, with marble-paved squares and steep cobbled streets.

Risnjak and Paklencia National Parks: both have excellent areas for hiking, the latter has excellent rock climbing opportunities.

Rovinj: an active fishing port, an excellent collection of marine life can be found at the aquarium.

Split: Diocletian's Palace, Maritime Museum.

Zagreb: the capital of Croatia, with a whole host of museums.

Cuisine of the region

Brodet: mixed fish stewed with rice

Burek: a layered pie made with meat or cheese

Cesnjovka: garlic sausage

Kulen: paprika-flavoured salami

Manistra od bobica: beans and fresh maize soup

Piroska: cheese doughnut

Struki: baked cheese dumpling

Virtually every region produces its own varieties of wine.

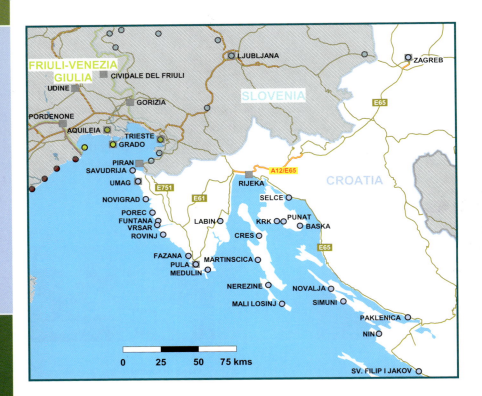

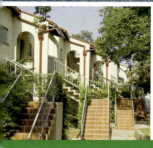

camping on the adriatic

Experience the Mediterranean in its originality

Campsites:
Camping Lanterna ***, Poreč
Camping Orsera ***, Vrsar
Camping Marina ***, Labin
Camping Puntižela, Pula
Camping Ježevac ***, Krk
Camping Solitudo ***, Dubrovnik

Hostel:
Camping Puntižela, Pula

Naturist campsites, apartments and rooms:
Naturist Resort Solaris ***, Poreč
Naturist Camping Istra ***, Funtana
Naturist Camping Politin ***, Dubrovnik

Mobile homes:
Camping Lanterna ***, Poreč
Camping Marina ***, Labin
Camping Ježevac ***, Krk

T +385 52 465 010   **F** +385 52 451 440
E camping@valamar.com
www.camping-adriatic.com

Istria
Green Mediterranean.

CROATIA

Baska

Camping Zablace

E Geistlicha 38, HR-51523 Baska (Kvarner) T: **051 856 909**. E: **campzablace@hotelibaska.hr**

alanrogers.com/CR6761

Camping Zablace is at the southern end of the beautiful island of Krk, in the ancient ferry port of Baska. Like most sites in Croatia it has direct access to a large, pebble beach and from the bottom row of pitches one has views over the Adriatic islands. The site has 534 pitches with 400 used for touring units. Zone 1 (nearest the beach) provides 100 individual pitches with electricity and water. The quietest zone, if further away (and across a public road that splits the site in two) has electricity and water taps. There is some shade. There are not many amenities on the site, but it is an easy five minute walk along the promenade to the centre of Baska where there are bars, restaurants and pizzerias and there is free entry to the Corinthia Hotel swimming pool. Well worth visiting is the little church on the top of the hill, where there are beautiful views over the bay and the Seniska Vrata channel.

Facilities

Five toilet blocks with toilets, open plan basins and controllable hot showers (key access for the toilets nearest the beach). Facilities for disabled visitors. Motorcaravan service point. Shop. Kiosks with fruit, cold drinks, tobacco, newspapers and beach wear. Off site: Giant slide and games hall. Tennis and minigolf 200 m. Windsurfing. Diving. Marked hiking and cycle routes. Free swimming pool and fitness 100 m.

Open: 1 April - 15 October.

Directions

On Krk follow the no. 29 road south to Baska, then good signs to site. GPS: 44.96668, 14.74512

Charges 2010

Per unit incl. 2 persons and electricity	Kn 125,00 - 233,00
extra person	Kn 30,00 - 49,00
child (7-11 yrs)	Kn 15,00 - 22,00
dog	free

Camping Cheques accepted.

Baska

Naturist Camping Bunculuka

Baska, HR-51523 Krk (Kvarner) T: **051 856 806**. E: **fkk-bunculuka@ri.hinet.hr** / **lolic@hotelibasta.hr**

alanrogers.com/CR6760

Bunculuka is on the opposite side of the port of Baska from Camping Zablace. In an enclosed environment, bordered by trees on one side and the sea on the other, it has 400 pitches (270 for touring units) in two areas. One is open and sloping downwards to the sea, the other is wooded and more hilly to the rear of the site (and mainly used for tents). The front row of pitches has beautiful views over the sea and the private pebble beach. Varying in size from small to average, most pitches are fairly level, although the ground is a little rocky.

Facilities

One newer and two refurbished toilet blocks with toilets, open style wash basins and controllable hot showers. Supermarket. Bar/restaurant with covered and open air terrace. Snack bar. Bread kiosk at beach. Newspaper, fruit and tobacco kiosks. Tennis. Minigolf. Fishing. Off site: Baska with bars, restaurants and shops 500 m.

Open: 1 May - 30 October.

Directions

On Krk follow 29 road south to Baska and then site signs. Turn right before Baska, then left (east) and follow signs for ferry and site. GPS: 44.96923, 14.76702

Charges guide

Per person	€ 4,00 - € 5,00
child	€ 2,00 - € 2,50
pitch	€ 8,00 - € 9,00
incl. electricity	€ 9,40 - € 10,50
dog	€ 3,20

Cres

Camping Kovacine

Melin I/20, HR-51557 Cres (Kvarner) T: **051 573 150**. E: **campkovacine@kovacine.com**
alanrogers.com/CR6765

Camping Kovacine is located on a peninsula on the beautiful Kvarner island of Cres, just 2 km. from the town of the same name. The site has 750 numbered, mostly level pitches, of which 632 are for tourers (300 with 12A electricity). On sloping ground, partially shaded by mature olive and pine trees, pitching is on the large, open spaces between the trees. Some places have views of the Valun lagoon. Kovacine is partly an FKK (naturist) site, which is quite common in Croatia, and has a pleasant atmosphere. Here one can enjoy local live music on a stage close to the pebble beach (Blue Flag), where there is also a restaurant and bar. The site has its own beach, part concrete, part pebbles, and a jetty for mooring boats and fishing. It is close to the historic town of Cres, the main town on the island, which offers a rich history of fishing, shipyards and authentic Kvarner-style houses. There are also several bars, restaurants and shops.

Facilities

Modern, comfortable toilet blocks (two refurbished) offer British style toilets, equipped with solar power, open plan washbasins (some cabins for ladies) and hot showers. Private family bathroom for hire. Facilities for disabled people plus facilities for children. Laundry sinks and washing machine. Fridge box hire. Motorcaravan service point. Car wash. Mini-marina and boat crane. Supermarket. Bar, restaurant and pizzeria. New swimming pool. Playground. Daily children's club. Evening shows with live music. Boat launching. Fishing. Diving centre. Motorboat hire. Free WiFi. Airport transfers. Off site: Wellness and fitness centre 0.5km. Historic town of Cres with bars, restaurants and shops 2 km.

Open: 27 April - 15 October.

Directions

From Rijeka take no. 2 road south towards Labin and take ferry to Cres at Brestova. Continue to Cres and follow site signs. GPS: 44.96188, 14.39650

Charges guide

Per person	€ 5,00 - € 9,80
child (3-11 yrs)	€ 2,40 - € 3,90
pitch	€ 4,80 - € 9,20
dog	€ 1,00 - € 3,00

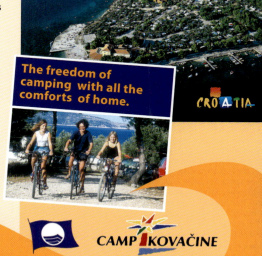

Dubrovnik
Camping Solitudo

Vatroslava Lisinskog 17, HR-20000 Dubrovnik (Dalmatia) T: **020 448 686**. E: **camping-dubrovnik@valamar.com**
alanrogers.com/CR6890

Solitudo belongs to the 'Camping on the Adriatic' group and is located on the north side of Dubrovnik. There are 238 pitches, all for touring units, all with 12A electricity and 30 with water, arranged on four large fields that are opened according to demand. Field D is mainly used for tents and pitches here are small. Field A has pitches of up to 120 sq.m. and takes many motorcaravans (long leads required). From some pitches here there are beautiful views of the mountains and the impressive Dr. Franjo Tudman Bridge. All pitches are numbered, some are on terraces and most are shaded by a variety of mature trees.

Facilities

Attractively decorated, clean and modern toilet blocks have British style toilets, open washbasins and controllable, hot showers. Good facilities for disabled visitors. Laundry. Motorcaravan service point. Shop. Attached restaurant/bar. Snack bar. Tennis. Minigolf. Fishing. Bicycle hire. Beach with pedalo, beach chair, kayak and jet ski hire. Excursions organised to the Elafiti Islands. WiFi. Off site: Outdoor pool 500 m. Bar, disco and restaurant 500 m.

Open: 1 April - 1 November.

Directions

From Split follow no. 8 road south towards Dubrovnik. Site is very well signed, starting 110 km. before reaching Dubrovnik, and throughout the city.
GPS: 42.661883, 18.07135

Charges guide

Per person	€ 3,74 - € 7,00
child (4-10 yrs)	free - € 4,90
pitch with services	€ 9,63 - € 15,30
dog	€ 2,92 - € 4,73

Camping Cheques accepted.

Fazana
Camping Bi-Village

Dragonja 115, HR-52212 Fazana (Istria) T: **052 300 300**
alanrogers.com/CR6745

Camping Bi-Village is large holiday village, close to the historic town of Pula and opposite the Brioni National Park. The location is excellent and there are some superb sunsets. The site is landscaped with many flowers, shrubs and rock walls and offers over 1,000 pitches for touring units (the remainder taken by bungalows and chalets). The campsite is separated from the holiday bungalows by the main site road which runs from the entrance to the beach. Pitches are set in long rows accessed by gravel lanes, slightly sloping towards the sea, with only the bottom rows having shade from mature trees and good views over the Adriatic. The pitches are separated by young trees and shrubs.

Facilities

Four modern toilet blocks with toilets, open plan washbasins and controllable hot showers. Child-size washbasins. Baby room. Facilities for disabled visitors. Washing machine. Shopping centre (1/5-11/10). Bars (1/5-30/9) and restaurants. Bazaar. Gelateria. Pastry shop. Three swimming pools. Playground on gravel. Playing field. Trampolines. Minigolf. Jet skis, motorboats and pedaloes for hire. Boat launching. Games hall. Sports tournaments and entertainment organised. Massage. Internet point.
Off site: Historic towns of Pula and Rovinj are close. Fishing 3 km. Riding 15 km.

Open: 5 March - 31 October.

Directions

Follow no. 2 road south from Rijeka to Pula. In Pula follow site signs. Site is close to Fazana.
GPS: 44.91717, 13.81105

Charges guide

Per person	€ 4,00 - € 8,50
child	free - € 4,50
pitch incl. electricity and water	€ 5,50 - € 16,00
dog	€ 2,00 - € 3,00

Camping Cheques accepted.

Check real time availability and at-the-gate prices...
www.alanrogers.com

Funtana

Naturist Camping Istra

Grgeti 35, HR-52452 Funtana (Istria) T: **052 465 010**. E: **camping@valamar.com**
alanrogers.com/CR6726

Located in the tiny and picturesque village of Funtana, this peaceful site is part of the 'Camping on the Adriatic' group. Istra has a fine array of facilities and, although there is no pool, it is surrounded by sparkling sea water on three sides. The formally marked pitches ring the peninsula and some are directly at the water's edge giving great views of the island off to the south (early booking is advised). There are 1,000 pitches on site with 745 for tourists, most with ample shade and varying in size from about 60-120 sq.m. The ground is undulating and some areas have been cut into low terraces.

Facilities

Five old and five new sanitary buildings provide toilets, washbasins, showers (hot and cold), hair dryers and some facilities for disabled campers. Laundry facilities. Small supermarket. Restaurant and bars. Play areas. Entertainment for children in high season. Organised sport. Minigolf. Tennis. Massage. WiFi near reception. Dogs are allowed in some areas. Off site: Fishing. Riding 1 km. Shops and restaurants in Funtana short walk from the gate. Porec 7 km. with regular bus service from the village.

Open: 1 April - 8 October.

Directions

Site is signed off the Porec - Vrsar road 6 km. south of Porec in the village of Funtana. Access for large units could be difficult when turning off the main road from the direction of Porec. If this looks as if it might be difficult, go past the signed turning and turn around in the night club car park a few metres further on. The problem is less when approaching from Vrsar. GPS: 45.17464, 13.59869

Charges guide

Per person	€ 3,35 - € 5,80
child (4-10 yrs)	free - € 3,90
pitch incl. electricity	€ 5,70 - € 13,10
incl. full services	€ 8,25 - € 14,10
dog	€ 3,35 - € 4,75

Prices for pitches by the sea are higher.

Hvar

Camp Vira

HR-21450 Hvar (Dalmatia) T: **021 741 803**. E: **viracamp@suncanihvar.com**
alanrogers.com/CR6865

Camp Vira has been recommended to us by our Croatia agent and we plan to undertake a full inspection next year. Located only 4 km. from the town of Hvar, it is said to be a nature lovers' paradise that combines Hvar's natural beauty and clean sea with an environmentally friendly array of modern amenities. Solar powered units supply the bulk of the camp's energy needs, while pine trees provide natural shade for the 90 pitches and 72 camping places. Vira's private cove has a pebble beach making it ideal for sunbathing, swimming and variety of water activities.

Facilities

Amenities include newly renovated shower and bathroom facilities. Laundry and ironing services. Grocery shop and souvenir shop. Aloe Vera bar and grill. Playground. Recreation rentals and beach shop. Fridge hire. Tent hire. Off site: Bus service to Hvar.

Open: 15 May - 31 October.

Directions

Site is 4 km. northwest from the town of Hvar. From Hvar go forward leaving the central car park on the left and follow roadside directions to site. GPS: 43.19087, 16.43032

Charges guide

Per person	€ 6,00 - € 7,00
child (3-11 yrs)	€ 3,00 - € 4,00
pitch	€ 11,00 - € 22,00
dog	€ 4,00 - € 5,00

Jezera Lovisca

Autocamp Jezera Lovisca

HR-22242 Jezera Lovisca (Dalmatia) T: **022 439 600**. E: **info@jezera-kornati.hr**

alanrogers.com/CR6840

Jezera Lovisca is a 75-acre family site with 400 informal pitches and would be a good choice for a beach holiday as it is on the island of Murter. In high season the site provides an entertainment program for children with games, music, drawing and swimming. For adults there are live musical nights at the bar/restaurant which has a large, welcoming terrace from where there are beautiful views of the lagoon. There are 360 grass and gravel pitches for touring units, all with 10A electricity (long leads may be necessary). They are mostly on level terraces, built with low rock walls in the shade of mature trees.

Facilities

Six modern and comfortable toilet blocks have British style toilets, open washbasins and controllable, hot showers (free) – all of a very high standard. Campers' kitchen. Fridge box hire. Shop. Bar/restaurant and takeaway. Tennis. Minigolf. Entertainment program for children. Internet access. Fishing. Watersports. Diving centre. Boat launching. Bicycle hire. Excursions. Live music nights. Barbecues permitted only in communal area. Off site: Harbour town of Jerz 500 m. Buses from gate to local attractions.

Open: 15 April - 15 October.

Directions

From Rijeka take no. 8 coast road south (Zadar and Split). 58 km. south of Zadar is Pirovic. Turn right 4 km. south of Pirovec (O Murter). Continue through Trisco keeping to coast road and on to Jereza Lovisca. Site is through village. GPS: 43.791533, 15.6279

Charges guide

Per person	Kn 33,80 - 55,50
pitch incl. car	Kn 52,50 - 97,50
electricity	Kn 28,90

Site does not accept euros.

Korcula

Autocamp Kalac

Dubrovacka cesta 19, HR-20260 Korcula (Dalmatia) T: **020 726 693**. E: **kalac@htp-korcula.hr**

alanrogers.com/CR6874

Close to the historical town of Korcula, Camping Kalac is a good choice for a relaxing holiday on the Dalmatian coast. Not one of the typically large sites of the area, this is a modestly sized one with only 230 pitches. Most of these are suitable only for tents or reserved for the season, but 70 pitches are available for tourers. Located under trees, there is sufficient shade and all have electricity connections. Many visitors leave their cars outside the camping areas as the pitches are fairly small and not always easy to access. A restaurant and several bars are close to the sea.

Facilities

The two sanitary blocks are modern and convenient, but lack facilities for disabled persons or special areas for children. Washing machine. Fridge hire. Large shop. Restaurant and bars. On-site entertainment is limited. Scooter, bicycle and boat hire. Minigolf. Torches are advised at night. Off site: Town 2 km.

Open: 15 May - 1 October.

Directions

The island of Korcula can be reached by ferry from Orebic. Leaving ferry, the main road winds up to Korcula town via a loop through the forest. The access road to the site is on the right (signed, near Hotel Bon Repos) in the built-up area 500 m. from the ferry landing. GPS: 42.950633, 17.14505

Charges guide

Per person	Kn 19,50 - 45,00
caravan or motorcaravan	Kn 30,00 - 72,00
electricity	Kn 19,50

Krk

Camping Jezevac

HR-51500 Krk (Kvarner) T: **052 465 010**. E: **camping@valamar.com**

alanrogers.com/CR6757

Camping Jezevac is a seaside site located close to the pretty town of Krk. This is a large site extending over 11 hectares with 670 pitches (80-120 sq.m). In high season the atmosphere is lively and the site's 800 m. private beach is a focal point. Jezevac has benefited from some renovation work in recent years. The reception area has been modernised and a quantity of mobile homes was added in 2008. A children's club is run for most of the season with a varied programme of activities. A good sports centre can be found 300 m. away.

Facilities

Heated toilet block with hot showers. Washing machines. Shops (1/4-15/10). Restaurants (1/5-1/10) and bars. Takeaway (1/5-30/9). Tennis. Playground. Activity and entertainment programmes and children's club (May - Sept). Fishing. Bicycle hire. Boat launching and sailing. Off site: Sports centre 300 m.

Open: 18 April - 15 October.

Directions

From Ostrovica: Upon entering Krk, follow signs to the town centre. Take the second right turn and continue ahead for 2.2 km. At the first roundabout take the second exit. Continue for 600 m. following signs to Camp Jezevac. GPS: 45.01964, 14.57072

Charges guide

Per unit incl. 2 persons and electricity	€ 18,10 - € 27,70
extra person	€ 4,40 - € 6,10

Krk

Naturist Camping Politin

HR-51500 Krk (Kvarner) T: **052 465 010**. E: **camping@valamar.com**

alanrogers.com/CR6758

Politin is an attractive naturist site on the wooded peninsula of Prniba, quite close to the centre of Krk. There are 250 touring pitches here, not all with electricity, and ranging in size from 70-110 sq.m. The site has its own 'blue flag' accredited private beach. There is an activity programme for children during the high season. On-site amenities include a shop, renovated toilet blocks and a bar/restaurant. Boat trips to the neighbouring islands of Rab and Cres are possible and can be arranged on site.

Facilities

Restaurant, bar and shop (all 1/5-30/9). Tennis. Playground. Children's activity programme (May-Sept). Fishing. Boat launching. Sailing. Free WiFi internet access. Off site: Fitness centre 1.5 km. Sports centre 2 km. Krk town centre.

Open: 15 April - 30 September.

Directions

Cross bridge from mainland to the island of Krk, head for the island's capital, Krk (28 km). On arrival head to first traffic junction and turn right. After 500 m. turn left (beyond petrol station). Continue on this road for 800 m. to site. GPS: 45.02440, 14.59280

Charges guide

Per unit inc. 2 persons and electricity	€ 18,10 - € 32,20
extra person	€ 4,40 - € 6,35
child (4-10 yrs)	free - € 4,35

Labin

Camping Marina

Sveta Marina bb, HR-52220 Labin (Istria) T: **052 879 058**. E: **camping@valamar.com**

alanrogers.com/CR6747

Camping Marina is a very quiet site with a somewhat steep approach. Overlooked by high, tree clad hills and adjoining a small bay, there are views of the rocky coast and the island of Cres. The 293 pitches are of all types, from those in the central area on level marked areas with electricity and water, to the cliff top pitches on the outskirts of the site. The particularly clear water where there are shipwrecks and caves to explore has made Marina a haven for divers and the campsite diving club, which has a diving school, won Croatia's best diving club award in 2004/5/6.

Facilities

The single toilet block houses British style toilets, free controllable showers and washbasins. Toilet for children and baby room, Facilities for disabled people. Washing machine and ironing area. Motorcaravan service point and points for washing diving/snorkelling equipment. Restaurant/bar. Church. Play area. WiFi. Dog shower and garden. Off site: Well stocked supermarket on the left at start of the entrance road to the site. Places to visit are Lapin, the old town. Rabac, a popular seaside resort during the time of Tito, with hotels, restaurants, bars and a small harbour.

Open: 4 April - 4 October.

Directions

Site is 10 km. south/southeast of Labin. From E751/21 Pula - Opatija road turn off to Lapin and follow signs for Rabac. On outskirts of Labin site is signed sharp right and up a cobbled road. Follow signs for Marina SV. Turn off the country road for site and Marina SV is well signed to the left. GPS: 45.033391, 14.157976

Charges guide

Per person	€ 3,80 - € 5,70
child (4-10 yrs)	free - € 3,30
pitch	€ 5,80 - € 18,90

Mali Losinj

Camping Poljana

Poljana bb, Mali Losinj, HR-51550 Losinj (Kvarner) T: **051 231 726**. E: **info@poljana.hr**

alanrogers.com/CR6772

Autocamp Poljana lies on the narrow strip of land in the southern part of Losinj island, just north of the pleasant town of Mali Losinj. With 600 pitches, this site is bigger than it looks. The camping area has been newly laid out with some flat areas and some terraces. The pitches are marked with flowers and shrubs. There are some mature trees for shade and 600 electricity connections. Campers may be able to experience both sunset and sunrise from the same pitch! The toilet facilities are new and well maintained, while a shop and a series of bars and restaurants are available close by.

Facilities

New toilet blocks, including solar panels for hot water, are entirely up-to-date and adequate. Facilities for disabled people. Baby rooms. Motorcaravan service point. Washing machine (expensive). Daily entertainment programmes. Bicycle hire. WiFi. Rock beach with cocktail bar. Marina. Off site: Riding and canoeing 6 km. Boat excursions. Losinj 4 km.

Open: 1 April - 18 October.

Directions

About 2 km. north of the town, the site occupies both sides of the road along the waterline and opposite the little marina. GPS: 44.55555, 14.44166

Charges guide

Per unit incl. 2 persons and electricity	€ 16,00 - € 33,00
extra person	€ 4,00 - € 8,30
child (3-9 yrs)	€ 2,00 - € 6,20
dog	€ 3,50 - € 7,00

Martinscica
Camping Slatina
Martinscica, HR-51556 Cres (Kvarner) T: 051 574 127. E: info@camp-slatina.com
alanrogers.com/CR6768

Camping Slatina lies about halfway along the island of Cres, by the fishing port of Martinscica on a bay of the Adriatic Sea. It has 370 pitches for tourers, many with 10A electricity, 50 new individual ones (29 fully serviced) off very steep, tarmac access roads, sloping down to the sea. The pitches are large and level on a gravel base and enjoy good shade from mature laurel trees, although hardly any have views. Whilst there is plenty of privacy, the site does have an enclosed feeling. Some pitches in the lower areas have water, electricity and drainage. Like so many sites in Croatia, Slatina has a private diving centre.

Facilities
Four new and two refurbished blocks provide toilets, open style washbasins and controllable hot showers. Facilities for disabled visitors. Laundry with sinks and washing machine. Fridge box hire. Car wash. Shop. Bar, restaurant, grill restaurant, pizzeria and fish restaurant. Playground. Minigolf. Fishing. Bicycle hire. Diving centre. Boat launching. Pedalo, canoe and boat hire. Excursions to the 'Blue Cave'. Off site: Martinscica with bars, restaurants and shops 2 km.

Open: Easter - 10 October.

Directions
From Rijeka take no. 2 road south towards Labin and take ferry to Cres at Brestova. From Cres go south towards Martinscica and follow site signs.
GPS: 44.82333, 14.34083

Charges guide
Per unit incl. 2 persons, electricity and water	€ 14,21 - € 23,46
extra person	€ 4,71 - € 7,68

Medulin
Medulin Camping Village
Osipovica 30, HR-52203 Medulin (Istria) T: 052 572 801. E: marketing@arenaturist.hr
alanrogers.com/CR6734

Medulin is part of the Arenaturist group and it has a fabulous setting near Pula on the tip of the Istrian peninsula, enjoying great views of the offshore island and the twin church towers in the town above. Consisting of a peninsula about 1.5 km. long and a small island accessed by a road bridge, the site is thickly wooded with mature pine trees producing a carpet of needles. Pitches are marked and separated into three sizes. The land is undulating but there is no shortage of level areas. There are 1,106 touring pitches, all with 10/16A electricity and some mobile homes which are not intrusive.

Facilities
The sanitary blocks are kept clean but are really in need of renovation. Toilets are mostly dated Turkish style and the search for British styles is tedious. Washbasins and showers are a mixture of outdoors and under cover. Most have hot water (relying on solar power). Shop, market and produce stalls. Eight restaurants or snack bars provide a large range of fare. Cocktail bar. Ice for sale. Fridge rental. Watersports. Barbecues are not permitted on pitches. Off site: Golf, fishing (with permit) and riding nearby. Restaurants and bars n Medulin village or in Pula.

Open: 27 March - 17 October.

Directions
Approaching from the north (Koper, Rovinj), on outskirts of Pula turn to follow signs for Medulin and site. Site is at far end of village and is well signed.
GPS: 44.81437, 13.93214

Charges 2010
Per unit incl. 2 persons and electricity	€ 17,70 - € 35,00
extra person	€ 4,50 - € 7,70
child (4-10 yrs)	€ 3,00 - € 4,50
dog	€ 2,70 - € 4,80

Medulin
Camp Kazela
Kapovica 350, HR-52203 Medulin (Istria) T: 052 576 050. E: info@campkazela.com
alanrogers.com/CR6735

Camp Kazela is partly naturist and is situated close to Medulin, an attractive old fishing port. The site can accommodate over 1,700 units on large, unmarked pitches, taking 1,250 touring units with 1,000 electricity connections (10A) and 100 pitches with electricity, water and drainage. The remaining pitches are used for chalets, seasonal guests and tour operators. The site is open with young trees and some pitches have pleasant views over the sea. Some clusters of mature trees provide a little shade, but generally this site is something of a sun trap.

Facilities
Six adequate toilet blocks have British and Turkish style toilets, open washbasins with cold water only and controllable hot showers (but they could be cleaner). Motorcaravan service point. Shopping centre with supermarket and restaurants. Two aquaparks. Sailing and diving schools. Water skiing. Parasailing. Trampolines. Entertainment team. Games hall. Disco. Live music. Off site: Historic towns of Medulin 2 km. and Pula 10 km. Visit Venice by hydrofoil.

Open: 4 April - 10 October.

Directions
Follow the road south from Pula to Medulin. At Medulin, follow the signs for the hotels and the site is 1 km. after the hotels. GPS: 44.80540, 13.95550

Charges guide
Per person	€ 3,50 - € 7,30
pitch	€ 5,80 - € 12,70
incl. electricity	€ 7,80 - € 14,10
dog	€ 2,80 - € 4,30
Camping Cheques accepted.	

Nerezine
Camping Rapoca

Rapoca, Nerezine, HR-51554 Losinj (Kvarner) T: **051 237 145**. E: **rapoca@lostur.hinet.hr**
alanrogers.com/CR6773

Camping Rapoca is located beside the historic town of Nerezine, an ancient seafaring and shipbuilding settlement, close to Mount Osorscica on the east coast of the Losinj island. This private site offers an oasis of tranquillity when compared to its bigger, commercial brothers. It has just 250 pitches, including 100 for tourers with 10A electricity. The touring pitches are in a separate area from the seasonal units, on one large, open field with little shade. The pitches are marked, level and vary in size, but are not separated. The site has its own restaurant with good value meals and a small bar.

Facilities
Two modern, comfortable toilet blocks have toilets, open style basins with cold water only and preset hot showers. Shop, newspaper stand and fruit kiosk. Restaurant and bar. Fishing. Small playground. Boat launching. Beach and promenade. Off site: Historic town of Nerezine with shops, bars and restaurants.

Open: 1 April - 31 October.

Directions
On Cres take no. 58 road south towards Mali Losinj. Site is on the left in Nerezine and has a sharp, narrow left turn to it which may be difficult for large units. GPS: 44.66455, 14.39810

Charges guide
Per person	€ 5,50 - € 7,00
child	€ 2,75 - € 3,50

Nin
Camping Zaton

Draznikova Ulica 76T, HR-23232 Nin (Dalmatia) T: **023 280 215**. E: **camping@zaton.hr**
alanrogers.com/CR6782

Zaton Holiday Village is a newly-built, family holiday park, close to the historic town of Nin and just a few kilometres from the ancient city of Zadar. This park itself is more like a large village and has every amenity one can think of for a holiday on the Dalmatian south coast. The village is divided into two areas separated by the shopping centre and a large parking area, one for campers close to the sea, the other for a complex with holiday bungalows. Zaton has 1,030 mostly level pitches for tourers, all with electricity, water and waste water.

Facilities
Five modern and one refurbished toilet blocks have British and Turkish style toilets, washbasins (some in cabins) and controllable hot showers. Child-size washbasins. Facilities for disabled visitors. Campers' kitchen with gas hobs. Motorcaravan service point. Car wash. Shopping centre. Restaurants, bars and kiosks. Water play area for older children. Heated swimming pool. Mini-car track. Riding. Trim track. Scuba diving. Professional animation team (high season). Teen club. Games hall. Internet point. Live shows by beach. Off site: Historic towns of Zadar and Nin.

Open: 1 May - 30 September.

Directions
From Rijeka take no. 2 road south and leave at exit for Zadar. Drive north towards Nin and Zaton Holiday Village is signed a few kilometres before Nin. GPS: 44.23477, 15.16437

Charges guide
Per person	€ 5,10 - € 9,90
child	€ 2,60 - € 7,70
pitch incl. electricity	€ 9,70 - € 35,00
dog	€ 4,40 - € 8,50

Novalja
Camp Strasko

Novalja, HR-51291 Otok Pag (Dalmatia) T: **053 661 226**. E: **turno@turno.hr**
alanrogers.com/CR6776

Strasko is a very large, part FKK, part textile campsite, close to Novalja on the Dalmatian island Pag. The naturist part is separated from the textile area by a high, rock wall. All 2,000 pitches (1,800 for touring units, 1,000 with electricity) are in the shade of mature oak, pine and olive trees. Just 200 pitches are marked and numbered, on grass and gravel off hard access roads. The site can get very busy in July and August and the lack of marked pitches may make it difficult to find space in high season. The beauty of this site is clearly its 1,650 m. long sand and pebble beach.

Facilities
Ten traditional toilet blocks, three new and seven refurbished, provide British and Turkish style toilets, open style washbasins and controllable hot showers. Three washing machines. Large supermarket and several kiosks. Bars, restaurant, self-service restaurant and pizzeria. Sports centre. Trampolines. Aerobics. Minigolf. Bicycle hire. Gymnastics. Games machines. Daily children's club. Art workshops. Dance nights. Bungalows to rent. Off site: Novalja with bars, restaurants and shops is close.

Open: 1 May - 30 September.

Directions
Take no. 2 coast road south from Rijeka and at Prizna take the ferry. From the ferry follow signs for Novalja and site. GPS: 44.53883, 14.88627

Charges guide
Per person	€ 3,20 - € 6,30
child	free - € 3,90
pitch	€ 5,00 - € 18,00
dog	€ 3,00 - € 4,00

Novigrad
Camping Mareda
Mareda, HR-52466 Novigrad (Istria) T: **052 735 291**. E: **camping@laguna-novigrad.hr**
alanrogers.com/CR6713

Backed by oak woods and acres of vineyards, Camping Mareda is located on the coast just north of the small picturesque town of Novigrad. The site is on hilly ground with 800 sloping grass and gravel pitches, most with shade from mature trees and some with views of the sea. There are 600 pitches for touring units, all with 16A electricity and 28 also with water and drainage. Some are marked and numbered on two areas near the sea, the others are for free camping in other areas of the site where it may be difficult to find space in high season.

Facilities
Four modern toilet blocks with British and Turkish style toilets, open plan washbasins and hot showers. Child-size toilets and basins. Laundry with sinks and washing machine. Motorcaravan service point. Supermarket. Coffee bar and normal bar with terrace. Restaurant. Play area. Tennis. Fishing. Boats, kayaks, canoes and pedaloes for hire. Games hall with video games. Organised entertainment. Off site: Bicycle hire 4 km. Golf and riding 10 km. Historic towns of Pula, Novigrad and Rovinj are close.

Open: 1 May - 30 September.

Directions
From Novigrad travel north towards Umag. After 4 km. the site is signed to left. GPS: 45.34363, 13.54815

Charges guide
Per person	€ 4,00 - € 6,90
child (5-9 yrs)	free - € 3,80
pitch	€ 3,00 - € 11,50
electricity	€ 3,00
dog	€ 3,10 - € 4,80

Novigrad
Camping Park Umag
Karigador bb, HR-52466 Novigrad (Istria) T: **052 725 040**. E: **camp.park.umag@istraturist.hr**
alanrogers.com/CR6715

This extremely large site is very well planned in that just half of the 127 hectares is used for the pitches, resulting in lots of open space around the pitch area. It is the largest of the Istraturist group of sites. Of the 1,800 pitches, 1,440 of varying sizes, all with 10A electricity, are for touring units and there are 350 seasonal pitches. Some pitches have shade. Some noise is transmitted from the road alongside the site and there is a late night disco which may disturb some campers (choose your pitch carefully). The site is very popular with the Dutch and a friendly and happy atmosphere prevails, even in the busiest times.

Facilities
Ten toilet blocks include two bathrooms with deep tubs. Two blocks have children's WCs. Facilities for disabled campers. The site has plans to update these facilities. Fresh water and waste water points only at toilet blocks. Motorcaravan service point. Shops and supermarket. Bars, snack bars and restaurant (musical entertainment some evenings) all open early morning to midnight (one until the small hours). Swimming pool complex. Tennis. Fishing (permit from Umag). Minigolf. Off site: Riding nearby.

Open: 25 April - 4 October.

Directions
Site is on the Umag - Novigrad road 6 km. south of Umag. Look for large signs. GPS: 45.36707, 13.54716

Charges guide
Per person	€ 3,80 - € 7,50
child (5-11 yrs)	€ 2,00 - € 4,50
pitch incl. electricity	€ 8,70 - € 18,50
dog	€ 2,00 - € 3,20

For stays less than 3 nights in high season add 10%.

Omis
Autocamp Galeb
Vukovarska bb, HR-21310 Omis (Dalmatia) T: **021 864 430**. E: **camping@galeb.hr**
alanrogers.com/CR6860

Galeb is 25 km. south of Split and sits below the Cetine Canyon which can deliver strong winds from the east. The river Cetine is just to the north of the site and the pretty port where river meets sea is another powerful attraction, complemented by the ancient forts and pirate buildings above. A dramatic 1,000-metre rock backdrop to the whole site reflects the light differently as the day progresses and the superb sunsets here paint it with amazing orange and red hues. The 500 touring pitches are informal and security was a little relaxed when we stayed. Flat and mostly shady, some pitches are right at the water's edge and very long electricity leads are often required.

Facilities
Three sanitary blocks have been renovated to a good standard, two have facilities for disabled campers. Hot water for showers is plentiful and there is a regular cleaning routine. Motorcaravan service point. Shop. Restaurant. Pizzeria. Tennis. Play areas. Bicycle hire. Entertainment all season. TV. Security boxes. Cold boxes. Exchange. Beach. Boat launching and boat hire. Windsurfing. Sailing. Off site: Busy village 100 m. Port 1 km. Island of Brac.

Open: 1 June - 30 September.

Directions
Site is off the main coast road between Split and Dubrovnik, about 25 km. southeast of Split and is well signed from the road. GPS: 43.440617, 16.680283

Charges guide
Per person	Kn 31,50 - 42,50
child (5-12 yrs)	Kn 20,50 - 25,50
pitch	Kn 30,50 - 58,50
electricity	Kn 10,00
car	Kn 20,50 - 31,00

Orebic

Autocamp Nevio

Dubravica bb, HR-20250 Orebic (Dalmatia) T: **020 713 100**. E: **info@nevio-camping.com**
alanrogers.com/CR6875

This little campsite is a first-class option in the southern part of Dalmatia. Everything on the site is quite new (2005) including a comfortable main building with a bar, restaurant and terrace (summer only). The 120 level pitches are slightly terraced and of 80-120 sq.m. All have electricity and water, ten also have sewerage connections. There is little shade as yet, but this will develop. Located on the peninsula of Peljesac, there is the atmosphere of Dalmatia and its islands without the need for a ferry from the mainland to reach the site. A tarmac road winds all the way down to the shore.

Facilities

New sanitary facilities include rooms for children and babies. Fully equipped unit for disabled persons. Small kitchen. Washing machine and dryer. Small bar and restaurant with terrace (summer). Fridge hire. Bicycle hire. Boat launching. Mobile homes for hire. Outdoor swimming pool (May-Oct). Off site: Shop 100 m. Orebic with further shops and tourist facilities within 2 km. The historical town of Korcula is easily reached by local ferry. Dubrovnik 125 km.

Open: All year.

Directions

Approaching from the mainland, site is just over 1 km. before the town of Orebic, on the left (signed). GPS: 42.98120, 17.19930

Charges guide

Per unit incl. 2 persons and electricity	€ 17,00 - € 27,00
extra person	€ 4,00 - € 5,50
child (3-12 yrs)	€ 1,00 - € 4,00
Camping Cheques accepted.	

Paklenica

Kamp Paklenica

Dr. Franje Tudmania 14, HR-23244 Paklenica (Dalmatia) T: **023 209 050**. E: **alan@bluesunhotels.com**
alanrogers.com/CR6830

This is a relatively small site next to the Alan Hotel in Paklenica. It has 250 pitches, all for tourers and 150 with 16A electricity, on level, grass and gravel ground (firm tent pegs needed) under mature trees that provide useful shade. The front pitches have beautiful views of the blue waters of the Adriatic. Paklenica is only 100 m. from the entrance of the Paklenica National Park and excursions to the Park and to the Zrmanja Canyon can be booked on the site. Paklenica has its own beach, paved with rock plates, that gives access to a sheltered lagoon for swimming and boating.

Facilities

Two good toilet blocks provide British and Turkish style toilets, open washbasins and controllable, hot showers. Child-size toilet, shower and basin. Excellent facilities for disabled visitors. Fridge box hire. Motorcaravan service point. Bar/restaurant and pizzeria. Pool (150 sq.m) with paddling pool. Playground (on gravel). Tennis. Minigolf. Fishing. Bicycle hire. Jet ski, boat and scooter hire. Children's club. Live entertainment night. Games room. Communal barbecue area. Off site: Supermarket 200 m.

Open: Easter - 15 October.

Directions

From Rijeka, take no. 8 coast road south along the Dalmatian coast towards Starigrad-Paklenica. In town turn right at sign for 'Hotel Alan'. Turn right to site. GPS: 44.287267, 15.447617

Charges guide

Per person	Kn 20,50 - 49,00
child (3-12 yrs)	Kn 11,50 - 30,00
pitch incl. car	Kn 37,50 - 71,50

Porec

Naturist Resort Solaris

Lanterna bb, HR-52440 Porec (Istria) T: **052 465 110**. E: **camping-porec@valamar.com**
alanrogers.com/CR6718

This naturist site is part of the 'Camping on the Adriatic' group and has a most pleasant feel and when we visited in high season there were lots of happy people having fun. A pretty cove and lots of beach frontage with cool pitches under trees makes the site very attractive. Of the 1,445 pitches, 550 are available for touring, with 600 long stay units. There are 145 fully-serviced pitches (100 sq.m) available on a 'firstcome, first served' basis, an ample supply of electricity hook-ups (10-16A) and plentiful water points. As this is a naturist site, single men and groups consisting of men only are prohibited and there are restrictions on photography.

Facilities

Thirteen excellent, fully-equipped toilet blocks (four upgraded in 2007) provide toilets, washbasins and showers. Some have facilities for disabled visitors. Washing machines and ironing facilities. Restaurants, grills and fast food, and supermarkets. Swimming pool. Tennis. Bicycle hire. Riding. Play areas. Boat launching. Car wash. Entertainment. Dogs are restricted to a particular area and are not allowed on the beach. Off site: Excursions. Riding and fishing 500 m.

Open: 1 April - 10 October.

Directions

Site is 3 km. off the Novigrad - Porec road about 8 km. south of Novigrad and is well signed. Camping Lanterna is also down this road so signs for this site may be followed also. GPS: 45.29126, 13.5848

Charges guide

Per person	€ 3,00 - € 6,15
pitch incl. electricity	€ 6,10 - € 17,50
Prices for pitches by the sea are higher.	

Porec

Camping Lanterna

Lanterna, HR-52440 Porec (Istria) T: 052 465 010. E: camping@valamar.com

alanrogers.com/CR6716

This is one of the largest sites in Croatia with an amazing selection of activities and high standards and is part of the 'Camping on the Adriatic' group. Reception is buzzing in high season as around 10,000 guests are on site. Set in 90 hectares with over 3 km. of beach, there are 3,000 pitches of which 2,600 are for touring units. Pitches are 60-120 sq.m. with some superb locations right on the sea, although these tend to be taken first so it is advisable to book ahead. Some of the better pitches are in a 'reserved booking' area. Terracing has improved the view in many areas. Electrical connections are 10A. Facilities at Lanterna are impressive with the whole operation running smoothly for the campers. The land is sloping in parts and terraced in others. There is a large pool and pretty bay with rocky beaches and buoyed safety areas. Some of the marked and numbered pitches are shaded and arranged to take advantage of the topography. Many activities and quality entertainment for all are available both on and off site – you are spoilt for choice here, including a vast choice of places to eat. Prices tend to be higher than other sites in the area but you get value for money with the supporting facilities.

Facilities

The fourteen sanitary blocks are clean and good quality. Children's facilities and baby care areas. Facilities for disabled people. Three supermarkets sell most everyday requirements. Fresh fish shop. Four restaurants, bars and snack bars and fast food outlets. Swimming and paddling pools. Sandpit and play areas, with entertainment for all in high season. Tennis. Bicycle hire. Watersports. Boats hire. Miniglcf. Riding. Internet café. Jetty and ramp for boats. Off site: Novigrad, 9 km. Hourly bus service from the reception area. Fishing. Riding 500 m.

Open: 1 April - 15 October.

Directions

The turn to Lanterna is well signed off the Novigrad to Porec road about 8 km. south of Novigrad. Continue for about 2 km. down the turn off road towards the coast and the campsite is difficult to miss on the right hand side. GPS: 45.29672, 13.59442

Charges guide

Per person	€ 3,85 - € 6,60
child (4-10 yrs)	free - € 4,65
pitch incl. electricity	€ 6,60 - € 14,95

Prices for pitches by the sea are higher.

New mobile homes

camping lanterna ***

istria · lanterna / poreč

T +385 52 465 010 **F** +385 52 451 440
E camping@valamar.com
www.camping-adriatic.com

Porec
Camping Puntica
Rade Koncara 12, Funtana, HR-52449 Porec (Istria) T: **052 445 720**. E: **ac.puntica@plavalaguna.hr**
alanrogers.com/CR6719

Puntica is a small, unassuming and old-fashioned campsite in a superb location. Everything is modest here and, if small is your thing, you will love it. There are 250 pitches, with 104 for tourers. Some of the flat, variably sized pitches (80-120 sq.m) are shaded amongst trees which could test larger units but the waterside pitches are wonderful. Electricity box positioning demands long leads in some areas (10A). The marina alongside is very attractive, as are the views from the terraces of the rustic restaurant and bar. There is a paved area around the tip of the site for sunbathing and ladders give access to deeper water.

Facilities
One main sanitary block is kept clean and has reasonable facilities but is short on hot water for washing. British and Turkish style toilets with one locked unit for disabled campers. Washing machines and dryers operated by the 'laundry lady'. Small shop. Restaurant and bar. DIY motorcaravan services. Fishing. Basic playground. Gas barbecues permitted. Fridge box hire. Boat launching. Marina facilities. Bicycle hire. Watersports. Scuba diving. Off site: Bicycle hire 500 m. Riding 500 m. Funtana 500 m.
Open: 23 April - 1 October.

Directions
Site is on the main road between Porec and Vrsar, near the village of Funtana, 7 km. south of Porec. Just watch for the yellow camping signs. GPS: 45.17665, 13.60099

Charges guide
Per person	€ 2,90 - € 5,00
child (4-10 yrs)	free - € 3,10
pitch	€ 3,40 - € 8,20
incl. electricity	€ 4,60 - € 13,70

Porec
Naturist Centre Ulika
Cervar, HR-52440 Porec (Istria) T: **052 436 325**. E: **reservations@plavalaguna.hr**
alanrogers.com/CR6720

This naturist site is well located, occupying a small peninsula of some 15 hectares. This means that there is only a short walk to the sea from anywhere on the site. The ground is mostly gently sloping with a covering of rough grass and there are 1,000 pitches with 6A electricity connections, 420 also have water and drainage. One side of the site is shaded with mature trees but the other side is almost devoid of shade and could become very hot. There are many activities on site and an excellent swimming pool. The reception office opens 24 hours for help and information.

Facilities
Six toilet blocks provide mostly British style WCs, washbasins (half with hot water) and showers (some with controllable hot water). Facilities for disabled visitors. Laundry. Motorcaravan service point. Supermarket (daily). Restaurant, pizzeria and snacks. Swimming pool. Massage. Tennis. Minigolf. Watersports. Boating and sailing - marina on site. Off site: Riding 3 km. Bicycle hire 6 km. Porec is 6 km. (a must to visit) with bus service from site reception.
Open: One week before Easter - 10 October.

Directions
Site is about 3 km. off the main Novigrad - Porec road, signed in village of Cevar. GPS: 45.25676, 13.58317

Charges guide
Per person	Kn 29,40 - 55,90
child (4-10 yrs)	free - Kn 38,50
pitch	Kn 43,80 - 166,90
electricity	Kn 18,10 - 25,70
dog	Kn 24,20 - 43,80

Porec
Autokamp Zelena Laguna
HR-52440 Porec (Istria) T: **052 410 101**. E: **mail@plavalaguna.hr**
alanrogers.com/CR6722

A busy medium-sized site (by Croatian standards), Zelena Laguna (green lagoon) is very popular with families and boat owners. Part of the Plava Laguna Leisure group that has eight other campsites and seven hotels in the vicinity, it is long established and is improved and modernised each year as finances permit. The 1,100 pitches (540 for touring units) are a mixture of level, moderately sloping and terraced ground and range in size from 40-120 sq.m. There are plenty of electrical hook-ups (10A). 42 super pitches are very popular and in other areas there are many water points. Slopes will be encountered on the site with quite a steep hill leading to the highest point.

Facilities
The sanitary blocks are good and some have been refurbished. The washbasins have hot water and there are free hot controllable showers in all blocks. Toilets are mostly British style. Facilities for disabled campers. Supermarket and shop. Restaurants and snack bars. Swimming pool. Sub-aqua diving. Tennis. Bicycle hire. Riding. Boat hire. Boat launching. Entertainment programme. Off site: Small market and shops immediately outside site. Supermarkets in Porec (4 km). Fishing 5 km. (by permit). Riding 300 m.
Open: 19 March - 7 October.

Directions
Site is between the coast road and the sea with turning 2 km. from Porec towards Vrsar. It is very well signed and is part of a large multiple hotel complex. GPS: 45.19529, 13.58927

Charges guide
Per person	€ 3,80 - € 7,00
child (4-9 yrs)	free - € 4,90
pitch	€ 5,60 - € 13,20
electricity	€ 2,30 - € 3,20

235

Porec

Camping Bijela Uvala

Bijela Uvala, Zelena Laguna, HR-52440 Porec (Istria) T: 052 410 551. E: mail@plavalaguna.hr

alanrogers.com/CR6724

Bijela Uvala is part of the Plava Laguna Leisure group and is a large friendly campsite with an extensive range of facilities. The direct sea access makes the site very popular in high season. The 2,000 pitches, 1,476 for touring, are compact and due to the terrain some have excellent sea views and breezes, however as usual these are the most sought after so book early. They range from 60-120 sq.m. and all have electricity, 400 also have water connections. Some are formal with hedging, some are terraced and most have good shade from established trees or wooded areas. There are also very informal areas where unmarked pitches are on generally uneven ground. The topography of the site is undulating and the gravel or grass pitches are divided into zones which vary considerably. As the coastline winds along the site, the rocky and intermittently paved sea access increases with boat launching facilities, beach volleyball and various eateries dispersed along it. The smaller of the two pools is in a busy complex adjacent to the sea which includes a large entertainment area and a family style restaurant. There are many sporting facilities and fairground style amusements (some at extra cost). The adjoining campsite Zelena Laguna is owned by the same organisation and access to its beach (including a naturist section) and facilities is via a gate between the sites or along the beach. A large sports complex is also within walking distance. This site is very similar to Camping Zelena Laguna but with fewer permanent pitches.

Facilities

Eight sanitary blocks are clean and well equipped with mainly British style WCs. Free hot showers. Washing machines. Facilities for disabled visitors. Motorcaravan service point. Gas. Fridge boxes. 2 restaurants, 3 fast food cafés, 2 bars and a bakery. Well-equipped supermarket and a shop. Two swimming pool complexes. Tennis. Playground. Amusements. TV room. Entertainment centre. Off site: Zelena Laguna campsite facilities. Sports complex 100 m. Naturist beach 25 m.

Open: 19 March - 7 October.

Directions

The site adjoins Zelena Laguna. From the main Porec to Vrsar coast road turn off towards coast and the town of Zelena Laguna about 4 km. south of Porec and follow campsite signs. GPS: 45.19149, 13.59686

Charges guide

Per person	€ 3,80 - € 7,00
child (4-9 yrs)	free - € 4,90
pitch	€ 5,60 - € 13,20
electricity	€ 2,30 - € 3,20

Primosten

Camp Adriatic

Huljerat bb, HR-22202 Primosten (Dalmatia) T: 022 571 223. E: info@camp-adriatic.hr

alanrogers.com/CR6845

As we drove south down the Dalmatian coast road, we looked across a clear turquoise bay and saw a few tents, caravans and motorcaravans camped under some trees. A short distance later we were at the entrance of Camping Adriatic. With 530 pitches that slope down to the sea, the site is deceptive and enjoys a one kilometre beach frontage which is ideal for snorkelling and diving. Most pitches are level and have shade from pine trees. There are 212 numbered pitches and 288 unnumbered, all with electricity. Close to the town of Primosten the site boasts good amenities and a fantastic location.

Facilities

Four modern sanitary blocks provide clean toilets, hot showers and washbasins. Facilities for disabled visitors. Bathroom for children. Washing machine and dryer. Kitchen facilities. Small supermarket (15/5-30/9). Restaurant, bar and takeaway (all season). Sports centre. Miniclub. Beach. Diving school. Sailing school and boat hire. Entertainment programme in July/Aug. Internet point. Off site: Primosten 2.5 km. Sibenic 25 km. Riding 15 km.

Open: 1 May - 15 October.

Directions

Take A1 motorway south and leave at Sibenik exit. Follow the 33 road into Sibenik, then go south along the coast road (no. 8), signed Primosten. Site is 2.5 km. north of Primosten. GPS: 43.606517, 15.92095

Charges guide

Per person	Kn 34,00 - 60,00
child (3-12 yrs)	Kn 25,00 - 45,00
pitch incl. car, electricity (10/16A)	Kn 54,00 - 105,00
Camping Cheques accepted.	

Check real time availability and at-the-gate prices...

www.alanrogers.com

Pula

Camping Stupice

Premantura, HR-52100 Pula (Istria) T: **052 575 101**. E: **marketing@arenaturist.hr**

alanrogers.com/CR6737

Camping Village Stupice, part of the Arenaturist group, is situated in a delightful strip of coast on the Istrian peninsula near the small village of Premantura. Most of the site is covered with undulating, dense pinewood providing ample shade with a carpet of pine needles. There are 1,000 pitches in total with 588 touring pitches in three sizes (ranging from 60-120 sq.m). They are sloping or level and about a fifth have sea views. Access roads are bitumen or gravel. A narrow pebble beach separates the sea from the site and it is not crowded due to the length of the sea access.

Facilities

The six toilet blocks are clean but need updating, with a mixture of Turkish and British style toilets. The few hot showers are unisex. Washing machines. Kiosk, small bars and grills. Good supermarket. Minigolf. Playground. Activities for children, disco and live entertainment in high season. Rock and pebble beach. Marina, boat launching, jetty and scuba diving. Bicycle and beach buggy hire. Aquapark. Off site: Premantura 1 km. Bicycle hire 500 m.

Open: 29 March - 25 October.

Directions

Site is 11 km. southeast of Pula. Follow signs to Premantura from Pula where there are site signs. GPS: 44.7978, 13.91366

Charges 2010

Per unit incl. 2 persons and electricity	€ 17,10 - € 33,40
extra person	€ 4,30 - € 7,30
child (4-12 yrs)	€ 2,90 - € 4,60
dog	€ 2,60 - € 4,50

Pula

Camping Indije

Banjole, HR-52100 Pula (Istria) T: **052 573 066**. E: **acindije@arenaturist.hr**

alanrogers.com/CR6739

Camping Indije is on the beautiful Adriatic coast in Banjole (Medulin), only a few kilometres from the historic centre of Pula. Medulin fronts a beautiful bay, dominated by a bell tower, with a wealth of little peninsulas and islands, all melting together with the blue sea and the green of the Mediterranean vegetation and Banjole is on one edge of it. All 353 grass and gravel pitches (50-120 sq.m) are for tourers are most are well shaded. All have 10A electricity and 16 are fully serviced. From many pitches there are wonderful open views over the sea to the islands.

Facilities

Three comfortable toilet blocks with British and Turkish style toilets, open plan washbasins and showers. Washing machine. Motorcaravan service point. Supermarket and newspaper stand. Bar and restaurant. Miniclub. Live music. Rock plateau beach. Diving centre. Boat mooring. Fishing (with permit). Boat launching. Off site: Historic towns of Pula and Rovinj are close. Riding 10 km. Golf 15 km.

Open: 24 April - 20 September.

Directions

From Pula follow signs for Premantura and Banjole southwards. From Banjole follow site signs. GPS: 44.82382, 13.85078

Charges guide

Per unit incl. 2 persons and electricity	€ 15,80 - € 30,70
extra person	€ 2,60 - € 6,70
dog	€ 2,40 - € 4,10

Pula

Camping Stoja

Stoja 37, HR-52100 Pula (Istria) T: **052 387 144**. E: **acstoja@arenaturist.hr**

alanrogers.com/CR6742

Camping Stoja in Pula is an attractive and well maintained site on a small peninsula and therefore almost completely surrounded by the waters of the clear Adriatic. In the centre of the site is the old Fort Stoja, built in 1884 for coastal defence. Some of its buildings are now used as a toilet block or laundry and its courtyard is used by the entertainment team. The 708 touring pitches here vary greatly in size (50-120 sq.m) and are marked by round, concrete, numbered blocks, separated by young trees. About half have shade from mature trees and all are slightly sloping on grass and gravel.

Facilities

Five toilet blocks with British and Turkish style toilets, open-plan washbasins with cold water only and controllable hot showers. Child-size basins. Facilities for disabled visitors. Laundry and ironing service. Fridge box hire. Motorcaravan service point. Supermarket. Bar/restaurant. Miniclub and teen club. Bicycle hire. Water skiing. Boat hire. Boat launching. Surfboard and pedalo hire. Fishing (with permit). Off site: Pula (walking distance). Riding 8 km. Golf 10 km.

Open: 4 April - 2 November.

Directions

From Pula follow site signs. GPS: 44.85972, 13.81450

Charges guide

Per person	€ 4,30 - € 7,50
child (4-12 yrs)	€ 2,90 - € 4,70
pitch incl. electricity	€ 8,80 - € 19,10
dog	€ 2,60 - € 4,70

Croatia

Punat

Camping Pila

Setaliste Ivana Bruscia 2, Punat, HR-51521 Krk (Kvarner) T: **051 854 020**. E: **pila@hoteli-punat.hr**
alanrogers.com/CR6755

Autocamping Pila is right beside the bustling seaside resort of Punat on the biggest Croatian island Krk, which is connected to the mainland by a bridge. Krk is the first island you reach as you travel south into Croatia and the Romans called it the 'Golden Island'. Autocamp Pila is just 100 m. from the Adriatic and has 600 pitches for tourers, all with 10A electricity on grass and gravel, plus some new individual pitches with water and waste water. Some are slightly sloping. Some 250 of the pitches are marked and numbered, most with shade from mature trees. The remainder are unmarked on a separate field. It can get very busy in high season and pitching can become cramped.

Facilities

Four modern, comfortable toilet blocks with toilets, basins and showers. Child-size showers and basins. Baby room. Facilities for disabled visitors. Campers kitchen with cooking rings. Motorcaravan service point. Supermarket, bar with terrace and restaurant (all season). Snack bar. New play area with basketball. Minigolf. Aerobics and aquarobics. Video games. Daily evening programme for children. Internet. Lessons in the Croatian language. Pebble beach. Off site: Punat (shops, bars, restaurants). Boat hire 200 m.

Open: 1 April - 15 October.

Directions

On Krk follow no. 29 road and take exit for Punat. In Punat follow good site signs.
GPS: 45.01663, 14.62873

Charges guide

Per unit incl. 2 persons and electricity	€ 17,40 - € 27,50
extra person	€ 3,90 - € 6,50
child (7-12 yrs)	€ 1,80 - € 4,20
Camping Cheques accepted.	

Punat

Naturist Camping Konobe

Obala 94, Punat, HR-51521 Krk (Kvarner) T: **051 854 036**. E: **konobe@hoteli-punat.hr**
alanrogers.com/CR6756

Naturist Camping Konobe is situated south of the historic fishing port of Punat on the island of Krk in a remote and quiet location. Access is down a long, tarmac road which leads to a landscaped terrain, with terraces built from natural stone. The 800 slightly sloping pitches are part open, part wooded, with some shade from mature trees and some with beautiful views over the Adriatic. Unmarked pitches for tents are on small terraces, with numbered pitches for caravans and motorcaravans of 80-100 sq.m. on gravel hardstanding off tarmac access roads. The remote location makes this site ideal for quiet camping among the wild charm of a rocky and still green environment.

Facilities

Three modern, comfortable toilet blocks with toilets, open basins and preset showers. Child-size washbasins. Facilities for disabled visitors. Campers' kitchen with connections (no rings). Gas. Supermarket. Bar/restaurant with open air terrace. Tennis. Minigolf. Fishing. Pebble beach. Boat launching. Evening entertainment programme for children. Croatian language lessons. Off site: Punat 4 km.

Open: 1 May - 1 October.

Directions

On Krk follow 29 road and take exit for Punat and follow main road through town. Site is 4 km. south of Punat and well signed. GPS: 44.99107, 14.63065

Charges guide

Per unit incl. 2 persons	€ 17,40 - € 29,00
extra person	€ 3,90 - € 6,50
Camping Cheques accepted.	

Rovinj

Naturist Camping Valalta

Cesta Valalta-Lim bb, HR-52210 Rovinj (Istria) T: **052 804 800**. E: **valalta@valalta.hr**
alanrogers.com/CR6731

This is a most impressive site for up to 6,000 naturist campers, which has a pleasant, open feel. The passage through reception is efficient and this feeling is maintained around the well organised site. A friendly, family atmosphere is to be found here. Valalta is a family oriented campsite. All pitches are the same price with 16A electricity, although they vary in size and surroundings. The variations include shade, views, sand, grass, sea frontage, level ground, slopes and terracing. It is not possible to reserve a particular pitch and campers do move pitches at will. The impressive pool is in lagoon style.

Facilities

Twenty high-quality, new or refurbished sanitary blocks of which four are smaller units of plastic 'pod' construction. Hot showers (coin operated). Facilities for disabled campers. Washing machines and dryers. Supermarket. Four restaurants (one specialising in seafood). Pizzeria. Two bars. Large lagoon style pool complex. Beauty saloon. Fitness club. Massage. Minigolf. Tennis. Sailing. Play area. Bicycle hire. Marina. Internet. Entertainment all season. Kindergarten. Dogs are not accepted. Off site: Riding 7 km.

Open: 25 April - 26 September.

Directions

If approaching from the north turn inland (follow signs to Rovinj) to drive around the Limski Kanal. Then follow signs towards Valalta about 2 km. east of Rovinj. Site is at the end of the road and is well signed. GPS: 45.122233, 13.6308

Charges 2010

Per unit incl. 2 persons	€ 18,00 - € 33,50
extra person	€ 8,00 - € 14,50
child (4-14 yrs)	€ 2,50 - € 4,75

261

238

Rovinj

Camping Vestar

Vestar bb, HR-52210 Rovinj (Istria) T: **052 829 150**. E: **vestar@maistra.hr**

alanrogers.com/CR6733

Camping Vestar, just 5 km. from the historic harbour town of Rovinj, is one of the rare sites in Croatia with a partly sandy beach. Right behind the beach is a large area, attractively landscaped with young trees and shrubs, with grass for sunbathing. The site has 650 large pitches, of which 500 are for tourers, all with 6/10A electricity (the rest being taken by seasonal units and 60 pitches for tour operators). It is largely wooded with good shade and from the bottom row of pitches there are views of the sea. Pitching is on two separate fields, one for free camping, the other with numbered pitches. The pitches at the beach are in a half circle around the shallow bay, making it safe for children to swim. Vestar has a small marina and a jetty for mooring small boats and excursions to the islands are arranged. There is a miniclub and live music with dancing at one of the two bar/restaurants in the evenings. The restaurants all have open air terraces, one covered with vines to protect you from the hot sun.

Facilities

Six modern and one refurbished toilet block with mainly Turkish style toilets and some British style, open washbasins and controllable hot showers. Child-size facilities. Baby rooms. Family bathroom. Facilities for disabled people. Laundry service. Fridge box hire. Motorcaravan services. Shop. Two bar/restaurants. Large swimming pool. Playground. Tennis. Fishing. Boat and pedalo hire. Miniclub (5-11 yrs). Excursions. Internet access in reception. Off site: Riding 2 km. Rovinj 5 km.

Open: 1 April - 1 October.

Directions

Site is on the coast 4 km. south east of Rovinj. From Rovinj travel south in the direction of Pula. After 4 km. turn right following campsite signs.
GPS: 45.05432, 13.68568

Charges guide

Per person	€ 5,00 - € 9,20
child (5-12 yrs)	free - € 6,90
pitch incl. electricity	€ 7,00 - € 22,00
dog	€ 3,10 - € 6,20

Camping Veštar *Rovinj*

Istria
Green Mediterranean.

CRO ATIA

Luxury sanitary facilities!
Pitch with water supply and drain!

ONLINE BOOKING

This campsite has a special charm – a warm welcome is guaranteed, in a stunning beachside setting.

tel: +385 (0)52 800 200 / fax: 800 215 / vestar@maistra.hr

www.CampingRovinj.com

Rovinj

Camping Amarin

Monsena bb, HR-52210 Rovinj (Istria) T: **052 802 000**. E: ac-amarin@maistra.hr

alanrogers.com/CR6730

Situated 4 km. from the centre of the lovely old port town of Rovinj this site has much to offer. The complex is part of the Maistra Group. It has 12.6 hectares of land and is adjacent to the Amarin bungalow complex. Campers can enjoy the facilities afforded by both areas. There are 670 pitches for touring units on various types of ground and between 80-120 sq.m. Most are separated by foliage, 10A electricity is available. A rocky beach backed by a grassy sunbathing area is very popular, but the site has its own superb, supervised round pool with corkscrew slide plus a splash pool for children. Boat owners have a mooring area and launching ramp and a breakwater is popular with sunbathers. The port of Rovinj contains many delights, particularly if you are able to contend with the hundreds of steps which lead to the church above the town from where the views are well worth the climb.

Facilities

Thirteen respectable toilet blocks have a mixture of British style and Turkish toilets. Some blocks have a unit for disabled visitors. Fridge box hire. Washing machines. Security boxes. Motorcaravan service point. Supermarket. Small market. Two restaurants, taverna, pizzeria and terrace grill. Swimming pool with flume. Watersports. Bicycle hire. Fishing (permit). Daily entertainment. Massage. Hairdresser. Barbecues are not permitted. Dogs are not allowed on the beach. Off site: Hourly minibus service to Rovinj. Excursions including day trips to Venice. Riding 2 km.

Open: 25 April - 27 September.

Directions

Follow signs towards Rovinj and if approaching from the north turn off about 2 km. before the town towards Amarin and Valalta. Then follow signs to Amarin and the campsite. Watch for a left turn after about 3 km. where signs are difficult to see. GPS: 45.10876, 13.61988

Charges guide

Per unit incl. 2 persons	€ 15,50 - € 28,60
extra person	€ 4,50 - € 7,80
child (5-11 yrs)	free - € 4,80

For stays less than 3 nights in high season add 10%.

Rovinj
Camping Valdaliso

Monsena bb, HR-52210 Rovinj (Istria) T: **052 805 505**. E: **info@rovinjturist.hr**

alanrogers.com/CR6736

Unusually Camping Valdaliso has its affiliated hotel in the centre of the site. The pitches are mostly flat with shade from pine trees and the site is divided into three sections all with 16A electricity. The choice of formal numbered pitches, informal camping or proximity to the sea impacts on the prices. The kilometre plus of pebble beach has crystal clear water. The entertainment programme is extremely professional and there is a lot to do at Valdaliso, which is aimed primarily at families. The variety of activities here and the bonus of the use of the hotel make this a great choice for campers. The fine Barabiga restaurant within the hotel offers superb Istrian and fish cuisine and the pool is also within the hotel. You are close to the beautiful old town of Rovinj and parts of this site enjoy views of the town. A water taxi makes exploring Rovinj very easy, compared with the impossible parking for private cars. A bus service is also provided but this involves considerable walking.

Facilities

Two large clean sanitary blocks have hot showers (coin operated). The northeastern block has facilities for disabled campers. Hotel facilities. Shop. Pizzeria. Restaurant. Tennis. Fitness centre. Bicycle hire. Games room. Children's games. Summer painting courses. Exchange. Boat rental. Watersports. Boat launching. Fishing. Diving school. Internet in both receptions. Water taxi. Bus service. Dogs are not accepted. Off site: Town 1 km.

Open: 4 April - 3 October.

Directions

Site is 7 km. north of Rovinj on the main coast road between Vsrar and Rovinj. Watch for the signs to Monsena and the site. GPS: 45.104267, 13.625183

Charges guide

Per person	€ 4,50 - € 8,00
child (5-12 yrs)	free - € 5,00
pitch	€ 6,50 - € 16,00

Rovinj
Camping Polari

Polari bb, HR-52210 Rovinj (Istria) T: **052 801 501**. E: **polari@maistra.hr**

alanrogers.com/CR6732

This 60-hectare site has excellent facilities for both textile and naturist campers, the latter having a reserved area of 12 hectares called Punta Eva. Prime places are taken by permanent customers but there are some numbered pitches which are very good. Many pitches have been thoughtfully upgraded and a new pitch (100 sq.m) is now offered with full facilities. Pitches are clean, neat and level and there will be shade when the young trees grow. There is something for everyone here to enjoy or you may prefer just to relax. An impressive swimming pool complex is child friendly with large paddling areas. Part of the Maistia Group, the site has undergone a massive improvement programme and the result makes it a very attractive option. Enjoy a meal on the restaurant terrace with panoramic sea views.

Facilities

All the sanitary facilities have been renovated to a high standard with plenty of hot water and good showers. Washing machines and dryers. Laundry service including ironing. Motorcaravan service point. Two shops, one large and one small, one restaurant and snack bar. Tennis. Minigolf. Children's entertainment with all major European languages spoken. Bicycle hire. Watersports. Sailing school. Off site: Riding 1 km. Five buses daily to and from Rovinj (3 km). Golf 30 km.

Open: 1 April - 2 October.

Directions

From any access road to Rovinj look for red signs to AC Polari (amongst other destinations). Site is about 3 km. south of Rovinj. GPS: 45.06286, 13.67489

Charges guide

Per unit incl. 2 persons and electricity	€ 18,00 - € 40,80
extra person (18-64 yrs)	€ 5,00 - € 8,90
children and seniors according to age	free - € 8,50
For stays less than 3 nights in high season add 20%.	

Check real time availability and at-the-gate prices...

www.alanrogers.com

Savudrija
Autocamp Pineta

Istarska bb, HR-52475 Savudrija (Istria) T: **052 709 550**. E: **camp.pineta@istraturist.hr**

alanrogers.com/CR6711

One of the older sites at the western end of Istria, Pineta is part of the Istraturist group and has been greatly improved over the last few years. It is of medium size (17 hectares) and gets its name from its setting amongst a forest of fully mature pine trees around two sides of a coastal bay. There are 460 pitches of which 160 are occupied on a long stay basis. Pitches are numbered and are 80-120 sq.m. all having access to electricity (10A). This is a site for those who prefer cooler situations as the dense pines provide abundant shade.

Facilities

Toilet blocks have been refurbished to a high standard. Hot and cold showers (plus showers for dogs). Mostly British style WCs and a few Turkish style. Excellent facilities for disabled campers. Fresh water at toilet blocks only apart from 'blue coded' pitches. Motorcaravan service point. Supermarket. Six bars, three restaurants and snack bar. Tennis. Fishing (permit). Barbecues on communal areas only. Activities centre. Evening music. Off site: Gas at local garage 500 m. from the site entrance. Riding 3 km. Golf 3 km.

Open: 25 April - 4 October.

Directions

From Trieste - Koper (Capodistra) - Umag road look for Savundrija signs. Site is 6 km. north of Umag. GPS: 45.48674, 13.49246

Charges guide

Per person	€ 3,50 - € 7,80
child (5-11 yrs)	€ 2,00 - € 4,80
pitch incl. electricity	€ 6,70 - € 15,80

For stays less than 3 nights in high season add 10%.

Selce
Autocamp Selce

Jasenova 19, HR-51266 Selce (Kvarner) T: **051 764 038**. E: **kamp-selce@ri.t-com.hr**

alanrogers.com/CR6750

Autocamp Selce is a small site in the village of Selce on the Dalmatian Coast. It has 500 pitches, all with 10A electricity, with 300 used for touring units and the others taken by seasonal guests. The pitches are mostly on level terraces on the steeply sloping terrain on a grass and gravel surface (firm tent pegs may be needed). They are under low trees that provide useful shade in the hot Mediterranean summer. Pitches are 50-80 sq.m. and there are several gravel hardstandings for larger units. From the top of the site it is an easy ten minute stroll downhill to the seaside promenade.

Facilities

Seven good toilet blocks with British and Turkish style toilets, open style washbasins and controllable, hot showers (free). Laundry service. Fridge box hire. Shop. Bar/restaurant with covered and open-air terrace. Barbecues permitted only in communal area. Fishing. A reader reports loud live music until midnight. Off site: Boat rental and water skiing 150 m. Boat launching and jetty 500 m.

Open: 1 April - 1 November.

Directions

From Rijeka, follow the no. 8 coastal road south towards Senj. In Selce, follow the site signs. GPS: 45.1541, 14.725133

Charges guide

Per person	€ 3,50 - € 6,10
child (5-13 yrs)	€ 2,20 - € 3,50
pitch	€ 4,50 - € 9,40
electricity	€ 2,00

Simuni
Camping Simuni

Otok Pag, HR-23251 Simuni (Dalmatia) T: **023 697 441**. E: **info@camping-simuni.hr**

alanrogers.com/CR6778

Camping Simuni is landscaped with low rock walls alongside the access roads and many varieties of shrubs and flowers, giving it a pleasant, welcoming atmosphere. It is close to the fishing port of Simuni and just 8 km. from Pag on the island of Pag. There are 800 pitches, most for tourers, about half with electricity and with a water tap between four pitches. Tent pitches are small, pitches for caravans are larger and fairly level, most with hardstanding and off tarmac or paved access roads. Shade is provided by mature laurel trees and all pitches are separated by low rock walls on grass and gravel.

Facilities

Three new sanitary blocks should now be open. Laundry service from reception. Supermarket and fruit kiosks. Bar, pizzeria and restaurant. Tennis. Bicycle hire. Aerobics. Boat launching. Trampolines. Football tournaments for children. Off site: Simuni (walking distance) and Pag 8 km.

Open: All year.

Directions

Take no. 2 road south from Rijeka to Prizna and take the ferry to Pag. From ferry follow signs for Pag and site. GPS: 44.46520, 14.96712

Charges guide

Per unit incl. 2 persons and electricity	€ 12,10 - € 37,00
extra person	€ 2,90 - € 8,20
child (3-12)	€ 1,40 - € 5,80

Camping Cheques accepted.

Sv. Filip I Jakov

Autocamp Rio

Put Primorja 66, HR-23207 Sv. Filip I Jakov (Dalmatia) T: **023 388 671**. E: **autocamp_rio@hotmail.com**
alanrogers.com/CR6833

In a village close to Biograd, the small Autocamp Rio provides 54 pitches of which 29 are available for tourers. All have old-type (two-pin) electricity connections. The fairly unofficial reception, the toilet block and the house of the Croatian owner are situated on the street front while behind, the site ends on a cliff directly above the sea. Below, a little sandy beach and a pier for boats are accessible from the site and used by campsite guests only. The partly shaded, marked pitches are laid out in two wings around a central grassy area so nobody is entirely surrounded by campers.

Facilities	Directions
Decent but simple toilet block has showers with curtains but no facilities for babies or disabled visitors. Washing machine. No bar or restaurant. Off site: Village within walking distance. City of Zadar 25 km. Komati Archipelago National Park. Vransko Jezero bird reserve 10 km. **Open:** Easter - 15 October.	From centre of Sv Filip I Jakov village, leave main coast road and follow signs for 'centar' and little site sign for Rio. Continue around a little park and keeping right (in southeastern direction, parallel to the sea) for almost 1 km. Rio is on the right, not far from the end of the village. GPS: 43.95604, 15.43521

Charges guide

Per person	€ 3,00
child (under 12 yrs)	€ 1,00
pitch	€ 5,00
electricity	€ 3,00

Trogir

Camp Seget

Hrvatskih zrtava 121, HR-21218 Trogir Seget Donji (Dalmatia) T: **021 880 394**. E: **kamp@kamp-seget.hr**
alanrogers.com/CR6850

Seget is a simple site which is pleasant and quiet with only 120 pitches, just 2 km. from the interesting old harbour town of Trogir. The site is set up on both sides of a tarmac access lane that runs down to the sea. Pitches to the left are arranged off three separate, gravel lanes. They are fairly level and from most there are views of the sea. Pitches to the right are slightly sloping and mostly used for tents. Of varying sizes (50-100 sq.m) the pitches are on grass and gravel (firm tent pegs may be needed), mostly in the shade of mature fig and palm trees and some are numbered.

Facilities	Directions
Two sanitary blocks (one half remaining a Portacabin style). British style toilets, washbasins and controllable, hot showers (free). Facilities for disabled visitors. Campers' kitchen. Shop (1/5-31/10). Bicycle hire. Beach. Fishing. Boat rental. Barbecues only on communal area. Off site: Bus at gate for touring. Golf 1 km. Boat launching 500 m. **Open:** 15 April - 15 October.	Follow no. 8 coastal road south from Zadar towards Split and in Trogir look for site signs, finishing in a sharp right turn. GPS: 43.5186, 16.224167

Charges 2010

Per unit incl. 2 persons and electricity	Kn 150,00 - 200,00

Umag

Naturist Camping Kanegra

Kanegra bb, HR-52470 Umag (Istria) T: **052 709 000**. E: **camp.kanegra@istraturist.hr**
alanrogers.com/CR6710

Situated almost on the Slovenian border, this could be said to be the first and last campsite in Croatia. Part of the Istraturist group, the smart air conditioned reception sets the tone for this very pleasant naturist site. It is located alongside the large Kanegra bungalow complex, and campers are able to share its comprehensive facilities. There are 190 level pitches here on sandy soil with sparse grass (90 are seasonal). They vary in size (80-100 sq.m) and are marked and numbered, with 10A electricity. The site has an open aspect with little shade and clear waters off the rocky beach which runs its total length.

Facilities	Directions
Two well equipped toilet blocks are kept very clean. Washing machine. Beach showers. No facilities for disabled campers. Motorcaravan service point. Supermarket. Two bars, three snack bars and two restaurants, all open until late. Nightly 'Tropic' disco in the adjacent bungalow complex but reportedly not disturbing the campsite. Playground in beach area. Use of all sporting facilities in the bungalow park. Many watersports. Off site: Riding and golf 3 km. Boat launching 1 km. Fishing. Tennis in Umag. **Open:** 25 April - 4 October.	From Koper, follow signs to Umag, but turn north towards Kanegra 5 km. before Umag. If approaching from south, after Umag follow main coast road north towards Savudrija (do not turn off towards this town) and then Kanegra. GPS: 45.4797, 13.571

Charges guide

Per person	€ 3,50 - € 8,40
pitch incl. electricity	€ 7,20 - € 18,20
For stays less than 3 nights in high season add 10%.	

243

Umag

Camping Stella Maris

Savudrijska cesta bb, HR-52470 Umag (Istria) T: **052 710 900**. E: **camp.stella.maris@istraturist.hr**

alanrogers.com/CR6712

This extremely large, sprawling site of 4.5 hectares is split by the Umag - Savudrija road. The camping site is to the east and reception and the amazing Sol Stella Maris leisure complex, where the Croatian open tennis tournament is held (amongst other competitions), is to the west. Located some 2 km. from the centre of Umag, the site comprises some 575 pitches of which 60 are seasonal and 20 are for tour operators. They are arranged in rows on gently sloping ground, some are shaded. Campers select their pitches all of which have 10A electricity. Many improvements over the last few years have made a huge impact on the standard of camping here.

Facilities

Three sanitary blocks of a very high standard. Hot water throughout. Excellent facilities for disabled visitors. Large supermarket. Huge range of restaurants, bars and snack bars. International Tennis centre. Watersports. Fishing (permit from Umag). Entertainment programme for children. Communal barbecue areas. Excursions organised. Off site: Land train every 15 minutes into Umag. Local bus service to coastal towns. Golf 1 km. Riding 0.5 km.

Open: 25 April - 4 October.

Directions

Site is 2.5 km. north of Umag. On entering Umag look for signs on main coast road to all campsites and follow Stella Maris signs. GPS: 45.45003, 13.51994

Charges guide

Per unit incl. 2 persons	
and electricity	€ 10,10 - € 30,00
extra person	€ 2,00 - € 7,00

For stays less than 3 nights in high season add 10%.

Umag

Camping Finida

Finida bb, HR-52470 Umag (Istria) T: **052 725 950**. E: **camp.finida@istraturist.hr**

alanrogers.com/CR6714

Finida is part of the Istraturist group and is a contrast to other sites in the area in that it is small and unassuming with a rustic Croatian feel on just 3.3 hectares. Many improvements have been made over the last few years. The beach runs the length of the site. It is heavily wooded affording abundant shade. Large motorcaravans will be tested in reaching some areas of the site due to narrow roads and leaning trees. There are 285 marked pitches (90-100 sq.m), all with 10A electricity, 103 also have water and TV connection. The lack of a swimming pool is not a problem as the site is alongside the sea.

Facilities

Three new toilet blocks contain mostly British style WCs and a few Turkish style with all modern facilities. Facilities for disabled campers. Washing machines. Motorcaravan service point (a bit tight to drive onto). Small but well stocked supermarket. Bar, snack bar and restaurant. Minigolf. Fishing (permit). Boats may be moored off the beach. Pedalos. Bicycle hire. Communal barbecue areas. Off site: Five buses per day into Umag and Novigrad. Golf 10 km. Riding 3 km.

Open: 25 April - 4 October.

Directions

Site is on the right off the Umag - Norigrad, 4 km. south of Umag. GPS: 45.39263, 13.54196

Charges guide

Per unit incl. 2 persons	
and electricity	€ 14,20 - € 30,00
extra person	€ 3,50 - € 7,00
child (5-11 yrs)	€ 2,00 - € 4,20
dog	€ 2,00 - € 3,50

Vrsar

Naturist Park Koversada

Koversada, HR-52450 Vrsar (Istria) T: **052 441 378**. E: **koversada-camp@maistra.hr**
alanrogers.com/CR6729

According to history, the first naturist on Koversada was the famous adventurer Casanova. Today Koversada is an enclosed holiday park for naturists with bungalows, 1,700 pitches (all with electricity), a shopping centre and its own island. The main attraction of this site is the Koversada island, connected to the mainland by a small bridge. It is only suitable for tents, but has a restaurant and two toilet blocks. Between the island and the mainland is an enclosed, shallow section of water for swimming and, on the other side of the bridge, an area for mooring small boats. The pitches are of average size on grass and gravel ground and slightly sloping. Pitches on the mainland are numbered and partly terraced under mature pine and olive trees. Pitching on the island is haphazard, but there is also shade from mature trees. The bottom row of pitches on the mainland has views over the island and the sea. The site is surrounded by a long beach, part sand, part paved.

Facilities

Seventeen toilet blocks provide British and Turkish style toilets, washbasins and controllable hot showers. Child-size toilets and basins. Family bathroom (free). Facilities for disabled visitors. Laundry service. Supermarket. Kiosks with newspapers and tobacco. Several bars and restaurants. Tennis. Minigolf. Boats, surf boards, canoes and kayaks for hire. Paragliding. Club for children. Live music. Internet access in reception. Off site: Riding 2 km.

Open: 25 April - 3 October.

Directions

Site is just south from Vrsar. From Vrsar, follow site signs. GPS: 45.14288, 13.60527

Charges guide

Per person	€ 5,00 - € 7,00
child (5-18 yrs)	free - € 5,25
pitch	€ 7,00 - € 18,00
dog	€ 3,10 - € 5,50

Naturist park Koversada *Vrsar*

Istria — Green Mediterranean. CROATIA

New seaside lots! Children's clubs and playgrounds!
ONLINE BOOKING

A Mediterranean paradise in a superb natural setting; the gentle climate and clean seas have made this a favourite summer holiday destination for many generations of naturists.

tel: +385 (0)52 800 200 / fax:800 215 / koversada-camp@maistra.hr

www.CampingVrsar.com

Vrsar

Camping Porto Sole

Petalon 1, HR-52450 Vrsar (Istria) T: **052 426 500**. E: **petalon-portosole@maistra.hr**
alanrogers.com/CR6725

Located near the pretty town of Vrsar and its charming marina, Porto Sole is a large campsite with 800 pitches and is part of the Maistra Group. The pitches vary; some are in the open with semi shade and are fairly flat, others are under a heavy canopy of pines on undulating land. There is some terracing near the small number of water frontage pitches. The site could be described as almost a clover leaf shape with one area for rental accommodation and natural woods, another for sporting facilities and the other two for pitches. There is a large water frontage and two tiny bays provide delightful sheltered rocky swimming areas. In peak season the site is buzzing with activity and the hub of the site is the pools, disco and shopping arcade area where there is also a pub and both formal and informal eating areas. The food available is varied but simple with a tiny terrace restaurant by the water.

Facilities

Five completely renovated toilet blocks are clean and well maintained. The low number of showers (common on Croatian sites) results in queues. Facilities for disabled visitors and children. Laundry. Large well stocked supermarket (1/5-15/9). Small shopping centre. Pub. Pizzeria. Formal and informal restaurants. Swimming pools (1/5-29/9). Play area. Tennis. Minigolf. Massage. Disco. Entertainment in season. Miniclub. Scuba-diving courses. Off site: Marina, sailing 1 km. Vrsar 2 km. Riding 3 km.

Open: 25 April - 3 October.

Directions

Follow signs towards Vrsar and take turn for Koversada, then follow campsite signs. GPS: 45.142117, 13.602267

Charges guide

Per person	€ 5,00 - € 7,40
child (5-12 yrs)	free - € 4,30
pitch	€ 7,50 - € 23,50
dog	€ 3,10 - € 6,50

Vrsar
Camping Valkanela
Valkanela, HR-52450 Vrsar (Istria) T: **052 445 216**. E: **valkanela@maistra.hr**
alanrogers.com/CR6727

Camping Valkanela is located in a beautiful green bay, right on the Adriatic Sea, between the villages of Vrsar and Funtana. It offers 1,300 pitches, all with 10A electricity. Pitches near the beach are numbered, have shade from mature trees and are slightly sloping towards the sea. Those towards the back of the site are on open fields without much shade and are not marked or numbered. Unfortunately the number of pitches has increased dramatically over the years, many are occupied by seasonal campers and statics of every description, and these parts of the site are not very attractive. Most numbered pitches have water points close by, but the back pitches have to go to the toilet blocks for water. Access roads are gravel. For those who like activity, Valkanela has four gravel tennis courts, beach volleyball and opportunities for diving, water skiing and boat rental. There is a little marina for mooring small boats and a long rock and pebble private beach, with some grass lawns for sunbathing. It is a short stroll to the surrounding villages with their bars, restaurants and shops. There may be some noise nuisance from the disco outside the entrance and during high season the site can become very crowded.

Facilities
Fifteen toilet blocks of varying styles and ages provide toilets, open style washbasins and controllable hot showers. Child-size toilets, basins and showers. Bathroom (free). Facilities for disabled visitors. Laundry facilities. Two supermarkets. Souvenir shops. Newspaper kiosk. Bars and restaurants with dance floor and stage. Pâtisserie. Tennis. Minigolf. Fishing (with permit). Bicycle hire. Games room. Marina with boat launching. Boat and pedalo hire. Disco near entrance. Daily entertainment programme for children up to 12 yrs. Excursions organised. Off site: Riding 2 km.

Open: 25 April - 3 October.

Directions
Site is 2 km. north of Vrsar. Follow campsite signs from Vrsar. GPS: 45.16522, 13.60723

Charges guide
Per person	€ 4,50 - € 7,00
child (5-18 yrs)	free - € 5,30
pitch incl. electricity	€ 5,50 - € 18,50
dog	€ 2,50 - € 6,00

246
Check real time availability and at-the-gate prices...
www.alanrogers.com

Vrsar

Camping Orsera

Sv. Martin 2/1, HR-52450 Vrsar (Istria) T: **052 465 010**. E: **camping@valamar.com**
alanrogers.com/CR6728

Part of the Camping on the Adriatic group, this site is very close to the fishing port of Vrsar, and there is direct access from the site. This is a 30-hectare site with 833 pitches of which 593 are available to touring units. Marked and numbered, the pitches vary in size with 90 sq.m. being the average. The sand and grass ground slopes towards the sea and there is some terracing. Ample shade is provided by mature pines and oak trees. Over 200 pitches have 16A electricity and water and 60 pitches also have waste water drainage. The views of the many small islands from the site are stunning.

Facilities

Many of the toilet blocks have been renovated and one completely new block provides very good facilities. Mainly British style WCs, washbasins and showers, mostly with hot water. Some have facilities for disabled campers. Facilities for babies and children. Laundry. Supermarket (1/5-15/9). Bar/restaurant (1/5-15/9). Sports centre. Cinema. Bicycle hire. Fishing. Watersports (no jet skis). Gas barbecues only. Off site: Golf 7 km. Riding 3 km. Excursions. Shops in Vrsar.

Open: 1 April - 8 October.

Directions

Site is on the main Porec (7 km) - Vrsar (1 km) road, well signed. GPS: 45.15548, 13.61032

Charges guide

Per person	€ 3,45 - € 6,15
child (4-10 yrs)	free - € 4,50
pitch incl. electricity	€ 5,75 - € 13,65
incl. water	€ 8,55 - € 14,65

Prices for pitches by the sea are higher.

Zagreb

Motel Plitvice – Autokamp

Lucko Bb, HR-10250 Zagreb (Central) T: **016 530 444**. E: **motel@motel-plitvice.hr**
alanrogers.com/CR6600

This is a typical transit site or possibly a site for a visit to the Croatian capital. As they put it themselves, this is the only campsite around Zagreb. Nothing special, the logistically efficient location (on the motorway) fortunately does not stand in the way of a normal night's rest, as the site is far enough from the road to reduce noise to acceptable levels. The pitches are of average size and have electricity connections, the toilet building is fairly old but acceptable. Despite the name, this site has nothing to do with the Plitvice Lakes National Park that is roughly 150 km. south from here.

Facilities

Shop, restaurants and bars in the Motel facilities connected to the site. Off site: Zagreb.

Open: 1 May - 30 September.

Directions

Motel Plitvice is located above and on both sides of motorway 1 circling Zagreb, just southwest of the capital between the junctions with motorway 12 to Karlovac (E65) and with National Road 4 (E70) to Ljubljana, Slovenia. Site is signed.
GPS: 45.77437, 15.87833

Charges guide

Per person	€ 5,00
pitch incl. electricity	€ 22,50

Zivogosce

Kamp Dole

Zivogosce bb, HR-21331 Zivogosce (Dalmatia) T: **021 628 749**
alanrogers.com/CR6870

Camping Dole is a basic site in southern Croatia, close to the beautiful island of Hvar. It has 500 pitches, of which 400 are for tourers, the other pitches taken by Czech tour operators. The beachside pitches are numbered and marked, the remainder are used informally and are mostly in the shade of mature trees. There are great views of the sea as the site is raised seven metres above the pebble beach which stretches for over a kilometre in front of the site. The pitches at the back have beautiful views of the impressive mountains. Close to reception is a welcoming bar with terrace for drinks. There is no restaurant on site but two restaurants are nearby.

Facilities

Four toilet blocks, three of which have been renovated to a reasonable level and offer high quality British WCs, washbasins and controllable, hot showers (free). The fourth block should now be completed. Fridge box hire. Several kiosks and supermarket. Bar. Jet ski hire. Paragliding. Pedalo and canoe hire. Full entertainment programme in high season. Excursions to Korcula. Barbecues only in communal area. Off site: Boat launching 200 m. Paintball next to site.

Open: 1 May - 30 September.

Directions

From Split take no. 8 coast road south towards Dubrovnik. Site is on the right in Zivogosce, 12 km. southeast of Makarska, and signed both 4 km. before village and in village. GPS: 43.170833, 17.196333

Charges guide

Per person	Kn 21,00 - 32,00
child (5-12 yrs)	Kn 12,50 - 20,00
pitch	Kn 60,00 - 140,00
electricity	Kn 22,00

Check real time availability and at-the-gate prices...
www.alanrogers.com

Accommodation

Over recent years many of the campsites featured in this guide have added large numbers of high quality mobile homes and chalets. Many site owners believe that some former caravanners and motorcaravanners have been enticed by the extra comfort they can now provide, and that maybe this is the ideal solution to combine the freedom of camping with all the comforts of home.

Quality is consistently high and, although the exact size and inventory may vary from site to site, if you choose any of the sites detailed here, you can be sure that you're staying in some of the best quality and best value mobile homes available.

Home comforts are provided and typically these include a fridge with freezer compartment, gas hob, proper shower – often a microwave and radio/cassette hi-fi too but do check for details. All mobile homes and chalets come fully equipped with a good range of kitchen utensils, pots and pans, crockery, cutlery and outdoor furniture. Some even have an attractive wooden sundeck or paved terrace – a perfect spot for outdoors eating or relaxing with a book and watching the world go by.

Regardless of model, colourful soft furnishings are the norm and a generally breezy décor helps to provide a real holiday feel.

Although some sites may have a large number of different accommodation types, we have restricted our choice to one or two of the most popular accommodation units (either mobile homes or chalets) for each of the sites listed.

The mobile homes here will be of modern design, and recent innovations, for example, often include pitched roofs which substantially improve their appearance.

Design will invariably include clever use of space and fittings/furniture to provide for comfortable holidays – usually light and airy, with big windows and patio-style doors, fully equipped kitchen areas, a shower room with shower, washbasin and WC, cleverly designed bedrooms and a comfortable lounge/dining area (often incorporating a sofa bed).

In general, modern campsite chalets incorporate all the best features of mobile homes in a more traditional structure, sometimes with the advantage of an upper mezzanine floor for an additional bedroom.

Our selected campsites offer a massive range of different types of mobile home and chalet, and it would be impractical to inspect every single accommodation unit. Our selection criteria, therefore, primarily takes account of the quality standards of the campsite itself.

However, there are a couple of important ground rules:

- FEATURED MOBILE HOMES MUST BE NO MORE THAN 5 YEARS OLD

- CHALETS NO MORE THAN 10 YEARS OLD

- ALL LISTED ACCOMMODATION MUST, OF COURSE, FULLY CONFORM WITH ALL APPLICABLE LOCAL, NATIONAL AND EUROPEAN SAFETY LEGISLATION.

For each campsite we given details of the type, or types, of accommodation available to rent, but these details are necessarily quite brief. Sometimes internal layouts can differ quite substantially, particularly with regard to sleeping arrangements, where these include the flexible provision for 'extra persons' on sofa beds located in the living area. These arrangements may vary from accommodation to accommodation, and if you're planning a holiday which includes more people than are catered for by the main bedrooms you should check exactly how the extra sleeping arrangements are to be provided!

Charges

An indication of the tariff for each type of accommodation featured is also included, indicating the variance between the low and high season tariffs. However, given that many campsites have a large and often complex range of pricing options, incorporating special deals and various discounts, the charges we mention should be taken to be just an indication. We strongly recommend therefore that you confirm the actual cost when making a booking.

We also strongly recommend that you check with the campsite, when booking, what (if anything) will be provided by way of bed linen, blankets, pillows etc. Again, in our experience, this can vary widely from site to site.

On every campsite a fully refundable deposit (usually between 150 and 300 euros) is payable on arrival. There may also be an optional cleaning service for which a further charge is made. Other options may include sheet hire (typically 30 euros per unit) or baby pack hire (cot and high chair).

IT62485 Camping Conca d'Oro

▶ see report page 22

Via 42 Martiri 26, I-28835 Feriolo di Baveno

AR1 – MAXICARAVAN ECONOMY – Mobile Home

Sleeping: 3 bedrooms, sleeps 4: 1 double, 2 singles, sofa bed, pillows and blankets provided

Living: living/kitchen area, heating, TV, air conditioning, shower, WC

Eating: fitted kitchen with hobs, coffee maker, fridge

Outside: table & chairs

Pets: not accepted

AR2 – MAXICARAVAN TOP – Mobile Home

Sleeping: 3 bedrooms, sleeps 5: 1 double, 2 singles, sofa bed, pillows and blankets provided

Living: living/kitchen area, heating, TV, air conditioning, shower, WC

Eating: fitted kitchen with hobs, coffee maker, fridge

Outside: table & chairs

Pets: not accepted

Other (AR1 and AR2): bed linen, cot, highchair to hire

Open: 26 March - 27 September		
Weekly Charge	**AR1**	**AR2**
Low Season *(from)*	€ 385	€ 420
High Season *(from)*	€ 735	€ 875

IT62440 Camping Solcio

▶ see report page 25

Via al Campeggio, I-28040 Solcio di Lesa

AR1 – MAXICARAVAN – Mobile Home

Sleeping: 2 bedrooms, sleeps 5: 1 double, 2 singles, sofa bed

Living: living/kitchen area, air conditioning, shower, seperate WC

Eating: fitted kitchen with fridge

Outside: table & chairs, parasol

Pets: not accepted

Open: 8 March - 17 October	
Weekly Charge	**AR1**
Low Season *(from)*	€ 385
High Season *(from)*	€ 658

IT64190 Camping River

▶ see report page 30

Localitá Armezzone, I-19031 Ameglia

AR1 – BUNGALOW – Bungalow

Sleeping: 2 bedrooms, sleeps 5: 1 double, 3 singles, sofa bed, pillows and blankets provided

Living: heating, shower, WC

Eating: fitted kitchen with fridge, freezer

Outside: table & chairs, barbecue

Pets: accepted (with supplement)

AR2 – CH 4+2 A CN 6 – Mobile Home

Sleeping: 2 bedrooms, sleeps 6: 1 double, 4 singles, sofa bed, pillows and blankets provided

Living: living/kitchen area, heating, air conditioning, shower, WC, seperate WC

Eating: fitted kitchen with fridge, freezer

Outside: table & chairs, parasol, barbecue

Pets: accepted (with supplement)

Other (AR1 and AR2): cot to hire

Open: 27 March - 3 October		
Weekly Charge	**AR1**	**AR2**
Low Season *(from)*	€ 245	€ 399
High Season *(from)*	€ 680	€ 1130

IT64030 Camping Baciccia

Via Torino 19, I-17023 Ceriale

▶ see report page 32

AR1 – 2 PERSONS BUNGALOW CHALET – Chalet	AR2 – 5 PERSONS HOLIDAY HOME – Mobile Home
Sleeping: 1 bedroom, sleeps 2: 1 double, pillows and blankets provided	**Sleeping:** 2 bedrooms, sleeps 5: 1 double, 1 single, bunk bed, pillows and blankets provided
Living: living/kitchen area, heating, TV, shower, WC	**Living:** living/kitchen area, heating, TV, air conditioning, shower, WC, seperate WC
Eating: fitted kitchen with hobs, coffee maker, fridge, freezer	**Eating:** fitted kitchen with hobs, microwave, coffee maker, fridge, freezer
Outside: table & chairs	**Outside:** table & chairs, 2 sun loungers
Pets: not accepted	**Pets:** not accepted

Other (AR1 and AR2): bed linen, cot, highchair to hire

Open: 15 March - 3 November		
Weekly Charge	**AR1**	**AR2**
Low Season *(from)*	€ 329	€ 413
High Season *(from)*	€ 619	€ 924

IT64120 Villaggio Camping Valdeiva

Localitá Ronco, I-19013 Deiva Marina

▶ see report page 33

AR1 – BUNGALOW – Bungalow	AR2 – CHALET – Chalet
Sleeping: 1 bedroom, sleeps 4: 1 double, bunk bed, sofa bed, pillows and blankets provided	**Sleeping:** 2 bedrooms, sleeps 4: 2 doubles, pillows and blankets provided
Living: living/kitchen area, heating, TV, shower, WC	**Living:** living/kitchen area, heating, TV, shower, WC
Eating: fitted kitchen with hobs, oven, fridge, freezer	**Eating:** fitted kitchen with hobs, microwave, fridge
Outside: table & chairs, 2 sun loungers	**Outside:** table & chairs, 2 sun loungers
Pets: not accepted	**Pets:** not accepted

Other (AR1 and AR2): bed linen, cot, highchair to hire

Open: 10 February - 5 November		
Weekly Charge	**AR1**	**AR2**
Low Season *(from)*	€ 350	€ 300
High Season *(from)*	€ 760	€ 740

IT64010 Camping Villaggio dei Fiori

Via Tiro a Volo 3, I-18038 San Remo

▶ see report page 35

AR1 – TYPE A/B – Bungalow	AR2 – TYPE C/D – Mobile Home
Sleeping: 2 bedrooms, sleeps 4: 1 double, 2 singles, sofa bed, pillows and blankets provided	**Sleeping:** 2 bedrooms, sleeps 4: 1 double, 2 singles, bunk bed, pillows and blankets provided
Living: living/kitchen area, heating, TV, air conditioning, shower, WC	**Living:** living/kitchen area, heating, TV, air conditioning, shower, WC
Eating: fitted kitchen with hobs, fridge	**Eating:** fitted kitchen with hobs, microwave, fridge, freezer
Outside: table & chairs	**Outside:** table & chairs
Pets: not accepted	**Pets:** not accepted

Other (AR1 and AR2): bed linen, cot, highchair to hire

Open: All year		
Weekly Charge	**AR1**	**AR2**
Low Season *(from)*	€ 320	€ 650
High Season *(from)*	€ 707	€ 910

IT63600 La Rocca Camp

▶ see report page 44

Localita San Pietro, I-37011 Bardolino

AR1 – CHARME 24 M² – Mobile Home

Sleeping: 2 bedrooms, sleeps 6: 1 double, 2 singles, bunk bed, sofa bed, pillows and blankets provided

Living: living/kitchen area, heating, air conditioning, shower, WC, seperate WC

Eating: fitted kitchen with hobs, coffee maker, fridge, freezer

Outside: table & chairs, parasol, 2 sun loungers, barbecue

Pets: accepted

AR2 – DELUXE 33 M² – Mobile Home

Sleeping: 2 bedrooms, sleeps 4: 1 double, 2 singles, sofa bed, pillows and blankets provided

Living: living/kitchen area, heating, TV, air conditioning, shower, WC, seperate WC

Eating: fitted kitchen with hobs, microwave, coffee maker, fridge, freezer

Outside: table & chairs, parasol, 2 sun loungers, barbecue

Pets: not accepted

Open: 26 March - 4 October

Weekly Charge	AR1	AR2
Low Season (from)	€ 455	€ 525
High Season (from)	€ 973	€ 1113

IT62550 Camping La Quercia

▶ see report page 50

I-37017 Lazise sul Garda

AR1 – MAXICARAVAN 5 LETTI – Mobile Home

Sleeping: 1 bedroom, sleeps 4: 1 double, 2 singles, pillows and blankets provided

Living: living/kitchen area, heating, shower, WC

Eating: fitted kitchen with hobs, fridge

Outside: table & chairs

Pets: not accepted

AR2 – BUNGALOW 5 LETTI – Bungalow

Sleeping: 2 bedrooms, sleeps 5: 5 singles, pillows and blankets provided

Living: living/kitchen area, shower, WC

Eating: fitted kitchen with hobs, fridge

Outside: table & chairs

Pets: not accepted

Open: 28 March - 4 October

Weekly Charge	AR1	AR2
Low Season (from)	€ 323	€ 280
High Season (from)	€ 711	€ 541

These images are general pictures of the region

IT62600 Camping Europa Silvella

▶ see report page 61

Via Silvella 10, I-25010 San Felice del Benaco

AR1 – TULIPANO – Chalet

Sleeping: 2 bedrooms, sleeps 5: 2 doubles, sofa bed, pillows and blankets provided

Living: living/kitchen area, shower

Eating: fitted kitchen with hobs, fridge

Outside: table & chairs

Pets: accepted (with supplement)

AR2 – MAGNOLIA – Mobile Home

Sleeping: 2 bedrooms, sleeps 5: 2 doubles, 1 single, pillows and blankets provided

Living: living/kitchen area, TV, air conditioning, shower, seperate WC

Eating: fitted kitchen with hobs, fridge

Outside: table & chairs, barbecue

Pets: accepted (with supplement)

Open: 29 April - 19 September

Weekly Charge	AR1	AR2
Low Season (from)	€ 259	€ 371
High Season (from)	€ 805	€ 1106

These images are general pictures of the region

IT62260 Camping Punta Lago

▶ see report page 66

Via Lungo Lago 42, I-38050 Calceranica al Lago

AR1 – VENEZIA – Mobile Home

Sleeping: 2 bedrooms, sleeps 6: 2 doubles, 2 singles, pillows and blankets provided

Living: living/kitchen area, heating, TV, air conditioning, shower, WC

Eating: fitted kitchen with hobs, microwave, fridge

Outside: table & chairs

Pets: accepted (with supplement)

AR2 – CAPRI – Mobile Home

Sleeping: 2 bedrooms, sleeps 6: 2 doubles, 2 singles, pillows and blankets provided

Living: living/kitchen area, heating, TV, air conditioning, shower, WC

Eating: fitted kitchen with hobs, microwave, fridge

Outside: table & chairs

Pets: accepted (with supplement)

Open: 25 April - 26 September		
Weekly Charge	**AR1**	**AR2**
Low Season *(from)*	€ 280	€ 350
High Season *(from)*	€ 630	€ 700

These images are general pictures of the region

IT62120 Camping Latsch an der Etsch

▶ see report page 69

Reichstrasse 4, Via Nazionale 4, I-39021 Laces-Latsch

AR1 – CHALET-MOBILHEIM – Mobile Home

Sleeping: 2 bedrooms, sleeps 5: 1 double, 2 singles, sofa bed

Living: living/kitchen area, heating, TV, shower, WC

Eating: fitted kitchen with hobs, fridge

Outside: table & chairs, parasol

Pets: accepted

Other (AR1): bed linen to hire

Open: All year	
Weekly Charge	**AR1**
Low Season *(from)*	€ 406
High Season *(from)*	€ 504

IT62100 Camping-Park Steiner

▶ see report page 69

J.F. Kennedy Strasse 32, I-39055 Laives - Leifers (Bolzano)

AR1 – TYPE A – Bungalow

Sleeping: 2 bedrooms, sleeps 4: 1 double, 2 singles, pillows and blankets provided

Living: living/kitchen area, heating, WC

Outside: table & chairs

Pets: accepted

Open: 21 March - 6 November	
Weekly Charge	**AR1**
Low Season *(from)*	€ 294
High Season *(from)*	€ 364

IT62290 Camping Lévico

see report page 70

Localitá Pleina 5, I-38056 Lévico Terme

AR1 – CHALET LEVICO – Chalet

Sleeping: 2 bedrooms, sleeps 5: 1 double, 3 singles

Living: living/kitchen area, heating, TV, air conditioning, shower, WC

Eating: fitted kitchen with hobs, microwave, coffee maker, fridge

Outside: table & chairs

Pets: not accepted

AR2 – MOBILE HOME LEVICO – Mobile Home

Sleeping: 2 bedrooms, sleeps 5: 1 double, 2 singles, sofa bed

Living: living/kitchen area, heating, TV, air conditioning, shower, WC

Eating: fitted kitchen with hobs, microwave, coffee maker, fridge

Outside: table & chairs

Pets: accepted (with supplement)

Other (AR1 and AR2): bed linen, cot, highchair to hire

Open: 1 April - 10 October		
Weekly Charge	AR1	AR2
Low Season *(from)*	€ 504	€ 392
High Season *(from)*	€ 840	€ 728

IT62040 Camping Seiser Alm

see report page 78

Saint Konstantin 16, I-39050 Völs am Schlern

AR1 – HOBBY LANDHAUS 2006 – Mobile Home

Sleeping: 1 bedroom, sleeps 6: 6 singles, pillows and blankets provided

Living: living/kitchen area, heating, TV, WC

Eating: fitted kitchen with hobs, microwave, dishwasher, coffee maker, fridge

Outside: table & chairs, parasol, 2 sun loungers

Pets: accepted (with supplement)

AR2 – TYPE A OR B – Appartment

Sleeping: 1 bedroom, sleeps 3: 2 singles, sofa bed, pillows and blankets provided

Living: living/kitchen area, heating, TV, shower, WC

Eating: fitted kitchen with hobs, dishwasher, coffee maker, fridge

Outside: table & chairs, 2 sun loungers

Pets: accepted (with supplement)

Other (AR1 and AR2): bed linen to hire

Open: 20 December - 2 November		
Weekly Charge	AR1	AR2
Low Season *(from)*	€ 350	€ 455
High Season *(from)*	€ 525	€ 560

IT60020 Camping Aquileia

see report page 80

Via Gemina,10, I-33051 Aquileia

AR1 – B3/B1 – Bungalow

Sleeping: 1 bedroom, sleeps 4: 4 singles, bunk bed, pillows and blankets provided

Living: living/kitchen area, shower, WC

Eating: fitted kitchen with hobs, oven, coffee maker, fridge, freezer

Outside: table & chairs, parasol

Pets: accepted (with supplement)

AR2 – MAXICARAVAN VENEZIA /MAUI – Mobile Home

Sleeping: 2 bedrooms, sleeps 4: 1 double, 2 singles, sofa bed, pillows and blankets provided

Living: living/kitchen area, heating, air conditioning, shower, WC

Eating: fitted kitchen with hobs, oven, coffee maker, fridge, freezer

Outside: table & chairs, parasol

Pets: accepted (with supplement)

Other (AR1 and AR2): highchair to hire

Open: 25 April - 15 September		
Weekly Charge	AR1	AR2
Low Season *(from)*	€ 420	€ 455
High Season *(from)*	€ 490	€ 525

IT60065 Camping Tenuta Primero
Via Monfalcone, 14, I-34073 Grado

see report page 82

AR1 – BUNGALOW A – Bungalow	AR2 – BUNGALOW B – Bungalow
Sleeping: 2 bedrooms, sleeps 5: 3 singles, bunk bed, pillows and blankets provided	**Sleeping:** 3 bedrooms, sleeps 5: 1 double, 4 singles, pillows and blankets provided
Living: living/kitchen area, TV, shower, WC	**Living:** living/kitchen area, TV, shower, WC
Eating: fitted kitchen with hobs, coffee maker, fridge, freezer	**Eating:** fitted kitchen with hobs, coffee maker, fridge, freezer
Outside: table & chairs, 1 sun lounger	**Outside:** table & chairs, 1 sun lounger
Pets: not accepted	**Pets:** not accepted

Other (AR1 and AR2): bed linen, cot, highchair to hire

Open: 1 April - 3 October		
Weekly Charge	**AR1**	**AR2**
Low Season *(from)*	€ 525	€ 665
High Season *(from)*	€ 980	€ 1190

IT60050 Villaggio Turistico Camping Europa
Via Monfalcone 12, I-34073 Grado

see report page 83

AR1 – CHALET – Chalet	AR2 – MAXICARAVAN – Mobile Home
Sleeping: 2 bedrooms, sleeps 6: 1 double, 2 singles, sofa bed, pillows and blankets provided	**Sleeping:** 2 bedrooms, sleeps 6: 1 double, 2 singles, sofa bed, pillows and blankets provided
Living: living/kitchen area, heating, air conditioning, shower, WC	**Living:** living/kitchen area, heating, air conditioning, shower, WC
Eating: fitted kitchen with hobs, fridge	**Eating:** fitted kitchen with hobs, fridge
Outside: table & chairs, 2 sun loungers	**Outside:** table & chairs, 2 sun loungers
Pets: not accepted	**Pets:** not accepted

Other (AR1 and AR2): cot, highchair to hire

Open: 24 April - 26 September		
Weekly Charge	**AR1**	**AR2**
Low Season *(from)*	€ 490	€ 420
High Season *(from)*	€ 945	€ 875

IT60080 Camping Sabbiadoro
Via Sabbiadoro 8, I-33054 Lignano Sabbiadoro

see report page 84

AR1 – TYPE H – Mobile Home	AR2 – TYPE F – Mobile Home
Sleeping: 1 bedroom, sleeps 2: 2 doubles, 1 single, pillows and blankets provided	**Sleeping:** 2 bedrooms, sleeps 5: 1 double, 3 singles, pillows and blankets provided
Living: living/kitchen area, shower, WC	**Living:** living/kitchen area, heating, air conditioning, shower, WC
Eating: fitted kitchen with hobs, fridge	**Eating:** fitted kitchen with hobs, fridge
Outside: table & chairs, parasol	**Outside:** table & chairs, parasol
Pets: not accepted	**Pets:** not accepted

Open: 6 February - 2 November		
Weekly Charge	**AR1**	**AR2**
Low Season *(from)*	€ 336	€ 651
High Season *(from)*	€ 504	€ 945

IT60100 Camping Capalonga

▶ see report page 88

Via della Laguna 16, I-30020 Bibione-Pineda

AR1 – GOLDEN SUITE – Mobile Home

Sleeping: 2 bedrooms, sleeps 6: 1 double, bunk bed, pillows and blankets provided

Living: living/kitchen area, heating, air conditioning, shower, WC

Eating: fitted kitchen with hobs, microwave, dishwasher, fridge, freezer

Outside: table & chairs, parasol, 2 sun loungers, barbecue

Pets: not accepted

AR2 – SUITE CARAVAN DELUXE – Mobile Home

Sleeping: 2 bedrooms, sleeps 6: 1 double, bunk bed, pillows and blankets provided

Living: living/kitchen area, heating, air conditioning, shower, WC

Eating: fitted kitchen with hobs, microwave, dishwasher, fridge, freezer

Outside: table & chairs, parasol, 2 sun loungers, barbecue

Pets: not accepted

Other (AR1 and AR2): bed linen, cot, highchair to hire

Open: 23 April - 26 September

Weekly Charge	AR1	AR2
Low Season *(from)*	€ 483	€ 546
High Season *(from)*	€ 889	€ 994

IT60140 Villaggio Turistico Internazionale

▶ see report page 90

Via Colonie 2, I-30020 Bibione

AR1 – ANNA PLUS – Bungalow

Sleeping: 2 bedrooms, sleeps 6: 4 singles, sofa bed, pillows and blankets provided

Living: living/kitchen area, heating, TV, air conditioning, shower, WC

Eating: fitted kitchen with hobs, microwave, coffee maker, fridge, freezer

Outside: table & chairs, parasol, 2 sun loungers

Pets: accepted (with supplement)

AR2 – MAXICARAVAN PLUS – Mobile Home

Sleeping: 2 bedrooms, sleeps 6: 1 double, 2 singles, sofa bed, pillows and blankets provided

Living: living/kitchen area, heating, TV, air conditioning, shower, WC

Eating: fitted kitchen with hobs, microwave, coffee maker, fridge, freezer

Outside: table & chairs, parasol, 2 sun loungers

Pets: accepted (with supplement)

Other (AR1 and AR2): bed linen, cot, highchair to hire

Open: 10 April - 26 September

Weekly Charge	AR1	AR2
Low Season *(from)*	€ 525	€ 455
High Season *(from)*	€ 1456	€ 1155

IT60030 Centro Vacanze Pra'Delle Torri

▶ see report page 93

P.O. Box 176, I-30021 Caorle

AR1 – APARTMENT COMFORT – Apartment

Sleeping: 2 bedrooms, sleeps 4: 2 doubles, sofa bed, pillows and blankets provided

Living: living/kitchen area, heating, TV, air conditioning, shower, WC, seperate WC

Eating: fitted kitchen with hobs, oven, microwave, dishwasher, coffee maker, fridge, freezer

Pets: not accepted

AR2 – BUNGALOW DE LUXE – Bungalow

Sleeping: 1 bedroom, sleeps 4: 1 double, sofa bed, pillows and blankets provided

Living: living/kitchen area, heating, TV, air conditioning, shower, WC, seperate WC

Eating: fitted kitchen with hobs, microwave, coffee maker, fridge, freezer

Outside: table & chairs, 2 sun loungers

Pets: not accepted

Other (AR1 and AR2): cot, highchair to hire

Open: 27 March - 2 October

Weekly Charge	AR1	AR2
Low Season *(from)*	€ 700	€ 538
High Season *(from)*	€ 1652	€ 1372

IT60110 Camping San Francesco

▶ see report page 92

Porto Santa Margherita, I-30020 Caorle

AR1 – PINETA/BEACH – Mobile Home	AR2 – M50 – Chalet
Sleeping: 2 bedrooms, sleeps 5: 1 double, 2 singles, sofa bed, pillows and blankets provided	**Sleeping:** 2 bedrooms, sleeps 5: 4 singles, sofa bed, pillows and blankets provided
Living: living/kitchen area, heating, air conditioning, shower, WC	**Living:** living/kitchen area, heating, air conditioning, shower, WC
Eating: fitted kitchen with hobs, fridge, freezer	**Eating:** fitted kitchen with hobs, fridge, freezer
Outside: table & chairs, parasol	**Outside:** table & chairs, parasol
Pets: not accepted	**Pets:** not accepted

Other (AR1 and AR2): bed linen, cot, highchair to hire

Open: 24 April - 25 September

Weekly Charge	AR1	AR2
Low Season *(from)*	€ 322	€ 315
High Season *(from)*	€ 1057	€ 1008

IT60200 Camping Union Lido Vacanze

▶ see report page 96

Via Fausta 258, I-30013 Cavallino-Treporti

AR1 – CAMPING HOME PATIO – Mobile Home	AR2 – CAMPING HOME DESIGN – Mobile Home
Sleeping: 2 bedrooms, sleeps 7: 1 double, 2 singles, bunk bed, sofa bed, pillows and blankets provided	**Sleeping:** 2 bedrooms, sleeps 6: 1 double, 2 singles, sofa bed, pillows and blankets provided
Living: living/kitchen area, heating, TV, air conditioning, shower, seperate WC	**Living:** living/kitchen area, heating, TV, air conditioning, shower, seperate WC
Eating: fitted kitchen with hobs, microwave, dishwasher, fridge, freezer	**Eating:** fitted kitchen with hobs, microwave, dishwasher, fridge, freezer
Outside: table & chairs, 2 sun loungers	**Outside:** table & chairs, 2 sun loungers
Pets: not accepted	**Pets:** not accepted

Other (AR1 and AR2): bed linen, cot, highchair to hire

Open: 30 April - 26 September

Weekly Charge	AR1	AR2
Low Season *(from)*	€ 679	€ 665
High Season *(from)*	€ 1057	€ 1015

IT60220 Camping Village Portofelice

▶ see report page 103

Viale dei Fiori 15, I-30020 Eraclea Mare

AR1 – CHALET WILMA – Chalet	AR2 – MAXI CARAVAN – Mobile Home
Sleeping: 2 bedrooms, sleeps 6: 1 double, 2 singles, sofa bed, pillows and blankets provided	**Sleeping:** 2 bedrooms, sleeps 5: 1 double, 2 singles, sofa bed, pillows and blankets provided
Living: living/kitchen area, heating, TV, air conditioning, shower, WC	**Living:** living/kitchen area, TV, air conditioning, shower, WC
Eating: fitted kitchen with microwave, coffee maker, fridge, freezer	**Eating:** fitted kitchen with microwave, coffee maker, fridge, freezer
Outside: table & chairs, 2 sun loungers, barbecue	**Outside:** table & chairs, 2 sun loungers
Pets: not accepted	**Pets:** not accepted

Other (AR1 and AR2): bed linen, cot, highchair to hire

Open: 8 May - 15 September

Weekly Charge	AR1	AR2
Low Season *(from)*	€ 511	€ 281
High Season *(from)*	€ 1414	€ 1027

IT60410 Camping Village Europa

see report page 100

Via Fausta 332, I-30013 Cavallino-Treporti

AR1 – WILLERBY – Mobile Home

Sleeping: 2 bedrooms, sleeps 5: 1 double, 2 singles, sofa bed, pillows and blankets provided

Living: living/kitchen area, heating, air conditioning, shower, WC

Eating: fitted kitchen with hobs, oven, microwave

Outside: table & chairs, parasol

Pets: not accepted

AR2 – MAXI CARAVAN CHALET EUROPA – Chalet

Sleeping: 2 bedrooms, sleeps 6: 1 double, 2 singles, sofa bed, pillows and blankets provided

Living: living/kitchen area, heating, TV, air conditioning, shower, WC

Eating: fitted kitchen with hobs, oven, microwave, fridge

Outside: table & chairs, parasol

Pets: not accepted

Open: 4 April - 30 September

Weekly Charge	AR1	AR2
Low Season *(from)*	€ 287	€ 420
High Season *(from)*	€ 641	€ 713

These images are general pictures of the region

IT60470 Camping Scarpiland

see report page 101

Via A. Poerio 14, I-30010 Cavallino-Treporti

AR1 – PRESTIGE ELITE – Mobile Home

Sleeping: sleeps 7: 1 double, 3 singles, bunk bed, sofa bed, pillows and blankets provided

Living: living/kitchen area, heating, TV, air conditioning, shower, WC

Eating: fitted kitchen with hobs, microwave, coffee maker, fridge

Outside: table & chairs

Pets: not accepted

AR2 – CHALET GIALLI – Bungalow

Sleeping: sleeps 6: 1 double, 3 singles, bunk bed, pillows and blankets provided

Living: living/kitchen area, heating, TV, air conditioning, shower, WC

Eating: fitted kitchen with hobs, microwave, coffee maker, fridge

Outside: table & chairs

Pets: not accepted

Other (AR1 and AR2): bed linen, cot, highchair to hire

Open: 24 April - 18 September

Weekly Charge	AR1	AR2
Low Season *(from)*	€ 210	€ 210
High Season *(from)*	€ 511	€ 539

IT60530 Camping Fusina

see report page 104

Via Moranzani 79, I-30030 Fusina

AR1 – MAXICARAVAN CONCORDE – Mobile Home

Sleeping: 2 bedrooms, sleeps 6: 1 double, 2 singles, sofa bed, pillows and blankets provided

Living: living/kitchen area, heating, shower, WC

Eating: fitted kitchen with hobs, fridge, freezer

Outside: table & chairs

Pets: not accepted

Open: All year

Weekly Charge	AR1
Low Season *(from)*	€ 552
High Season *(from)*	€ 672

These images are general pictures of the region

IT60370 Camping Jesolo International

▶ see report page 106

Viale A. da Giussano, I-30016 Lido di Jesolo

AR1 – HOLIDAY HOME – Mobile Home

Sleeping: 2 bedrooms, sleeps 5: 2 doubles, 1 single, sofa bed, pillows and blankets provided

Living: living/kitchen area, heating, TV, air conditioning, shower, WC

Eating: fitted kitchen with hobs, oven, microwave, grill, dishwasher, coffee maker, fridge, freezer

Outside: table & chairs, parasol

Pets: not accepted

Other (AR1): bed linen, cot, highchair to hire

Open: 1 May - 30 September

Weekly Charge	AR1
Low Season *(from)*	€ 560
High Season *(from)*	contact site

IT60450 Camping Marina di Venezia

▶ see report page 108

Via Montello 6, I-30013 Punta Sabbioni

AR1 – DE LUXE – Bungalow

Sleeping: 2 bedrooms, sleeps 7: 1 double, bunk bed, sofa bed, pillows and blankets provided

Living: living/kitchen area, heating, TV, air conditioning, shower, WC

Eating: fitted kitchen with hobs, microwave, coffee maker, fridge, freezer

Outside: table & chairs

Pets: not accepted

AR2 – GREENHOUSE – Mobile Home

Sleeping: 2 bedrooms, sleeps 4: 1 double, 2 singles, pillows and blankets provided

Living: living/kitchen area, heating, TV, air conditioning, shower, WC

Eating: fitted kitchen with hobs, coffee maker, fridge, freezer

Outside: table & chairs

Pets: not accepted

Other (AR1 and AR2): bed linen, cot to hire

Open: 24 April - 30 October.

Weekly Charge	AR1	AR2
Low Season *(from)*	€ 529	€ 389
High Season *(from)*	€ 1120	€ 822

IT60560 Camping Miramare

▶ see report page 110

Via Barbarigo 103, I-30015 Sottomarina di Chioggia

AR1 – MAXICARAVAN – Mobile Home

Sleeping: 2 bedrooms, sleeps 5: 1 double, 2 singles, sofa bed, pillows and blankets provided

Living: living/kitchen area, heating, TV, air conditioning, shower, WC

Eating: fitted kitchen with hobs, fridge, freezer

Outside: table & chairs

Pets: not accepted

AR2 – CHALET – Mobile Home

Sleeping: 2 bedrooms, sleeps 5: 1 double, 2 singles, sofa bed, pillows and blankets provided

Living: living/kitchen area, heating, TV, air conditioning, shower, WC

Eating: fitted kitchen with hobs, fridge, freezer

Outside: table & chairs

Pets: not accepted

Other (AR1 and AR2): bed linen to hire

Open: 1 April - 20 September

Weekly Charge	AR1	AR2
Low Season *(from)*	€ 300	€ 335
High Season *(from)*	€ 846	€ 895

IT68040 Camping Village Eurcamping

 see report page 176

Lungomare Trieste Sud, I-64026 Roseto degli Abruzzi

AR1 – TRAMINER – Mobile Home	AR2 – SAUVIGNON BLANC – Mobile Home
Sleeping: 2 bedrooms, sleeps 4: 1 double, 2 singles, pillows and blankets provided	**Sleeping:** 2 bedrooms, sleeps 4: 1 double, 2 singles, pillows and blankets provided
Living: living/kitchen area, TV, air conditioning, shower, WC	**Living:** living/kitchen area, TV, air conditioning, shower, WC
Eating: fitted kitchen with hobs, coffee maker, fridge	**Eating:** fitted kitchen with hobs, coffee maker, fridge
Outside: table & chairs	**Outside:** table & chairs
Pets: not accepted	**Pets:** not accepted

Other (AR1 and AR2): bed linen to hire

Open: 1 April - 31 October

Weekly Charge	AR1	AR2
Low Season *(from)*	€ 324	€ 400
High Season *(from)*	€ 931	€ 1085

IT69160 Sporting Club Village & Camping

 see report page 196

Ctra Bocca Arena, I-91026 Mazara del Vallo

AR1 – MARINA 5+1 – Mobile Home	AR2 – MONO LINEAR 2 – Mobile Home
Sleeping: 2 bedrooms, sleeps 6: 1 double, 3 singles, bunk bed, pillows and blankets provided	**Sleeping:** 1 bedroom, sleeps 2: 2 singles, bunk bed, pillows and blankets provided
Living: living/kitchen area, TV, air conditioning, shower, WC	**Living:** living/kitchen area, air conditioning, shower, WC
Eating: fitted kitchen with hobs, fridge	**Eating:** fridge
Outside: table & chairs, parasol	**Outside:** table & chairs, parasol
Pets: not accepted	**Pets:** not accepted

Open: 1 April - 10 October

Weekly Charge	AR1	AR2
Low Season *(from)*	€ 336	€ 252
High Season *(from)*	€ 1183	€ 632

IT69190 Camping Scarabeo

 see report page 198

I-97017 San Croce Camerina

AR1 – MOBILE HOME – Mobile Home
Sleeping: 2 bedrooms, sleeps 4: 1 double, 2 singles
Living: living/kitchen area, air conditioning, WC
Eating: fitted kitchen with hobs, fridge
Outside: table & chairs, parasol
Pets: not accepted

Other (AR1): bed linen to hire

Open: All year

Weekly Charge	AR1
Low Season *(from)*	€ 315
High Season *(from)*	€ 805

IT69140 El Bahira Camping Village

see report page 199

Ctra da Makari - Localitá Salinella, I-91010 San Vito Lo Capo

AR1 – MOBILE HOME – Mobile Home

Sleeping: 2 bedrooms, sleeps 5: 1 double, 2 singles, sofa bed, pillows and blankets provided

Living: living/kitchen area, heating, air conditioning, shower, WC, seperate WC

Eating: fitted kitchen with hobs, fridge

Outside: table & chairs, parasol, barbecue

Pets: accepted

AR2 – BUNGALOW – Bungalow

Sleeping: 1 bedroom, sleeps 6: 1 double, bunk bed, sofa bed, pillows and blankets provided

Living: living/kitchen area, heating, TV, air conditioning, shower, WC

Eating: fitted kitchen with hobs, oven, fridge, freezer

Outside: table & chairs, parasol, barbecue

Pets: accepted

Other (AR1 and AR2): bed linen, cot, highchair to hire

Open: 1 April - 30 September

Weekly Charge	AR1	AR2
Low Season *(from)*	€ 340	€ 360
High Season *(from)*	€ 980	€ 1070

IT69145 Camping Village La Pineta

see report page 200

Via del Secco, 88, I-91010 San Vito Lo Capo

AR1 – BUNGALOW – Bungalow

Sleeping: 3 bedrooms, sleeps 6: 1 double, 2 singles, bunk bed

Living: living/kitchen area, heating, shower, WC

Eating: fitted kitchen with hobs, fridge

Outside: table & chairs

Pets: not accepted

Other (AR1): bed linen to hire

Open: 1 May - 30 September

Weekly Charge	AR1
Low Season *(from)*	€ 490
High Season *(from)*	€ 700

CR6731 Naturist Camping Valalta

see report page 238

Cesta Valalta-Lim bb, HR-52210 Rovinj

AR1 – MOBIL HOME – Mobile Home

Sleeping: 2 bedrooms, sleeps 4: 1 double, 2 singles, pillows and blankets provided

Living: living/kitchen area, TV, air conditioning, shower, WC

Eating: fitted kitchen with hobs, coffee maker, fridge, freezer

Outside: table & chairs

Pets: not accepted

AR2 – MOBIL HOME LUX – Mobile Home

Sleeping: 2 bedrooms, sleeps 5: 1 double, 3 singles, pillows and blankets provided

Living: living/kitchen area, TV, air conditioning, shower, WC

Eating: fitted kitchen with hobs, coffee maker, fridge, freezer

Outside: table & chairs

Pets: not accepted

Other (AR1 and AR2): bed linen, cot to hire

Open: 25 April - 25 September

Weekly Charge	AR1	AR2
Low Season *(from)*	€ 427	€ 469
High Season *(from)*	€ 805	€ 945

Mobile Homes & Chalets

Low Cost Flights

An Inexpensive Way To Arrive At Your Campsite

Many campsites are conveniently served by a wide choice of low cost airlines. Cheap flights can be very easy to find and travellers increasingly find the regional airports often used to be smaller, quieter and generally a calmer, more pleasurable experience.

Low cost flights can make campsites in more distant regions a much more attractive option: quicker to reach, inexpensive flights, and simply more convenient.

Many campsites are seeing increased visitors using the low cost flights and are adapting their services to suit this clientele. An airport shuttle service is not uncommon, meaning you can take advantage of that cheap flight knowing you will be met at the other end and whisked to your campsite. No taxi queues or multiple drop-offs.

Obviously, these low cost flights are impractical when taking all your own camping gear but they do make a holiday in campsite owned accommodation much more straightforward. The low cost airline option makes mobile home holidays especially attractive: pack a suitcase and use bed linen and towels provided (which you will generally need to pre-book).

Pricing Tips

- Low cost airlines promote cheap flights but only a small percentage of seats are priced at the cheapest price. Book early for the best prices (and of course you also get a better choice of campsite or mobile home)

- Child seats are usually the same costs as adults

- Full payment is required at the time of booking

- Changes and amendments can be costly with low cost airlines

- Peak dates can be expensive compared to other carriers

Car Hire

For maximum flexibility you will probably hire a car from a car rental agency.

Car hire provides convenience but also will allow you access to off-site shops, beaches and tourist sights.

Travelling

When taking your car (and caravan, tent or trailer tent) or motorcaravan to the continent you do need to plan in advance and to find out as much as possible about driving in the countries you plan to visit. Whilst European harmonisation has eliminated many of the differences between one country and another, it is well worth reading the short notes we provide in the introduction to each country in this guide in addition to this more general summary.

Of course, the main difference from driving in the UK is that in mainland Europe you will need to drive on the right. Without taking extra time and care, especially at busy junctions and conversely when roads are empty, it is easy to forget to drive on the right. Remember that traffic approaching from the right usually has priority unless otherwise indicated by road markings and signs. Harmonisation also means that most (but not all) common road signs are the same in all countries.

Your vehicle

Book your vehicle in for a good service well before your intended departure date. This will lessen the chance of an expensive breakdown. Make sure your brakes are working efficiently and that your tyres have plenty of tread (3 mm. is recommended, particularly if you are undertaking a long journey).

Also make sure that your caravan or trailer is roadworthy and that its tyres are in good order and correctly inflated. Plan your packing and be careful not to overload your vehicle, caravan or trailer – this is unsafe and may well invalidate your insurance cover (it must not be more fully loaded than the kerb weight of the insured vehicle).

CHECK ALL THE FOLLOWING:

- **GB sticker.** If you do not display a sticker, you may risk an on-the-spot fine as this identifier is compulsory in all countries. Euro-plates are an acceptable alternative within the EU (but not outside). Remember to attach another sticker (or Euro-plate) to caravans or trailers. Only GB stickers (not England, Scotland, Wales or N. Ireland) stickers are valid in the EU.

- **Headlights.** As you will be driving on the right you must adjust your headlights so that the dipped beam does not dazzle oncoming drivers. Converter kits are readily available for most vehicle, although if your car is fitted with high intensity headlights, you should check with your motor dealer. Check that any planned extra loading does not affect the beam height.

- **Seatbelts.** Rules for the fitting and wearing of seatbelts throughout Europe are similar to those in the UK, but it is worth checking before you go. Rules for carrying children in the front of vehicles vary from country to country. It is best to plan not to do this if possible.

- **Door/wing mirrors.** To help with driving on the right, if your vehicle is not fitted with a mirror on the left hand side, we recommend you have one fitted.

- **Fuel.** Leaded and Lead Replacement petrol is increasingly difficult to find in Northern Europe.

Compulsory additional equipment

The driving laws of the countries of Europe still vary in what you are required to carry in your vehicle, although the consequences of not carrying a required piece of equipment are almost always an on-the-spot fine.

To meet these requirements we suggest that you carry the following:

- FIRE EXTINGUISHER
- BASIC TOOL KIT
- FIRST AID KIT
- SPARE BULBS
- TWO WARNING TRIANGLES – two are required in some countries at all times, and are compulsory in most countries when towing.
- HIGH VISIBILITY VESTS – now compulsory in France, Spain, Italy and Austria (and likely to become compulsory throughout the EU) in case you need to walk on a motorway.

Insurance and Motoring Documents

Vehicle insurance

Contact your insurer well before you depart to check that your car insurance policy covers driving outside the UK. Most do, but many policies only provide minimum cover (so if you have an accident your insurance may only cover the cost of damage to the other person's property, with no cover for fire and theft).

To maintain the same level of cover abroad as you enjoy at home you need to tell your vehicle insurer. Some will automatically cover you abroad with no extra cost and no extra paperwork. Some will say you need a Green Card (which is neither green nor on card) but won't charge for it. Some will charge extra for the Green Card. Ideally you should contact your vehicle insurer 3-4 weeks before you set off, and confirm your conversation with them in writing.

Breakdown insurance

Arrange breakdown cover for your trip in good time so that if your vehicle breaks down or is involved in an accident it (and your caravan or trailer) can be repaired or returned to this country. This cover can usually be arranged as part of your travel insurance policy (see below).

Documents you must take with you

You may be asked to show your documents at any time so make sure that they are in order, up-to-date and easily accessible while you travel. These are what you need to take:

- Passports (you may also need a visa in some countries if you hold either a UK passport not issued in the UK or a passport that was issued outside the EU).
- Motor Insurance Certificate, including Green Card (or Continental Cover clause)
- DVLA Vehicle Registration Document plus, if not your own vehicle, the owner's written authority to drive.
- A full valid Driving Licence (not provisional). The new photo style licence is now mandatory in most European countries.

Personal Holiday insurance

Even though you are just travelling within Europe you must take out travel insurance. Few EU countries pay the full cost of medical treatment even under reciprocal health service arrangements. The first part of a holiday insurance policy covers people. It will include the cost of doctor, ambulance and hospital treatment if needed. If needed the better companies will even pay for English language speaking doctors and nurses and will bring a sick or injured holidaymaker home by air ambulance.

An important part of the insurance, often ignored, is cancellation (and curtailment) cover. Few things are as heartbreaking as having to cancel a holiday because a member of the family falls ill. Cancellation insurance can't take away the disappointment, but it makes sure you don't suffer financially as well. For this reason you should arrange your holiday insurance at least eight weeks before you set off.

Whichever insurance you choose we would advise reading very carefully the policies sold by the High Street travel trade. Whilst they may be good, they may not cover the specific needs of campers, caravanners and motorcaravanners.

Telephone 01580 214006 for a quote for our European Camping Holiday Insurance with cover arranged through Green Flag Motoring Assistance and Inter Group Assistance Services, one of the UK's largest assistance companies. Alternatively visit our website at www.insure4campers.com

Travelling continued

European Health Insurance Card (EHIC)

Make sure you apply for your EHIC before travelling in Europe. Eligible travellers from the UK are entitled to receive free or reduced-cost medical care in many European countries on production of an EHIC. This free card is available by completing a form in the booklet 'Health Advice for Travellers' from local Post Offices. One should be completed for each family member. Alternatively visit www.dh.gov.uk/travellers and apply on-line. Please allow time to send your application off and have the EHIC returned to you.

The EHIC is valid in all European Community countries plus Iceland, Liechtenstein, Switzerland and Norway. If you or any of your dependants are suddenly taken ill or have an accident during a visit to any of these countries, free or reduced-cost emergency treatment is available - in most cases on production of a valid EHIC.

Only state-provided emergency treatment is covered, and you will receive treatment on the same terms as nationals of the country you are visiting. Private treatment is generally not covered, and state-provided treatment may not cover all of the things that you would expect to receive free of charge from the NHS.

Remember an EHIC does not cover you for all the medical costs that you can incur or for repatriation - it is not an alternative to travel insurance. You will still need appropriate insurance to ensure you are fully covered for all eventualities.

Travelling with children

Most countries in Europe are enforcing strict guidelines when you are travelling with children who are not your own. A minor (under the age of 18) must be accompanied by a parent or legal guardian or must carry a letter of authorisation from a parent or guardian. The letter should name the adult responsible for the minor during his or her stay. Similarly, a minor travelling with just one of his/her parents, must have a letter of authority to leave their home country from the parent staying behind. Full information is available at www.fco.gov.uk

Open All Year

The following sites are understood to accept caravanners and campers all year round. It is always wise to contact the site to check.

ITALY

Piedmont & Aosta

Dalai Lama	19
Glair	28
Gofree	24
Gran Bosco	25
Mombarone	28
Orta	24

Ligúria

Dei Fiori (Pietra Ligure)	34
Dei Fiori (San Remo)	35
Miraflores	34
Sfinge	33

Trentino - Alto Adige

Antholz	65
Cevedale	68
Gamp	67
Lago-Molveno	71
Olympia	77
Sass Dlacia	75
Sexten	76

Veneto

Alba	87
Alba d'Oro	106
Fusina	104

Emília-Romagna

Castagni	116
San Marino	117

Tuscany

Boschetto di Piemma	139
Finoria	132
Michelangelo	132
Mugello Verde	140
Panoramico	130
Soline	126
Toscana Village	136

Lázio

Castelfusano	165
Fabulous	166
Flaminio	169
Roma	168

Abruzzo & Molise

Genziana	172
I Lupi	177
Vecchio Mulino	175

Campania

Zeus	181

Puglia & Basilicata

Baia di Gallipoli	184
Dei Trulli	183
Masseria	184

Calabria

Costa Verde	190
Il Salice	189
Vascellero	189

Sicily

Dello Stretto	197
Jonio	194
Marinello	198
Nettuno	194
Panorama	193
Pineta	200
Rais Gerbi	195
Sabbiadoro	194
Scarabeo	198
Valle dei Templi	193

Sardinia

Agritourism C'tiolou	207
Cernie	206
Spinnaker	208

SLOVENIA

Dolina Prebold	217
Kamne	216
Koren	215
Ljubljana Resort	216
Moravke Toplice	217
Terme Catez	214
Terme Ptuj	218

CROATIA

Nevio	233
Simuni	242

Dogs

For the benefit of those who want to take their dogs with them or for people who do not like dogs at the sites they visit, we list here the sites that have indicated to us that they do not accept dogs. If you are, however, planning to take your dog we do advise you to contact them first to check – there may be limits on numbers, breeds, etc. or times of the year when they are excluded.

Never – these sites do not accept dogs at any time

ITALY

C'tiolou	207
Al Boschetto	99
Alberello	118
Argentario	122
Athena	180
Baia Domizia	179
Bella Italia	58
Bellamare	159
Ca'Pasquali	100
Ca'Savio	90
California	165
Capalbio	125
Capalonga	88
Cevedale	68
Cisano & San Vito	45
Dei Fiori	35

Dei Fiori	95
Del Garda	57
Delle Piscine	140
Delle Rose	49
Europe Garden	176
Framura	34
Garden Paradiso	98
Gasparina	43
Green Garden	160
Holiday	173
Ideal Molino	62
Il Tridente	88
Internazionale	160
Isamar	104
Isuledda	205
Italy	96
Jesolo	106
Lido	88

Lido Village	163
Lo Stambecco	20
Malibu Beach	105
Marelago	94
Mediterraneo	99
Miramare	
Punta Sabb.	102
Montescudaio	136
PicoBello	158
Portofelice	103
Pra' Delle Torri	93
Puntala	138
Punta Lunga	186
Residence	94
Riva di Ugento	186
Riva Nuova	174
Riva Verde	156
Rubicone	119

Saint Michael	143
Salinello	177
Sant'Angelo	99
Serenella	44
Settebello	169
Stella Maris	160
Tahiti	115
Tenuta Primero	82
Union Lido	96
Villa al Mare	95
Voltoncino	121
Waikiki	105

CROATIA

Valalta (Naturist)	238
Valdaliso	241

Maybe – not accepted in high season

ITALY

Baia Gabbiani	141
Baia Verde	138
Baita Dolomiti	75
Butteri	141
Capo Ferrato	207
Cieloverde	135
Cigno Bianco	209

Conca d'Oro	22
Costa Ponente	195
Costa Verde	190
Don Antonio	174
Europa	144
Free Time	134
International	175
Italia	143

Jonio	194
Lido	56
Mareblu	129
Maremma	128
Marinello	198
Mariposa	203
Miramare (Chioggia)	110

Molino a Fuoco	146
Pionier Etrusco	165
Rais Gerbi	195
Riccione	118
San Nicola	184
Steiner	69
Tripesce	145
Vascellero	189

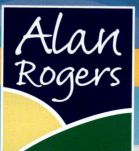

FIND YOUR PERFECT PITCH

- ■ **Sites Finder – The UK's biggest online directory!**
- ■ **Easy-to-use with over 4700 sites**
- ■ **Search by region, type of pitch or site facilities**

More and more people are choosing UK holidays and *Caravan* magazine's new online directory, Sites Finder will make finding your ideal campsite easy! So if you're looking for a pet-friendly campsite or one that's open all year round, Sites Finder will help you to find that perfect pitch.

Check out Sites Finder at caravanmagazine.co.uk/sitesfinder

TRY 3 ISSUES FOR JUST £3

Trentino-Alto Adige
page 64

Friuli-Venezia Giúlia
page 79

Lake Garda
page 42

SLOVENIA
page 210

CROATIA
page 220

Lombardy
page 37

Veneto
page 86

Piedmont &
Valle d'Aosta
page 16

Emila-Romagna
page 111

Ligúria
page 29

Marche
page 155

Tuscany
page 120

Umbria
page 147

Abruzzo & Molise
page 171

Lazio
page 162

Campania
page 178

Puglia & Basilicata
page 182

Sardinia
page 201

Calabria
page 187

Sicily
page 192

Town and Village Index

Index by Campsite Region and Name